EBURY PRESS

HAMID

Hamid Ansari has a master's degree in management studies with a specialization in operations and supply chain management from Mumbai University, as well as a second MBA degree in human resources from the Narsee Monjee Institute of Management Studies, Mumbai. Hamid has worked with NGOs like the Rotary Club and been a volunteer with the United Nations. He is currently part of the visiting faculty at a junior college in Mumbai, and is a motivational speaker who is working towards becoming an entrepreneur.

Geeta Mohan is a journalist, covering international relations and diplomacy. She is currently the foreign affairs editor at *India Today*, TV Today Network. Apart from heading the desk, she also anchors the show *World Today*. Passionate about sharing real stories from the ground, she is widely recognized for her reporting.

ADVANCE PRAISE FOR THE BOOK

'In this spellbinding account, co-authored with senior journalist Geeta Mohan, Hamid Ansari tells the harrowing story of his six-year captivity in Pakistan, and of the people on both sides of the border who strived to free him. Standing for hope and understanding over suspicion and hatred, *Hamid* is an eye-opening testimony to the ordinary people who are harmed by the unfeeling forces of international politics. Having met his anguished parents during his captivity, I am more than happy he has been able to tell his story as a free man.'—Shashi Tharoor, Congress MP and renowned author

'This is a compelling story, veering between hope and tragedy, suffering and faith. Hamid Ansari's poignant story is a reminder that India and Pakistan may be divided by competing nationalisms but are united in the end by humanity. Told with rare empathy, this is a book that will tug at your heart and broaden the mind.'—Rajdeep Sardesai

'Hamid's story is a gripping narrative of an ordinary Indian's heroic fight by undertaking a daring journey that took him from Kabul to the badlands of Peshawar, only to be arrested and then charged with being a RAW agent. It then chronicles, in vivid detail, Hamid's battle to save his life and survive the shockingly inhuman treatment he was subjected to in Pakistani jails for three years. It is also a heart-warming story of hope as activists and journalists from both sides of the border came together to help his distraught family, particularly his brave mother, secure his release. This is real-life drama, packed with raw emotions and with the twists and turns of a Bollywood film that make for riveting reading—I read it from start to finish in one go. The style of the narrative, which is a combination of engrossing first-person details from Hamid and Geeta Mohan's flair for journalistic detail, makes this book a must-read.'—Raj Chengappa

'The true story of Hamid Ansari's arrest and capture in Pakistan has been told for the first time in such vivid detail through his own words. Geeta Mohan's years of experience covering India–Pakistan ties shines through in the book as the reader navigates how exactly Ansari landed up in a Pakistani jail, how he was treated and how he came home. A must-read.'—Nidhi Razdan

'There is nothing more cruel than the crushing of ordinary people's dreams under the feet of large States engaged in conflict. There is nothing more heart-warming than the determination of individuals to overcome those difficulties in the name of humanity. For those journalists who covered Hamid Ansari's journey to Pakistan, his incarceration and his mother's struggle to somehow bring him home, every twist has been heart-stopping. The ordeal has been recounted brilliantly by Hamid Ansari and Geeta Mohan here. A must-read!' Suhasini Haidar, diplomatic editor, *The Hindu*

'Hamid Ansari's case is an excellent example of how people from two countries can stand up for each other and help with a human touch in distress, even though the two nations may not be on good terms politically. If Hamid's case is widely publicized and made known to people on both sides of the borders, it would contribute richly in harmonizing the relationship between the two neighbouring countries. My hearty congratulations to both Fauzia and Nehal Ansari and best wishes to Hamid for his future.'—Advocate Majeed Memon, ex-MP, Rajya Sabha

'This is the heart-wrenching true story of a young man who crossed the Line of Control illegally for love. His journey is a painful read and grim reminder of how bloodshed and hostility between two neighbours with a shared history and border can shape the destiny and destroy the lives of ordinary citizens and several other Hamids caught in the Indo-Pakistan political conflict. A powerful memoir penned by Hamid Ansari and Geeta Mohan, who followed the story of this inspiring family closely as a journalist.'—Smita Sharma

'Hamid's story is essentially a story of hope and possibilities as much as it is a story of an individual caught in the cross-hairs of two nations. It tells us to see the people of India and Pakistan as separate from their governments. Just as Indians worked for his release, so did Pakistanis. Hamid's return is a telling comment on how activists and opinion-makers can intervene and change the course of personal-political histories on both sides of the border, and make truth triumph. Hamid's story is a reminder too that India and Pakistan must be humane towards prisoners, especially fish workers, women and senior citizens languishing in jails in each other's countries. As Hamid was, such prisoners too should be released.'—Jatin Desai, senior journalist and former secretary, Pakistan–India Peoples' Forum for Peace and Democracy (PIPFPD)

'Rukhshanda and I happened to meet in Kathmandu at a SAFHR meeting and I was able to hand over relevant documents of the case that Fauzia had sent. Subsequently, on several occasions when we met through our many common networks, Fauzia was able to send, through me, medicines and other essentials to Rukhshanda for Hamid in jail in Pakistan. It was a very long journey and thanks to Rukhshanda and the determination of Fauzia to not give up, Hamid is back home and has resumed his life with dignity. I believe that the civil society networks that connect us across hostile borders made an important contribution.'—Rita Manchanda, human rights activist

'Hamid Ansari's life was about to change. The former engineer and member of the Rotary International travelled from his home in Mumbai to the tribal region of Pakistan on what he believed to be a life-changing humanitarian mission. But he never expected to be remanded in custody of Pakistan's Intelligence Service for over three years and subsequently be convicted of "spying", for which he was sentenced to solitary confinement for three and a half years . . . A true story of horrendous cruelty, injustice, brutality, torture, gross abuse of human rights, and the determination of the human spirit and its resolve to survive the most appalling custodial conditions while being denied any contact with his family in India. Hamid's parents courageously battled relentlessly for his release and repatriation.'—Jas Uppal, founding trustee of Justice Upheld, a British human rights charity

'No young man should rot in jail. No mother should suffer the trauma and live in fear of losing her son. I met Fauzia, Hamid's mother, much ahead of his release from jail. Her tears broke my heart and left me helpless. Helpless at the system which condemns a man caught on the wrong side of a piece of earth which God created for all without discriminating against its inhabitants. But this fascinating book is not just about agony and angst at being deceived by those you trust. It is more about the triumph of love and humanity over hatred and enmity. If loving someone is no crime, risking one's own life to save the life of a young accused deserves to be celebrated. The book celebrates that spirit of angelic love and care Hamid received while he spent countless desperate, depressing hours in prison. His story needed to be shared uncensored and full. I am glad Hamid collaborated with journalist and writer Geeta Mohan to tell it.'—Mohammed Wajihuddin, journalist, *Times of India*

'Hamid Ansari's case was one of the most important fights of my journey in human rights. As a human rights activist, it was my duty to help Fauzia Ansari, a strong and dedicated mother, who took the initiative into her own hands to find and bring back her son. As soon as Fauzia Ansari found out the whereabouts of her son, she contacted many authorities to prove his innocence. I would like to thank Mr Ansari's family who showed faith and trust in me.'—Jayesh C. Mirani, president, All Maharashtra Human Rights Welfare Association, member of United Nations, Department of Public Information, USA

'Hamid Ansari's case is a unique one . . . It is an honour and privilege for me to know that Hamid's desperate mother, Fauzia Ansari, received my call when she was pleading at the doors of the Kaaba in Makkah for her son's safe recovery. She considered me a Divine help, an answer to her prayers. In this heart-wrenching, dark phase of Hamid's life, I am proud to say I was also a part of helping a mother meet her son . . . This book is a must-read, an eye-opener, an inspiration with the message of humanity, brotherhood, peace and harmony for both countries.'—Zeenat Shehzadi, freelance investigating reporter and peace activist at PIPFPD

'Hamid Ansari's story of pain, hardships, patience and faith is much more than a love story. It is a deeply disturbing and profoundly humanizing tale of the fraught relations between India and Pakistan. By narrating it in a book, he and Geeta Mohan have rendered a great service to the cause of India–Pakistan normalization. I cannot wait to see it made into an international blockbuster movie.'—Sudheendra Kulkarni, activist for Indo-Pakistan peace

'This is the honest account of a man who has been through hell and back. It takes courage to revisit such a traumatic past. But Hamid Ansari doesn't hold back, and that's what makes this story so engaging. Every chapter is a roller-coaster ride of emotions. The ending reminds us that truth prevails. Always.'—Gajanan Kirtikar, leader of Shiv Sena, MP, Lok Sabha, Mumbai

HAMID

THE STORY OF
MY CAPTIVITY,
SURVIVAL
AND FREEDOM

HAMID ANSARI
WITH
GEETA MOHAN

EBURY
PRESS

An imprint of Penguin Random House

EBURY PRESS

USA | Canada | UK | Ireland | Australia
New Zealand | India | South Africa | China | Singapore

Ebury Press is part of the Penguin Random House group of companies
whose addresses can be found at global.penguinrandomhouse.com

Published by Penguin Random House India Pvt. Ltd
4th Floor, Capital Tower 1, MG Road,
Gurugram 122 002, Haryana, India

First published in Ebury Press by Penguin Random House India 2020

ISBN 9780143450153

Typeset in Adobe Garamond Pro by Manipal Technologies Limited, Manipal

Printed at Repro India Limited

Contents

Introduction

Hamid Ansari

Time can turn your destiny upside down. I had never imagined that I would author a book one day, let alone one on the sufferings and betrayals of my own life. A decade ago, I was a different man—just a young engineer in Mumbai, getting by happily in the world I had made for myself, living with Ammi, Abbu, and my brother, Khalid. Life was speeding by in a city that was always on the move, and writing down my thoughts on paper was far from my mind.

That I would be putting pen to paper to chronicle not fiction but the true story of a nightmarish life experience was something I could not have fathomed back then. Even now, when I close my eyes, I can clearly see the prison cells in which I was put into solitary confinement, an atmosphere of death all around me, and no hope of returning home.

'We know you are innocent, but your only crime is that you are an Indian Muslim, and Indian Muslims are a bigger threat to us because Muslims blend into our culture and we cannot identify them easily.' I heard these words from many Pakistani authorities, and that is why I wanted to tell the world my side of the story. I wanted to write down the details of each and every incident, every session of torture, trauma and injustice. Then, I had no pen and paper with me, so I started making mental notes of some dates and events, and writing on dusty jail walls with my nails, scratching out code words which only I knew how to decipher.

When wounds bleed, they soothe the pain of the heart. This untold story of mine, an innocent victim's ordeal, tells the bitter truths of betrayal by trustworthy friends, and the backstabbing of opportunists and hypocritical well-wishers. These emotions needed to be conveyed, especially in a world where expressing humanity is considered a weakness.

The world may know a bit of my story due to print and electronic media, that a boy called Hamid Ansari had entered Pakistan to save a friend who was in extreme despair, that he was caught and went missing, and later alleged to be an Indian spy.

While my screams, sobs, appeals and pleadings fell on the deaf ears of Pakistani officials during numerous interrogation sessions, I vowed to scream out the truth one day, to make sure the world heard me when I was free. I vowed to write my story once I was released. However, for security reasons, some names in the book have been changed. Since none of the army officers in Pakistan ever revealed their identities, names have been assigned to them so they can be identified while reading the book.

After three and a half years of solitary confinement in a dingy cell 20 feet below ground level, I was brought to the surface—and sent to civil prison in a most uncivilized manner. But that meant I finally got a glimpse of nature and the outside world, which I hadn't seen for what felt like an era. Apart from the company of a few good people in the prison, I also got news about my case in the Peshawar High court in Pakistan.

Then I came to know about angels like Zeenat Shehzadi, Advocate Qazi Anwar and Advocate Rukhshanda Naz. I was thrilled by their noble gestures. They were not my relatives; they were in fact from the same land of Pakistan where I was betrayed and labelled an Indian spy. Before meeting them, I had given up on life. But they stood by my side and gave me new hope. Advocate Qazi Anwar, through fifty years of legal practice, had fought thousands of cases but never visited prison to meet a client, but he visited me there thrice, waiving off all fees and taking care of me like an elder guardian would.

Advocate Rukhshanda Naz was my counsel, and she really made me feel like I had a mother's protective hand over my head. When she visited me in prison, she registered her relationship with me as one of *insaniyat*, or 'humanity'.

The little angel with a big heart, young journalist Zeenat Shehzadi, never knew me. A mother's tears had melted her heart. She decided to help my family once she was convinced that I had been duped by people I had considered friends. Aware that my intention was only to help a troubled Pakistani girl, she stayed the course of the fight till one day she herself became the victim—losing her brother to suicide and even being kidnapped herself.

Such heartfelt examples of humanity also need to be seen and celebrated, and that is another big reason I was compelled to write the book.

After six years of this dark phase of my life, when I was repatriated to India on 18 December 2018, I was welcomed by the then external affairs minister of India, Sushma Swaraj. Even she advised me to pen down my experiences in Pakistan. There was no turning back. Meanwhile, in the *India Today* office, journalist Geeta Mohan offered her assistance in this endeavour. The spark was fanned into a fire.

Through this book, I also want to convey an important message to the world: not everyone behind bars is a criminal. There could be many who fell prey to someone else's animosity, jealousy or greed and were deemed to be on the wrong side of the law. But society shouldn't forget the truth of history, that many freedom fighters, noble men and women, saints, prophets and social reformers have faced the hardships of prison life for acts of humanity.

All innocent souls who have been wrongly kept behind bars must be accepted back in society and helped to overcome the stigma caused by a jail term. Those who have been punished for acts that are not criminal should be helped by their governments, NGOs and civil societies to recover from the losses and damages inflicted on them.

The agony of prison life and complete loss of freedom are compounded by thoughts of what might have been. After being deprived for years of the support of family and friends, and the ability to establish oneself professionally, the nightmare does not end upon release. With no money, housing, transportation, health services or insurance, and a false criminal record that is rarely cleared despite innocence, the punishment lingers long after innocence has been proven. Society has a responsibility to restore the lives of wrongfully convicted prisoners.

In the end, I must emphasize the fact that I have been repatriated to my country by my government and many more people, but I regret to say I haven't got justice yet.

Geeta Mohan

This book was conceptualized in the basement of a guest house in New Delhi, where Hamid Ansari's parents, Fauzia and Nehal Ansari, met me on one of many occasions when they were in Delhi for Hamid's case. I had been following the case since it came to light, and was in awe of the grit and determination of Hamid's mother. With the case concluded and the sentence delivered, there was hope that Hamid Ansari would be coming home after spending six years inside Pakistani prisons.

While the world knew bits of the story, there was so much more to tell. The Ansaris and I discussed the idea of a book that could encapsulate Hamid's journey and that of the family's once he was repatriated to India. Hamid had not spoken yet; we didn't know what he had gone through.

The book was firmed up when I met Hamid upon his return. He came across as a young man whose spirits were unshaken despite the ordeal he had gone through in Pakistan. His smile was endearing, but the conversation I had with him gave away the fears he had about what lay ahead. When I told him that he had to tell his story to the world, not only did he agree, he was quite eager to do it. It felt like he had decided while he was still in Pakistan that he wanted to share his experience with the world.

But nothing about this story can be complete without including the struggle of three women: Fauzia Ansari, Zeenat Shehzadi and Rukhshanda Naz.

Fauzia Ansari's fighting spirit, her undying faith in justice and the belief that she would see her son again. The dedication and determination of Zeenat Shehzadi, a young Pakistani journalist whose investigations revealed for the first time that Indian national Hamid Ansari was in Pakistani custody. She paid a heavy price for speaking truth to power. And of course, the much-needed legal fight put up by Rukhshanda Naz along with well-known senior advocate Qazi Anwar. Rukhshanda's presence in those final years of Hamid's prison term gave him a new lease of life. Her warmth gave him the strength to fight.

There were many others who played a critical role in bringing Hamid back, among them advocate Qazi Anwar. When nobody was willing to touch the case of an Indian who had been declared a spy, Qazi Sahab came forward and showed the country and the world what it meant to take an oath to uphold the law of the land and defend a person in the best possible way. There were others too who the couple had approached but couldn't afford because of the huge sums of money they demanded. Despite the pressures and knowing the implications of fighting an Indian's case, Qazi Anwar, highly regarded across Peshawar and Pakistan, took it up (pro bono) and won.

The other factor at play was the active civil society in India and particularly in Pakistan that took up the cause of Hamid Ansari and sought justice for him. Beena Sarwar, I.A. Rehman, Hina Jilani and others. They demanded that his case be moved from military court to civilian court if Hamid was indeed not a spy. This was a call made by some journalists from India and Pakistan as well.

Jatin Desai, a founding member of the Pakistan–India Peoples' Forum for Peace and Democracy, worked a lot on the case in India. He connected Hamid's parents to various journalists in Mumbai and Delhi. It was through him that they got in touch with TV journalist Rajdeep Sardesai, who time and again raised the issue of Hamid's release on various platforms, including at an interaction with Pakistan Prime Minister Imran Khan at the Kartarpur Sahib groundbreaking ceremony in November 2018. That was where the final assurance of Hamid's timely release came—from none other than the Pakistani premier himself. And twenty-one days later, Hamid walked free.

In India, from the moment the news came to light of an Indian national being caught by the Pakistani administration, the Ministry of External Affairs and the Indian High Commission in Pakistan worked actively to get Hamid released, but the effort lacked political momentum. It was after 2014, when the BJP administration came to power and Sushma Swaraj became the external affairs minister, that new blood was pumped into the effort to fight for Indians languishing anywhere in the world.

Sushma Swaraj's outreach to Indians stranded abroad and her focus to ensure they got home safe were what gave Fauzia, who was exhausted with her efforts, new hope. Sushma Swaraj had kept in constant touch with her officers in Delhi and in Islamabad, and gave them clear instructions that the mission has to do all it can to 'bring the boy back', as she would tell them.

During one of their first meetings, she told Fauzia that she herself was a mother and understood her pain. She gave Fauzia her word and said, 'I will bring your son back. Take my word for it. Don't worry and just follow what the officers ask you to do.'

Swaraj wanted to keep the entire process a quiet affair since it was a sensitive issue, and while she knew Hamid was not a spy and should be brought home, she did not want to be seen encouraging youth to carry out any illegal acts of entering other countries without following proper procedures. She stood by the family with the steely resolution of bringing Hamid back.

There were many others whose paths crossed Fauzia and Nehal's. Many are mentioned in the book, some may not have been. This is the story of the effort of people who came together to make Fauzia's will turn into reality.

I was inspired and honoured to be a part of the story as I witnessed the struggle of this couple, who overcame emotional, financial, societal and legal pressures and took their fight across the country.

Diplomatic ups and downs between India and Pakistan have always played an important role in how a case is treated in both countries. Unfortunately, things were on a downward spiral when it came to ties between the two nations while Hamid was in custody. Fauzia's fears were visible every time she heard of an adverse development in relations between the two countries.

Things took an ugly turn with the terror attacks in Uri and Pathankot, and the nabbing of Kulbhushan Jadhav by Pakistan. But an undeterred Fauzia in India and the unfazed Qazi Anwar and Rukhshanda in Pakistan did not let such events affect the case. They moved ahead with the same vigour and fought on the grounds of evidence collected by Zeenat Shehzadi.

The chapters in the book move between Hamid's first-person narratives and the third-person accounts of the family, the Indian government, the counsels in Pakistan and Zeenat Shehzadi. The chapter on Fiza (name changed), the girl Hamid went to Pakistan to rescue, has been written on the basis of phone and text conversations between Hamid, Fiza and her sister.

Writing this book was a tiring and an exhilarating experience. While I covered the story extensively, nobody knew the inside details of their struggle. Hamid's six years in Pakistan, the torture he faced, his family's painstaking efforts to be heard—these were all difficult to write about. But the initiatives and efforts leading to the events taking a positive turn displayed the audacity of people to seek freedom for Hamid prevailed amidst the India–Pakistan diplomatic quagmire.

Sometimes, reality is not exactly what it appears to be. There are a lot of pulls and pushes to drive individuals towards certain actions. This book will take you down the road of a real-life experience. It is as surreal as it is real.

1

Forbidden Love

To experience freedom in my bones again . . . Would I ever be able to breathe the air of my country again, feel the embrace of my mother? These were the constant questions on my mind.

I felt her warm hand on my head and woke up with a start, staring at the ceiling of my dingy underground military cell in Peshawar, Pakistan. The feel of my mother's warmth soon waned and the frigidity of the 6'x6' room crept in, bringing with it the burden of regrets, remorse and all the 'I shouldn't haves'.

Fiza . . . I thought of her. Was it worth risking my entire being? Fiza . . . what must have become of her? I couldn't believe that two years had passed with no news from anyone. It felt like I had vanished from the face of this Earth and nobody knew what had really happened to me. Allah, please forgive me for putting Ammi through whatever she must be going through. Does she think I am dead? Do they know where I am?

A journey that started in 2011 had left me with questions and fear of the unknown. Uncertainty in an unknown land, an enemy state . . . Pakistan.

It all started with innocence, friendship, hope and love.

~

It was just another day in November 2011. I was a global replenishment senior executive at Hettich GmBH in Mumbai. With no responsibility of handling family and home expenses, since both my parents worked, I had all my earnings to myself. And at twenty-seven, life seemed great! When I offered to start paying at home, Ammi said, 'The money is yours. Do whatever you want with it. But just be wise with it.'

One day, my neighbourhood friends and I planned a two-day biking trip to Matheran, which is 80 kilometres from Mumbai. We reached Matheran in the evening. As with most boys in their twenties, we were soon talking about girls. I had briefly had a girlfriend but things did not progress beyond a point. I was curious about how some of my friends were meeting and speaking to so many girls.

We come from a community and a neighbourhood where having a girlfriend is not really something that is openly talked about. Clandestine relationships that often end in failure is the fait accompli of most couples.

That night, Samir, one of my friends, showed me an online chat platform called NIMBUZZ. He said that this was where they chatted with women, and some even ended up dating them. The same night, I went to my room in the hotel and downloaded the mobile app. I started exploring the platform, which was quite similar to online chat rooms in the past such as Yahoo. You could choose your location, and so I entered the Mumbai chat room. I wasn't particularly on the lookout for someone. I just wanted to see what the hype was about. It was an uneventful experience.

The next morning, I pushed myself to get out of bed before the hotel restaurant closed its breakfast service. Samir saw me walk to the table and smiled at me. I wondered what that was about. When I placed my plate on the table and sat beside him, he started, 'So, how was last night? Did you meet anybody online?'

I brushed him off, saying, 'It was boring as hell! But let's see if something comes up in the next couple of days.'

The afternoon was a lot of fun with the boys. We went sightseeing and then rode home. That evening, when I was home, I logged on to NIMBUZZ again. As soon as I entered the Mumbai chat room, I received a personal message from someone whose profile name was just a number (6586192). It was just a 'hi'. I had logged in as 'Hamid'. So to respond to a number felt a little weird. Who could it be on the other side? But then, I had nothing to lose, so I wrote back, 'Hi.'

Promptly came the next question: 'ASL?'

I might have been new to this platform but not to online chatting. I knew what that meant, and I immediately responded with my age, sex and location: '27 M Mum' (27 years old, male, Mumbai). I asked the person behind the number, 'ASL?'

The response was, '25 F Kohat.'

'Where the fuck is this Kohat?' I said aloud. I tried to think where it could be. Not in Mumbai for sure. Was it a small town or village in Maharashtra? I googled to find out where Kohat was. It showed up somewhere near Pitampura in Delhi. Well, who cared. I had a girl talking to me! I thought, 'This bloody thing is for real. It works! *Samir bevaqoof nahi hai.*' (Samir is not as daft as I imagined.)

I asked her what she was doing in life. She said she was a student. I told her I worked in an MNC.

She asked, 'What is an MNC?' I found the question very strange. Who didn't know what an MNC was? She was certainly not from the city.

I explained, 'It is a multinational company.'

She said, 'You must be a big businessman or something.'

I laughed and told her that I was just an employee in the company, although I did have a wallet manufacturing business of my own. 'You must have heard or seen the Le Rico brand of wallets on Flipkart. I make them.'

She asked, 'What is Flipkart?' I thought she was kidding. I jokingly asked if she was familiar with the Internet, as it was impossible to not know Flipkart. She said she didn't like using the Internet.

I said, 'If that is the case, what are you doing on NIMBUZZ? Anyway, what are you studying at the age of twenty-five? Shouldn't you have completed your studies by now? Did you flunk a few years?'

She said she had completed her studies. 'I am now studying to become a teacher.'

'For someone who does not know how to use the Internet, I wonder what you teach your students,' I said, trying to be funny. Turned out the humour wasn't well received. She was miffed. I apologized but added that knowledge of the Internet was essential these days. She finally concurred.

I wanted to move on to a lighter topic. So I asked her where she had graduated from. She said, 'Islamabad.' I was stunned into silence. Had I heard her right? Did she just say Islamabad?

Hesitantly, I asked, 'Did you say Islamabad? Islamabad in Pakistan? You went all the way to Pakistan for higher studies?'

She said, 'No. I am from Pakistan.'

'That can't be. I googled Kohat. It showed up as a place in Delhi . . . in India!' I blurted out, a little shocked.

She laughed and swung a jibe at me, 'So much for your Internet and Google. Hahaha . . .'

But she also checked Google to find a Kohat in India as well. I laughed at the whole misunderstanding. Something had happened. Unfamiliar territory, unwelcome neighbour, but there was a strange pull at that moment. I finally typed, 'What is your name?'

'Fiza,' she said. She typed back asking me my name.

I wrote, 'Hamid.'

'Mashallah, a very nice name,' she wrote.

I asked, 'Who all are there in your family?'

She said, 'Abbu, Ammi, a brother, and we are six sisters. Two have been married off. I am the third. One younger brother and three younger sisters. What about your family?'

I replied, 'Abbu, Ammi and a brother.'

She suddenly told me she needed to attend to chores in the house and would chat tomorrow. So I bade her goodbye. But I wanted to talk more. This felt different.

I lay down on my bed that night thinking of what could become of such a relationship. While I had questions, it did not feel absolutely alien. The concept of families in India and Pakistan visiting each other was not completely unfamiliar territory. Even we had neighbours with families on the other side of the border.

Somehow, this felt doable. In hindsight, it feels like absolute naïveté on my part. What was I thinking? But I couldn't stop going over our brief chat. I went to bed thinking about her and woke up looking forward to our conversation in the evening.

The next day, she added me to her friends' list (with my guidance) from an ID with her real name. I was happy to read her name on my screen. Fiza.

I typed, 'How are you?'

Her curt response was, '*Koi salaam dua nahi. Yeh kaun sa tareeqa hai mulaqat ka?*' (No pleasantries. Is this a civilized way to start a conversation?)

I found this endearing. I simply wrote, '*As-salaam alaykum.*' (Peace be upon you.)

From thereon, there was no stopping us. We would chat about what food we ate and at what time, whom we spoke to and what we did all day; we discussed everything under the sun. She would always say that we were good friends, and friends had a right over each other. But I knew there was more. She was becoming a part of my daily life . . . a part of my being. And I could feel the indispensability of my presence in her life. There was nothing or no one more important to her than me.

But I hadn't heard her voice. I knew she was shy. So I didn't want to come on too strong. It was a weekday and I was at work when she messaged me. I told her I was in office. She said she would connect later as she also had to study. I thought this was the right time to ask her if she was okay with exchanging numbers.

'Will you give me your number? I want to talk to you. I want to hear your voice,' I asked.

Without any resistance, she promptly shared her number. I stared at it for a very long time, thinking about whether I should call her. An international number that started with the digits +92 was certainly not one I had thought I would dial one day. This was far from a regular long-distance relationship. It was a distance that neither of us knew how to bridge. But then, the heart ruled over the mind, emotion over logic, desperate desire over common sense . . . and more.

I dialled the number. The phone rang for a while, and then I heard the sweetest voice on the other side saying, 'As-salaam alaykum.' My heart stopped beating and then, before I knew it, started thudding like it was going to explode. She said, 'Hello', wondering if I was there. I replied, '*Wa-alaikum-salaam.*' (Peace be upon you too.)

As it was November, the weather in Mumbai was brilliant. I came back from work, had dinner and then went to my room to speak to Fiza. I called her and asked how she was doing. She said, 'It is very cold here. The temperatures have been dipping to unbearable levels at night.' I wondered what the weather was like out there in Kohat. We had a long conversation. I asked her to keep warm and stay covered.

'Have you eaten anything?' I asked. To my surprise, she said, 'Yes, Maggi. Only because you insisted.' And I thought of all the things common between India and Pakistan—Maggi was one of them, but not love.

Even as I hung up, one thought stayed with me: the cold temperature there. After getting off the phone, I googled it. It said Kohat was very cold at 6 degrees Celsius. *Wow, that's crazy.*

We started asking a lot of details about each other's health, if we were eating well, and how everyone was doing at home. I always pictured her talking to me, but was yet to muster up the courage to ask her how she looked. Would it be rude? Or would she understand my curiosity? I wondered.

In December 2011, I hadn't heard from Fiza for a few days, till I got a call from her saying that her grandmother had passed away and she had gone with her family to their village in a place called Karak.

~

One night, her name flashed on my mobile screen.

'Hi,' came a meek voice from the other side.

I asked her if everything was all right. 'Why are you sounding so low, Fiza? Is something wrong?' I asked.

Soft laughter escaped her lips when she said, 'No, no . . . I am fine. It is just very cold here and I have to step outside to talk to you since the entire house is full of family members from everywhere.'

I heaved a sigh of relief. But something didn't feel right. I made light of the situation by saying, 'Come on, how cold can it be?' I was in a quilt, saving myself from the Mumbai cold of 18–19 degrees, while she was sitting in the open, under the sky at night, when the temperatures must have hit chilling lows.

All this effort and pain only for me. There was certainly more than friendship here. I felt my heart melt. But something about our conversation still kept tugging at me. Her voice was different, melancholic.

Such purity of heart and innocence of being. She was an honest soul. And her dedication towards this relationship made me yearn for more. I wanted to see her.

The next day, I requested Fiza to share a picture of herself, but was faced with extreme resistance. I thought it was unwarranted but she was adamant. There would be no sharing of any kind of photograph. I was so pissed. 'What the hell! Why the hell not?' I nearly screamed into the phone.

'You don't seem to trust me. Why else would you not share your picture?' I shot off these words at her and banged the phone down.

She called back and tried to explain, 'I cannot share my picture. Please try to understand. Can we talk about something else? If not, then I can't help you. I will leave,' she said.

I said 'Okay,' and hung up on her.

Our first fight. I couldn't believe that she was being so stubborn about such a simple demand. This fight led to a temporary halt in communication between the two of us. I was desperate to call her and hear her voice but then decided against it.

A few days later, Fiza called, 'Are you still mad at me? Am I important or my picture?'

I quietly replied, 'I just want to see you. That's all.'

My phone beeped. I had a new image on WhatsApp. I opened it to see a photograph of a girl standing at a distance, wearing a salwar kameez, her head wrapped in a black dupatta. Big beautiful eyes, pink lips . . . she was a dream.

Fiza, unsure of herself, said, 'Don't make fun of my pic.'

I told her, 'If this is indeed your picture then you look heavenly, and if it is not, even then you are beautiful.'

Shocked, she said, 'You don't think I have sent my own photo?'
I told her that I was joking and that she was astoundingly pretty.

That night, I kept staring at her photograph, and before I knew it,
I had fallen asleep with the phone in my hand, thinking of Fiza.

2

Fiza

On that cold December night when Fiza had called Hamid from her grandmother's house in Karak, things hadn't been fine. Whether for death or celebration, any occasion where a family gets together is an opportunity to discuss marriage. This time, it was Fiza who was under fire. She vehemently refused to have any conversation about getting married, leading to heated arguments and some amount of violence. The tension in the house was palpable.

'I don't want to talk about marriage right now. I want to complete my education and have a career. Don't shatter my dreams,' she screamed. Her proud Pashtun father, Sadiq-ur-Rahman, wouldn't take no for an answer. He stormed towards her and slapped her across the face, growling at her, 'Nobody asked you for your opinion.' The entire room fell silent. He looked at Fiza's mother, giving her a cold stare as he walked out of the room.

Fiza, a BEd student at Sir Syed College in Kohat, was a Pashtun from the most orthodox, backward and dangerous part of Pakistan. She was not going to have it easy in fighting tradition and finding her own path towards having a career as a native of Karak, a district in Pakistan known to be inhabited primarily by one tribe of Pashtuns: the Khattak tribe.

While her ancestral home was in Karak, Fiza's family had moved to Kohat, just 77 kilometres away, due to her father's job. Both cities fall under the Kohat division of Khyber Pakhtunkhwa; the latter is the capital of Kohat district. The majority of Kohat's population is from the Bangash tribe of Pashtuns. Sadiq-ur-Rahman was the revenue officer at the Water and Power Development Authority (WAPDA).

With two siblings married off, Fiza was the third in line. She was very close to her sister Abida, in whom she would confide everything going on in her life.

Distraught and troubled, Fiza ran up to the terrace on that bone-chilling wintry night when the temperature was less than 4 degrees Celsius. Abida rushed after her. She walked on to the terrace and found Fiza fiddling with her mobile phone. As soon as she came closer, a startled Fiza hid it.

'What is it, Fiza? What are you doing with the phone? Are you hiding something from me?' asked Abida.

Fiza was staring at the floor, fidgeting with her mobile. 'It's nothing,' she said, looking away.

'You are lying and I know it. What is wrong? It's more than just the wedding talk, and why the hell did you talk back? You had it coming. He is not getting you married off right away. Tell me, what is it?' demanded Abida.

Fiza pulled Abida to one side and sat down on the carpet placed by the door to the terrace. She looked sheepishly at Abida and said, 'I've been talking to a boy. Just hear me out before you bite my head off. It is more complicated than that. I really like him. He is a good guy.'

Abida interrupted Fiza, 'Are you out of your mind? Do you know what they will do to you if they find out? Get you married off to the first animal they find on the street. Or they might just kill both of you to save the honour of the family. This is crazy.'

'That's not it,' said Fiza. She looked Abida in the eye and said quietly, 'He is from India.'

'India! You sure have a death wish,' she snarled.

'Please help me and try to understand. I can't help what I feel for him. I have never felt like this before. I won't be able to live without him,' she said, tears rolling down her cheeks.

Abida could not bear to see Fiza cry. She hugged her tightly and then asked her the boy's name. 'Hamid,' said Fiza, coyly wiping her tears away. The little sister smiled and the two embraced each other in a tight hug. 'Will you help me? I cannot live without him,' Fiza asked. Abida nodded but her apprehension was evident. She wanted her sister to be happy.

At night, the two sisters slept after offering a small *dua*, a prayer for peace and love.

The next morning, Fiza and Abida kept giggling while serving breakfast to the elders. Their mother frowned and pinched Fiza, reminding her that the house was in mourning, but the girls just couldn't help themselves. They quickly finished their chores and ran to the backyard for some peace and quiet.

Even in the crowded city dwelling, the small backyard of this old house had a few guava trees and the light of a warm winter sun that made Fiza feel dizzy with love. The girls spread out a rug and sat with their cups of tea and morning roti. Abida asked Fiza if she had a photo of Hamid. Fiza, giving her a naughty look, told her she did. She pulled out her phone and showed it to her. Abida smiled, looking at the phone, and approved. The two girls chatted till it was time to help the other women prepare lunch for the entire household of relatives.

During lunch, one of Fiza's uncles broached the idea of marriage and a suitable boy for Fiza. She heard this and stormed out of the room. 'I know why he is doing this . . . because he and his wife know that I hate the idea of getting married right now and they will do all it takes to create a scene. Such nuisance mongers,' she snapped when Abida came running into the bedroom.

Fiza stayed hungry the whole day, not eating a morsel of food. That night, she called up Hamid, with Abida sitting right next to her. 'I don't think I can live like this. I can't live without you,' she said to Hamid, who asked her what had happened in a worried tone. She narrated the whole story and told him that her sister had learnt about them and that she was on their side. 'She will help us, Hamid,' said Fiza.

Abida gestured that she wanted to speak to Hamid. Fiza asked Hamid if that was okay, and he agreed. 'Salaam, Hamid Bhai, I am Abida.

Hope you are well,' she said, according him the respect one does to a brother.

Hamid smiled at the affable voice on the other side and replied with the same pleasantries. 'Salaam, Abida, I am fine. How are you? Hope both of you are keeping well. I am worried about Fiza. Is all okay?' he asked.

'No. Everything is not fine. There is a lot of talk about marriage in the house, which is straining relations between Abbu and Fiza. She hasn't eaten anything since morning. I am worried for her. I want to help the two of you but I don't know how. Staying hungry is certainly not the solution, I know that,' said Abida when Fiza snatched the phone from her.

'Fiza, come on, you cannot starve yourself to death. Eat something. We will try to figure things out together,' reassured Hamid.

'If you say so . . . but Hamid, I am telling you that I will take some drastic step if my family forces me to marry anyone else. You are my world and I won't have it any other way,' she said firmly.

'Okay, my dear. May Allah's blessings be upon you. Eat something and sleep well,' said Hamid.

Fiza held the phone to her heart and kissed it. She put it inside her pocket and rubbed her hands as she walked down the stairs from the terrace. As she entered the passageway, she saw her uncle there, looking at her questioningly. She quickly went to the room where all the girls were asleep and snuck into bed beside Abida.

A few days later, Fiza was helping her mother in the kitchen while her brother and father were taking an afternoon nap, when they heard some boys in the neighbourhood creating a ruckus while playing cricket right outside their house. An angry Sadiq-ur-Rahman went out screaming blue murder but to no avail. 'This is not the time to play. Get out of here, else you'll have hell to pay,' he howled. The young lads laughed at the old man's protestations and continued their game. Sadiq went back inside and complained, sitting beside his son, Gauhar, who was lying down on the bed. Suddenly getting furious, Fiza's brother stormed out with a gun in his hand and fired at them. One of the boys was shot, and he died on the spot. The others ran away. Hearing gunshots, the neighbours came running; some peeped out of their windows to see a boy on the ground and Gauhar standing by his door, holding a pistol.

Gauhar ran inside the house and told his father what had happened. Sadiq slapped his son and shook him hard while screaming into his ears, 'What have you done? Do you know what you have brought upon this family? We are ruined.'

'I did it for your honour,' Gauhar screamed back, while his father pushed him and then kicked him to the floor. 'You fool,' said Sadiq, not expecting the reaction that was to follow. Gauhar trained the gun on his father and fired a shot. Luckily, the bullet just grazed his head near his earlobe and hit the wall behind him. Sadiq started bleeding.

Hearing all the gunshots and commotion, the women of the house ran out to see Sadiq on the floor. Gauhar darted out of the house. The neighbours called an ambulance and Sadiq was rushed to the hospital.

The pillars of the house had fallen, the foundation had been shaken. Seven women were left to fend for themselves.

~

After a few days, Fiza heard a knock on the door. She opened it to find a village elder standing there with a few other men. 'Call your mother,' he said.

Her distraught mother walked to the door. She was informed by the men that a jirga (a tribal council, which is all-powerful in such areas) was being formed to decide the fate of her son and that she should be present there with a male member of the house. She burst into tears and said that her husband was in the hospital. She was told that her husband's brother had been informed.

The next morning, Fiza's uncle and aunt arrived (the same uncle and aunt who wanted Fiza married off). Her mother got ready, wore her veil and stepped out to go to the village council. The elders and the chief of the council were sitting on benches while other villagers stood around them in a semicircle. On one side stood the family of the boy who had been killed, an inconsolable mother and father. On the other side stood Fiza's uncle and mother. The families knew each other, and had even broken bread together. But today, one mother stood against the other in this court, seeking justice for the blood of her son. Revenge. Compensation.

With the men of the family absent and no money to offer, the jirga invoked the custom of *wani* (or *wanni*), giving a girl's hand in marriage or servitude to the aggrieved party as a form of compensation. That was decided as the punishment. Fiza was to be married off to an elder male of the dead boy's family as punishment for the murder of one of the sons of that family.

The judgement was final. No questions were asked, and there were no protests. Fiza's family came back home. Abida ran to the door upon seeing her mother and uncle walk in. Fiza brought them water. They all sat on the charpoy in the courtyard. Her mother hugged Fiza and started wailing. The two girls also started crying. Through her tears, Fiza kept asking what had happened at the council meeting.

Her uncle finally spoke. 'The jirga has decided that you are to be married into that family as wani for your brother's crime,' he said with tears in his eyes.

Fiza's world came crashing down.

3

Hamid

In my twenties, life was as good as it could get. Living with my mother, father and brother, I did not have any responsibilities to bear. They gave me everything within their means to make me the man I was.

My mother, Fauzia Ansari, was a lecturer in junior college, and my father, Nehal Ansari, was a marketing manager in Bank of India. My brother and I received a good education and even went abroad for higher studies. I completed my engineering degree and went to Dubai for an MBA internship, and my brother, Khalid, studied dentistry in Pune, India, and implantology in New York, USA.

I was an active member of the Rotaract Club, which is a derivative of Rotary International, and volunteered in many social projects like teaching at regional-language schools, helping students from weaker sections of society, cleaning the streets, etc. I had a good set of friends and we all did a fair bit of voluntary work.

With the help of my club members, I played host to students from universities across the globe. I made friends with exchange students from Japan, Hong Kong, Afghanistan and other countries. That's where I came across Hamdan Khan, who promised to host me if I ever visited his country, Afghanistan.

Fiza . . . where was she?

Having not experienced the burden of responsibility that comes with adult life, I felt weighed down by the events of the past couple of months. The sense of responsibility towards another human being. The need to ensure she was safe. Where was she? How was she? These thoughts were killing me.

Days passed, but there was no news from Fiza. I went online every half an hour to check if there was a message from her but there was none . . . No communication from anywhere. All I had was a mobile number which was not responsive. My messages went undelivered, and devastating thoughts of death, forced marriage and suicide flooded my mind. I needed to find a way to reach her.

Every day was a brutal assault on my being. I was crushed. I was losing hope, and with it, my mind, appetite, health and sanity. Ammi and Abbu were visibly worried about me. Khalid came to me one day and sat me down. As instructed by Ammi, Khalid asked, 'Are you possessed? What is up with you? We are all worried.'

Citing work-related tension, I said, 'Don't worry, Bhai. I am not doing drugs and am not involved in any kind of substance abuse. The distance and timing of my work is just taking a toll on me. That's all,' I said.

~

Two months passed with no word from her. On 22 February 2012, with no hope but only by force of habit, I went online to check if there was any message. Nothing. Suddenly, Fiza came online and wrote, 'Hamid, I am in deep trouble. I am the sacrificial lamb in this wani custom of ours. Please come and rescue me or I will die. I don't want to be a victim of wani.'

She quickly typed all these words and went offline, giving me no time to respond or even ask her any questions.

I did not know what this wani custom was. I was troubled and needed to speak to someone. So, I called up one of my friends from college, Shabnam, and asked her to meet me. I desperately needed advice.

The next day, we met for coffee at Café Coffee Day. I narrated the entire story to her. She sat in silence for a while and then said, 'Hamid, do you know what you have got yourself into? Are you sure about the girl? What if this is not real?' she inquired.

I told her that I knew Fiza was in trouble and that I needed to help her.

'If you are so confident then see how you want to go about it. But I am warning you. You could get into trouble. Pakistan is not safe,' she said with concern.

Only two scenarios played out in my mind. Either I went ahead alone, or I sought help and had somebody guide me through this so I could eventually rescue Fiza. I did not share my plans with Shabnam but I promised her that I would be careful.

While taking the local train back home, I kept wondering what could have happened to her. Feeling suffocated, I decided to go to the beach and sit there for a while.

I was deep in thought when I saw a man walk past me carrying cages filled with exotic birds. Fiza came to mind. I couldn't bear the sight. I bought one of the birds and set it free. But it didn't help. If anything, I felt worse thinking of Fiza in a similar situation. I cried all the way home. Why had life come to such a pass?

Later that night, I determined to draw up a plan. First, I wanted to find out a little more about Fiza's town and her community. So I started my research. I went back to recollecting our conversations to figure out where to start. 'Pashto. We speak Pashto,' she had said once.

I went online and typed 'Pashto, Pashtun, Kohat, Pakistan' and clicked the search button. I started reading up on the culture of the place. It was then that I came across an explanation of wani, which left me feeling cold and numb. I reached out to a man called Shah Sahab on the Internet, who explained the practice to me.

'It is prevalent among the tribals of Afghanistan and Pakistan. It involves women being given away in marriage as compensation for crimes committed by male members of their family. More often than not it is in cases of murder,' said Shah Sahab.

'What about the laws of the land?' I asked in shock.

'The laws don't apply in these parts of the country. It is the jirga that controls the administrative and judicial systems. They follow their own law and are supreme. The rulings of the jirga cannot be defied,' came the response.

'What happens if the girl defies them?' I asked, knowing that my plans depended on his answer.

'Death. The girl is hunted down and killed in the most brutal manner imaginable. The family is ostracized and the other girls of the house are left unbetrothed. Why do you ask?' he said.

'I was just doing some research and wanted to understand this wani system,' was my effortless reply since I had prepared myself for such a question.

But I was also constantly questioning myself. Was I doing the right thing? In hindsight, I should have done things very differently, and maybe not have acted upon the desires of my heart. But back then, my heart didn't know better. Thus, I began planning.

That evening when I got home, Ammi came running to me. Stuffing a piece of mithai into my mouth, she said, 'I have some good news for you.'

I smiled and asked, 'What is it, Ammi? What's all the celebration about?'

'We have fixed Khalid's marriage. We don't have the dates yet but the girl is very nice and they both seem to like each other,' my mother said as she swayed in joy.

I looked at Khalid; he smiled. We hugged each other. I was so happy for him. 'We need to talk, my man. How did this happen? Finally!' I exclaimed.

'There is so much to do,' Ammi said aloud like a little girl. Then she looked at the three of us staring at her—Khalid, Abbu and I. She composed herself and said, 'Let me not get ahead of myself. One step at a time.'

The three of us roared with laughter. The sound of that soothed my aching heart a little.

We all had dinner. Ammi had prepared Khalid's favourite mutton qorma and my favourite dessert, kheer.

After dinner, we chatted for a while and then Khalid and I went into his room. 'Tell me everything,' I said.

He pulled out a photograph of the girl. 'I really like her. I am so excited. We have to plan a lot of things. I know how I want my wedding to be. You better get your act together. And get out of the funk you have been in,' he warned me with the warm look of an elder brother.

I hugged him and wished him goodnight. 'Dream about your girl,' I teased him and left the room.

I was very happy for my brother. But I had to get on with my plan. I was a man on a mission.

4

The Search

I woke up the next morning determined to make some headway. The first thing I did was go online to check if there was any message from Fiza.

But there was no word from her. I kept speculating about the trouble she could be in. I had no idea. But I only hoped and prayed it wasn't what Shah Sahab had told me: a case of forced marriage.

'If I have to go to Pakistan, I have to do it right,' I said to myself.

I went online and checked the Pakistan High Commission's website for the documents needed to apply for a visa. It was clearly specified that for any personal travel, I would require an invitation from someone in Pakistan. So, I got thinking.

It struck me that I could use my membership of the Rotaract Club in Mumbai. I went through the Rotary database and found a fellow Rotarian from across the border—Peshawar, in particular—who could help me with my visa.

In the Rotary database, Pakistan was divided into two districts: 3271 and 3272. There were two prominent individuals on the 3272 list, which included Lahore, Islamabad and Peshawar: Mr Ahsanullah from Islamabad, and Advocate Abdul Rauf Rohaila from Peshawar. I decided to connect with the lawyer since he was from Peshawar in Khyber Pakhtunkhwa, where Fiza said she lives.

I found his mobile number from the club directory and wrote to him. 'Hello, Rotarian Rohaila. I am Rotaractor Hamid Ansari, club president from Mumbai, India. I wish to visit Rotary Peshawar. Would you be able to help me with an invitation letter for my visa? It would greatly help facilitate the process. I would be obliged.'

Promptly came the answer in the affirmative. He sent me a text message which read: 'I invite Rotaractor Hamid Ansari to Rotary Club, Peshawar.'

'Is this a joke?' I cried out loud. Fuming, I wrote back, 'Rohaila Sahab, I would require the invitation to be on the Rotary letterhead and not just via text message.'

'I am sorry, Hamid. I am no longer on the board of the club and therefore cannot send you an invite on the letterhead. You should get in touch with our DG, Ahsanullah Sahab,' he replied, sending the contact number of the man.

It was March 2012, the time of year when most district conferences in Rotary clubs across the world took place. I thought I was in luck. I sent a message to DG Rotarian Ahsanullah that I wanted to attend the district conference in Islamabad and requested an invitation for the same to apply for a visa.

The next day when I opened my inbox, I saw an email from Ahsanullah. I couldn't believe it was happening. I opened the mail to find his 'letter of invite' attached to the mail. '*Shukriya*,' I muttered under my breath, heaving a sigh of relief.

I looked up the contact details of the Pakistan High Commission and called the number.

'Salaam, Pakistan High Commission. Whom do you wish to speak to?' asked a man's voice.

'Hello, my name is Hamid Ansari. Could you put me in touch with the officer in charge of visas? I am from the Rotaract Club and wish to attend a conference in Pakistan.'

'Do you have an invitation?' he asked.

I told him that I did. The officer then told me that I should fax the invite to them for their perusal.

'Should I send my visa application form and the requisite documents?'

'Not necessary. Just send the invite first. We will send it further on. Only after clearance from Islamabad will you be able to apply for a visa.'

I did the needful. The next day, I called to check if they had received my letter.

The call was put on hold and then I heard a voice saying, 'Hello, how can I help?'

'Hello, I am from the Rotaract Club of India and wish to attend a conference on 30–31 March in Pakistan. Whom am I speaking with, sir?' I asked.

The voice said, 'I am Kamaal. We have received the invitation letter by fax, but for any visa issuance, we need clearance from our interior ministry.'

'How long could that take?' I asked.

'I don't know. It depends. We will keep you posted. I have all your details. You can reach me on this number for any further inquiry,' said Kamaal.

I felt a sense of relief along with some anxiety. Would I be able to go to Pakistan by the end of the month?

~

Days passed with no response from the mission. Closer to 30 March, I started calling Kamaal almost every day, only to get the same reply—it was still with the Ministry of Interior and the moment they heard from Islamabad, they would issue the visa.

India–Pakistan became a regular topic of conversation I would broach with anyone willing to listen. I would never reveal too much. This was how I learnt of Jatin Desai, an active member of the India–Pakistan peace forum. I thought maybe he could help me with my visa.

The only journalist I knew at that time was a distant cousin, Shabana, who was working with *DNA*, a Mumbai-based newspaper. I called her to find out if she knew about him. She did, and I noted down his phone number. I quickly ended the call with Shabana and dialled Jatin Desai to introduce myself. I told him that someone I knew in Pakistan was in trouble and I was trying to get a visa to go there. I inquired if he could help. He agreed to meet.

Two days later, I met him at the Fun Republic Mall. After exchanging pleasantries, I told him, 'There is a girl in Pakistan who's in trouble and she happens to be my close friend.' I also told him that I suspected this was a case of wani. Jatin was a kind, soft-spoken man and was shocked to hear this. He told me that Khyber Pakhtunkhwa and the tribal areas were dangerous terrain where the writ of tribal leaders was the law. So if anything went wrong, he said, 'One would be pretty much on their own.'

Jatin also told me that it was quite difficult for Indian nationals to get a Pakistan visa. However, with proper documents and a genuine invitation letter, it could work out. On learning that my destination was Kohat, he was a little apprehensive. But he told me he would try to do whatever he could. I followed up with him for a while but nothing came of it.

On 30 March, I had just about lost all hope. I was extremely disappointed in the Pakistani administrative system. How inefficient could they be? I had provided all the documents! Little did I know that there was no intention on their part to issue me a visa in the first place.

The disturbing thought of Fiza being in trouble kept creeping in. Now I started feeling bad for her as a human being. How could life be so unjust? What barbarism was this that was probably destroying the lives of so many young women in Pakistan?

I called up Ahsanullah Sahab for advice. He told me that since I had missed the Rotary district conference, I could attend the district conference for Rotaract Club, which was to be held in May. He asked me to contact Rotaractor Adnan Saboor Rohaila, a barrister, whose letter would hold more value than letters from any other member of the club. He was the son of Abdul Rauf Rohaila. I messaged him. Wasting no time, he sent me an invite for the conference scheduled in May 2012.

I was so excited. Ahsanullah's words rang in my head: 'His letter is more important than anybody else's.' I thought I had winged it. I forwarded the invitation letter directly to the High Commission of Pakistan, New Delhi, and then called Kamaal.

'Good afternoon, Kamaal Sir, I have sent a fresh invitation letter for a conference to be held in May. Since the date of the last conference is over, you might require a fresh invitation to consider my visa request,' I said.

'Oh, I thought you had missed the conference so you no longer require the visa,' said Kamaal matter-of-factly.

'No. I do require a visa to travel to Pakistan. I want to participate in the Rotaract conference there. I have sent you a fresh invitation. Please see it,' I replied.

After a couple of moments of silence, Kamaal told me that there was no need for another invitation letter as my previous letter and application was still up for clearance from the Ministry of Interior.

There was uncertainty in his voice. But I was confident that this new invitation would hold me in good stead. I had to prepare myself for the journey. Where should I start? Well, learning a little more about the area's language and culture would be a good beginning.

I planned my days such that I could return from work every day and spend time researching on the Internet. Ammi, like most worried mothers, would ask me what I was up to. I would just say that work was keeping me busy.

I started looking for websites that could teach me Pashto, the language people primarily spoke in Kohat. With great difficulty, I found one that taught basic conversations. But I had to learn more than just pleasantries. So I looked for a contact on the website and found an email address. I wrote to the person, seeking more help. The owner of the website responded with the email address of the person responsible for Pashto content.

That was a start. I immediately wrote to the address, reiterating my request, and got an offer of help from a man called Rahmat Khan. As time passed and our familiarity grew, I found him to be a very kind-hearted soul from Afghanistan. I told him the entire story about Fiza and me. He said that even though he was an Afghan, he lived in Peshawar and knew one of the elderly imams of a mosque in Kohat. Imams are highly respected in the tribal areas and their word is considered sacrosanct.

A glimmer of hope. I shared details of where Fiza had said she lived, and also told him what I knew of her family and their place of origin, Karak. I told him about my struggle to obtain a visa for Pakistan.

He assured me he would do his best. That was the first time I actually discussed all these things with someone. I felt lighter, like somebody was there to share my burden, someone who understood my problem and why I wanted to save Fiza.

While I waited for my visa, I started doing my own search of Fiza's exact whereabouts. All I had was her phone number. So, I started by finding out which company the number belonged to. Google showed Telenor as the telecom service provider. The next thing I did was go on Facebook and search for 'Telenor'. I got multiple results—details of the company, employees, pages, posts, etc. I messaged a few of the employees that I needed help, but got no answer.

I waited a day to see if anything came up. The next day, after I returned from work, I quickly had dinner and went to my room. I turned on my computer to check for responses. None whatsoever. I was stymied.

I lay down on the bed, thinking of newer ways to hunt out information. I went online and checked if I could find someone working in Telenor. I left a few messages, saying I needed to get in touch with a friend who was in trouble.

The next morning when I woke up and checked my inbox, lo and behold! I had a bunch of messages from men and women. I thought it best to reach out to one of the women. Afreen, an employee of Telenor from Lahore, was willing to help me. I struck up an informal conversation to verify whether it was a genuine or fake account. Once I was convinced, I explained the situation my friend Fiza was in. I shared Fiza's contact number with Afreen, and she said she would try finding out more details and get back in a day or two.

I was quite pleased with the progress I had made through open-source intelligence (OSINT), just using the Internet to my advantage. I didn't feel like I was doing anything wrong. I was trying to save a girl, an innocent soul who was being thrown into a life she didn't ask for.

Life was on autopilot. I was numb; nothing excited me any more. I was becoming a little irritable and wasn't my usual jovial self. My brother and mother both noticed it. Khalid came to my room one night and asked again, 'Hamid, what's up with you? You have changed a lot. Is there something you want to talk about? Is there a girl? Are you seeing someone?'

I shot him a look and feigned a laugh. 'Not at all. I really am tired with all the work. Frankly, I think I want to look at doing my wallet business full-time, Bhai. Let's see.'

Khalid and I spoke for a while and then he called it a night since he had an early morning the next day at the clinic.

I logged in to my account and saw a message from Afreen. Excited, I read it, only to realize that she wanted something from me. 'Hamid, I am writing to you for some help. You told me you are into social service. Would it be possible to help an NGO that I am associated with? It does a lot of work to help deprived persons,' said her message.

I was absolutely disheartened since I was yet to get any information about Fiza. But I told her that transferring money was not an option for me. Instead, I connected her with some of the Rotarians in Lahore.

A few days later, I received another message from her which I hurriedly opened to find some details about Fiza—and the phone numbers of her friends and family members. The number that Fiza was using was registered in the name of her father, Sadiq-ur-Rahman, which confirmed that Fiza had not lied to me. But I still did not have her location.

I messaged Afreen, 'Thank you, Afreen. But how do I get her location?' She replied, 'The best way to get that is to contact the National Database and Registration Authority [NADRA], the agency that maintains such records.'

I thanked her for all her help and bade her goodbye.

I followed the same OSINT procedure with NADRA, searching for it on the web and connecting with some of its employees on social media. I found an employee named Nawaz who seemed to be in a senior position. I wrote to him, 'Hello, I am Hamid Ansari and I have been trying to locate my friend who belongs to Kohat. Could you help me with the address if I share the CNIC [Computerized National Identity Card] number with you? This is urgent. Please help, if you can. Look forward to hearing from you.'

There was no response. So I logged out and went to bed. The next morning, I checked my inbox and saw a reply from Nawaz. He had asked for the CNIC number. I shared all the details with him before leaving for work.

Later that evening, when I returned home and sat in front of my computer, I saw a mail from Nawaz. He had not only sent me her location but also a screenshot of Form B of that CNIC number which had details of the entire family—the number of family members, their names, photographs, addresses, dates of birth, spouse details, etc.

The only thing that confused me was that the registered address was in Karak, whereas I remembered her telling me that they had moved to Kohat because of her father's job. It all boiled down to the same question: Where could Fiza be? Karak or Kohat, which were an hour's drive from each other?

I again took to the Internet and searched for Karak through my social media profile. I messaged people who were from the place. Someone called Atta-ur-Rahman responded. His profile picture showed a middle-aged, portly looking man with a round face and a moustache, wearing a cap. Rahman told me that he was a native of Sargodha but had moved to Karak when he was very young. He was a journalist with *Dastak*, a local newspaper.

'Rahman Sahab, I am very worried for my friend. Will you please find out if she is okay? She didn't tell me much but I only know that her father, Sadiq-ur-Rahman, and her entire family are in trouble. She mentioned something about wani. What is it? Will you please find out and let me know?'

'Don't worry, Hamid. Let me get more details. We have reporters across the district. I will touch base with my reporters in Karak and let you know.'

Slowly, we became good friends. One day, I decided to tell him the truth about Fiza and me. This was beyond friendship, I told Atta-ur-Rahman.

He replied, 'As a journalist, I had once helped another couple. Hamid, don't worry, my reporters are finding out about Fiza and her family. Let us see what they come up with.'

I asked, 'Do I need to be there to help Fiza or can it be done in any other way?'

He said, 'A local would never dare to help a girl, especially one who has been given away in wani, as ordered by the jirga. The chances of getting caught are very high. But if you come and we prepare a foolproof plan then it will never come back to us. It is best that you come here. We just need to figure out how.'

Meanwhile, I also found another individual on Facebook who was from Karak and happened to be a medical student in Islamabad, Dr Shazia. I sent her a personal message on Facebook and told her I was seeking help for Fiza. After a few days, she replied saying that she would help me in any way possible.

I was glad to have another source in Pakistan.

It was nearing May, which was when the second conference was to be held, so I called up the Pakistan High Commission in New Delhi to get an update on my visa status. I got the same reply, 'Clearance has not come from Islamabad.'

I lost my cool and yelled into the phone, 'Am I a terrorist? I volunteer for an NGO and only want to attend a conference. This is how you treat someone who works for peace?' I hung up in anger.

Once I had cooled off, I regretted my actions since it was not the visa officer's fault that I wasn't being granted a visa. But I couldn't undo my actions. I felt there was no hope there.

I tried a few more things, like getting in touch with UNESCO to see if they had a study project anywhere in Pakistan, and checking with UNESCO Islamabad to see if they needed volunteers or workers, but to no avail.

Through Facebook, I learnt about the Kohat University of Science and Technology. Since it was the biggest institute in Kohat, I thought the university would be able to get me a visa if it invited me for a project. I called to discuss my proposal. The man in charge of the exchange programme and seminars was Mr Khattak, who sounded very rude and arrogant on the phone but gave me a hearing nonetheless.

I even went to the extent of sourcing the number of Rehman Malik, the then interior minister of Pakistan, and reached out to him since somebody told me that he had once helped an Indian journalist get a visa upon her request to him on Twitter. I called up the number and spoke to Malik's secretary. I told him about the trouble I was going through for a simple visa. But he told me that they did not interfere in the current visa process as it was a matter of national security.

Facebook was flooded with news of Imran Khan coming up as a new leader in Pakistan. I even tried to reach out to him but his party representatives on social media said that since they were not in power there was precious little they could do.

Meanwhile, a Rotary member, Farzana Jafar from Islamabad, came into my horizon. I discussed my concerns with her and updated her about the invitation letters. She said that she would be happy to have me there and would definitely help me with the clearance as she knew someone in the Ministry of Interior. A few days later, she said that the ministry was trying to reach the person who had invited me to confirm the authenticity of the invitation but Adnan Rohaila had not responded to their requests. And all this while I had been blaming the Pakistani administration. But then again, I didn't know whom to believe and whom to blame any more.

There was only one moment of clarity that emerged from all these efforts. Getting a visa for Pakistan was not an option. I would have to find another way to rescue Fiza.

5

Rescue Mission: Failed Attempt

It was the third week of May when Atta-ur-Rahman left a message for me on social media. I could see the words 'bad news'. I quickly opened my inbox.

'Hamid Bhai, I have found out that Sadiq-ur-Rahman and his son Gauhar have been tried by the jirga because of the killing of a young boy from the neighbourhood in a cricket-pitch scuffle, where he opened fire in rage. Sadiq is out on bail after accepting that he did it. The village council has ordered that Fiza be married off as compensation, as part of the wani tradition here. You were right that the family is in big trouble, Hamid Bhai,' the message read.

My fears had come true. I sat on my bed and stared at the wall for a long time, till I saw that Rahman was online. My fingers shivered at what I had just learnt.

I typed, 'Why Fiza? Is this the final decision? Did her father not do anything to save her?'

He explained, 'The actual incident had taken place in February. However, the matter got delayed since the father was in hospital. That wretched boy shot at his own father. Sadiq-ur-Rahman had a narrow escape, and as soon as he recovered, the first thing he did was take the blame on himself and ensure that there was no case against his son. That is when the jirga was called to take up the matter. By the time he was out of hospital and on bail, tragedy had already befallen his family.'

All that rang in my ears was Fiza saying, 'I will die!' Feeling numb, I thought to myself that I would have to find a way to reach her. What if she killed herself?

I told Atta-ur-Rahman about the visa situation. He then suggested that if I did not get a visa for Pakistan, I could also try to enter the country through Afghanistan via the Torkham border. I told him I would think about it. He said goodnight and reminded me that I had very little time to plan things and even lesser time to execute them.

I only caught snatches of rest that night. This would be illegal. What if I got caught? The thought of leaving my family behind without a word was killing me.

The next morning, I sent in a resignation letter to my office. My mother could see that something was not right about my behaviour. She gave me tea and asked, 'Son, what is wrong with you? You look like you haven't slept a wink. You have been acting very different for the past few months. Tell me. Maybe I'll be able to help.'

I looked into the kind eyes of my mother and thought of the betrayal I was going to put her through. I couldn't bear to think about it.

My father and Khalid walked into the room for breakfast. 'You haven't left for the clinic yet?' I asked Khalid.

He said he would leave a little later. 'Why do you look like death? What is the matter?' he asked.

'I said the same thing. This is more than work,' chided my mother.

I looked at my brother and gestured to drop the topic right now. *We will talk later*, I signalled. He quickly picked up on it and said, 'He must just be tired. You should look for a new job if this one is keeping you so unhappy,' he said. I concurred.

My father didn't understand what was happening. He just added, 'Do what makes you happy.' We all smiled at that.

It had always been a relief to have Khalid around. He was only two years older than me, but he had taken care of me all through my school years when we would return home early while my parents were still at work.

I missed having him around when he left for Pune to pursue dentistry. I kept in touch with him on a regular basis. My father had given him a mobile phone—a rare possession in those days. I would call him from our landline almost every day to fill him in on what was happening.

We were close, but somehow I couldn't get myself to tell him about Fiza or my plans. I had to keep it a secret. I knew if I told him, he would never allow me to take such a drastic step and would inform my parents. So, I kept everything to myself.

His phone rang and I saw him smile. Assuming it was a call from his fiancée, we let him leave the table and go to the other room.

I finished breakfast and then went to my room. The moment I thought of Afghanistan, I could only think of one man—my friend Rahmat Khan, who had introduced me to the Pashto language. I immediately called him and told him about my situation. I wanted his advice on whether crossing over from Afghanistan was a good idea. He said, 'It is dangerous, but possible. You need a foolproof plan. I found out from the imam in Kohat that the girl and her family are in trouble and also untraceable. I suppose they are in hiding.'

He added that I had some time since Ramzan and Eid was around the corner and any action would only take place after the festival. 'You have three months to come here and rescue Fiza. Move fast.'

So, it was certain that Afghanistan was the only option. Now, I had two Herculean tasks in front of me: convincing my family, and getting a visa for Kabul.

The next morning, I told my parents that while I was job hunting in India, I would also like to explore the idea of going abroad.

Ammi and Abbu looked at each other and wondered what that meant. Ammi said in an encouraging tone, 'That is very good to hear. But what do you have in mind?'

I asked them to come to my room and turned on the computer. They walked in wondering what I was up to. I opened websites with job offers in Afghanistan. 'Look, there is ample opportunity in Kabul. I want to go there and see if things work out for me,' I said.

'Absolutely not,' said Ammi. 'Haven't you seen the news? It is dangerous to go there. What is wrong in working here? Find something here,' she said, shaking her head in disapproval.

My father was quiet for a while and then said, 'Look at the pros and cons first. And then decide whether you want to take such a big step.'

Ammi glared at Abbu and turned back to me. 'It is a no! You are not going to Kabul. Find work here,' she said and left the room.

But I was determined to go and was just getting them used to the idea that I would go abroad for work.

Later, I called the Afghanistan consulate in Mumbai and inquired about the visa procedure and requirements. I told the officer that I wanted to travel to Kabul to explore business options. He told me that the consulate did not handle business visas, only visitor visas, but since I did not have family in Afghanistan, that was not an option. He said that business visas were issued only in New Delhi. I called up the embassy in Delhi and was connected to the concerned officer who explained that I would have to travel to Delhi and apply in person.

That evening, my father, mother and brother were sitting and chatting over cups of tea. I walked up to my mother and sat down next to her. 'Ammi, I have been exploring job options in Kabul. I found a job at the airport. I will be paid well. I need to do this. Please let me go. I'll have to go to Delhi for the visa. Please.'

My mother looked visibly upset. My father intervened. Although Ammi is the boss of the house and Abbu very rarely disagrees with her, he came to my rescue. 'If you have thought it through then you should give it a try,' he said. He turned to my mother and said, 'Let him go. He is a grown, wise man. He wants to do something on his own.'

Khalid looked at me. He saw the plea in my eyes and shrugged. 'Ammi, let him go. We need to find our own paths. He seems to have a plan.'

Ammi hesitatingly approved. 'If you insist. But I will be worried sick. And it's not fair to put me through that,' she said.

I took that as a yes and prepared to travel to Delhi. I booked a train ticket for the next day and left with all my documents. Being the proprietor of a wallet business, I had the requisite papers to apply for a business visa.

Upon reaching Delhi, I immediately headed to the Afghanistan embassy where I was asked to meet the commercial attaché since my case was for a business visa. I walked through the gate after clearing security and was taken to a room. Ahmad Fardin Zalali was waiting for me in his spacious room, which had an Afghani carpet on the floor. This was the first time I felt things were moving in the right direction.

'Good afternoon, sir. Thank you for meeting me and giving me time,' I said and handed over my documents.

He went through the papers and asked for the invitation letter from Kabul.

I looked puzzled and asked, 'What invitation?'

'You need an invitation from the company that wishes to do business with you, my friend,' he said.

'I am not going to do business with one individual or company. I want to go there and explore market opportunities and develop my business,' I explained.

He plainly refused and said that the rules did not allow him to issue a visa without an invitation and that I needed to either get an invitation from Kabul or a letter from the Indian Chamber of Commerce to authenticate my claim of purpose.

I started thinking of what to do even as Zalali spoke. I sought some time from him and left the room. I stepped out of the embassy complex and immediately called Rahmat Khan in Kabul.

He said he could arrange an invitation from a friend's company but that would take time.

I was so miffed that I called up the Afghanistan consulate in Mumbai and blasted the person who picked up the phone. 'You said that I could get a business visa here. I have come with all the documents but nobody told me about an invitation letter,' I shouted.

The voice on the other side said he was not familiar with my case. He connected me to the commercial attaché in Mumbai, Farooq Rohaila.

'Hello, yes. Please tell me, what is the matter?'

'Sir, I was told that business visas are issued only in Delhi so I travelled here from Mumbai with all the documents that the consulate specified. Now they want an invitation letter as well. I only want to explore business opportunities in Afghanistan. How many Indians are looking at that? This will only enhance trade between the two countries,' I said, sounding very stressed.

Rohaila calmly said, 'Mr Ansari, I was not aware of your case. Please come back to Mumbai. I will issue you a visa from here. But I will certainly require an invitation letter.'

I was stunned to hear that business visas were issued in Mumbai as well. 'Your office told me that Mumbai does not handle business visas,' I said.

A miscommunication, misunderstanding or an ill-informed official—whatever it was, I had ended up losing time and money. Since I happened to be in Delhi, I decided to go to the High Commission of Pakistan to meet Kamaal and see if there had been any movement on my visa application. There was a window on the side of the building that was for visa applicants. The person in charge asked me to wait. A while later, Kamaal came to the room from the main building which was well within the compound.

'I was in Delhi so I thought I would come and check on my visa status, Mr Kamaal,' I said. His response was the same, 'You should've called. There is no development. We are still awaiting clearance from Islamabad.'

I went back to the station and managed to book myself on the next train to Mumbai, which was the following day. I spent the night in the railway dormitory.

I reached home the day after that, exhausted. Ammi asked me what had happened. I told her that I had to wait for some documents to come from Kabul. I crashed on my bed. Later that night, I logged on to the Internet to see if there was any message from Fiza or a mail from Rahmat Khan. There was nothing.

Two days later, I saw Rahmat Khan's name pop up in my mailbox. Excited, I opened the mail to find an invitation letter from a company called Symbol Solutions. My heart took a leap. I quickly took a printout of the document, put it in my file and got ready to go to the consulate.

Farooq Rohaila met me there, and the entire visa process turned out to be smooth. I submitted all my documents and was asked to come again the next day. My passport was stamped and I was ready to fly. I went home and started looking at ticket options for Kabul. I wanted to travel light so I only packed a backpack with three sets of clothes, toiletries, documents and around 15,000 Indian rupees. Rahmat Khan had said that he would take care of everything and I wouldn't require more than this amount since my job should be over in a day or two.

On 25 July 2012, I took an early flight to Delhi since all India–Afghanistan flights took off from the national capital. My flight left at 2 p.m. and landed in Kabul at 4.30 p.m. During the flight, I spoke to my co-passenger, Qudratullah Sirat. He asked me the purpose of my visit and was fascinated to learn that I wanted to do business with the Afghans. I asked him to help me with a SIM card when we landed. As soon as the SIM card was activated, I called Rahmat Khan to inform him that I was in Kabul. He told me he was at the airport and that he was wearing white.

When I stepped out of the airport, I saw a fair, middle-aged man with a brown beard waving at me. He came and hugged me. 'Welcome to Kabul, Hamid Bhai,' he said.

My tense body eased a little with the warmth that he showed. I felt like I was in safe hands and was reassured about the journey I would shortly embark upon. He took me to a hotel in an area called Shahr-e Naw in northern Kabul where a room had been booked for me. I left my bag there and the two of us went for dinner to a nearby restaurant.

When we were walking back to the hotel, Rahmat Khan informed me that he had some bad news. I stopped in my tracks. 'Rahmat Bhai, what is it?'

He said, 'I am being told that the Torkham border has been closed because of the NATO supply. When the supply trucks move, the borders are shut for any civilian or commercial movement.'

I was really disappointed. Seeing my forlorn face, Rahmat Khan said, 'Don't look so sad. I am just telling you what I have been informed of. I will try to find a way for you to cross. You get some sleep. And don't go close to the windows at night. It is not safe when bombs go off. The first thing to break is glass.' He laughed loudly and left the room.

I sat there looking at the windows. Wow, what a country. It was so alien. Never had I felt so insecure sitting in the confines of a nice, snug room. And then the thought of Fiza came to mind. If she could endure so much then so would I.

The next day, I got ready and called up Rahmat Khan. 'Where are you, Rahmat Bhai?' I asked.

'I am about to reach in a couple of minutes.'

He had carried breakfast, but he didn't look his usual jovial self. 'Hamid Bhai, you can't possibly cross the border today. It is completely closed for civilians. NATO supplies coming from Pakistan is serious business. Not a single civilian is allowed. And checking also becomes very strict,' he said.

I kept staring at my plate, wondering what to do. The fear of losing time, the fear of what must be happening in Pakistan played on my mind. I finally nodded in agreement.

Rahmat Khan pulled out a few packets of dry fruits and said, 'Take this home for your family. I will keep you informed on the situation here.'

I was gutted. Any tangible hope I had shattered in front of me.

I booked my flight back and returned an absolutely disappointed man.

6

The Final Attempt

26 July 2012

As soon as I landed in Mumbai, I changed the SIM card in my phone to the India number and called my mother.

'Ammi, I am back and headed home,' I told her over the phone. She inquired about the visit and if I had set up any business transactions. 'I made some contacts. Will discuss when I get home,' I said.

The journey back home was tedious and heartbreaking. The pain of my failure weighed on me. But things were only going to get worse. Soon, Rahmat Khan would break off all communication with me, blowing me off. He wouldn't answer my calls or reply to my messages and emails. It would feel like the end of the road.

At home, I rang the doorbell. My mother opened the door and asked me about the trip and the job interview. I opened my bag and pulled out the dry fruits. 'These are samples I have got from there to see if there are buyers in India. Let's see if things work out. I also have got leads for jobs there. The interview for the airport was good.'

My brother was relieved to see me. We chatted for a while and then called it a night. Before going to bed, I dropped a message to Rahmat Khan, thanking him for all his help and requesting him to keep an eye on the opening of the border.

~

The next morning, when I woke up and checked my phone, there was no response from Rahmat Khan. I then messaged him several times, tried calling and even sent mails and messages, but to no avail. I never heard from him again.

The pressure on the home front was ever growing. I decided to be gainfully employed and simultaneously continue looking for ways to go back. I remembered Rahmat Khan's words that I had three to four months' time because of Ramzan and Eid.

I got in touch with the *Dastak* journalist Atta-ur-Rahman, who was my sole support now. He said, 'This is terrible, Hamid Bhai. You are losing precious time. Do something and come as soon as possible. I only hope that you are able to rescue that poor girl from this hell. I'm hoping it could lead to some gain for me too. I am a very small reporter here.'

I was a little confused with his last sentence. Gauging my silence, he said, 'I mean, doing this good deed might earn me some blessings.'

I told him that I was trying to find a way and would get back to him as soon as I found someone. I constantly engaged with Atta-ur-Rahman but he never lost his cool. The support was immense.

When I asked him about Fiza, he said, 'The entire family is underground. The father is trying to pursue the jirga members and sort the matter out. But the victim's family does not want a settlement. They are insisting on wani and Fiza's hand in marriage. Although right now it does not look like a wedding is in the offing.'

'Then what is happening?' I asked.

'Actually, what the father was trying to do was pay the victim's family 70 lakh rupees as blood money. But the other side is adamant.

They straight out refused. In fact, they are not nice people. I don't think their intentions are right.'

That left me worried.

~

A few weeks passed and I finally got a job as an assistant professor at an MBA college in Mumbai. While I had resigned to my fate and lost hope, I didn't stop thinking about Fiza or figuring out ways to get to her. One day, I was reminded of Hamdan Khan, the Afghani I had befriended last year at the Rotaract exchange programme. I looked up his contact details on my phone and sent him a message. He immediately called back. 'Hamid Bhai, how are you? It is so nice to hear from you. I am still in Mumbai. The programme gets over only by next year. But I am glad to hear that you will be visiting my country. I insist that you stay at my place if you ever visit Jalalabad.'

I felt relief knowing that there was someone I could reach out to in Afghanistan. My phone buzzed after I hung up, and I saw a message from Hamdan with his father's contact details and address.

I also remembered Dr Shazia and messaged her on Facebook again. She promptly replied, asking what the status was.

'I have tried very hard to obtain a Pakistani visa but it has been impossible. The only way out is for me to travel to Afghanistan and then try to enter Pakistan. I am trying to work out a way,' I wrote.

She replied, 'Hamid, I tried to find out about Fiza. There has been talk of wani in Karak but I am still trying to get more details. It is the worst thing they can do to that poor girl. I will do my best to help. If you manage to reach Afghanistan and intend to cross over, I can drive down to the Torkham border to pick you up. That way at least you will be safe.'

That sounded like a good plan. But first I had to sort out my travel.

I approached the Afghanistan consulate for a visa for the second time. Rohaila was there and he issued me a visa on the basis of my previously submitted documents. I told my family that I had been called to Kabul for an airport assistant's job. Meanwhile, I also got in touch with some Rotary members in Afghanistan who were interested in starting a school in Kabul. I looked at it as a potential business or job prospect.

This time, my family was happy to see me finally find a good job. I was to fly to Kabul on 1 November 2012. Khalid and Ammi insisted on dropping me to the airport. Halfway there, Ammi asked me if my papers were in order. 'Oh shit!' I yelled. My brother, who was driving, got startled and asked what happened. I had just remembered that my wallet was left on the table at home. In the time it took to turn back and collect the wallet, I missed my flight. Was that a message, a sign? I didn't read it as one. Should I have? Well . . . No use thinking about it now.

I booked the next flight for 4 November. This time I made no mistake and ensured I got on the plane. My mother called me to check if I had boarded. She gave me her blessings to do well. 'May Allah be with you, beta. Call or message as soon as you land,' she said and disconnected.

I remembered that I needed an entry pass to submit at the airport in case I was leaving Afghan territory and coming back. But there was nobody at the counter. A piece of paper stuck to the window had on it a phone number. I reported the matter to the on-duty officer, that the concerned officer was not on his seat. The duty officer, Shahid, gave me his number and said that I should get in touch with him at the time of my departure from Kabul and he would provide the documents.

I took a cab and went back to the same area where Rahmat Khan had put me up. It was a long distance from the airport. Kabul was a different kind of city, quite green, but one could sense the tension because of the massive security presence. I had never experienced the feeling of such an ever-present threat, which was part of the daily lives of Afghans. But the city was far from what I had imagined. From the news broadcasts and newspapers I had seen, I expected a town in a shambles, with broken buildings and shattered windows. It was not like that. But it was tough to get used to the extreme cold of the city, especially as I was from Mumbai. It felt like I had been stuffed into a freezer.

The cab driver took me to Hotel Hairat Faisal in Shahr-e Naw, where I went through security checks before entering. By the time I reached, it was already dark. The receptionist was an old Pathan who wore a turban and salwar kurta. He was a fair man with lots of wrinkles. While he was taking down my details, I asked for the login ID of the lobby WiFi. After connecting, I immediately messaged Dr Shazia on Facebook that I was in Kabul and would be leaving for the border the next morning. I asked her for her coordinates and whether she was going to pick me up.

The receptionist completed his formalities and handed over the keys to my room to a young attendant. We took the stairs. The young lad told me that he was the son of the receptionist and that it was a family-run business. An affable boy, he opened the door to my room, smiled and asked me if I needed anything.

The room was clean and within my budget—about 2000 Afghanis (Afghanistan's currency), which was approximately $30—but it was freezing cold. Looking at me shiver, the boy turned on the heater. It didn't seem too effective so I requested him to get me more heaters. With all the windows shut and three heaters in the room, I still shivered under the quilt, but soon exhaustion took over and I fell asleep.

The next morning, I went to the lobby (the only place where WiFi was available) to check if Dr Shazia had responded, but there was no message from her. I went back to my room, and after breakfast, tried to call Hamdan Khan's father, Haji Sahab, but the number was unreachable. I thought there was no use wasting time so I planned to travel to Jalalabad, which is 151 kilometres from Kabul. Before checking out of the hotel, I did another check for a reply from Dr Shazia, but there was nothing. I didn't want to waste more time so I exchanged around 2000 Indian rupees for 1700 Afghanis. I then sought help from the old receptionist to get to the taxi stand, where there were shared cabs waiting for passengers. I heard a man shouting, 'Nagrahar, Nagrahar, Nagrahar', and saw people paying him money and boarding a red Toyota Corolla.

I asked if the cab would go to Jalalabad. One of the bystanders said Jalalabad and Nagrahar were the same, so I paid the driver 250 Afghanis and got in. There was one person already sitting in the car. We had to wait for a while till two more passengers entered, dressed in bright salwar kurtas and Peshawari caps.

The journey was through the hills, which were barren but beautiful. There was a river to one side of the road. It looked green, and the air was fresh and cold. But the windows were rolled up and the car felt warm and cosy. I wondered if Haji Sahab would meet me. But it was worth a try.

Three and a half hours later, I reached Jalalabad. It was around four o'clock in the evening. I called up Haji Sahab again. This time, he picked up. With a sigh of relief, I introduced myself. He said his son had told him about me and he would come and pick me up. He asked me my location. Unfamiliar with the area, I sought help from a shopkeeper, who guided Haji Sahab to the location.

After some time, I saw a gentle, elderly soul step out of a Toyota and wave in my direction. 'As-salaam alaykum, Haji Sahab, I am Hamid. Thank you so much for picking me up,' I said.

He showed me to the car. It was a pleasant drive. 'Son, not a problem at all. You are like one of my sons. I hope my son Hamdan is focusing on studies in Mumbai. I have sent him there with great difficulty. I hope he makes good use of the opportunity. Look around you . . . there are no opportunities here. Outsiders have ruined our nation. I am lucky to still be alive and even more blessed to have all my children alive. Life is difficult in these parts.'

I was quietly listening to him speak. He probably wanted to vent. We reached his house, which had a walled compound. Most houses here had such compounds for security purposes and for privacy. Afghanistan was a conservative society.

The main house was where the family lived. I was taken to the adjacent structure, which had the guest bedroom, or what they call the *hujra*. From the corner of my eye, I could see young girls peeking at me and giggling. This new Urdu-speaking man who didn't look like he was from around there had made them quite curious.

But there was clarity about their place in the house. Not one soul stepped into my area. It was a conservative household, strongly observing the strictures of Islam and the purdah system (veils were mandatory if they needed to come out of their areas).

After dinner, I called up Atta-ur-Rahman. He had asked me to inform him before I left for Peshawar and then once I reached.

~

On the morning of 6 November 2012, I went to the Rotary office in Jalalabad and interacted with a Rotarian, Mohibullah Israr. He had proposed establishing an educational institute in Kabul. I was intrigued. There was so much to do there. I wished I had visited the place in different circumstances.

I went back to Hamdan's house and had lunch with Haji Sahab. During the meal, I told him about my impending secret voyage. He looked a bit stunned.

'Do you have documents to travel to Pakistan, son?'

'I tried very hard to get a visa, Haji Sahab, but I didn't succeed. I am left with no choice but to go without papers.'

The old man looked unconvinced and worried. He didn't fancy being an accomplice in such a dangerous plan. He then inquired if I had my entry papers to return to Afghanistan from the border. I replied in the negative. That made him all the more uncomfortable.

'What in the world are you thinking, son?!' he exclaimed. 'Does Hamdan know of your plans? We could get into a lot of trouble. Have you thought it through? You may never come back if you are caught. I will never be able to forgive myself if something happened to you.'

'But I have people helping me on the other side of the border.'

'I pray that things work out for you. Alas, it is time for us to part ways,' he said, hinting at the fact that he no longer wanted to be associated with me.

I understood where Haji Sahab was coming from. So, the next morning, I bade the family goodbye and thanked him for his hospitality. 'If you are ever in Mumbai, please be our guest,' I said.

'Allah willing, we will see you return safely,' the man said, blessing me.

I figured it was essential for me to get an entry pass. So I took a cab to the Kabul airport, which took me approximately two and a half hours.

Upon reaching, I called up the duty officer, Shahid, and sought his help. He kept his word and got me the pass.

We got talking and he asked me where I was headed. I told him that I would look for a hotel to stay the night. He offered me a place to stay and said I could pay him instead. At first, I objected since I didn't want to intrude but when he insisted, I accepted his offer. I felt a bit of relief at the fact that it was safer to be with a cop than staying alone in a hotel.

Shahid made a quick call and then told me that his brother Zaman would come to pick me up. I stepped out and waited at the entrance of the airport. A while later, a blue car approached me with three young men sitting inside. They all stepped out and one of them asked if I was Hamid Ansari. 'I am Zaman. My brother asked me to pick you up and take you home. Welcome!' he said.

He introduced the other two as Waleed, his future brother-in-law (Zaman was to marry Waleed's sister), who had come home from London to visit his parents on their return from Hajj, and Zafr, a friend who was also a cop like Shahid and Zaman.

We left the airport and went to a marketplace. There, I recharged my mobile talk time and called up Atta-ur-Rahman. He asked me to call him once I reached Peshawar. Later that evening, Shahid came home. We got talking, and after he learnt I was an engineer, he pulled out a brand new phone and asked me to help transfer his photos into it. I first did a trial run by transferring one photo of Shahid, Zaman and Zafar in uniform on to my phone, and once I succeeded, I moved the data to his phone.

Unfortunately, I forgot to delete the photo of these Afghans in uniform from my own phone. A heavy price would be paid for this lapse in judgement later.

It turned out that the three of them were planning a trip to the nearby Qargha Lake a couple of days later. I went along with them. It was cold but beautiful, and the temperatures dipped even further as we got close to the water body. We spent a few hours around the lake and ate a meal on the shore. I kept smiling to myself at the thought of Fiza, thinking of her laughter and her beauty.

Zaman looked at me and asked what I was smiling about. I didn't think I had made it so obvious. Turning away, I said, '. . . looking at a beautiful and promising future.'

We drove back and arrived in Kabul around 8.30 p.m. The streets were deserted. Unlike Mumbai, the city that never sleeps, life here came to a standstill at 7.30–8 p.m. The winter chills added to the dreary, haunted look and feel.

In the distance, there was an army checkpost, where soldiers stopped our vehicle for a routine check. Zaman spoke to them, pointed towards me and explained that I was an Indian visiting Afghanistan for work. The moment they heard 'Indian', they smiled and wished me a good stay. They let us go. We reached Shahid's home, and over dinner, I told him that I wanted to go to Jalalabad. He said Waleed would also be leaving the next day after the Friday prayers since his parents' flight from Saudi Arabia had been delayed.

On 9 November 2012, we left as planned, after the Friday prayers. The road from Kabul to Jalalabad was winding, treacherous and full of sharp bends, but the natural beauty around us was mesmerizing. Who could tell that the people of this country, this beautiful land, continued to suffer one of the worst cases of conflict and terrorism? They were so warm and nice. Where were the bloodthirsty terrorists, the Taliban? One couldn't tell. But in the silence of the mountains and the rush of the river that flowed on one side, there was a sense of uneasiness too. The air was ominous.

We reached Jalalabad around seven in the evening, and its streets were deserted by that time. Upon entering Waleed's house, I was surprised to find throngs of people. I was told that there was a *daawat* (feast) awaiting us since it was customary to have a feast when someone returned after performing the Hajj pilgrimage. Waleed's family and friends were all there. His younger brother took care of the family business, while his elder brother was employed somewhere else.

Again, similar to Haji Sahab's house, none of the womenfolk came out, not even to serve dinner, which was done by Waleed's younger brother. At that point, I broached the topic of going to Pakistan.

'I have a confession to make. I want to go to Peshawar. I do not have travel documents. Could you guide me how to go about it?' I told the three men.

They looked at each other and thought for a while. They asked me what the reason was for such a high-risk decision. I told them, 'There is this girl in Kohat who is my friend, and she is in extreme trouble, I want to help her. She is being forced to marry someone against her wishes under the wani custom. I must go there to rescue her. I have someone waiting in Peshawar to help me.'

Waleed held my hand and confidently said, 'Don't worry. There is a direct bus service from Jalalabad to Peshawar called the Dosti bus service. It has become very easy to travel to Peshawar. You can also get a pre-activated Pakistani SIM card at the border itself before you leave for Peshawar.'

One of his cousins told me that he could have accompanied me to Peshawar but since my destination was Kohat, it did not make sense for him to come along. I was relieved to hear all of them say that travel to Peshawar would be incident-free.

After breakfast the next morning, I was dropped to the bus station around 10 a.m., only to find that the last Dosti bus for Pakistan had departed at 8 a.m. Another day missed. I had to stay back in Jalalabad. I was constantly in touch with Atta-ur-Rahman, and would call him up and ask how Fiza was doing. He said things were not fine and that I should try to be there as soon as possible.

I then called up Ammi and told her that I was fine and work was keeping me busy. I felt very guilty. She sounded happy that I was doing well at my job. She told me what was happening at home and that I better be back for all of Khalid's wedding preparations. I promised her that I would return soon. With a heavy heart, I put the phone down.

I had time to kill, so Waleed took me to his brother's vermicelli factory where the workers had some horrid stories to tell about the torture and ill treatment of Afghans at the hands of the Pakistani establishment. One worker said that he had visited Lahore and was put through hell because his passport contained an Indian visa.

A thought flashed in my head when they were saying these things. What if I got caught? But I knew that I had a good friend in Atta-ur-Rahman.

Everyone at the factory spoke very highly of India and shared their cherished memories of visits there. The conversation was genuine. I could see that they truly loved India and Indians, and were not simply saying this because an Indian stood before them.

We then headed to the market, where I got some Pakistani currency exchanged. The next morning, Waleed came to the room while I was getting ready to leave. It was early and extremely cold. He sat on the bed and watched me pack. I told him that Atta-ur-Rahman had advised me not to keep any Indian documents on my person. Waleed agreed and said it would be too dangerous. So I decided to leave them in Waleed's custody. He promised to take care of all the belongings till my return.

On 11 November 2012, I was dropped off at the same bus stop by Waleed's younger brother, who got me a ticket on the Dosti bus service. I was scared and excited at the same time. I called up Atta-ur-Rahman as soon as the bus started from Jalalabad and informed him that I had left. All this while I had been in touch with my family, and tonight would be the first time I would not be calling Ammi. She would be worried sick. But I knew that I had to do this for Fiza. While it felt selfish to make my parents worry, it would have been worse if I told them I would not be able to contact them for a few days. I thought I would explain once I returned from Pakistan.

With a few clothes in my backpack, some Pakistani and Afghan currency in my wallet, my BlackBerry and another basic Nokia mobile phone, I boarded the bus and was off on the most dangerous journey of my life.

7

The Crossover

11 November 2012

'Pak-Afghan Dosti bus service', said my ticket. My heart felt faint but I gathered all the courage I had. Fiza would be waiting for me. But what if it was too late? With these questions in mind, I boarded the bus.

I looked for my seat and quietly sat beside a burqa-clad woman without making any eye contact. In my jeans, shirt and jacket, I surely didn't look like a local. While I wanted to remain inconspicuous, that was not to be.

Something felt strange. All eyes were on me. As somebody from Mumbai, the sight of so many women covered from head to toe was not something I was used to. The burqas looked like long sheets of cloth draped in a single flow, covering every inch of the person. There were a lot of women on the bus, most of them of large build. My neighbour looked like that too. But she was taken aback when I sat next to her.

Figuring out that I was a foreigner, the conductor of the bus came up to me and asked if I was related to the woman beside me. I looked at her from the corner of my eye and looked back at the conductor. 'No. We are not related at all. Why, is something wrong?' I asked.

'You cannot sit here if you are not a blood relative or her immediate family, Bhai Jaan,' he explained and gave me a seat in the last row, beside an old man in Pathan attire. I was relieved that they didn't find me suspicious. It was a window seat, so I fixed my eyes outside.

The bus left the station, and as we drove out of the city, the view outside changed to beautiful snow-capped mountains. I felt exhausted from lack of sleep. The night before had passed chatting with the boys all night long, followed by an early morning. And now that I was on the bus to Pakistan, sleep was the last thing on my mind. I had flashes of Fiza, my mother, my father, Khalid. He was to be married the next month. I shut my eyes and prayed that I would succeed in my mission and go back safely.

It was cold outside, but the bus was warm even though some of the windows were open. The view was mesmerizing. I had never experienced such beauty and such dipping temperatures. The cold breeze brought in the freshness and fragrance that teased my senses, which had dulled with the smells of the city.

The journey from Jalalabad to the border took two hours. I turned to look at the rows of people on the bus, men beside men and women beside women; it was a strange sight. Almost all of the passengers had fallen asleep. Some of them had children on their laps, some had bundles tied up in sheets. It was evident that they needed to rest before they got drawn into the hustle and bustle of life beyond the border.

I had my guard up and noticed every small and big thing. It just occurred to me that none of the passengers was carrying a smartphone. My BlackBerry would certainly draw attention. In order to remain low-key, I quickly slid the phone into my backpack under the clothes.

I was losing my nerve as we got closer to the border. I shut my eyes tight to mute the noises in my head, when I heard a loud sound followed by the worst kind of smell. The old man had farted. The godawful smell had spread to the entire row. While I was startled and afraid, I couldn't help but laugh quietly to myself, putting my head down on the backrest of the seat in front of me. When I looked up, there was a child a few rows ahead staring at me over her mother's shoulders. I got frightened. Was I that obvious? Did I look that different? What if I got caught? What if the people on the bus got to know and informed the authorities? What if there was someone from the intelligence agencies on this bus?

It was quiet on the road but my mind was ever so restless. The worried thoughts went on and on, and I kept looking out for any suspicious movements or looks from anyone. I was tense as the bus inched closer to the Torkham border. There were buildings on either side with Afghan and Pakistani flags atop them. I started to get cold feet, but there was no going back.

As the bus approached the gates, I recalled a conversation that I had had with Atta-ur-Rahman, where he was frustrated with my delays and said, 'Are you Indians always this scared?' I was determined to rescue Fiza, and no, I was not scared, I said to myself.

There was a long queue of vehicles waiting to cross over. I was trying to see what was happening when I heard the sounds of young boys trying to sell something. I couldn't understand what they were saying till I heard the words 'phone' and 'SIM'. I sprung up and tried to search for the voice that had said those two words. I called out to him.

Signalling the boy to get me a SIM, I asked him with hand gestures if it was pre-activated. He said 'Ao, ao', nodding to mean yes. I paid him 150 Afghans for a UFone SIM. I quickly inserted it in my Nokia phone, hoping to call Atta-ur-Rahman. But there was no signal.

This was the crucial test. I had to pass immigration. Just as I was preparing to get up and disembark, I saw the door of the bus open and the conductor give way to a man wearing all-black Pathani clothes and a black cap. At this point, my hands started shivering, so I folded my arms and looked down. I thought I would be caught and taken away. That the immigration officials had information on me. When I moved my head up slightly to see what was happening, the officer had not moved an inch. He stood on the stairs, ran his eyes around the bus and stepped out, after giving a nod. The door closed and the conductor signalled for the bus to move through. I had mixed feelings. How was that easy? Wasn't this the world's most dangerous area? How was this possible? Heaving a sigh of relief at the same time, I thanked Allah for the countless blessings on this arduous journey. Memories of the time I had spent with my four new friends in the last couple of days flashed through my mind. The joyous drive and the laughter-filled evenings . . .

But suddenly I panicked and thought something had to be wrong. It could not be this simple. Did the guard recognize me and inform his seniors? Did they know? Did they have information about an illegal entrant? What would I do? I remembered Atta-ur-Rahman telling me, 'Don't be scared, Bhai, this is like an open border. There are no checks. One can walk across freely.' And then I saw the bus pass the building without stopping.

I had crossed over.

Then began a rough ride. The moment we entered Pakistan, I could see the infrastructure was in a sorry state. While we navigated through mountains with no buildings, I saw that the roads were broken in some parts and non-existent in others. A two-way drive without a divider. Being driven around in Afghanistan was a joyride compared to this roller coaster. The mountainous ghats twitched and turned in random fashion. But the driver drove like he was doing this journey for the millionth time. And then I saw the first few officers of the Pakistan army in their fatigues. As we moved ahead, they were visible at regular intervals—in black uniforms with black caps.

Finally, the roads became a little better as we hit civilization, but the infrastructure continued to be a total disappointment. But there were signs of life beyond the armed forces, and the bus stopped at a marketplace for refreshments. I wanted to know where we were, but for fear of being found out, I kept to myself. I didn't step out. I just wanted to reach Peshawar. The bus started to move again. My destination wasn't far so I started scanning the roads for army men and cops. But in the city area, they were rare to spot, which put me a tad at ease. I suddenly thought of Ammi and her blessings before I left for Kabul. Maybe it was her hand on my head that had kept me out of harm's way.

By now the sun was up and the weather had turned warmer as compared to Afghanistan. The air felt cool. Having entered without any problem, my nerves eased and I fell asleep, with the fresh air grazing my face. Suddenly, I woke up with a start when I heard the bus conductor shouting, 'Pekhawar! Pekhawar!' The bus had come to a halt at the depot. I got off, took out the Nokia phone from my pocket and checked for a signal. There wasn't any. I panicked. Atta-ur-Rahman would be waiting for me. So I went to the shop nearby and asked the shopkeeper, 'Bhai Sahab, is there a PCO booth here?' The man looked at me quizzically. Then I realized those things were long gone. Nobody needed to go to a calling booth in this era of mobile phones.

Some of the men there looked at me with suspicion. I knew I had made a mistake. But no one asked me my nationality. I was directed from one place to the other till I stopped in my tracks on seeing a checkpost with seven or eight army men and four to five cops. I rushed back to the shopkeeper and quietly requested him for his mobile. 'Bhai Jaan, my friend is supposed to pick me up but my mobile does not have network. Could I please borrow your phone? I will just make one call,' I said.

He gave me his mobile phone. I quickly pulled out Atta-ur-Rahman's number from my phone and called him. He picked up. 'Atta Bhai, I have reached Peshawar. I am at Haji Camp Adda. Are you coming to pick me up?' I asked.

He replied, 'Welcome, Hamid Bhai. I am stuck at work, so I will not be able to come. I am sending my friend Imtiaz, who will be there shortly. He will take you to another bus stop from where he will put you in a taxi to Rawalpindi. From there, you will have to hire a taxi to come to my house in Karak.'

I was flummoxed. This was an all-new plan that I knew nothing about. Why should I be going all the way to Rawalpindi when Karak was just two or three hours from Peshawar? I was visibly disturbed and could see the shopkeeper looking at me. Since I did not want to raise suspicion, I agreed. Before hanging up, Atta said, 'Hamid Bhai, Imtiaz does not know anything about you, so don't tell him anything.'

I said, 'Okay,' and cut the call.

I thanked the old shopkeeper for his kindness and offered to pay for the call but he refused to take any money. I bought a bottle of water and a few packs of biscuits. As I was walking away, the shopkeeper hollered at me and said, 'Let's give your mobile a shot.'

I ran back to him. He said, 'We should try refilling cash on the SIM number using the direct mobile or easy top-up service.'

I didn't understand exactly what he meant but nodded in agreement. He tried adding 100 rupees using his cell phone, and bingo! The top-up was successful. I now had a balance amount of 100 rupees and my SIM was activated.

I wanted to hug the old man. But I resisted and instead thanked him profusely. I then called Atta and told him that my number was active. I could be in touch with him till I reached his house in Karak. This was my chance to ask him about the change in plans.

'Atta Bhai, why do I have to go all the way to Rawalpindi? I can just take a taxi directly to Karak from here or even travel back with Imtiaz,' I asked.

Atta-ur-Rahman calmly explained, 'There are too many checkposts, Hamid Bhai, from Peshawar to Karak via Kohat. The route is through a tunnel which was made by China; a few years back there was a blast in the tunnel and that's where the army checkposts are. These checks cannot be avoided under any circumstances, and if they stop you for documents then you are bound to get caught. So the only way out is to go to Rawalpindi's Peer Wadai Adda (bus stop) and then take a cab to Karak. That way you can avoid the tunnel and the army checkposts.'

I asked him about the police within the city. He asked me if I was carrying enough cash. I answered in the affirmative. He sounded relieved and said, 'If they stop you, just pay 100 rupees and they will not bother you.' I went through the entire route with him once again. Just as we were finishing our conversation, the call ended. I checked the balance and saw that I had consumed the entire amount.

I went back to the shopkeeper and got another recharge of 100 rupees before I left the depot. Atta had shared Imtiaz's number with me. As I called him, I saw a young man on a bike looking for someone. I had a feeling he was there for me. I waved at him and he waved back and rode up to me.

'Salaam, Hamid Bhai, blue jeans, shirt and leather jacket,' he pointed at my clothes and laughed. That must have been Atta's description of me.

I laughed along with him and hopped on to his bike. We were riding to the other bus stop. We passed the same army checkpost outside the depot. I stiffened and prayed that we would not be stopped. But the confidence with which Imtiaz rode past it made me feel safe.

It was a short journey, past a few crossroads and junctions. A little further down, cops stopped us for a routine check. Imtiaz asked me to sit quietly. He handled the cops deftly, as though this was a regular affair. He pulled out his press card and it worked like magic. No questions.

After moving ahead, I asked him what that was all about. He said, 'In Pakistan, a reporter's ID card has a lot of value. Even the cops don't mess with someone holding a press card.'

'But what was our offence?' I asked. He said, 'Double-riding on bikes is banned in Pakistan. A lot of antisocial elements use motorbikes, pillion-riding on them, as their mode of transport,' he said.

I was shocked. I had thought it was because we weren't wearing helmets. I started thinking, what if they had checked us if they suspected we were terrorists and found me not just without documents but someone from the enemy state India? What an ugly turn things would have taken.

That was when it struck me that I was completely dependent on one man and one man alone: Atta-ur-Rahman.

I was lost in these thoughts when the bike stopped. We had reached our destination.

'This is the Charsadda Adda, Hamid Bhai. This is where we also get taxis. But before you travel ahead, let us have lunch together,' he said.

Imtiaz showed me to the bus stop canteen, which was a fairly large space where they served tea, coffee, cakes, biscuits and even main course meals. He ordered lunch. I wasn't hungry so I didn't order any food. He insisted that I share his meal. But I was tense about the onward journey and had lost my appetite.

After he finished lunch, he ordered tea for both of us. We drank it and then headed towards the vehicles section of the adda. We asked for regular cars or cabs for Rawalpindi. But the transport guy behind the counter said that all the cars had left for the day and no small vehicle was available for Rawalpindi.

He, however, guided us to the buses, where one bus was ready for departure. We both looked at each other and then ran to the bus. I clambered on in the nick of time.

Imtiaz spoke to the bus conductor and arranged a seat for me. I asked for the fare and the conductor told me it was 250 rupees. I thanked Imtiaz for his kindness and we parted ways.

I took my seat. This was unlike my bus ride in Afghanistan, where the passengers were separated based on gender. Here men and women (wearing their *chadri*—a long cloth to cover the head, wrapped around the neck) sat together, but I could tell that the woman who sat beside me felt odd since I was not dressed in the traditional Pathani outfit.

I didn't want her to create a scene and have everyone's eyes on me, so I just pretended to sleep, hoping that nobody would disturb a sleeping soul. Thankfully, I was right. The conductor asked the woman to move instead. I was relieved.

Some distance away, the bus stopped and more passengers boarded it. A young man in his early twenties sat next to me. He seemed to be high on life and his questions did not stop. At the time, I thought of him as quite immature, but in hindsight I question who was the real buffoon. Alas!

He chatted me up like we were childhood buddies. He told me his name was Sunny.

'I am from Rawalpindi. I was visiting my uncle in Peshawar. The only problem with travelling to these parts is that if you don't reach on time, you miss all the cabs and are stuck in a bus,' he said grumpily.

I asked him, not out of curiosity but more for information, 'What difference does it make?'

He explained that the bus route was longer since it took the GT Road and went through the cities, whereas cars took the motorway to Rawalpindi, which almost halved the journey time.

I noticed that by now the bus was running smoothly and had picked up speed. The journey from Peshawar to Rawalpindi had started. I called up Atta-ur-Rahman and updated him on the slight change in the mode of transport and told me I could be late. He asked me to keep him posted and said he would be there to receive me.

'Check out my phone. I have the best collection of music,' said Sunny as I put my mobile back into my pocket.

Without warning, he plugged one of the earphones into my ear and the other into his own and played some hardcore Punjabi remixes which I couldn't understand a word of but nonetheless I listened to, giving him a thumbs-up. I had a window seat again, so I looked out at the trees, farmlands, small shops and houses that we drove past.

I had no way of finding out where I was, and no access to the Internet. So I started reading the boards and signs on shops very carefully, particularly banks with branch names clearly spelt out. I didn't engage Sunny because I wanted to keep our interaction to a bare minimum.

The bus made quite a few stops to pick up and drop passengers. But the real trouble started when it was intercepted by a police patrol. I almost broke into a sweat but kept as calm as I possibly could. All kinds of thoughts came into my mind. I shut my eyes and started praying. My prayers were heard and the cops did not get on the bus. Sunny told me that this was just a routine check.

'The power play. They just do it to harass us and the transport guys . . . To make a quick buck. They are all in on it,' Sunny said.

I informed Atta of the check and he responded with a similar answer but added, 'Just maintain a low profile and you will be fine. See you soon.'

During the journey, Sunny kept fidgeting with his cell phone and at one point said that he had no balance. 'Could I make one call home to inform my mother that I will reach late since I am travelling by bus, please?' he pleaded.

I had no choice but to lend him my mobile. He called up a number and said, 'I will be late since I missed the cabs. I am not coming via the motorway. The bus is driving through GT Road so I will be late. Just wanted to inform you.'

He returned the phone and thanked me profusely. And then he wanted to chat some more. I had no strength to listen to his gibberish, so I closed my eyes. I wanted to desperately get some rest but the constant police sirens kept me on tenterhooks. I kept messaging Atta with location updates so he knew where I was. At one point, we crossed a bridge where the river had dried up. Atta seemed to know where I was. He then wrote that I had crossed Attock bridge and I needed to get to Peer Wadai Adda in Rawalpindi and let him know.

The journey continued in the company of Sunny, along with other intervals and interceptions, and by approximately 7.30 in the evening, we reached our destination. But the adda was some distance away. We disembarked and Sunny showed me where to hail a cab from. If this was Mumbai, we would have exchanged numbers. But given the circumstances, I wanted to fade into the night without a trace.

I took off in the direction he had shown and finally reached Peer Wadai Adda. I immediately called up Atta-ur-Rahman and told him that I was at the location. He guided me on how to get a shared cab ride to reach his place in Karak. There were some 'Costas'—twelve-seater minivans—standing by with destination plates displayed on the windshield: Kohat, Peshawar, Islamabad, Lahore and many others. But none were going to Karak.

After searching for a while, I found a car headed for Karak. The owner or driver sitting outside confirmed the destination but said it would leave at 11.30 p.m. I asked if there was any other ride available before that. The driver asked me to check for cars parked just behind a local shop. I went there and to my surprise found a Costa destined for Karak. But the driver was missing. So I waited near the car. A man sitting at a distance was staring at me. I felt uneasy and feared that I looked like a foreigner, an outsider. But then he called out and gestured to ask what I wanted. I told him that I was looking for the driver of the Costa. He said that he was the driver.

'When will you start from here?' I asked. He confirmed that the car would depart at 8.30 p.m. I messaged Atta and updated him and also told him that my cell phone battery was about to run out so I was switching it off to save the last bit for an emergency. Meanwhile, I picked up a few packs of biscuits and booked my seat in the cab.

With a delay of five to ten minutes, the final leg of the journey to Karak began. There were four more passengers. I could see signboards along the route pointing towards Kohat and Karak.

This had been no small feat. I felt a little relaxed knowing that I was soon to be in the care of Atta-ur-Rahman. I didn't want my heart to run free but I allowed it a bit of excitement.

The road from Rawalpindi to Karak had no streetlights. It was a two-way lane with no dividers. The driver relied only on the headlamps of the car. Cars on both sides drove on high beam and blinded the drivers. The only saving grace was that these drivers knew every inch of the route. We were travelling at a decent speed. I presumed we had crossed the city limits of Rawalpindi as the roads appeared very secluded. There were no shops, houses or signs of civilization.

I looked out of the window to see a star-studded sky. This was a rare sight. I couldn't believe that the sky had so many stars. In Mumbai, the skies at night had been driven to darkness because of the bright city lights. I wanted to capture this moment.

It was a long, never-ending journey. There was only one halt for refreshments in the middle of the forest, at a dhaba where candles and lanterns were being used as there was no electricity. Multiple charpoys were spread out and various local eatables were being served. It was a cold winter night and I got myself a hot cup of tea. After stretching our legs, we all got back into the car and the journey began again, cutting through the forest until we halted at a gas station.

I got off the vehicle to soak in the beautiful surroundings. Behind me was a thick forest leading up to the mountains. I kept my gaze fixed on the enormous cluster of stars that I had never seen before. Then I heard the driver call out to me as they were ready to leave. I switched on my phone and checked for network, but there wasn't any. However, I sent a message hoping it would get delivered whenever I got a signal.

It was past midnight when we reached an iron bridge, where a board read 'Kushal Gadh Pul'. I saw an army checkpost near it. As the car got closer to the checkpost, a soldier stepped out holding a rifle, while another soldier stood behind the sandbags, pointing his rifle at the approaching cars. The official signalled the driver to stop, peeped in and looked at all of us. Then he went back to the shack near the checkpost, giving us the green signal to move forward. As we crossed the post, I saw all of them huddled around a fire. The checks were just a formality.

The vehicle crossed the iron bridge, which rattled like a set of brittle bones. I asked the driver how long it would take to reach Karak. He told me approximately an hour.

As we drove, I saw railway tracks and then, at a distance, a compound with a chimney billowing smoke—perhaps an oil refinery or a chemical factory. The car halted there and two of the passengers got off. We continued ahead and a couple more disembarked at their respective destinations. The driver told me that he was also a resident of Karak. Meanwhile, I pulled out my phone to check for network. There was, but just then it went off. 'Shit!' I said out aloud. The driver turned to me and asked what the matter was. I looked miffed and sounded it too when I told him that my phone had no charge. He offered me his phone, but I needed Atta's number from mine so I tried to switch it on; luckily, it did. I quickly noted down the number before the phone died again.

I shared the number with the driver. He spoke to Atta and took down the exact location. Around 3 a.m., we reached a place where I saw two men standing on the roadside, both wrapped in shawls. I recognized one of them as Atta-ur-Rahman; the second man was unfamiliar. But I was so glad to see Atta. I had never been happier. After paying the driver, I stepped out and hugged him, and he introduced the man standing next to him as his elder brother.

'Yeh mere bhai Faiz-ur-Rahman hai. Peshe se hakeem hai.' (This is my brother Faiz-ur-Rahman, a traditional doctor by profession.)

I couldn't stop grinning. But aware of the surroundings even in the dead of the night, I contained my joy and walked with the two men through small lanes amid tall, walled compounds. The last house on the muddy track was theirs. The brother unlocked the house and let us in. Atta took me to his room. A while later, his brother entered with two cups of tea.

Hot tea was all I wanted on that frigid night. Atta-ur-Rahman said, 'We have so much to talk about, but first I am glad that you have reached safely. It is late and there's much to do tomorrow. You should—in fact, we all should get some sleep.'

I couldn't have agreed more. My bones were aching and my body was giving up. As soon as I lay on the bed, I fell asleep. Tonight, I had no thoughts, no worries. Exhaustion had got the better of me.

8

A Worried Mother

10 November 2012

It was 10 p.m. when the phone rang. Fauzia knew it was her son calling from Kabul. That was when he called her every night, keeping the promise he had made to her when he left for Afghanistan. This would be the last time he would speak with her before he crossed over into Pakistan.

'As-salaam alaykum, Hamid, how are you?' Fauzia asked as soon as she picked up.

Hamid was in Kabul. He was going to take the Dosti bus the next morning. Guilt jabbed at his heart when he heard his mother's worried voice. 'I am fine. How are you and everybody at home? Work is fine. I may get some orders,' he said, keeping his nerves steady.

'When will you be back?' she asked.

'I should be back by the 12th but if I get held up then I will be home latest by the 15th. Don't worry.'

'Stay safe. And come home soon,' said Fauzia before blessing him and disconnecting.

11 November 2012

Like the ritual it had become, Fauzia had waited for Hamid to call after she returned from college. When she sat for dinner with her husband,

Nehal Ansari, and Khalid, she expressed concern that Hamid hadn't called.

Khalid said, 'He must be busy. Don't worry. He will call when he finds time.'

An unconvinced Fauzia called up a few of Hamid's friends to check if they had heard from him.

12 November 2012

It was a Monday. When Hamid's number remained unreachable, the entire family was worried. His parents and brother started making calls to friends, acquaintances and former colleagues. By the evening, Fauzia was having a complete meltdown, imagining the most horrid circumstances in which Hamid could be caught in. She tried to brush those thoughts aside and said a prayer for her son's safety.

'He said he would be returning today. Why hasn't he called? We need to check with the airlines,' she told her husband.

Khalid, who was sitting beside his father, reminded Fauzia that he had said his return would be either by the 12th or latest by the 15th of November. 'This is irresponsible of him, but he must have got stuck somewhere. Let's wait another day,' he said.

They had dinner in silence. Later that night, Fauzia went to Khalid's room to talk to him since she was restless. As she entered, she saw Khalid sitting at his computer trying to figure out if he could find any electronic trace of Hamid. He looked at his concerned mother and put up a brave front. 'I am trying to connect with him online. I am sure he must be in a low-network area, or maybe there is a disruption in Internet supply; it is Afghanistan after all,' he said.

When Khalid went to bed, Fauzia sat in front of the computer to look up all the flights to and from Kabul. There were only two a week, on Thursdays and Sundays. She thought to herself, 'It is Monday so he couldn't have come today. Thursday would be 15 November. He must be on that flight. I'll check tomorrow morning with the airlines.' She left Khalid's room and went into the drawing room to sit in silence for a bit.

She tried Hamid's number again to see if it would ring. It didn't. It was now around 10.20 p.m. She suddenly had a sinking feeling sitting alone in the tiny drawing room. It felt like time had stopped. She looked up at the wall clock and saw that the seconds hand was not moving. Time indeed had stopped in that household. All the wall clocks of that house had stopped ticking. Fauzia was petrified. She didn't sleep that night, weeping alone and praying for her son's safety.

13 November 2012

Fauzia called in sick at work. She was determined to get some information on Hamid. She pulled out the number of Ariana Airlines and found the number of their Kabul office. Her fingers shook as she dialled. 'Please let him be on the list, please, please,' Fauzia kept muttering as the phone rang. It kept ringing for a very long time, till she finally heard a young male voice say, 'Hello, Ariana Airlines. How can I help you?'

'Hello, this is Fauzia Ansari calling from Mumbai, India. I wanted some information regarding a passenger. Could you check if he is on your Thursday flight to Delhi?'

'I am sorry. We do not give out passenger details. This is our company policy.'

'Son, I am calling since I am worried for my child. My son Hamid Ansari travelled to Kabul and was supposed to be back this week. He said he would be back by 15 November. Please help me. I only want to know if he is booked on the next flight. Please help!' It was the plea of a desperate mother.

'Hold the line, ma'am,' said the man.

She needn't have worried and could've waited a few days. But something did not feel right to her. Add to that the fact that Hamid was not reachable on his phone. She had a sinking feeling, like a part of her was being cut off. Her fears were taking on a life of their own and she was not able to concentrate on work. She wanted to ease her nerves by getting some information on Hamid.

The man came back on the line and said, 'Ma'am, could you share his details again?'

Fauzia did so. He put the phone on hold again and when he returned, he said, 'Madam, there is nobody with this name booked on our flight this coming Thursday.'

She was stunned into silence. Tears rolling down her cheeks, she said, 'Son, please check again. He must be on the list.'

There was silence on the other side, then the man said, 'I have the list in front of me. He might book a ticket later. There is time. He has two more days, Madam. Please don't worry. I am sure you will be able to connect with him soon.'

Fauzia was disheartened. She couldn't stop crying. She called up her husband, who had left for his job at the bank.

'I am worried for Hamid. He has not booked his flight. His name is not on the flyers' list. What do I do?' she started off as soon as Nehal picked up the phone.

'Calm down, Fauzia. How do you know that his name is not on the list?' he asked, puzzled.

'Well, I looked up the number of the airlines and called the Kabul office. The officer there said that his name was not on the list of people flying on Thursday. He told me this after I pleaded to him about Hamid. They are not supposed to share passenger details,' she said.

Nehal thought quickly. He was as worried as Fauzia but right now he had to be calm. He told her that maybe Hamid was caught up with work and would book the ticket closer to the date.

'That's what the airlines guy said. But that's not like him; won't the ticket cost more? I am worried. Something doesn't feel right,' she said.

'Let me come home and we will talk,' Nehal told her, asking her not to worry before disconnecting the line.

Fauzia again made a few calls to some of Hamid's friends to see if they had heard from him but to no avail. She frantically called Khalid and narrated the whole story again. Khalid was also disturbed about the situation but didn't want to worry his mother. 'Ammi, let's wait to hear from Hamid. Meanwhile, I will try to reach some of his friends,' he said.

When he came home and checked his email, he found one from Hamid. Relieved, he called his mother to the room and showed her the mail. It was brief. The family was happy to hear from Hamid but Fauzia was still concerned about the fact that she hadn't spoken to him.

She thought he would return on Thursday, 15 November. She said she would call the airline every Thursday and Sunday after the departure time so she could get them to check the passenger list. She asked Nehal if they should go to the Afghan consulate and check. When her husband and son looked quizzically at her, she said, 'After all, they gave him the visa. He is in their country. They could trace him and at least let us know where he is.'

They agreed, since there was nothing else they could do. He had not been online, his phone was not reachable and nobody knew where he was.

14 November 2012

Nehal took leave from his job at the bank and figured out the address of the Afghanistan consulate. While he got ready, Fauzia dialled the Ariana Airlines office in Kabul again.

The phone rang for a long time but there was no answer. She called again. The same young man picked up the phone. Fauzia didn't lose a breath before saying, 'Son, it is me . . . Fauzia Ansari. Just checking if Hamid Ansari's name is on the passenger list. Could you please check?'

'I hope you are fine, Madam. Let me check the list for you,' he said. He returned to the phone and said that there was no Hamid on the list.

Fauzia could sense her world turn turtle. This was not her Hamid. He would never do this unless he was in trouble.

~

The Afghan consulate in Mumbai was an old two-storey bungalow in Malabar Hills. The gate opened on to a small pathway leading up to the reception. Fauzia and Nehal told the guard the purpose of their visit. He sent word in.

After waiting for about twenty minutes, the guard received a call from inside. 'Do you have documents and details about your son?' he asked. Fauzia replied in the affirmative. He directed the couple inside to the reception area.

They went into the quiet room and sat on the couch at the reception, hoping they would get a hearing and learn of their son's whereabouts. The man at the reception asked if they had an appointment. Fauzia told him that they did not, but that it was a matter of grave importance and urgency. 'We need to meet any officer who is available at the embassy right now,' she said.

He informed someone on the phone and then asked them to hand over their documents. He said they would get a call whenever an official could attend to their request. The officials were caught up with other things and the couple would have to come back with an appointment.

Fauzia told the young man that she would not go until someone from the mission met them.

But they were instructed to leave the premises. Fauzia and Nehal stepped out of the gate reluctantly but Fauzia said clearly that they would not budge until they got a hearing.

They sat outside, near the gate, in the heat for hours. Time went by and Fauzia kept praying, hoping that her prayers would be heard. 'Where could he be?' This thought constantly ran through her mind. But she was certain about one thing. There was no way that she was leaving the consulate without meeting an official. They had never done this before so it was very embarrassing to sit on the ground while cars went in and out of the consulate building.

'My son is in their country and it is their responsibility,' she said, looking at Nehal. The helpless father nodded and continued to sit there, but he was also thinking to himself, 'What if there is bad news? What will I do? Fauzia will be shattered. Hamid shouldn't have gone to such a dangerous country.'

After about three or four hours, at around 2.30 p.m., the young man came out and told them that they were being called in. They were taken to a room and brought before an officer of the consulate, a middle-aged Afghan diplomat dressed in formal attire. He looked kind and was soft-spoken. Gesturing to them to sit, he pulled out a few papers and said, 'I went through your son's documents. He went to Kabul legally after applying for a visa at the consulate here,' he said, showing a copy of the visa issued to Hamid.

'We haven't heard from our son for the past few days. He was to return latest by 15 November but he hasn't booked his ticket yet. I mean, he is not on the airline's passenger list. My wife has been calling the airline and inquiring daily. We are really worried,' said Nehal.

'My son was given a visa by your consulate. His safety and security is your responsibility. You should know of his whereabouts. He must have mentioned his place of stay in the form. Please provide me all the details,' added Fauzia.

The officer listened to the couple intently and thoughtfully, and said, 'Look, the weather conditions in Kabul are pretty bad during winters, and more often than not, we have network issues. I'm almost certain that is the case.'

'Were you the officer who issued the visa to Hamid? Have you met him?' asked Fauzia.

'No, I have not met Hamid. Visa officers handle these cases. But I still think you should wait for your son to call. He will call. Don't worry,' he said.

They were given a copy of Hamid's visa and passport and were assured of assistance in the future. Fauzia and Nehal took the documents but left unsatisfied. They still had no information about their son and the consulate had not been of much help.

When they got home, Khalid was waiting for them. Fauzia told him what had happened. By then, Khalid had started suspecting that this was beyond just a business visit. Hamid was up to something else. But he was careful not to say this in front of his parents. Fauzia did not feel like cooking that night, so they ordered some food. She had lost her appetite. She did not eat and went in to pray.

15 November 2012

Fauzia called up Ariana Airlines again to check if Hamid was on the flight back. The same voice, the same disappointment. He was not on the list.

'He might be coming home next week, Madam,' said the young man who attended the calls in the Kabul office.

She prepared breakfast for the two men, and when they sat at the dining table, they saw she was weeping. 'He is not coming back,' she said and burst out crying. Her husband tried to console her. 'Let's not lose hope. We need to try and trace him. Today is the 15th. If you say he is not on the flight then we need to inform the Afghan consulate so they can take some formal action. Let's write to the officer.'

The letter was written and Khalid sent it through registered post.

The long wait for the Ansari family began. Calling Ariana Airlines had become a ritual for Fauzia. She called them up every Thursday and Sunday for months. She had to pick up the pieces and try to find her son, but she also had to make a living. She started going back to work but would call the airline every day before leaving for college. She soon realized that even though Hamid meant the world to her, his name was of no consequence to the rest of the world.

The person attending calls for Ariana Airlines had started recognizing her voice by now. Once, as he picked up the phone and was checking the passenger list, a voice from behind asked him who was on the line. He said, '*Pagal budhiya hai jo roz call karti hai.*' (The mad old woman who calls up every day.)

Fauzia heard him say this since he had not put her on hold. From that day onwards, she stopped calling the airline.

~

A few weeks passed. Fauzia started to think that Hamid might have become a victim of a bomb blast or an attack. 'He could be injured, maybe in a hospital? Or could he be dead? No, Allah would not do that to us.' This development could not be kept within the family any longer. They needed help and guidance. Finally, the extended family, which also lived in Mumbai, was informed.

The entire household was in shock. The joint search for Hamid began.

9

The Arrest

12 November 2012: Karak, Pakistan

I woke up at 8.30 a.m. and looked around, trying to figure out where I was. For a moment, I had forgotten. I was in a small, dingy room that smelt as though it had not been aired in days. The air inside was stale, but given the weather outside, it was unimaginable to keep the doors or windows open. The winter chill was unbearable for someone from Mumbai.

I sat on the bed and wondered what to do. When I opened the door, I saw a woman putting out clothes to dry in the courtyard. Knowing very well by now that the culture in this part of the world was very different, I immediately shut the door and waited inside for Atta to come and fetch me.

Sometime later, Atta-ur-Rahman stepped in and showed me the way to the bathroom. He asked me to freshen up while breakfast was being laid out. I was craving a good cup of tea. At breakfast, Atta asked if I had slept well. 'I was so tired that I must have dozed off the moment my head hit the pillow. So, yes, I did catch up on some sleep,' I said.

'I wanted to discuss our plan. How is Fiza? Any news of her?' I asked, sipping my tea.

'We will talk about it after you get ready. Go have a bath first,' he said.

Atta explained that since he did not have the keys to the hujra last night, he had sent me to his bedroom instead. Now he asked me to shift my things to the guest room which had been readied. It was a separate space, with a boundary wall to ensure that outsiders stayed away from the women of the family.

I asked Atta where I could bathe. He showed me to the bathroom in the guest space. I hesitated for a second, but then decided to ask, 'Atta Bhai, is there hot water? I am dying in this weather.'

'Hot water! I've never had a warm water bath in my life. Nobody here does. Real men don't need hot water,' he said.

I took it as a challenge and nodded at his dare. But as soon as I entered the severely cold bathroom, staring at the bucket of ice-cold water, I wondered if I should skip having a bath.

'Stupid Pathans. At least in Afghanistan they provided me with hot water to bathe. This is plain crazy,' I said to myself as I touched the water to see how cold it was.

I didn't think I would survive the bath. Anyhow, mustering up my courage, I got out of my clothes and poured the first mug of water on myself. I almost screamed when it touched my body. That was the quickest bath I ever had in my life. I rushed to the hujra to get dressed. After getting a little warm, I picked up the phone and called Atta, who was already in his office. He asked me to wait.

In some time, I heard the door of the guest compound open. I stepped out of my room to see who it was. Atta emerged, accompanied by a thin young lad. 'This is Zabiullah. He owns a mobile shop close by. He is my good friend. You can trust him,' said Atta.

I walked up to Zabiullah; we shook hands and hugged. Atta continued, 'I have some work in office so why don't you go to his shop and stay with him while I finish up?'

I pulled him aside and asked, 'Have you told him everything about me? What about Fiza and Sadiq-ur-Rahman? Do you have an update?' I went on, 'The plan was that your contact in Kohat and I, along with a few NGO people and Dr Shazia, will go there to take up the matter with the jirga. My nationality will be a secret. We will all go as a group of people who have heard the news of a girl being put through the evil custom of wani.'

'I have discussed everything with Zabi and you can trust him. Don't worry,' said Atta. I was unhappy that he was talking about me to others, but I couldn't do anything about it now.

He again asked me to go with Zabiullah while he finished work and got all the details from his reporter in Kohat. With nothing much to do at home, I agreed to accompany Zabi.

I went into my room to pick up a muffler, and then we all walked out of the compound. Zabi's shop was hardly a five-minute walk through the narrow lanes of the colony where Atta lived.

We didn't speak a word on the way. He opened the padlocks to a small shop in the corner of a street, and we entered. I found a stool in a corner of the room and sat there quietly, with the barest bits of conversation. I was tense and wondering if I was exposing myself too much. Zabi seemed to be an affable guy who kept trying to chat, but I picked up a paper and kept my eyes fixed on it.

Around afternoon, Atta came to the shop to pick me up. We went home and entered the hujra, where he had brought lunch from the main house. After eating, he was washing the utensils when I asked him, 'Atta Bhai, any update on Fiza and her family? When can we leave for Kohat? I can't continue staying here.'

Atta looked up from the other side of the small courtyard. 'I have not been able to reach the guy who is supposed to help us. I'll try again this evening. We can only go there once there is a local contact, otherwise it is very dangerous territory,' he said.

Meanwhile, I called up Shahid in Kabul to inform him that I had reached safely and was in Atta-ur-Rahman's residence in Karak. He asked if I was prepared. I told him that there was no clarity yet but maybe by the evening I would have a plan. He wished me luck. That was my last conversation with him. I went to my room.

A while later, Atta came in and asked if I wanted to go with him to his office where he had a small business matter to handle. I agreed. His office was just across the road, a small space. It was locked, and Atta had the key. Down a passageway was a small room with a few computers. He guided me to one with an Internet connection in case I wanted to check my mail. The very first thing I did was send an email back home since I was expecting my family members to be worried as my Afghanistan number was not working.

I emailed Khalid informing him that networks were down and I was fine.

> Dear all,
>
> Everything is fine here. Nothing to worry abt. Food, weather, stay, work. Some issue with the mobile network dats y fones are not working here. Insha Allah things shud b back on in a few days. Using internet frm a frnd's place bt cant com here v often to use net. Relax dont worry. Tel mom not to worry abt anything. I am actually enjoying here. Also tel her not to worry abt my toilet issue. Its al very hygienic here.
>
> Wil cal asap
> Love
> Hamid

I waited for Atta to finish work, and after a while, he came back to the room where he had left me. We returned to his residence. By 5 p.m., it was dark and the city was coming to a standstill. The entire day had gone by waiting for an update. The longer I stayed, the more dangerous it was for me. I knew that. I was scared I would get caught.

Around six o'clock, I could hear Atta on the other side of the compound talking to his wife. Then he entered the hujra with dinner. We were sitting down to eat when he spoke, looking a little ashamed, 'I am sorry, Hamid Bhai. I couldn't get an update. Tomorrow I will ensure that I connect with my contact in Kohat and we can then leave. Meanwhile, I am also getting an NIC made for you.'

'What is that?' I asked.

He said, 'It is the National Identification Card that everybody in Pakistan has.'

'But I have already crossed over. Where is the need for it now?' I inquired.

He said, 'It will help you not only in your travel here but also to go back to Afghanistan, in case there is checking. The NIC will ensure you are safe.'

I was sceptical about carrying a fake document with me, but then again, I had entered the country illegally, without any documents. Having an ID wouldn't be such a bad idea. With no news of Fiza and with thoughts of the dangers ahead, I called it a night.

13 November 2012

I woke up early, and decided to get Fiza's address out so it was easier to locate her. I transferred my Pakistani SIM card from the Nokia phone to my BlackBerry as it had all the details I had collected from Afreen, the telecom employee.

As I finished the process and put the phone by the pillow, Atta walked in and greeted me. 'Salaam, Hamid Bhai. I hope you slept well. Let's have breakfast and then I will connect with my guy in Kohat,' he said.

Wishing him a good morning, I told Atta-ur-Rahman of the details I had managed to gather which could help us locate Fiza.

He stepped out and returned with a tray that had tea and roti. We finished up and then I took out my BlackBerry to give him the seven or eight phone numbers I had. I told him that I had tried the numbers when I was in India to see if they were valid, and had managed to get through on only two of them. One was picked up by an elderly woman and the other by a young girl.

Atta started calling each number one by one. I told him to speak in Pashto. All but one were switched off; the one that rang was answered by a girl. He started talking in Pashto, mimicking a girl's voice, but after a short conversation he ended the call. I did not understand what he had said and asked if he had managed to get anything useful. He said that he had pretended to be a college friend of Fiza's and asked to speak to her about some college assignment. The girl on the other side sounded suspicious and asked, 'What college work? What is your name? How do you know Fiza?' Even before Atta could try to convince her, she had sternly told him not to ever call on that number again and disconnected the line.

'Oh my God! That was the rudest conversation I have ever had in my life,' said Atta. He added that there was no way out but to travel to Kohat and see if we could rescue Fiza.

I asked Atta why we couldn't go and check if they were in Karak since we were already there.

'The accident took place in Karak. Why can't we simply go to their home here instead of to Kohat?' I asked.

With a shocked look on his face, Atta explained, 'Everyone in that village is interrelated. We will be easily identified as outsiders. And an outsider approaching the house of a convict asking for a girl of the Khattak tribe! Hamid, you have come up with a brilliant plan to get both of us killed. We cannot afford any miscalculations. In fact, you were the one who said Fiza is from Kohat and has been untraceable. So why should we go all the way there? Let's just stick to the plan,' he added. 'Let me go to the office and get a report on the case against her brother and how far things have gone. Meanwhile, you go to Zabi's store and stay there,' he said.

I got dressed and we walked together to the shop. This time, the chirpy, talkative Zabi invited me in like we were old friends. Atta left for work and Zabi started asking about my Kohat plan. I was surprised at his questions, but since he was already aware of everything I told him the real reason. 'Well, Atta-ur-Rahman has planned to accompany me along with other journalist friends from the Rotary and a doctor from Islamabad. I am waiting for him and the team so we can proceed together,' I said. He looked at me for a while and then nodded.

I felt like a huge weight had been lifted off my shoulders. This was dangerous territory. Two days had passed and I had already started feeling unsafe and vulnerable, completely dependent on one person who was not sharing anything with me. Fear started creeping in and my mind was full of horrid thoughts and scenarios.

In the afternoon, my phone rang. I wasn't used to receiving calls, so much so that Zabi had to tell me that I was getting a call. It was Atta. He said we would leave within the hour. My heart started racing, and we went back home and had lunch. Atta gave me a new number and asked me to save it. 'Call me only on this number from now on,' he said, sounding very cautious.

'Is there a problem?' I asked, wondering if I had been exposed. Should I be working on another plan?

Atta assured me that journalists kept changing their numbers for security reasons. Just then, he received a call and stepped out to answer it. He came back in and to my surprise told me that I wouldn't be able to travel today. I frowned and was about to protest when he added that Zabi was hosting a dinner for me at his residence where his family would also be present. I told Atta not to discuss anything with the rest like he had with Zabi.

While I was left alone in the room, I spent the entire evening worrying about my fate. Pacing up and down, I questioned the trust that I had reposed in Atta. Feeling stripped of security and apprehensive about my dependence on a stranger in a foreign land, I wanted to weep. But I composed myself and was convinced that our plan was foolproof and we would be able to save Fiza.

Later that evening, in the cold winter night, Atta-ur-Rahman, his brother and I went to Zabi's house. It was similar to Atta's house, with high walls and a separate area for male guests. Almost immediately after our arrival, we sat on carpets with a lavish *dastarkhwan* spread in front of us.

It was a delicious meal, with chicken curry, roti and pulao as the main course, while dessert was a home-made sweet dish made with rice, very similar to kheer.

During dinner, Atta and the other family members started speaking in Pashto, which I was unable to understand. I guessed they were talking about me as I noticed some look at me from the corners of their eyes. I immediately asked Atta if I was being discussed. He denied it, but added that the stares and looks were because of my attire. I was the only one wearing jeans, a shirt and a jacket.

After dinner, the younger ones of the household came to us with an *aftaba* and *cheelam che* (a jug and bowl, as I found out) for us to wash our hands. Unlike the practice in India, in Pathan households people don't go to a basin to wash their hands. Observing these aspects of their culture was quite fascinating despite all my worries. The hospitality shown by all those I had met through the journey up until now was heart-warming but I couldn't enjoy it fully. I couldn't get the sense of fear out of my mind even for a moment.

After dinner, Atta's brother left but Zabi said he had arranged a movie screening for the three of us. I expected a Pashto movie, but to my surprise, it was Nicolas Cage's *Next*, dubbed in Urdu. In hindsight, like the plotline of the film, I wish I could have looked into the future to avert the disaster in my life.

Atta and I were walking back after the movie when a police patrol stopped us. A few cops jumped out and started searching us. I went numb. This would be the end of me, I was certain. Everything around me went quiet; all I could see was the men moving around and asking questions. My brain froze. I kept staring at the men unblinkingly. I knew that my time was up. I was in Western attire, with no legal documents or local identification. I was almost sweating on that cold, wintry night. This was it. But then, Atta pulled a card out of his pocket and flashed it at the officers. They looked at it and smiled at both of us, patting Atta on the back. He said something to them, and they sat in the vehicle and drove off.

I couldn't believe what had just happened. The moment we were alone again, I turned around, held him by his arm and asked, 'What just happened? What is that magic card you have?'

He grinned and pulled it out again. 'It is my media card. They don't mess with the press. I told them that you are my cousin from Lahore and we were returning from a daawat,' he said.

'Thank God,' I said.

'Well, either this or we could have just bribed them,' he laughed and I joined in.

He suddenly became serious and asked if I had enough money for situations like this. I replied in the affirmative but didn't reveal exactly how much I had. 'Don't worry, till the time you are with me it's fine, but in case I am not around, you have to be careful. That is why you need the NIC identification,' he said.

'But why would I ever be without you while I am here? I am not comfortable keeping a fake ID. I might get into much more serious trouble,' I argued.

'More trouble than the fact that you are Indian?' he asked, staring at me. Well, he did have a point, I thought.

14 November 2012

I woke up feeling uneasy and frustrated. Why the hell was I stuck in this godforsaken town when I was short on time and had to move fast on my plan? The more I stayed here, the greater the danger I was in.

When Atta came in with breakfast, I told him that I was not here on a holiday. 'Atta Bhai, we have to go to Kohat. For all you know, Fiza might be getting married as we speak. I am here for her sake. She will commit suicide if she is forced. We don't have time. We need to execute our plan to approach the jirga. You promised to help, Atta Bhai,' I pleaded with him.

'Hamid Bhai, I know. Please do not doubt my intentions. I am swamped with work and Dr Shazia has also not responded to our calls. Your friends from the Rotary club were expected to come from Islamabad and join us in Kohat but none of them have shown up yet,' he said.

Then, after a moment of silence, he looked at me and suggested I go to Kohat by myself. 'My friend, who is also a reporter, will help with everything there and I will arrange for your ID card at the earliest,' he said.

I protested and said that the plan was for all of us to go together. I refused to go alone.

'Please try to understand, Hamid Bhai. I have an urgent family dispute to attend to in Mianwali and I will leave as soon as I see you off,' he said and hurried out of the room.

I was shocked. Alone all the way to Kohat! What if I got caught? What if someone stopped to ask me something? I would be exposed. I didn't even speak Pashto.

I prayed and then sat quietly, staring at the empty walls of my tiny room. Suddenly, I heard a knock and Atta walked in. He had with him a fake NIC, a student's ID card and a new SIM card.

I held the card, which seemed to be a printout on a green paper held together by two plastic sheets stapled to each other. It looked fake. The card read 'Hamza Muhammad'. I looked questioningly at Atta, who said, 'This is the best I could do. We need to hide your identity.'

Then I picked up the student's I-card, where the 'Date of Birth' section was struck off. I again looked at Atta, and he said, 'Well, there was a minor mistake', pointing at the struck-out bit where I could make out the words '14 Nov. 2012'. They had put the current date instead of a birthdate.

This was a flawed exercise and would put me in harm's way, I thought. That was not all. The SIM card was registered in someone else's name and not in Hamza Muhammad's, which was supposed to be my identity in Pakistan. I decided not to take the documents.

But Atta assured me that this was the best way to go about it. He asked me to put the new SIM in and give him the old Pakistani SIM that I had picked up at the border. I asked him why he needed my SIM card. He said that he would destroy it and throw it away.

I wasn't comfortable with the idea but had no other option. I was in his house with nowhere to go. I took the SIM out, destroyed it and gave it to Atta. 'Here, I have destroyed the card myself,' I said to him.

I added, 'I am not taking these documents. They don't look authentic at all and will land me in greater trouble. Instead, I can just say that I forgot to carry my ID.'

Atta-ur-Rahman looked disappointed but insisted that I hold on to them. 'You never know when you'll require it,' he said and put it back in his own pocket.

He then mentioned that I needed to connect with his friend Abdullah in Kohat. 'Abdullah is the reporter I was telling you about who used to give me information about Fiza and her family. He just informed me over the phone that Fiza and her family are in Kohat. You should head there at the earliest. Abdullah will receive you in Kohat and help you in your mission. Inshallah, you will come back successful,' Atta said, patting my back.

In the afternoon, Zabi came and the three of us had lunch together. Atta and Zabi waited for me outside the hujra while I got ready, after which they escorted me to a stop from where I could hail a cab to Kohat. Before boarding the cab, Atta tugged on my jacket and pulled me aside. He said, 'Hamid Bhai, I will help you as much as I can and I hope you are successful in saving the girl, but if you get caught please do not take my name. I have a family to look after. Even if you do, I will deny having known you at all. Please try to understand and be careful.'

I again felt a tug at my conscience. Was I doing the right thing? Atta had failed to keep any of his promises. He hadn't turned up in Jalalabad, then he was a no-show when I had reached Haji Camp in Peshawar, and now he was not coming with me to Kohat. But then I made myself remember the things he had done for me: he had sent Imtiaz to help me; he told me how to avoid the army checkpost at the Kohat tunnel and had been waiting at 3 a.m. on a wintry night to receive me; he had taken a risk by letting me stay in his own house; and he had saved me from the cops after the dinner at Zabi's. I had no reason to doubt his intentions.

Zabi pulled out an envelope and pressed it into my hand. I gave a quick look inside to find some folded currency notes. I returned it, thanking him profusely for his hospitality and kindness. 'This is our culture. We cannot send you away empty-handed. You might need it in Kohat. Just keep it,' he said and shoved the envelope into my jeans' pocket and hugged me. I was suddenly reminded of my own brother, Khalid. He must be so so angry with me. But I knew he wouldn't have understood even if I had told him everything I was going through.

After some time, a Costa cab arrived. Atta-ur-Rahman spoke to the driver. I bade them goodbye and sat in it.

My journey to Kohat began in the late afternoon. It was not very long. I was told that I would be in Kohat in one and a half to two hours' time. As I stared out of the window at the beautiful landscape of the countryside, my phone rang. It was an unknown number. I hesitantly picked up and found out it was Atta calling from a new number. He asked me to save the number and to only use this one. After some time, I got an SMS with Abdullah's number.

I called Abdullah and told him that I was about to reach. He asked me to get off at Dewoo bus stop. Around 4 p.m., after an hour's journey, I reached the stop and called him. He asked me to wait there.

Four men walked up to me. One of them introduced himself as Abdullah and welcomed me with a hug. The others were also very warm. 'Hamid Bhai, so nice to meet you. These are my friends. Let us first go and get something to eat. We will sit and discuss things and then I will take you to my own hostel where I have reserved a room for you. It is a small place. Please don't mind. We do not have big hotels in Kohat,' Abdullah said.

One of them took my backpack and we walked to a small restaurant nearby for some tea and refreshments. 'Kaka ji', read the board. There were others who looked like they had also been travelling.

We sat around a rickety table. Abdullah didn't waste time and asked if I had a picture of Fiza. I pulled out the phone and showed him her photo.

'Yes yes, that is the daughter of Sadiq-ur-Rahman,' exclaimed Abdullah. There were stares from the other tables. Becoming aware of how loud he was, he leaned forward and whispered, confirming that the family was from Karak and that they were his neighbours.

I figured that was how he had been giving Atta the updates. 'Are you related?' I asked.

'No, no. We live in the same neighbourhood but we are not related,' he replied.

The other boys started asking me about my journey and looked very excited. I could see Abdullah making a few calls. He would get up from the table during his phone conversations. When he returned from one of them, he said, 'Hamid Bhai, I had asked my people to reserve a room for you in my hostel but now they are telling me that it won't be possible. So I have spoken to a hotel nearby. We will go there and get a room. Like I said, it might not be up to your expectations. I am sorry. But that is what I was busy with just now.'

'Please don't embarrass me. You are already doing so much. Thank you for everything,' I said.

Meanwhile, I called Atta on his new number and updated him. He wished me luck and said he would be leaving for Mianwali so his number would be unreachable. 'You have Abdullah who will help you with everything. Think of him as though it's me who is there with you. You are in safe hands. Take care. And Inshallah, I will see you soon,' he said.

We walked up to the main market of Kohat on Bannu Road, where two of Abdullah's friends parted ways from us. Abdullah, one of his friends and I walked further down the road. I could see a board of Khyber Bank, and quite a few electrical stores. A little further down, we turned left on to a smaller road where Palwasha Hotel stood.

'We are here. Please wait. Let me first go in and speak to the receptionist.' I waited outside while Abdullah filled in some details in a register.

He came out and told me that the room fare was 300 rupees per night. It was just for one night, I thought to myself and gave him the money.

He went back to pay for the room and came back with the room key. Handing it over, Abdullah said, 'Hamid Bhai, I have to go to finish a college assignment. Please stay in the room and do not venture out without me.'

'But where are you going? Can you not show me where Fiza lives before you go?' I asked. I was losing patience. I wanted to get this done as soon as possible and make my way home.

Abdullah hesitated and said that the assignment was important and urgent so the trip to Sadiq-ur-Rahman's house would have to wait.

'I promise you that my friends and I will go along with you as a team to rescue Fiza and ensure your safe return to Karak. But right now I have to go,' he said.

I took my bag and went up to my room. It was small, and the curtains were drawn. It was also cold. I sat on the bed and wondered if I should waste another day or at least try to do something about rescuing Fiza.

I started pacing the room. I looked out the window; there was nothing to see but cramped buildings. I didn't want to venture out alone since Abdullah had warned me not to. He had said that it was the time of Muharram (a mourning period for Shia Muslims that involves processions) and the city was under heightened security and checking. It was already dark. But then I thought I had already taken so many risks, and just going to see where she lived wouldn't do me much harm. I had my mobile phone in case I needed assistance.

I finally got up, thinking of the address that Fiza had given me a year ago. I left my bag, locked the room and went out. It was pretty cold; I felt like my ears would drop off. I was just not used to such extreme temperatures and wondered how people survived in these parts of the world.

After I stepped out of the hotel, I saw a small shop at the corner that led to the main road. I asked the shopkeeper the way to KDA Hospital (District Headquarters Hospital, Kohat Development Authority). It was a thirty-minute walk from where I stood but nobody told me that. They just gave me general directions. I didn't want to talk much and expose myself as a foreigner, but they had surely figured out I was not a local.

Switching two autorickshaws, I made my way to KDA Hospital. Finally, I reached a red-brick building surrounded by trees and barren hills. Opposite the hospital was a pathology lab, a chemist and a stationery shop. I went to the chemist and asked if he knew of Sadiq-ur-Rahman Sahab, an employee of WAPDA.

The chemist told me that he was new to the area and did not know any such person. However, an old employee would arrive soon and he could give me some information.

While I waited, the chemist asked in Urdu, 'You don't look like you are from around here. Where are you from?'

Relieved to hear Urdu, I responded with just one word, 'Lahore.'

Even as he started to ask another question, my phone rang. It was an unknown number. I picked up. It was Abdullah.

He sounded agitated; 'Hamid Bhai, where are you?'

'Abdullah Bhai, I am at KDA Hospital. Fiza stays close by. I thought I would just do a recce of the place rather than while away my time in the hotel room,' I answered.

'Don't go anywhere. Just stay at the hospital. I am headed there anyway,' he said and disconnected the phone.

After some time, Abdullah arrived with the friend who had been with us while booking the hotel room. The three of us went to the pathology lab. I asked him about his sudden arrival. 'You had said you were going to be busy with your assignments.'

Abdullah said that his friend wanted to get some blood tests done at the hospital. So we sat outside and waited for him. Then we saw two policemen drive up on a motorcycle. They stopped right in front of the pathology lab.

Before I could react, Abdullah looked at me and asked me to go away from there. I was shocked. 'Where do I go? I have no place to go or hide in! Don't abandon me. Just show them your press card,' I pleaded, holding his hand.

He brushed my hand off and asked me to stay away. 'Go away right now. We cannot get caught together. Leave me alone,' he said, raising his voice.

I thought it best to leave before the conversation attracted the attention of the cops. I stepped out of the pathology lab and saw a group of people walking in a particular direction. I joined the crowd and started walking with them. But one uniform-clad man followed me and flashed his torch at me. He asked me to stop.

When I turned, I saw that he held a torch in one hand and a revolver in the other. At a distance, I could see the other man near the bike pointing a rifle at me.

The cop with the torch said, 'Stop right there,' and rushed towards me. Before I could react, he started checking my pockets. He pulled out the envelope of money Zabi had given me. He pulled my cell phone and wallet out from the other pocket. When he checked the envelope, along with the cash, he retrieved the fake ID cards. I was in shock and trembling, but tried to keep my cool. I knew that disaster had struck because Abdullah had abandoned me and Zabi had betrayed my trust. I kept looking for Abdullah, hoping he would come to my rescue. But I couldn't see him anywhere.

The cop asked where I was headed. I told him that I was going to get a rickshaw from the other side of the road. 'You think I am a fool. Can you see rickshaws on the other side? There is no rickshaw stand

there, so stop lying!' He grabbed me by the arm and called his colleague
to bring the motorcycle to us.

He gestured to me to sit on it. I sat between the two cops, and as we
were driving out of the area, I saw Abdullah standing at a distance with
a vile look on his face, a look of revenge and hatred. A sense of betrayal
swept through my entire being. I was shivering and had tears in my eyes
as I was driven away by the cops.

An arrested Indian national with no legal documents. This was as
bad as it could get.

10

The First Encounter

14 November 2012

Sitting between the two cops, I tried to think of ways to escape. What would I tell them? Could I call Atta? Maybe he would be able to help me through his journalist contacts. But then I was reminded of his last words. He said he would disown me if I mentioned him. Disowned, abandoned, betrayed . . . Should I just be honest?

The bike entered a gated premise and halted. It was a police station. I was taken inside and made to sit on a chair. This was my first encounter with the Pakistani authorities. Before this, Atta had handled everything, but now I was left to my own devices. What was I to do?

The officer rested himself on the table in front of me and bent forward. He smiled and said, 'It is best you tell us the truth. We already have intelligence on you. We know about you.'

I was shocked and kept staring at the floor. My head hurt. I wanted to scream and cry but I also wanted to reason with them. Abdullah's face flashed in front of me, and the thought crossed my mind that this was an ambush set up by him. Why would he suddenly ask me where I was? Why did his friend need a blood test at that moment? The abrupt change of venue from a hostel to a hotel, and then the 'assignment'. 'Don't leave the room'—his words echoed in my mind. It was a trap.

The cops would have caught me in the room itself. I only delayed the process by stepping out. There was no point lying about my nationality, so I told them the truth.

'Sir, I am an Indian and have come here looking for a girl, a friend who is in trouble. I just want to help her. She is being married off forcefully under the wani custom. I tried very hard to get a visa for Pakistan but failed . . .' Even as I was speaking, a few men in civilian clothes arrived.

Among them was a senior-looking man in civil clothes, with a pleasant demeanour. He walked up to me and said softly, 'I was called in because my colleagues told me they have caught an Indian spy. What is the truth, my son? If you are honest with me, maybe I can help. I am in charge here.'

I was fumbling through my words in fear. 'I am not an Indian spy. I swear on Allah. I am from Mumbai in India. I am an engineer and I came here to rescue my friend Fiza, who is the daughter of Sadiq-ur-Rahman. His son killed a neighbour and now she is being offered in marriage as part of the wani custom . . .'

I went ahead and told him how I had planned and entered Pakistan through Afghanistan by researching on the Internet. I omitted the part about Atta-ur-Rahman. Most of the policemen were sneering and laughing. But the officer kept a serious face. I couldn't gauge whether he believed me or not.

I stopped to see what he had to say. He looked at me hard and asked, 'How is it possible that you entered Pakistan, not just Lahore or Karachi, but the interiors of Khyber Pakhtunkhwa, without any assistance? You will have to give us names.'

I was reminded of Atta-ur-Rahman's words about not taking his name and that he would deny knowing me even if I did. I didn't want to betray him so I told the officer that I did some research on the Internet and planned the whole thing on my own. I added, 'Sir, I am telling the truth. I am sure if you ask someone about Sadiq-ur-Rahman and his family, you will know. I came here for a humanitarian cause.'

The elderly officer was about to ask a question when a voice from behind interrupted him. 'Sir, Sadiq is my relative. I did hear about the problems he faced. He was injured, shot by his own son. It was during

that time that the jirga decided that Fiza's hand in marriage would have
to be given in wani. But as far as I know, no wedding has taken place yet
in that household and Sadiq is also out on bail.'

'Sir, I am not a spy,' I pleaded again. 'Now your own man is
confirming my story. Please help me. Please,' I said.

The officer turned around. He stepped out with the others, and
when they returned, the cop who was Sadiq's relative was not among
them. The senior officer handed over my hotel keys to one of his juniors
and asked him to get all my belongings.

'What is happening, sir? Please help me. I am innocent. I am not
here to harm anyone but to help a girl in need,' I said.

They started laughing. Another cop walked up to me and said that
the matter was out of their hands now and that another team was on its
way. 'They will come and deport you,' he said.

The senior officer said, 'Pay me 5 lakh and I will drop you to the
border in my own car.' There was another roar of laughter since they
knew that all I had was 5000.

So his pleasant demeanour had been a farce. The evil laughter was
enough for me to know that any amount of pleading now would only
end in ridicule. So I kept quiet. Meanwhile, I saw an officer come in
with some papers.

One of them started noting details in their register. I was officially
booked and arrested.

My rights were not read to me. I was only told of my arrest. Their
minds were made up. It was as though this was part of a larger scheme and
I had taken the bait unknowingly. Was everybody involved? Was Atta also
part of this plan? I sure as hell knew Abdullah was. He had ruined my life.

The questioning didn't stop even after I was booked. They asked
me about my family, where I lived, what I did, how I had got in touch
with Fiza.

One of them held up my fake ID and said, 'So this is not your real
identity. How did you get this ID card? What is your real identity? Are
you even a Muslim?'

'I paid an agent and bought the ID. I have given you my real name,
sir. I am Hamid Ansari. I am a Muslim,' I said.

They seemed very curious. Another officer said, 'You are an Indian. There are no real Muslims in India. So don't lie to us.'

I was shocked but now was not the time to argue. In a short span of time, the conversation had moved from me being an Indian without legal papers to questioning whether I was a Muslim or not.

They started asking questions about Islam. I answered all of them correctly. They were left with no choice but to accept what I said. Instead, one of them turned around and implied that I was a 'very well-trained spy'.

I was yet to fathom the severity of the situation and was dreading what lay ahead. But seeing the buffoonery of the cops, I blurted out, 'Do you know that Islam does not allow any Muslim to question or doubt someone's religious belief?'

They all stopped talking and stared at me. The senior officer raised his voice for the first time, 'Don't teach us what to do. You will be taught a lesson well and good.'

I froze. One of the officers took me to another room and asked me to strip. I couldn't believe what I had heard so I gave him a blank stare. He shouted and asked me to remove all my clothes. I had seen this in the movies. But I had never thought I would be at the receiving end of such a nightmarish experience.

My inner voice screamed 'rape!' I didn't know what to do. I pleaded with the cop, 'Please don't do this. I have done nothing wrong.'

The temperature had dipped by then. The room was cold and so was his stare. Without flinching, he said that this was procedural. They needed to search me for any chips. I saw that their minds were made up. They were convinced that I had come with some ulterior motive.

'Strip,' he said aloud.

I started to take off my clothes one piece at a time. I stood there in front of him in my underwear, my arms wrapped around my body as the biting cold pierced through my bones.

The officer pointed at the last remaining stitch of clothing and gestured to me to remove it. I protested, 'This is against Islam. You cannot expose someone's private parts.'

He retorted, 'For someone who has committed so many illegal acts, don't teach me Islam. Do as I say or suffer the consequences.'

I prayed for forgiveness and kept hoping I wouldn't be raped. The threat was enough for me to take off my underwear. I was bodily checked. All the while their hands were on me, I anticipated that I would be sexually harassed, but nothing of the sort happened. Moments later, I was asked to put on my clothes again.

I did so, crying. This was just the beginning. I wanted to know if I could call home or the Indian embassy in Pakistan. But first, I wanted them to hear me out.

Once I got ready, I was taken to an adjacent room. More men in civilian clothes were sitting there, along with cops in uniform. The questioning started again in the presence of the new set of people. I learnt that they were also cops.

I was asked the same questions, but the response of the new guys was different. They termed all my answers as cover stories and said that I was hiding the real mission for which I was sent to Pakistan.

One of the officers asked if I was Muslim. The officer who had checked me replied, 'I checked, sir. He has been circumcised.'

I was shocked. Had the body check only been a pretence? They had actually just wanted to see if I was Muslim or not? I felt disgusted. I cursed the people and the country that called itself the 'Islamic Republic of Pakistan'.

One of the officers, who seemed to be the seniormost in the new team, pulled out his cell phone and called someone. I heard him say in Urdu, '*Yaar, aap log jald se jald aa kar isse le jao aur mujhe farigh karo.*' (You guys, please come here as soon as possible and take him so I can be free of this responsibility.)

All that time while we waited for someone to come, I shut my eyes and mumbled words of prayer, seeking help from God. Sometime later, a few more officers in civilian clothes walked in. I had lost track of time but I knew it must be pretty late. They had taken all my belongings. The only thing they allowed me to keep were my spectacles since I had very high power (minus 5.5 progressive). I was practically blind without my glasses. By now, I was tired of all the questioning and my mind was racing. Of all countries to be stuck in, I was in Pakistan, that too on the wrong side of the law.

Everyone stood up. One of the officers who had just arrived seemed to be senior to the others. They saluted him. He looked at me and asked, '*Yahi hai kya?*' (Is this the guy?)

'*Ji janab, yahi hai. Kehta hai Musalman hai. Achhi tarah se sikha kar bheja gaya hai ise.*' (Yes, sir, he is the one. Says he is a Muslim. He has been trained well and sent here.)

I was handcuffed and taken out of the police station and shoved into a white Suzuki 800 with four others in white uniform. Being handcuffed felt unreal, yet the weight of the cuffs tugging at my hand as I sat uncomfortably in the car was a reminder of where I was.

We drove towards the Kohat cantonment. As soon as we entered the cantonment area, it dawned on me that I was being handed over to the Pakistan army. I was scared for my life. As we reached the gates, the man sitting next to me rolled down his window and signalled the guards to let them through the barricades. The car entered unchecked. I wondered what the signal meant that had eliminated all security checks. I started looking around. There was a board that read 'Islamabad' to the left and 'Peshawar' to the right. One of the officers noticed what I was doing. He asked me to remove my spectacles and blindfolded me with a black cloth. In fact, he covered my entire face.

I could only feel the car twist and turn before it finally came to a halt. Two people held me from either side and took me inside a building and made me sit on a chair. It was pitch-dark, but I could hear some sounds in the distance. Then I heard footsteps, and a male voice asking me if I wanted anything. I asked for a glass of water. He returned with a glass and removed the black cloth so I could drink. I asked him what would happen next as he took the glass from my hand and covered my face again.

I was sitting in the same place for a very long time with my hands cuffed behind my back and my face covered. Then I heard a heavy voice say in the most unkind manner, '*Kapda hatao iske muh se.*' (Remove the cloth from his face.) I dreaded opening my eyes, and when I did, everything was hazy since I didn't have my glasses. He pulled out my glasses from a tray and tried them on, only to exclaim, 'Oh my God! Your eyesight is really poor. You are literally blind.'

When I wore my glasses, I saw a hefty person sitting on the table in front of me, with one foot on my chair.

He started to ask me the same questions that I had already answered twice over, threatening me that if I didn't I would be labelled a spy and sent to die in prison. So I answered everything and also told him that I had proof of the purpose of my visit on my phone. He picked up my phone from the same tray and asked me to show him.

I opened all the pictures, chats and even the voice messages sent by Fiza. He still looked unconvinced.

'Quite a well-prepared cover you have,' he said, staring into my eyes. He pulled out my glasses and slapped me hard. I couldn't believe what had just happened. My head was spinning. He then pulled my hair and whispered in my ear, 'Don't teach us. We know who you are.'

I was shivering and tears rolled down my eyes.

'This is only the beginning. Wait and see what we do to you. Don't you ever think that you are going back, you Indian spy,' he said and stormed out of the room.

My head was again covered with the black cloth. I started crying and praying. This was hell. If this was the beginning, I didn't want to think about what was to follow. My world froze. I was dizzy.

Two men came in and held me by my arms. I was taken to another building and put into a brightly lit cell. My face was uncovered. I saw a small hole near the roof in the top corner for ventilation. There were no windows and the doors were sealed. I could hardly see without my glasses. After some time, a slit under the door opened and a small plate with some curry and chapati was pushed in.

'Eat,' said a heavy voice on the other side of the door. But I had lost my appetite. I was thirsty but there was no water. I didn't have the courage to ask. I kept crying and praying. I was restless and fatigued but sleep eluded me. I sat in the corner of that cell with only one thing ringing in my head: the officer saying I could forget about ever returning home.

I started thinking of the people I had read about who had got trapped in Pakistan and returned only when they were old, if at all— like the fishermen who were trapped across the borders on both sides and were allowed to come back no sooner than thirty to thirty-five years later, if they hadn't languished and died in prison by then.

I thought of my parents being shattered. Would they ever know where I was? I broke down again, thinking about what a fool I had been to commit such a mistake. 'Ammi,' I called out and wept. Just the thought of them suffering was unbearable. I fell on my knees and asked Allah for forgiveness. The men might not hear my truth but my Creator would, I thought, and kept praying.

A few minutes later, the door opened and a young man came in with three chairs. He asked me to get up and made me sit on the floor in front of the chairs. With my hands behind my back, I sat on the floor in a very uncomfortable position. The handcuffs were not the ones I had seen in the movies. They consisted of a steel rod with loops on either end which made manoeuvrability difficult.

Four more men entered. Three sat on the chairs and one stood behind me. All three of them had pen and paper in their hands. The one sitting at the centre told me that if I cooperated, I would not be harmed and the process would be easy for me. But if I played around then they would adopt techniques that I couldn't imagine even in my dreams.

Their manner of questioning was professional, but I was answering the same questions for the fourth time. They started by asking me my name, nationality and profession. They asked me how I had planned my mission. Although I was exhausted repeating myself, I told them exactly how I had planned it, only leaving out the contribution of Atta-ur-Rahman.

There was silence, and then the senior officer looked at the man standing behind me. I felt his hand on my face like a bolt of lightning. My ears buzzed. I lost my balance and fell to one side.

'You are a RAW [India's intelligence agency, R&AW, Research and Analysis Wing] agent. Tell us about your mission or we will take it out of you,' said the officer.

Another officer, an elderly man, said that the punishment for being a spy was a minimum of thirty-five years, but if I told them the truth, they could consider a relaxation of the sentence.

But I knew nothing about spying and would have been in bigger trouble if I admitted to something I hadn't done. So I stuck to my story and repeated the same thing.

'Believe me, sir, I was here only to save Fiza from wani. You can check my phone and all the messages and pictures,' I pleaded.

One of the officers alluded to the fact that Fiza could be involved in this and might be a RAW agent too. I was shocked. What had I done? Would she also be in trouble now?

The four men got up and left me with my disbelief. Before he left, the man standing behind me covered my face again.

Time went by and I kept sitting there, perhaps till the wee hours of the next day. I was waiting for a fate unknown, but the near future seemed bleak, fraught with danger, torture and humiliation. Life seemed very uncertain.

I was already a broken man. My life as I knew it had ended. The ordeal had just begun.

11

Torture: From Kohat to Peshawar

Thursday, 15 November 2012

I was locked in a small, suffocating room with no ventilation, and my face was covered the entire time. I couldn't bear to sit like that any more, but I did not have a choice. I hadn't slept a wink.

My ears were alert to any sound outside. I heard footsteps and then metal clanking at the door. A key turned and the door opened, the cold air hitting me. I dreaded what was in store. I didn't want to be beaten up. I prayed that I could prove my innocence.

The man who entered asked if I wanted to go to the washroom. *'Khana to tune khaya nahi hai to washroom kyun jaana hai? Chhota peshab karna hai?* (You haven't eaten anything but do you still want to go pee?) In a parallel universe, the phrase 'chhota peshab' would have left me in splits. But I no longer knew what a joke felt like.

I nodded. He pulled me up and guided me to the washroom. When we reached the door, he unlocked my cuffs and removed the blindfold. Keeping the door slightly ajar, he said, 'Don't turn around. Just go in and do your job.'

I asked him if I could shut the door. He refused, saying the door would have to remain slightly open. I was reminded of the humiliation I had faced at the police station. I couldn't urinate, and was just able to

94

perform my ablutions so I could offer namaz. When I stepped out, the man looked at me and asked why I hadn't answered nature's call. I told him I didn't feel like it. He held me by my hair and started beating me up there itself. 'If you didn't want to go then why did you waste my time?' he said, kicking me.

I was shocked. How was this allowed? He dragged me to the cell and threw me inside. I was handcuffed and blindfolded and left writhing in pain on the cold floor. I could feel blood on my lips and knew that my left under-eye area was swollen. I couldn't touch it to see how bad it was. My body hurt and I was experiencing shooting stomach cramps—aggravated by the lack of food and the kicks I had been subjected to.

The level of brutality shocked me. Was there no humanity in this land? But it was truly only the beginning. I finished my prayers and kept crying, thinking about my fate and my family. I finally cried myself to sleep.

I woke up to the sound of the door opening. The person who entered the room simply kicked me in the chest and said, '*Tu yahan aaram se sone aaya hai? Chal uth. Jasoos kahin ka.*' (Have you come here to sleep? Get up, you bloody spy.)

He pulled me up and dragged me to another cell a short distance away. I couldn't see anything, but the room reeked of sweat and blood. An interrogation room. For the fifth time.

Spy, RAW agent, cover story, real mission—these were the refrains I heard over and over again. My voice was lost in all these untruths.

'Tie him up,' I heard someone say. I panicked, shaking my head and moving back till I was dragged along by the man who had brought me to this cell. He held my arm and pushed me to a wall. Someone else held my other hand. My wrists were cuffed to a chain hanging from the ceiling and I was made to balance on a metal cube frame with my feet fastened to the two sides of the thin pipes. My knees gave way, and I was hanging by my arms. I heard a voice asking me to stand up. I did as I was told, but my legs were shaking. I expected them to come charging at me with their batons, but they didn't do that. There was silence. I must have stood there for hours. I felt faint and was convinced that they had left me to die, hanging like that.

To them, I was an Indian who had entered their country on a spying mission. They didn't even consider me Muslim. Hanging from the ceiling for hours, my hands became numb and my feet were in excruciating pain. I thought I would die in that position.

Finally, they brought me down, slapped on the handcuffs again and made me sit in a corner of the cell. They removed my blindfold and started kicking me and beating me up. But just then, a huge man entered the room dressed in a Pathani outfit, a waistcoat and long boots, and they stopped what they were doing. His messy hair fell to his shoulders, he had a long beard, a dark complexion and big, red eyes with dark circles. As soon as he entered, everyone stood at attention and saluted him. He didn't look like an army officer. I noticed the documents in his hand and wondered if he was part of the Taliban or if the Taliban had joined the Pakistan army. I was completely confused in my death-like situation.

He gave me a hard look and ordered the others to take me away. They quietly obeyed and helped me up. As I passed him, the officer extended his hand for a handshake. I reached out and shook it. He smiled, saying, 'Ham log tab tak kisi ke saath mujrimo wala sulook nahi karte jab tak uska jurm sabit na ho jaye.' (We don't treat anyone like a criminal until his crime is proven.) These were the only kind words I heard in a long time.

He added, 'I am from the same tribe as Fiza.' The Khattak tribe. I noticed that he had the ugliest set of teeth—a few were missing and two gold ones stuck out. Could he be trusted? What if he was just playing mind games? I hoped he would help me, at least let me inform my family. But I didn't say anything. I was taken out of the cell and, instead of being put in that dungeon of a room, led out of the building. I asked them where they were taking me. I could see the same white Suzuki 800 from earlier up ahead.

A flicker of positivity struck me—maybe they believed me and had decided to set me free. I was asked to sit in the car. Nobody answered my questions. And the gloom of despair filled me again. We drove to the hospital within the cantonment premises and emerged from the car, with two guards by my side at all times, pointing their rifles at me. Everything scared me. Nothing seemed normal. I had not seen so many guns, uniformed people and this culture of brutality, arms and force in my entire life.

I couldn't move. I felt paralysed. Two men helped me inside for medical tests, which they said were just procedural. A doctor looked at me and asked if I was on any medication or undergoing any treatment. I shook my head. He asked if I was in pain and if I was being ill-treated. My swollen face and bruised body answered his questions, but he didn't say anything, just signed a paper and handed it over to the men.

I was taken back to the car and then to a different compound which had several buildings with slanted roofs. One of the men in the car said that I would spend the night there and my case would be handled in the morning. Someone else told me that it was being taken up on priority, and he had therefore been instructed to send faxes and emails rather than use the mailing service to speed up paperwork.

I felt a sense of relief. 'Is that a good thing? Have my parents been informed?' There was silence.

Without saying anything further, they handed me over to the man in charge of the facility and left. A new set of guards stood at the entrance to escort me to my cell, which was part of a series of high-ceilinged ones with iron-grilled gates in front of wooden doors. The walls must have been 20 feet high, and the ceilings were supported by wooden planks. The place looked colonial.

There was a plastic dustbin in one corner of my cell. The room was large, unlike my last abode. There were bloodstains on the walls, along with other signs of damage, cobwebs on the ceilings and a stench that seeped into my skin.

Well, the Taliban-type officer certainly wasn't talking about me when he said that they didn't ill-treat those who were innocent. The room was whispering words of death into my ears. The more I looked around it, the more I feared that the end was near.

I shut my eyes, asking for forgiveness from my parents. But even as I broke down, something inside me shook me up. I had to fight. I was innocent. They would have to listen to me. I could not let them get the better of me. I was only worried about whether my parents had been or would be informed. I didn't want to be a nameless grave in an 'enemy state'. I wanted to go home. The Almighty knew I was innocent and He would come to my rescue, I told myself.

A while later, I went to the door and knocked on it softly. The guard on the other side asked me what I wanted. 'I want to offer namaz. Could I go to the washroom to perform *wuzoo* [ablutions]?' I requested.

He shouted, 'I am not your servant. And you anyway don't need to pray any more since your prayers will not be heard by anyone,' he said and laughed. He threatened me by saying he would break my bones if I knocked on that door again.

I thought what kind of Muslims these people were if they did not even allow someone to offer prayers. Even if I was not a Muslim, it was none of their concern how I prayed and if my prayers were heard or not.

After some time, the man in charge came in with his subordinate, who got me food. I told them that I wasn't hungry. I just wanted to wash up so I could offer my prayers. The officer thought I was avoiding food over fear of being poisoned. He took a small piece of roti, put it in his mouth and said, 'See, I am eating it. There is no poison in your food.'

I requested him to take me to the washroom. But he refused and walked away. The plate was left in the room and I was locked up again. Were they afraid that I would make an escape? It was impossible to get out of this garrison.

It was dark and the whole place had gone quiet. In the middle of the night, I really had to pee, but I knew I couldn't ask the guard. I spotted the dustbin and relieved myself. I was still not hungry. The only thoughts running through my head were, 'Have my parents and my brother eaten? What must they be thinking?'

Prayer is the best source of strength and mental peace. I did not have water, but I remembered that Islam allows Muslims to use soil for ablution if water is not available. I did so, rubbing my hands on the muddy floor. I didn't know which direction I was facing and I did not have the courage to ask. But I prayed anyway.

~

I cried so much that my eyes were swollen and my head hurt. Resting my back against the wall, I shut my eyes against the dim bulb in the room. But no sooner had I closed my eyes than I saw a nightmare of my parents crying in pain. I woke up with a start. Regret filled my mind, my body and my soul. Hitting the back of my head to the wall, I kept saying, 'What have I done, what have I done?'

Friday, 16 November 2012

I woke up to the *azaan* and offered namaz. Around afternoon, I heard the sermon and remembered that it was *jummah* (Friday).

I knocked on the door despite the guard's threat and requested him to allow me to offer Friday prayers. But he simply mocked me and said I was pretending to be a Muslim so the officers would be lenient with me. 'Don't pretend. You are not allowed to offer namaz since you aren't a Musalman,' he said.

'May you burn in hell,' I cursed him to his face. He could not do anything but stare at me.

After the Friday prayers, I heard voices outside the closed door. Someone asked if I wanted to eat anything but another person said that I should not get anything. I was not hungry for food, and the words I heard were full of hatred.

Around afternoon, the door opened to let in the same officers who had brought me to this facility. I was handcuffed, blindfolded and taken back to the earlier facility. By evening, the officers who had interrogated me there earlier came in.

They didn't say a word, but just started beating me with belts and batons. I didn't know what had brought this on. They asked me the same questions all over again. I kept screaming and wailing. At some point, I couldn't bear to hear my own screams.

I begged them to stop and asked them to cross-check all that I had said so far about Fiza and my travels. At one point, the skin on my wrists started bleeding because of the friction caused by the handcuffs.

Then the questions became very detailed, and they found that I couldn't remember the finer points. This led to more beating. They asked questions like what time I had made a particular call, what was the duration of that call, how much money I had carried from Jalalabad, how much I had spent during the journey and where, how much I had spent in Karak and how much I had left at the time of the arrest.

I couldn't give them the exact numbers. 'I was not keeping a detailed account so I will not be able to account for every penny. It isn't possible,' I told my interrogators.

There was a knock on the door and the beating stopped. The officer who had been beating me left the room and did not come back. Another person came in, asked if I wanted some water and said that it was all over and I could relax. But I was shivering in fear and could not relax. The brutal officer's subordinate, who was still in the room, charged at me and gave me a sharp whack on the face. I thought they were all psychotic.

The new officer intervened and asked the other man to back off. That was a relief. He told the subordinate officer that my innocence had been proved and I would be released the next day. I couldn't believe what I had just heard. I was offered a glass of water, and my blindfold was removed temporarily.

'Thank you so much for believing me. I know it was wrong to enter your country the way I did, but my intentions were honourable. I never wished anything bad for your country. I am sorry,' I pleaded.

The new officer said that some of the army officers had been sent to meet Fiza and her family to cross-check everything I had said. And Fiza had vouched for me and given a statement in my favour. She also admitted that she had called me to help her out of the grave situation she was in.

He added, 'Fiza was in tears when she heard about the state you were in. She appreciates what you did for her and has thanked you for your efforts. In fact, she also apologized for all the trouble you went through just to help her.'

I asked about her current situation. 'Has she been married off as part of wani. Is she in trouble like me? Is she being accused of being an Indian agent too?'

The officer simply told me that she was safe. I was relieved. I wanted to offer prayers to give thanks. I requested this good soul to allow me to perform my ablutions. I was taken to the washroom, allowed to answer nature's call with the doors closed and perform my ablutions. When I was taken back to the cell, I offered my prayers, thanking the Almighty for the good news I had heard.

Fiza was safe and I was being released. All my prayers had been answered. I was grateful she had spoken up for me. I knew this was the end for us but I prayed that she had a good life ahead. That night I had a chapati for dinner and went to sleep.

Saturday, 17 November 2012

I woke up feeling hopeful, which I had not been over the past few days. I offered prayers to the Almighty for saving me from this hell.

I couldn't stop smiling as I waited for the officers to come to take me to the border with India. I kept thanking Allah for everything and asking for forgiveness for the grave mistake that I had committed.

I heard the thud of boots. Four men walked into my cell and took me outside the building, this time to a pick-up truck and not the rickety old Suzuki 800. This could be because the journey was long, I told myself. I was made to sit between two men. Something about the situation was odd and the air was tense. The officers on either side of me had the barrels of their rifles stuck to my ribs. I wanted to ask where we were going but didn't. Maybe I was afraid of the answer. I desperately wanted my positive feelings to last a little longer.

The vehicle exited the Kohat cantonment. After driving some distance, as we approached the busy streets of the town, the officer sitting in the front seat pointed towards a house and said, 'That is where Fiza and her family live.'

I kept my eyes on the house till the vehicle turned and it was no longer visible. We drove through a huge tunnel, which made one of the officers boast, 'This tunnel was built by China as a gift to Pakistan. A few years ago, there was an attempt to blow it up, but nothing happened.'

Much later, I learnt that the Kohat Friendship Tunnel connecting Kohat and Peshawar was built by the Japanese and not the Chinese.

It was a very impressive tunnel, similar to the ones on the Mumbai–Pune expressway.

On the other side of the tunnel were army checkposts—the same ones Atta-ur-Rahman had told me about. The officer in the front seat gestured to the guards at the post and they made way for the vehicle to pass. Soon, the road seemed secluded and the entire landscape looked barren and arid, with only a few trees around, and not a single soul. Where were we going? I started to panic, thinking that they were planning to get rid of me in a fake encounter, and that's why we were headed to a secluded spot.

Scenes from movies flashed through my mind, the ones where the victim was asked to step out of the car and walk, only to be shot down when he started walking or running. I couldn't help myself. I blurted out, 'Are you planning an encounter?'

There was silence, followed by a roar of laughter. The officer turned around from the front seat and said, 'If we wanted to kill you, we could have done it in the cantonment. Where was the need to bring you out and expose ourselves to the public?'

He didn't say anything further about their plans and turned back to look at the road, gesturing to one of the guards to cover my face.

The gunman sitting to my right said, 'We are just taking you to finish some paperwork. After the formalities are complete, you will be released.'

I felt some relief, but then asked, 'If you know I am innocent, why do you have these guns pointing at me?'

Both men chuckled and removed the rifles from under my ribs. One of them asked if I was comfortable now.

The officer added, 'This is part of protocol. You are being taken to Peshawar where a routine questioning will take place and documents prepared for your release. I have the documents that prove your innocence right here,' he said.

After an hour's journey, the vehicle slowed down and I heard sounds that indicated heavy gates were being opened. I was taken out of the car and after just one step forward guided down a staircase by two men. I figured it was an underground area. We stopped at the end of the stairs, turned right and entered a room, where I was made to sit on a chair. My handcuffs were unlocked. I thought this was it. But they were immediately replaced with another set of handcuffs.

I couldn't see anything but I tried to move a little. I was shaking. The men held me down firmly until the cuffs were clasped. I could not understand what was happening. What kind of release procedure was this? I stood still. I did not want to spoil my chances.

A while later, I heard the door being locked. I tried to sense if anyone else was in the room—but I figured I was alone. Trying to remain positive, I thought maybe I had to go through one last round of questioning before being released.

I waited patiently . . . and waited . . . and waited . . .

12

From Intruder to Prisoner

I don't remember how long I sat blindfolded on that chair. My only hope was for someone to enter and ask me the same questions and then throw me out of the country. Little did I know what lay in store.

This was an underground facility. I remembered taking a flight of stairs down and then some more. So it should be at least 20 feet below ground level, I thought.

I heard footsteps approach the door. Then I heard it open and could sense a man standing before me. He asked me some basic questions such as my name, age, nationality and the reason for my visit.

I cleared my throat to speak. It was parched since I had had no water and been silent for a very long time. I responded to all the questions and, after they seemed to have ended, asked, 'When will I be released?'

He said, '*Agar tujhe chhorna hota to ye log tujhe yahan nahi latey. Un logon ne to bas apna kaam khatam kar ke tujhe ab humare hawaley kar diya hai. Ab yahan tera case chalaya jayega. Fir tujhe saza hogi aur jab teri saza poori hogi tab tu yahan se jayega.*'

(If you had to be released then you would not have been brought here. The men who brought you here did their job of delivering you to us. Now the real procedure begins. There will be a case initiated against you, and you will be sentenced. Only after completing your jail term will you be allowed to go back.)

Without saying anything else, he left the room. I thought he was trying to scare me. My heart sank and the blindfold became damp with tears. I couldn't believe what I had just heard.

Next, I heard the footsteps of a few men. They entered and removed my blindfold. It took some time for my eyes to adjust to the light. Everything was hazy because of my weak eyesight. But I could see that the walls of the room were orange. There was a table in front of me with a green tablecloth, across which sat two men in civilian clothes. There was a huge mirror on the wall behind the men. To my right was the door, and on the left there were many things hanging on the wall, but I couldn't see what they were without my glasses.

The men looked fiercely angry. One of them stood up. The other had contempt in his eyes and sat with a laptop in front of him. There was a small device attached to his laptop, but I couldn't make out what it was.

The first officer asked me to narrate the details of my entire journey. I did as asked. When I mentioned Fiza and that I was there to rescue her, the officer yelled at me, '*Humein ye cover story mat suna. Tere jaise bahut pakde hain humne. Sach sach humein apna asal mission bata de. RAW walo ne tujhe kya karne ke liye yahan bheja hai? Apne sathiyon ke naam bata. Warna humein aur bhi tarike atey hain sach nikalwane ke. Humein majboor na kar.*' (Don't give us this cover story. We know that you have been sent here by RAW. Tell us about your mission and the names of your accomplices here. If you don't, we know ways that will force you to divulge the truth.)

The officer with the laptop kept staring at me. I could not believe what was happening. The entire conversation sounded unreal. I thought I had convinced them. What happened? What changed?

The officer who was standing gestured towards the man with the laptop and said, '*Ye bade sahab yahan baithe hain, inko sab sach sach bata de. To hum teri saza aaj hi se shuru kar denge. Warna pata nahi tujhe kitna saal lagega.*' (He is our senior officer. Tell him the truth and maybe he'll be able to help you. Your sentence could begin today or it could take years for the case to be heard.) He saluted the senior officer and left the room.

The man looked at me and typed something. He then asked me to move forward and place all four fingers on the device, which turned out to be a fingerprint scanner. I had to repeat the process with the other hand and then the two thumbs.

He pulled out a slate, handed it to me and asked me to go stand against the wall. The slate had my name on it in Urdu. He asked me to hold it to my chest, and pulled out a camera and took pictures. I was made to stand facing him, then turn right and left. I knew what was happening. I was being treated like a criminal. They were beginning formal procedures to charge me.

I was called back to the chair and my thumb impressions were taken on paper. I wanted to protest but was too scared. While I was trying to not show fear, the man blindfolded me, collected everything he had come with and left the room.

I could hear murmurs outside. Another man entered the room and asked if I wanted something. In a faint voice, I said, 'Water.' He walked up to me with a glass of water, handed it over and left. Before leaving, he told me there was a mattress on my left by the wall and guided me to it. The room was cold and I had to feel around to find a blanket on the mattress. My hands and feet were numb. I wrapped the thin quilt around myself as I shivered and cried.

I had stopped requesting them to take me to the bathroom to perform my ablutions so I could offer namaz. Instead, I would rub my hands on the soil on the floor and pray. I asked the guard outside which side Makkah was so I could pray in the right direction. I had lost track of time, lost any sense of direction . . . My life had come to a standstill. I had been hoping for a miracle. But my hopes had died, on foreign soil, where they looked at me with hatred and labelled me a spy.

I heard someone enter the room and ask me to get up. I was in the midst of namaz, but I finished my prayer quickly and did as I was told. I was made to sit on the chair. Someone ordered my blindfold to be removed.

Across the table, I saw the same two officers from earlier, and a third man sitting between them. He was huge, with a round face, trimmed hair and a beard. He wore a navy blue kurta. His voice was deep and hoarse but he was polite.

He said, 'I am the judge who will be handling your case. Everything you say from now on will be part of it. I have nothing to do with your nationality or your religion; we both have to be honest. You be truthful with your answers and I will ensure justice is served. I also have to answer to the Almighty so I will not be partial or biased against you, rest assured.'

His attire and look did not seem to be that of a judge or anyone from the judiciary. But I was all ears. This formidable personality would be deciding my fate. I trembled but managed to ask, 'What is the guarantee that you will believe me? I have been speaking the truth, but look at how mercilessly I have been treated. How will you ensure I am not ill-treated if I tell the truth? How do I believe you?'

He heard me out and then smiled. 'Do you have a choice?'

After a moment, he added, 'Well, you might not have had a choice then or even now, but I am here to make sure justice is done. I will lay down three scenarios in front of you and you decide which one suits you best. One: You are completely innocent and did not come to Pakistan with any bad intentions. I will have to release you. Two: You came in with a bad motive and but did not go ahead with it. I will then give you the benefit of the doubt. Third: If you came with bad intentions and carried out your plans, you will be in great trouble and I will make sure nobody is able to help you.'

I replied, 'I fall in category one, sir. I came with no bad intentions.'

The officer smiled and said, 'Then we have nothing to worry about.'

There was silence before I added, 'I am being discriminated against for being an Indian. I have not even been allowed access to the bathroom to wash up for my prayers.'

He assured me that I need not worry about these things and left the room. Before he stepped out, I heard him instruct the commander to take me to the washroom. The commander put the blindfold back on me and led me to the toilet. Then I was brought back and made to sit on the mattress. It was one thing to feel suffocated when you were gagged and another when you were blindfolded.

The commander came in with a tray and said, '*Bade sahab bahut achhe insaan hain. Unhone tumhare liye chai aur biskut bheja hai.*' (Our senior is a very good human being. He has sent tea and biscuits for you.)

I had not experienced such kindness from a Pakistani official yet. I began to think there were kind souls too in this country. And then the beast of hope resurfaced. Maybe this new officer would do justice and the truth would prevail.

An elderly officer, who I realized was the guard, came into the room with food and asked if I wanted dinner. 'I don't feel like eating,' I said. He frowned and put the plate in front of me. 'Eat,' he said, lifting my blindfold and allowing me to see the room. To my left was the table where I was sitting sometime ago; towards the right was a light pink dental chair. The chair reminded me of my brother's clinic.

I was in no position to fight so I had half a roti with some curry, which was primarily water. I was again moved to the chair and table. The commander gave me sheets of paper and a pen. 'Bade Sahab has asked you to write everything about yourself: your childhood, where you grew up, your school, college, where you worked, your involvement with the Rotary and how you ended up in Pakistan.'

The word 'Rotary' stayed with me. If he knew about the Rotary, he wasn't unfamiliar with my case. And if he knew, they all knew. Was this just a psychological exercise to break me so I could agree to whatever they wanted me to admit?

I placed a sheet in front of me and started thinking about how to start. I didn't want to waste time. I thought the sooner I finished this exercise, the better it would be for me. So I started writing my autobiography. I was in tears thinking and writing about Ammi, Abbu and Khalid. I missed them terribly. I missed fighting with Khalid, joking with him and teasing Ammi and Abbu. My tears fell on the sheet and the ink got smudged. I dabbed it with my sleeve and continued writing.

Letting everything out was a cathartic experience but I didn't let my emotions get the better of me. As I approached the part where I had connected with Fiza, I sharpened my focus to ensure I didn't go wrong, didn't leave out anything or anyone. Atta-ur-Rahman came to mind. He had said that he would deny knowing me and then it would become my word against his. Who would they believe? A Pakistani, that too a journalist, or an alleged Indian spy?

So I decided to omit Atta's role entirely and concocted an entire story about how I had researched and done everything by myself. I feared this could play out badly, but if I took his name and he refused to know me, it would be worse.

~

One day became the next and then the next . . . The elderly guard sat in the room to monitor my activities, or the lack thereof. After the first couple of days, he started empathizing with me and served me tea at night to tolerate the cold, while I sat and wrote. But he was getting tired of monitoring me day and night. He asked me to stop after a certain time every night. When I did, he would take the paper and pen along with him and blindfold me again, leaving me to sleep in the cold, wintry night on a cold mattress with a thin quilt.

After a few days, word was sent to the judge that I had completed my assigned writing. Three days later, the same two officers walked in with the judge right behind them. I was made to sit on the chair and my blindfold was removed. The judge held the papers in his hands. He asked me, 'Have you been truthful?' I nodded.

They all sat down. I felt like they hadn't really felt the need to go through the documents to see what I had written. Every night, when the documents had been taken away, the officers would have got to see my words. The judge turned to the pages where I had written about entering Pakistan.

'In your testimony, you have written that you planned it all alone,' said the judge. I nodded.

He pulled out a few papers from another file and asked, 'Well, the phone records of the number you were using at the time you were apprehended have a different story to tell. Do you not know someone called Atta-ur-Rahman?'

He looked at the papers and then turned to me again. 'It seems like not only did you call his number, you even received calls from it. Also, your SIM was activated on 14 November and the very first call was an incoming one from Atta-ur-Rahman. So how did he get your number?'

I stared at the judge as my world came crashing down. My eyes welled up and I folded my hands, seeking mercy. 'Please forgive me, sir. Please. I fabricated that part because Atta had threatened me that he would deny knowing me, and I thought you would believe him and not me. That's why I did not write this.'

He gave me an intense look, which turned into disappointment and I saw him shaking his head. I could see that an innocent man had turned into a suspect in his eyes.

'I am sorry, son. I told you that this document would be precious and so you should be truthful. How could you have lied in a legal document? Now you have moved from scenario one of being innocent to scenario two, where your motives are questionable. You are now a suspect.'

I broke down. I was inconsolable. The room was silent, before the judge got up from his chair and screamed, 'Shut up! You have no right to cry. All you had to do was be honest.'

He was fuming. He bent to look me in the eye and said in a strange, hoarse voice, 'You have dug your own grave.' His large frame was intimidating.

He moved back to the table and sat beside the officer with the laptop, then beckoned me to their side of the table. I wiped my tears and walked around. There were a few photographs on the screen. He asked me to identify the persons in them. I went close to the screen, and immediately recognized the photograph, even without my spectacles. Filled with shame, I identified Atta-ur-Rahman (he was without his cap) and Abdullah.

Without a word, the judge got up and left the room. I was made to sit on the floor and blindfolded again. Before they could hear my pleas for mercy, the room emptied. I cursed myself and screamed. 'What have I done?' I slapped myself and pulled my hair, all the while calling myself an idiot. The whole night, I cursed and wept myself to sleep.

The next day, a few officers walked in. It was like Kohat all over again. They threw me on the ground and proceeded to inflict hours of torture on me: beating, kicking, abusing me, pushing my head to the ground with their boots and demanding that I spill the beans. Since I was blindfolded, I didn't know where the next blow would come from. Sticks, chains, belts, punches—I felt like they were bringing every piece of metal and wood down on me.

My screams echoed through the room. I'm sure anyone listening would have shuddered at the sounds. The beatings were unbearable, and caused me more pain because it was extremely cold.

For three days and three nights, I could only remember hearing my own screams, and feeling the seething pain as my skin tore. My hair was literally pulled out and I would find tufts of it on the floor when they were done. I begged, cried and pleaded, but nobody listened.

At night, the pain was so unbearable that it made me faint. I couldn't even see my wounds since I was always kept blindfolded. Every night, I thought I would not live to see the next day. But I did.

After three days of this hell, the interrogation started again. This time there wasn't one kind word said to me. The officers would all look at me with contempt, and then two of them would begin the questions; the rest would be there to beat or slap me when they felt like it.

They never stuck to the point. Sometimes they would ask me infuriatingly irrelevant questions like why Pakistan was hit by floods in 2010 or why China was hit by a severe earthquake. When I had no answer, they would beat me.

I snapped and retorted once, 'Do spies have the power to cause natural calamities?' I got a kick in response. 'I will ask whatever I wish to,' said the interrogating officer.

He added, 'What do you want to talk about?'

I said, 'Aerodynamics.' I felt silly even as I said it. But I knew I had invited trouble. I had no room or right to act smart. So I looked down at the floor and waited for the consequences of hurting the officer's ego.

The interrogation sessions continued. They would always end with one question: 'What was your real mission?'

While they had caught a lie of mine, they had no evidence to prove I was a spy. After a couple of days, the beatings reduced and then finally stopped.

~

Whenever I heard footsteps, I would jump up from the mattress, fearing that they were coming back to beat me. After some more days, two men pulled me out of the room and dragged me to the adjacent one. I was a lump of flesh and couldn't walk. I waited for the interrogation or torture to begin, but there was neither, and I wondered what was happening. The respite was short-lived. I could see through the gap of my blindfold and the bridge of my nose that the room looked like an observation room. After a couple of hours, they took me back to my room.

The next day, after lunch, I was resting on the mattress when a stick hit me so hard that I almost fainted. I was pulled up by my hair, and then the ruthlessness began all over again. I kept saying, 'I am innocent. I am not a spy. Please don't . . .' but my words fell on deaf ears. That day was one of the worst.

'I was just trying to save a girl,' I screamed. One officer spat on my face. 'Even if we were to believe you, you think you can just come here and take a Pakistani girl, you kafir? What if we picked up a girl from your family?' The torture continued. I was humiliated and broken.

After they got tired of beating me up, the interrogating officer asked, 'The Afghan visa on your passport is stamped as GRATIS. Why? This is only issued to diplomats and officials. So how come your passport has the same?'

I had never heard of the word and I didn't know what he was saying. I hadn't even seen the visa stamp that closely. 'I don't understand what you are saying. I went to Kabul on a business visa. I don't know any other details,' I said earnestly.

The officer shook his head and said, 'You are lying again.' The odds were against me, and the lies of the past didn't help. Even before I could refute the charges, I was hit on the head; this was followed by kicks and punches. My face was smashed to the floor. I collapsed. In a meek voice, garbled with blood and spit, I said, 'I don't know what this stamp is. I have never heard of it, I swear.'

They left me almost dead, lying on the floor. The next few days, nobody came to the room, but I sat in one corner and dreaded every moment.

~

One morning, the commander came running into the room and provided me with orange clothes and asked me to change into them. It was winter, we were 20 feet underground, and the clothes I was wearing were made of thin material. I hadn't eaten any proper food in ages—I could not feel my body. My limbs were numb with cold. My body hurt with the constant shivering.

I was told that some higher authorities were visiting the facility. Later that day, I was shifted to a cell adjacent to the interrogation room. The orange clothes and the move to an empty cell with my blindfold always on—they were all signs of impending doom.

I was again taken to the interrogation room and made to stand in the centre. As soon as I entered, I felt cold air—the fan and air conditioner were on at full speed. I protested, only to be met with a beating. 'Don't tell us what to do. Just keep standing till we allow you to sit.'

I stood in one place, in the cold, for hours, and then for three days—standing all day and all night. I thought that my life would end like this. There was no way out. I was not allowed to sleep or rest, or even to sit for a minute, not even for meals and namaz. I had swollen feet, and the pain later shot through my spine. I could feel tingles in my head. At times, I would collapse on the floor, only to be woken up with ice-cold water poured on me. Every day, a paramedic would come to check my vital stats. I used to hope and pray that he or a doctor would advise them to stop. But he would check me and give them the green signal.

It was like a game: Would he survive another day of torture? Yes, he would. And then, bang! It would begin again.

After the third day, they saw that my body was too weak to stand, so they provided me with a stool to sit on. I would sleep off while sitting on it. With the blindfold, nobody could see if my eyes were open or shut. But my body would jerk as I fell asleep while sitting, and they would slap me to wake me up. But staying awake had become an impossible task with the blindfold on and my eyes shut. This went on for a week.

One day, I woke up with the awareness that I had no blindfold on. There were blue skies above me; a sight I had not seen in a long time. I was in an open valley with trees and chirping birds. I got up and limped a bit further to find a beautiful water body. Suddenly, I heard growls. When I tried to concentrate on what was happening, I saw the judge sitting in front of me and talking to me. I couldn't understand what he asked me and what I answered. But, following this event, I was allowed to sleep.

When I woke up, the commander said that I had been asleep for more than twenty-four hours. He asked me to sit up and eat. When I sat up, I felt a shooting pain in my bottom.

'Was I injected with something?' I asked. He said that I had fallen unconscious so the doctor had administered some medicine to revive me. He added, 'You were running a very high fever. This happened two days ago when the judge visited around 3 a.m. and the interrogation went on till dusk.'

How was that possible? The valley, the blue skies, the water—it had all felt so real. Sleep deprivation must have led to hallucinations. I was allowed to rest for a couple of days. But then, soon enough, the same set of officers visited me again and ordered me to be shifted back to my cell. I had forgotten that I had been moved to another cell and made to wear the Guantanamo Bay–like orange uniform. The only relief was that I was no longer blindfolded 24/7.

I was back in the room with iron grills, crying every night, praying to be saved. One such night, an elderly officer came to me and said, 'There is no use crying. You will meet the fate of a spy. The next thirty-five years will be no better or worse than this.'

'My parents will die. My brother must be devastated. I don't even know if they have been informed. They will never forgive me,' I cried.

I had stopped eating, and was now a skeletal version of my earlier self. One evening, a guard asked me why I was not eating my meals at all. He and the other guards suspected that I wasn't eating because dinner every alternate night consisted of a sorry excuse for non-vegetarian curry with hardly any meat in it, and according to them I was a Hindu.

'Why aren't you eating? Because you are a Hindu and this has meat?' he asked.

I said, 'Food is the last thing on my mind. Right now I worry for my freedom and my parents. Also, I am a Muslim and I don't have to prove it by eating meat.'

After being kept in a dark room with no light, I felt my eyesight had become weaker. I had developed breathing trouble because of the extreme cold; my lungs had been infected but I was given no medical treatment.

~

I was taken to the washroom only once a day, after being given the choice of a morning or an evening visit. I chose to go in the mornings. Two guards and one commander with a stick would take me to the washroom, blindfolded and handcuffed. I once asked if I could bathe. One guard said I could, but there was no hot water. I went for days without a bath.

It was only when I heard screams from someone else that I figured I was not the only one being held there. The cells were diagonal to each other so nobody could see the person in another cell or interact with them.

One evening, I was taken to the interrogation room. I was shaking. What now? What had they found out? The commander walked in and removed my blindfold. I saw the judge sitting in front of me. He was smiling, and asked how I was doing.

I gave him a cold stare. By now I was hardened, or so I thought.

'I have been told that you have stopped eating. All you do is cry and pray. If your conscience is clear, why are you so worried?'

'Wouldn't your son have been worried if he was innocent and trapped in a foreign country and treated like an enemy?' I snapped.

There was silence. The judge responded, 'I have been sitting with your case for so many days. How can you say such a thing? All I am trying to do is ensure justice prevails. I was not the one who lied in my statement. You said one thing and the evidence pointed to another. Investigations on the ground threw up newer details that you had hidden. You, not me. It was not a minor omission; it was an obfuscation of facts. Do you understand what you did? I don't trust you.'

There was silence. The judge changed his tone again and spoke softly, 'Anyway, is there anything you want to eat?' I shook my head and kept looking down, tears falling on the floor.

He stood up and walked away. I was taken back to my cell.

~

A week later, I heard a huge blast, which shook the entire barracks. The shockwaves were so strong that I was tossed to the other side of the room. It felt like a missile had hit the facility. I stood still while the guards came and checked the locks on all the cells. This was dangerous territory.

At the end of January, I was given a set of Pathani kurta pyjamas to wear. I didn't know why, but one of the guards told me it was to distinguish those who were going to stay in prison for a longer time from those like me, who might be there for a shorter period.

Some days later, the two investigating officers told me that they had good news. 'The man who tried to help you, your accomplice from Karak, has been caught. He was planning on flying to Dubai,' said one of them.

My heart sank. Atta-ur-Rahman. Then the other officer said, 'We also checked the "gratis" stamp on your Afghan visa. It seems like they use this not just for diplomats but also for those seeking business visas. The Afghan embassy confirmed to us that there are no separate business visas.'

I looked up to decipher what they meant by this. I had no idea that I could be in trouble for the one legal document that I had. The other man congratulated me for the fact that at least this bit had been cleared up.

'Maybe you are innocent. Maybe you will be able to prove your innocence after all. And maybe you were indeed here to help Fiza and rescue her from wani. I might just start believing you,' he said.

I thanked them for understanding this and checking the facts.

~

Exactly three months passed. On 14 February 2013, one of the officers came in and told me that my case had been escalated to higher authorities and was awaiting signatures for clearance. Once that was done, I would be released. I wanted to jump for joy. 'Finally, finally, finally,' I kept saying and grinning from ear to ear.

A week later, on 21 February, the same officer came and said that my Afghan visa had been extended so I could be sent back via the same route. He said it was only a matter of time. 'Just be a little more patient,' he said.

I told the officer that I was having chest pains and breathing trouble. They took me to the Combined Military Hospital for a check-up of my vital stats: blood pressure, pulse, ECG, etc. But there was not a single test for breathing trouble. The doctor didn't even use a stethoscope. I was told the reports were normal. The officers looked at me suspiciously after being told this diagnosis.

The attitude of everyone around me suddenly became harsh. While earlier I had been told it was only a matter of time, now they expressed uncertainty. From March till May, my life continued in suspension.

These were strategies being used to break me, I figured. But why? I couldn't understand. Then one day, I heard two guards speaking outside my cell.

One of them said to the other, 'It has been too long. They should let the poor Indian guy go back.'

The other guard replied, 'That is not possible. Haven't you heard of the recent developments? He had stayed with cops before entering Pakistan.'

Cops! Who were they talking about? My head was buzzing. I had not known any cops. And then I realized they were talking about Shahid and his brothers in Kabul. Thinking about what would follow this revelation made me extremely nervous. I dreaded more torture sessions, but I knew there was no escape.

Every day, I lived in fear. Every day, I asked if this life was worth living. Every day, I sought forgiveness.

13

Family Discovers Pakistan Link

In November 2012, a cloud of despair descended upon the Ansari household in Mumbai. Fauzia would keep waiting for the phone to ring. Finally, it did. She ran to it, mumbling Hamid's name, expecting her son to be on the other side. Instead, a lady's voice greeted her. It was Khalid's soon-to-be mother-in-law.

'Salaam, Fauzia Baaji, *kaise ho*, how are you? I haven't heard from you in a while. The wedding is in December and there is a lot of work to do. We wanted to come and meet to finalize the preparations and arrangements,' she said.

Fauzia had not been expecting this call. She tried to wrap her head around what was being said. 'Salaam, I am so sorry for not having kept in touch. Nehal Sahab and Khalid have not come home yet. Let me speak to them and I will call you back,' she said and exchanged pleasantries before disconnecting.

She held her head and sat on the sofa in her tiny drawing room. They had stopped discussing the marriage after getting so caught up in the search for Hamid. Khalid was at home. She called him to come to her and told him about the call.

'Right now, our priority is Hamid. Let us first trace him. I will not get married without him. I will not get married if Hamid is in trouble. Our priority is to trace him,' he said.

'How do we do that?' Fauzia asked.

'Let me try logging into his social media accounts and see what he has been up to.'

'I will look at them with you. I need to see what this Facebook and other things on the computer are,' she said to Khalid.

Later that evening, Nehal was told about the phone call. 'Let us wait and find out exactly what has happened to Hamid and then decide on Khalid's marriage,' he said.

'I will not marry if Hamid is in trouble. He is my only brother.' Khalid went off to his room.

Fauzia broke down. Her husband tried to console her and told her that it was not the time to lose hope. But she couldn't stop worrying. 'Why are we going through this? Why us? Why us?' she kept saying.

That night, she went to Khalid's room while he was at the computer. He showed her Hamid's Facebook profile.

'How did you get it or get in? Don't you have to put in some details?'

'His password was saved on the system,' he replied.

She sighed in relief at this small mercy. Cracking the password would have been near impossible.

Khalid tried to figure out when Hamid had last logged in, while explaining the website to his mother. They started looking at all the conversations on his page. Khalid then opened the private conversations. Lo and behold! Hamid had chatted with quite a few people from Pakistan. There were too many messages for the two of them to take in. In her heart, Fauzia knew that Hamid was in deep trouble. Tears started rolling down her eyes. Khalid held his mother and asked her to be strong. 'Ammi, for Hamid. Let us not lose our nerve.'

Someone called Atta-ur-Rahman had called him to Pakistan. There was also a Dr Shazia, Saba Khan and Abdullah Zaid.

Fauzia's heart sank. She couldn't believe her eyes. She got angry. What had he been up to? But then the biggest fear crept in. What if he was not in Afghanistan? What if he was in . . . Pakistan?

She quietly said 'Pakistan' and Khalid repeated after her 'Pakistan . . .' For the next few moments, they stared at the screen and then at each other. Khalid was red in the face. He was shocked and angry and scared for his brother.

Fauzia tried to gather her wits about her. There was a lot to do. Picking up a pen and paper, she started writing down everything they had found. She first read his entire conversation with Atta-ur-Rahman and figured out that there was a plan to rescue a girl named Fiza. The word 'wani' kept appearing. She jotted that down.

There was a contact number for Atta-ur-Rahman. She noted that too.

His conversations were all about a girl called Fiza. How? How could he have been such a fool? she thought. He was an educated boy.

Khalid's face turned red out of embarrassment that Hamid had fallen into this situation. He turned to his mother and asked, 'Ammi, what if it was a trap? What if they have captured him? It's a dangerous place. What was he thinking?'

'Son, let us see if he followed through with these plans,' she said. They started looking at more conversations.

Soon, it was clear that he had indeed intended to cross into Pakistan. The plan had been clearly spelt out. This shocked Khalid and Fauzia. After a long pause, the son turned around and told his mother, 'Ammi, call off the marriage first thing tomorrow morning. We are in no state to tell anyone this truth and we cannot hide it from such a decent family. Without Hamid, I will anyway not go through with this. He is our first priority,' he said, holding her hand.

Fauzia understood how difficult this decision must have been for Khalid. Wiping her tears, she placed her hand on his head and asked him to make a copy of everything they had found on the computer. She cried the entire night.

The next morning, when Nehal saw her, he was shocked at her swollen eyes and dishevelled hair. She looked like death. 'What happened, Fauzia?' he asked, rushing to her.

'Hamid is in Pakistan. My foolish son is in Pakistan, apparently, to rescue a girl,' she said, looking out of the window.

'What?' exclaimed Nehal, stunned.

Fauzia explained what she and Khalid had discovered on Hamid's computer, the people he had contacted, the plan he had made and the certainty of him being in Pakistan.

'But what if it was a trap?' asked her distraught husband.

Fauzia told him that Khalid had said the same thing. She added, 'Khalid wants us to call off the marriage. The devil has his eyes on us . . . our happy home is in pieces.'

The wedding was duly called off.

~

Despite all the trouble on the home front, Fauzia and Nehal did not take leave from work. The work routine helped provide a distraction, even if for a short while, from the predicament of the family. Fauzia's college was very particular about attendance and she did not want anyone to get wind of her situation, so she put up a brave front.

Every day after work, it became a routine for her to try and find out more about her son and where he could be. Her steely determination gave strength to her husband and her elder son. All they had was each other and there certainly was no giving up.

This was unchartered territory. The fact that Hamid was Muslim and had gone missing in Pakistan didn't help matters. But she was going to fight and find out what fate had befallen her son, while praying for his safety and his life.

As soon as she would reach home from college, Fauzia would pull out all the papers she had compiled and start reading all the points she had made. She called on Atta-ur-Rahman's phone number but nobody answered. She called again but still got no response. She kept calling that number, but to no avail.

She had hit a dead end, but decided to start doing some research on the Internet. Khalid was not home, but she now knew the basics of using a computer. She fumbled her way through, driven to find out more. Somehow, she managed.

She figured out that Hamid and Fiza, a Pashtun girl, were emotionally involved, that she was about to be a victim of wani, that Fiza's brother had committed murder, that there had been a jirga trial . . . All these facts were from a completely new world for a simple family from Mumbai.

Fauzia told her husband that they needed to find a way to reach Atta-ur-Rahman in Pakistan. 'What if he isn't picking up your call because it is an India number?' wondered Nehal.

Fauzia nodded. 'Yes, maybe it is that. We should ask someone from another country to call.' They thought about whom they could take into confidence.

Nehal suggested Mahmood, a family friend who had moved to Dubai years ago. Fauzia concurred. He might be able to help. They called him and told him the whole story. He was shocked.

'Fauzia Baaji, I am sorry to hear this. How are you holding up?' he asked as Nehal handed over the phone to her after explaining the entire story.

She broke down and said, 'Mahmood Bhai, please help. My son is in trouble. We need to connect with this man Hamid was in touch with, Atta-ur-Rahman.'

He promised that he would call the number and update her if the man picked up. The next day, Fauzia's phone rang, and she saw that it was Mahmood calling. With some trepidation, she picked up and said, 'As-salaam alaykum, Mahmood Bhai, hope you are well. Any news of Hamid?'

He said that he had called the number a couple of times and finally Atta-ur-Rahman had picked up. 'And?' asked Fauzia.

'He confirmed that Hamid had gone to Pakistan to rescue some girl called Fiza. When I asked him where Hamid was, he was nervous. He said that he had dropped him off at a hotel and didn't know where he went after that.'

'Allah! What will I do now?' said a shocked Fauzia, sitting on the sofa. Nehal asked her what had happened and took the phone from her. He spoke to Mahmood and got all the details of the call. Then he kept the phone on the table and looked at his weeping wife.

The helpless couple sat and wondered what they should do next. Their son was in Pakistan. Fauzia wondered how he had got there.

Did he have the correct documents? She was determined to find out all these details.

'We have to inform the rest of the family,' said Nehal, looking troubled.

'We will but let me find out more. God forbid, if he has gone illegally then the authorities too will have to be told.'

'Good lord! We should also check with the Pakistan High Commission. I don't think they have an office in Mumbai. We'll have to check with Delhi,' he said.

Fauzia's tears were as unstoppable as her determination to find her son. She went back to the computer and started over. For someone who hadn't used a computer all her life, she had got the hang of it quite quickly.

She logged on to Facebook and went through all of Hamid's conversations again, making notes of everything she considered important, like the critical information regarding his travel plans. She stumbled upon the fact that he had been advised to enter Pakistan through Afghanistan because he was not getting a visa for Pakistan. The messages further said that he would have to enter without legal documents. At some point, Atta-ur-Rahman even advised him not to carry his Indian documents.

The entire conversation screamed trouble. Holding her head in her hands, she sat there, feeling like she was going to have a nervous breakdown. She was shaking and couldn't stop. Her eyes hurt, her head hurt and her heart ached. How could this be happening to her? She was wounded. But more than that, she was scared. She wondered if Hamid was safe. That night she sat in the drawing room and wept till dawn.

In the morning, she showed her husband the latest details she had found. Their world had come crashing down. This wasn't the kind of battle they wanted to fight so close to retirement. 'Why us? Why him?' Nehal echoed Fauzia's words with tears in his eyes.

Hesitantly, Fauzia said, 'We will have to call the elders and tell them.' She called up her in-laws and close relatives and asked them to gather at the Ansari residence that evening.

Once they were told, they just couldn't wrap their heads around this development. A flurry of questions followed: 'But how?', 'What was he thinking?', 'How did he get involved?', 'How Pakistan?', 'Did he not know the dangers involved?' and 'How did he come across this girl?'

Fauzia answered all their questions with tremendous patience and control. She looked around the room and said, 'The question is not how he landed in Pakistan, it is about what to do next. Should we approach the cops and get them involved? Or is there any other way out?'

There was silence. Then Nehal's youngest brother, Iftekhar, said, 'I think we should inform our own authorities because we are dealing with a foreign country, that too Pakistan.'

Everyone in the room agreed, but they did have a conversation about how bad it would look to have their young son in Pakistan. They were all in agreement that if the only reason he made the trip was to save a girl, and there was enough evidence to prove it, they should file a missing person report.

The brother-in-law added, 'Wait before going to the cops. I think we should first take advice from Majeed Memon, the NCP [Nationalist Congress Party] leader and well-known advocate. He might be able to guide us. His son Zaheer is my friend.'

The next day, Iftekhar called Zaheer and asked him to meet Fauzia and Nehal.

The couple, along with Iftekhar, went to Memon's residence in Bandra. Zaheer seemed unconvinced with the story and questioned them about Hamid's 'motives', asking them to tell him everything they had found out. The biggest obstacle, again, was that it was Pakistan.

Zaheer listened to Fauzia very carefully and asked her, 'I hope he has gone only for this reason and not for any subversive activity. I hope his intention is not misplaced because my father is a very reputed man and I will not have his image tarnished.'

Fauzia and Nehal were prepared for such comments, which questioned a Muslim boy's patriotism. Fauzia was nervous yet did not want to lose hope. She was clutching on to the last threads of what she saw as light at the end of a dark tunnel.

'Believe me, Zaheer, I am his mother and I know my son. I have everything to prove that his intentions were not misplaced,' she said.

Zaheer was convinced after a long conversation with Nehal and Iftekhar as well. He told them that he would try to convince his father. They stepped out of the house and Fauzia immediately turned to her brother-in-law as they walked to the car. 'Will he help?' she asked. Iftekhar nodded with mild assurance. They drove away.

The following day, Zaheer met Iftekhar and informed him that his father had agreed to meet the Ansaris but would charge them. Seeing the hesitation on Iftekhar's face, Zaheer handed him a business card and said, 'If you want to discuss it further, you can connect with my father directly. Here are his details.'

Iftekhar took the card and left. He called up Fauzia and informed her that he was coming over. When he entered the third-floor residence of the Ansaris and sat in the drawing room, Nehal and Khalid were also present. He said, 'Fauzia Bhabhi, salaam, I just met Zaheer and he told me that Majeed Memon has agreed to look into our case but . . .'

Fauzia caught on to his reticence and asked, 'But what?'

'But he has demanded a huge amount as his fee. He wants 5 lakh Indian rupees to help us.'

'Five lakh!' exclaimed Khalid.

Fauzia told Iftekhar that they didn't have so much in their savings. They would try to pay as much as possible, but they also had to see how to sustain their efforts. They could not exhaust all their resources on one person.

Iftekhar pulled out the card Zaheer had given him and pressed it into Fauzia's hand, asking her to write to Majeed Memon. 'If the letter comes from a mother, he may be able to understand your pain. You write to him,' he said.

Fauzia thanked her brother-in-law for everything. She served tea and snacks, and they all discussed what to write before Iftekhar left.

The family had limited resources and had to bank on them for this fight. Nehal said they would have to be careful since they did not know how long the battle would go on.

Fauzia sat with Khalid after dinner and wrote an email to Majeed Memon. After introducing herself and writing about the case and the situation they were in, she broached the subject of payment. She wrote,

'We cannot afford to pay five lakh, Majeed Sir. We are salaried people. I am a lecturer, my husband works at a bank. All our savings were spent in educating our two sons. Khalid is a doctor and Hamid is an engineer. Please, sir, take up my case on humanitarian grounds. My humble appeal to you.'

A day went by and there was no response. Fauzia called up Iftekhar to check if there was any word from Memon's office, but he said there was none. She was disheartened. She did not know where to go and who to seek help from.

The next day, Zaheer called Iftekhar and informed him that Memon had agreed. Iftekhar profusely thanked him and was told to come the next day. He immediately called up Fauzia. She looked up and thanked the Almighty and then blessed her brother-in-law for all his help.

He told her that Memon wanted to meet them. The next day, they reached Memon's office at Flora Fountain fort, one of the posh areas in Mumbai. Fauzia and Nehal took the lift to his third-floor office, where they were made to wait at the reception. A while later, Memon called them in and showed them to two chairs. Fauzia narrated the entire story and all that she had found out.

'Sir, my son has made a huge mistake. While I have found out that he is there, we don't know what circumstances led him to take such a step. He is a very sensible boy. Please help, Majeed Sahab, please guide us.'

He calmed down the pleadings of this helpless mother. He thought for a while and asked, 'Are you sure he went for love and not for terrorism? It just sounds unreal. This is not a movie.'

Nehal said they had proof on their computer and that his wife and son had been researching for days.

'Bring printouts of all that you have; only then will I decide if I can help you,' said Memon in a matter-of-fact voice.

The couple looked at each other and then at the advocate, who was unmoved by their expressions.

Finally, it was decided that they would come with all the documentary proof the next day.

They went home.

The first thing Khalid did when they returned was connect the printer to the computer. He and Fauzia printed out all the relevant conversations. They started preparing two sets of files: one for Majeed Memon and one for themselves.

They focused on the conversations that Hamid had had with four persons: Rahmat Khan, Atta-ur-Rahman, Dr Shazia and Saba Khan.

They had about 250 to 300 pages that were diligently marked and highlighted. Conversations in pink were proof that Hamid had gone there for love and not for terrorism. Those marked in green were about his visa and his plans for the journey.

The next day, they handed over all the documents to Memon.

'Could we start working on the case from today itself?' Fauzia asked humbly.

He looked at her and said, 'Don't worry. It will all be fine. I know a lot of people and we will make sure that we find your son.'

They waited a few days. When there was no response, Nehal called Memon's office to get an appointment. He was called in the next day.

They went to his office in the morning, before Fauzia had to head to college. They sat in the very same spots they had the first time around. The folder that Fauzia had made for him was on the table. He opened it in front of them and said, 'I have gone through this file. It does seem like your boy was in love and was trying to save the girl from a terrible situation.'

He advised them to file a police complaint immediately. He also wrote out letters on his letterhead to the then external affairs minister, Salman Khurshid, Interpol and the Mumbai Police commissioner, and attached Fauzia and Nehal's letters to them. Fauzia kept copies of the letters. As a teacher, she was meticulous with paperwork. She had maintained files and papers from the day she had started looking for her son. This day was no different.

Memon told them that they might have to travel to Delhi to meet a few people.

'Justice Katju and the IB [Intelligence Bureau] chief Asif Ibrahim are very good friends of mine. They might be able to take the case forward. Right now, we need to see if the Indian government is aware of the situation. If not, then they should know about it,' he said.

'So should we file a case?' Fauzia asked.

Memon was of the view that there first needed to be clarity that the government and the authorities were aware of the case.

They thanked Memon and left his office. Fauzia started to believe that there was hope. Weeks later, she would know that the ordeal had just begun.

On the evening of 31 December 2012, while Mumbai was readying to usher in the new year, the Ansaris reached Versova police station in Mumbai to lodge a missing person report. They walked up to the officer in charge, who seemed disinterested and pointed the couple to another room. They went there and Fauzia said, 'My son has gone missing. He had travelled to Kabul in Afghanistan and was supposed to return on 15 November but hasn't. We are really worried and want to register a complaint.'

The officer heard Fauzia out and then said that the matter didn't fall in his domain of work. He redirected them to another room. The tired couple went from pillar to post, with nobody appearing willing to register a simple missing person report. Finally, Fauzia walked up to one of the desks and said that she would not move till they did as she asked. The officer sitting behind the desk pointed to a 'complaint box' and said, 'Madam, write a letter and drop it in that box.'

Fauzia was aghast by the attitude. She looked at the cop sternly and said, 'I am not going to just drop a letter in a box. My son is missing. Last I spoke to him, he was in Kabul. So, no . . . I am not just dropping a complaint. You better register my complaint and give me a receipt of the letter I submit.'

They finally agreed. Fauzia detailed out what had happened and signed at the bottom of the letter of complaint. The officer gave the couple an acknowledgement by stamping on the copy of the original.

For days, there was no movement; the family did not know what to do. They continued going to work every day.

A few weeks later, there was a knock on their door. Nehal opened it and saw a bunch of men standing outside. 'Is this the house of Nehal and Fauzia Ansari?' asked one of them.

'Yes, what is the matter, sir?' asked Nehal.

'We are from Mumbai Police and have come here to discuss the case of Hamid Ansari. Can we come in?' he asked.

Nehal showed them in and shut the door. He was relieved to see that they were not in uniform. He called Fauzia out.

They learnt that the inquiry had been initiated at the behest of the Mumbai Police commissioner. They figured it was because of the letter written by Memon.

The Ansaris were called to the station for the first inquiry, after which the officers began coming home to take the investigation further. Fauzia disclosed everything she had found out. The family was prepared for all kinds of odd questions and suspicions about Hamid's motives. Pakistan was a red flag.

On 25 April, Fauzia and Nehal went to the Mumbai Police headquarters to meet the police commissioner.

Offering them a cup of tea, an officer sympathetically asked, 'Maa ji, have you eaten anything? With your son missing, I know it's not a priority, but do take care of your health.' They were warned as well to 'share every little detail, hide nothing'.

The moment the Mumbai Police had learnt of the case, they had alerted the Criminal Investigation Department, and in no time, the Maharashtra ATS (Anti-terrorism Squad) got involved. They were all very well behaved with the Ansaris. They knew that Fauzia was a teacher; and the nephew of one of the ATS officers was her student. They showed utter respect for their privacy and also sympathized with her.

The boy from Mumbai who had gone missing in Pakistan was suddenly big news in the media. The media attention also ensured that every agency looked into the case—from the National Investigation Agency (NIA), Mumbai's Anti-terrorism Squad, the Customs Department, the Mumbai Police Criminal Investigation Department to the local police. The Ansaris were subjected to questioning by all these agencies, either at their offices or at their own home.

After a thorough verification of the documents and notes compiled by Fauzia, the authorities alerted the international criminal investigation organization Interpol to issue a 'Yellow Notice'—to locate a missing person or to identify a person unable to identify himself/herself.

14

MEA, Family and the Media

January 2013

The PAI (Pakistan–Afghanistan–Iran) division of the Ministry of External Affairs (MEA) received a note from the Ministry of Home Affairs (MHA). Yash Sinha, additional secretary at the MEA, opened the file to read the contents and was shocked to see ATS Mumbai's missing person report filed by a couple with the name Ansari, whose son had gone missing in Pakistan.

Before taking it to the foreign secretary, Sinha picked up the phone and connected to the Indian High Commission in Islamabad. Deputy Chief of Mission Gopal Baglay was on the line. 'Gopal, I have just received a note. A twenty-seven-year old Indian boy has gone missing in Pakistan. Do you know about this?' he asked.

Baglay, who was known never to lose his cool, calmly responded, 'Boss, send the details across. We are not aware of such a case. Where does he hail from?'

'Mumbai. It is not the kind of case we normally deal with. Take a look at the details and get back to us. Meanwhile, I shall apprise the higher-ups of the situation,' said Yash.

The matter was shared with the then foreign secretary, Ranjan Mathai, who further informed the then external affairs minister, Salman Khurshid.

A few days later, Baglay received a copy of the MHA report in the weekly diplomatic bag (also called a dispatch). A diplomatic bag or a diplomatic pouch is a container in which official mails, documents and items are sent by a country to its missions and embassies abroad. It enjoys certain legal protections and is not subject to customs inspection or any other kind of checking.

Baglay knocked on the door of his boss's room. The head of the Indian High Commission in Pakistan, High Commissioner T.C.A. Raghavan, was an affable man who knew Pakistan very well since he had served as the joint secretary (JS), PAI, before coming to Islamabad.

'Come in,' said Raghavan.

'Sir, I have just received this note from headquarters. You may want to see it. It is a note from the MHA to JS, PAI. It says an Indian boy called Hamid Ansari has gone missing in Pakistan,' he said, handing it over.

'Did we know about this?' asked Raghavan.

'No, sir. The additional secretary, PAI, had called last week and asked about it, and he said he would be sending details. It seems the boy crossed over for a girl,' he said.

'A girl!' exclaimed Raghavan, and started going through the document. 'Good God! Entering Pakistan illegally for love. The boy must have been out of his mind. So, Pakistan has not informed us yet. Let's see . . . the note here says he went missing on 14 November. It is January already.'

As he continued reading, Baglay added, 'If the authorities have him, they should have informed us, else they are in violation of the Vienna Convention on Consular Relations. But if they don't have him then I wonder if he is alive at all.'

Raghavan looked up and thought about it. He asked Baglay to send a 'note verbale', an official communication, to the Ministry of Foreign Affairs (MoFA), Pakistan's foreign office, asking about the Indian national.

Baglay did that as soon as he reached his office, but he knew not to expect a response. Pakistan was known to stay silent on such matters. If they had an Indian national, Baglay knew it would take a lot more than a note verbale to elicit a response. But for now, that was the only device he had at his disposal.

~

The Ansaris had no news of Hamid. They had to routinely endure calls by the cops and the same old questions about Hamid's motives. In the process of trying to trace her son, Fauzia was duped by many who promised to help. She had given away her money but not got any of the promised help in return.

The saving grace was that they lived in a nice neighbourhood where everyone was sympathetic to the family's plight. The neighbours loved Hamid, who had always been a helpful young man.

Every night, like a ritual, Fauzia would sit in front of the computer and try looking for new links and hints to where her son could possibly be. She found the contacts of a lot of Rotarians in Pakistan who Hamid had been in touch with. She diligently started taking down names and sourcing their numbers. One night, she looked through the drawers of the computer table and found a printout of a letter of invitation addressed to Hamid from a Pakistani barrister called Adnan Saboor Rohaila.

It was the same printout that Hamid had taken to fax to the Pakistani High Commission in New Delhi when he had requested for a visa. Fauzia thought this had to be a crucial document. The man seemed important. He had to be, if he was inviting Hamid to Pakistan for a Rotary event.

The top left corner of the letter had his address and contact details. He was from Peshawar. Fauzia picked up her phone and called the number. A man answered.

With trepidation, Fauzia spoke, 'Hello, could I speak to Barrister Adnan Saboor Rohaila?'

'That's me. Who is this?' came the heavy voice of a man who didn't sound very old.

'My name is Fauzia Ansari. I am the mother of Hamid Ansari. The Indian boy to whom you sent an invitation to visit Pakistan for a Rotary event,' she said.

'Yes, yes, I remember. He was very keen to attend the conference last year. Did something happen? How can I help?' he asked, sensing something wasn't right.

'He is missing. He didn't get a visa to go to Pakistan but he went nevertheless. I last spoke to him in November last year, when he was in Kabul. Now we have learnt from all his online chats that he crossed over into Pakistan illegally and is now untraceable,' she said, trying to hold back her tears.

'Why would he do that? If he didn't get the visa to attend one Rotary event, he could have tried for next year or the year after that,' he said, sounding utterly befuddled.

'Well, well . . . it was not for an event. He wanted to go there to rescue a girl from trouble,' she said hesitantly.

'Are you serious? Did he not think of the consequences? Madam, I am very sorry to hear this but I had no role to play in it. I sent him the invitation specifically for a formal event,' said the man, desperate to prove his innocence. He could land in major trouble if this news got out.

'Rohaila Sahab, I know that. I am sorry if you thought I was calling to accuse you. I am calling to seek help. My son is lost . . . In your country . . . You are a barrister in Peshawar. Would you be able to help me find my son?' she pleaded.

He told her that he would think about it and get back to her.

Fauzia waited for a week. There was no word from him. She was losing hope. But her determination was steadfast. 'He will have to help,' she told herself.

One afternoon, during a free period, she went into an empty classroom and locked the door from inside.

She then sat down and continuously dialled Rohaila's number. He finally answered. Fauzia pleaded, cried, begged him for help. Rohaila finally agreed, on one condition: She should not call him on his mobile. Any communication would have to be through email and WhatsApp.

'Thank you so much, Rohaila Sahab, I will abide by all your conditions but please help us.'

In a day or two, Fauzia emailed him to find out if there had been any development. His one-line reply was, 'I am trying my level best.'

Meanwhile, Fauzia had started writing to the consular division at the Indian mission in Islamabad seeking help to trace Hamid. 27 August was another such day when she wrote to the embassy, saying, 'Sir, almost a year is going to be completed. In spite of my continuous, rigorous efforts, I haven't seen a ray of hope. The situation is still as it was on day one . . .'

The mail went on to seek advice on how to travel to Pakistan and search for Hamid.

Acquino Vimal, who was the counsellor at the Indian High Commission in Islamabad, responded on 10 September, saying, 'As we had informed you earlier, we have again reminded the Pakistani authorities about the seriousness of the case and to expeditiously look into the case of your son and inform us about his whereabouts.'

He further asked for Fauzia's contact details so MEA officials in New Delhi could get in touch with her. The couple continued their effort on both ends, with the Indian government and the Pakistani lawyer.

One day, Rohaila messaged and advised that a habeas corpus petition be filed in the Peshawar High Court on her behalf. It would cost four thousand dollars.

Meanwhile, the Ansaris started meeting politicians and leaders who gave them the time of day. They met local MLA Krishna Hegde (state representative) and MP Priya Dutt (parliamentary representative), and local MP Gajanan Kirtikar, who later approached Sushma Swaraj, as well as Hyder Azam, a BJP leader in Mumbai. They also met other MPs like Kirit Somaiya, Supriya Sule, Shashi Tharoor, Shahnawaz Hussein, and Rajya Sabha MPs Salim Ansari and Munavvar Saleem, who in turn wrote letters to people they knew. Priya Dutt said she would write to the external affairs minister.

When the Ansaris met Hegde, he insisted on looking at all the documents and transcripts of conversations between Hamid and Atta-ur-Rahman and Dr Shazia Khan. 'This is a difficult one. I hope your son is safe,' he said and directed his office to draft a letter for them addressed to Salman Khurshid.

Interestingly, Hegde had played an important role in the repatriation of another Indian prisoner from Pakistan, Bhavesh Parmar from Mumbai. But Hamid's case was different and he knew that.

On Saturday, 26 January, Republic Day, the Ansaris had an appointment with Congress leader and Mumbai (north-west) MP Gurudas Kamat (who passed away in August 2018). As was the case with most politicians, there were a lot of people at his MP bungalow. The Ansaris were made to wait in a small room. When he met them a while later, he heard the couple out and said he would do what was possible. Salman Khurshid received a letter from him as well.

In the same month, Fauzia and Nehal decided to go to Delhi. To manage their jobs, they had to reserve travel plans for the weekends. If need be, they took a day off on Friday or Monday.

Money was another important consideration. The Ansaris had limited resources and some savings for a rainy day. That day had come, when clouds of doom brought a downpour the family never anticipated.

For their first trip to Delhi, they decided to take leave for a few days. They booked train tickets for Delhi and found a small, inexpensive place to stay in. After reaching, they called up the residence and office of External Affairs Minister Salman Khurshid, seeking an appointment, but to no avail. The persistent Fauzia told her husband that they should go to his residence and see if they would be given an audience.

On a cold, wintry morning, they stepped out of their hotel room near New Delhi Railway Station, hailed an autorickshaw to House No. 2, Kushak Road, in the heart of Delhi's posh Lutyens's Bungalow Zone, Khurshid's residence. The harsh air of Delhi's winter hit their faces as the autorickshaw sped on. They reached their destination to find many people outside the residence and inside.

Nehal asked someone what was happening. 'He is meeting his constituency people. He does that on weekends,' replied the man.

Fauzia tugged at her husband's sweater. Calling this an opportunity, she insisted that they go in and join the crowd. So they did. They stood there waiting for their turn. As soon as Khurshid reached them, Fauzia implored the minister to look into the case of their missing son.

He tried to walk on, saying his office would look into it. But Fauzia wouldn't let go. She opened the file she was carrying and told Khurshid that her son was innocent and was trapped by certain people in Pakistan. After a while, Khurshid snapped and said, '*Toh phir kya hum jang kar de?*' (Should we wage a war?)

Fauzia retorted, '*Ji zaroorat pade toh woh bhi kar dijiye.*' (If needed, do that too.)

Nehal held her hand and pulled her back. They had to go for another appointment, so they left.

Hoping that their prayers would be heard, the next day, the two of them again went to the Khurshid residence. The minister was not home, but his wife called them in.

The couple had forgotten what it was like to be treated with kindness. This harsh, transactional world was breaking their belief in empathy. But unlike her husband, Louise Khurshid spoke to them with compassion. It was a relief.

She held Fauzia's hand and asked, 'Tell me what happened.'

Fauzia gave an account of what they were going through and how desperate she was to find her son. She broke down and said, 'At least we should know if he is dead or alive.'

Louise consoled her and told her not to imagine such things. 'You are his mother. Be strong. I can understand what you are going through.' Fauzia thanked her and told her about her interaction with Khurshid.

'There is a difference between men and women. But I assure you that my husband will look into the case. Give me your letter and I will see if we can do something,' she said.

Since they were in Delhi, they thought of approaching the Pakistan High Commission as well. They also intended to apply for a visa.

On Monday morning, they reached Shanti Path in Chanakyapuri, where a white building with blue domes and minarets stood. When they approached the window at Gate 1, they were told to go to the gate on the left-hand side of the building, where the visa section was located. But nobody was there to meet them. They tried to apply for a visa, but the person at the window was not forthcoming.

Fauzia hoped for a miracle. She saw a small gate open some distance away, and a tall man in white Pathani attire step out. People rushed to him, asking about their visas and other applications. Fauzia and Nehal also ran to him. Without wasting a moment, Fauzia started, 'Sir, my son is missing in your country, Pakistan. I have come from Mumbai to seek your help but I am not being allowed to go inside. Please help me meet someone in your office who can help.'

The man heard them out patiently and took them inside.

Visa officer Noorul Hassan heard them out. He shook his head and said, 'This is all a cover story. Anybody can write the Facebook conversation you are showing me, Madam.'

Undeterred, she showed him Atta-ur-Rahman's phone number, the email details of *Dastak News* and Atta-ur-Rahman's Facebook profile with his photo. She pleaded, 'Sir, *aap khud check kar lein yeh* genuine *hai ya nahi.*' (You can check for yourself if these are genuine or not.) The visa officer took all the documents and their contact details, promising to look into it. They went back to their hotel and rested for a bit before Fauzia got back to writing letters and calling people up.

The next morning, Fauzia's phone rang. It was a landline number that belonged to the Pakistan High Commission. She answered and was told to visit at noon.

She and Nehal reached the gate at the appointed time and declared that they had an appointment with the visa officer Noorul Hassan. A while later, they entered the premises after going through security checks. It was a nice, spacious area with a fountain at the entrance, and they were taken into a room where a young lady officer was seated.

'Salaam, I am Saima Syed. I am a diplomat at the mission,' she said as she walked up to them and introduced herself.

They had a long conversation about the case. This was the first time they were meeting her, but she promptly shared her direct office number with them.

'If there is anything you need or any new development in the case, please feel free to get in touch with me,' she said.

'Will we get visas to travel to Islamabad? I will plead to the authorities there of my son's innocence. We at least need to know if they have him, if he is dead or alive,' said Fauzia.

Saima assured them that the authorities would look into her son's case. Meanwhile, there was no basis on which a visa could be issued. The couple were asked to wait till the mission heard from headquarters.

They returned to Mumbai. Fauzia called Saima on a regular basis. But there was no word or clearance from Islamabad.

When Fauzia told Saima that their visa applications would never be considered because they didn't have invitations or references, the consulate officer told her to put her name in the references column. It was nice to speak to an officer who understood a mother's woes.

Meanwhile, Fauzia started looking at advocacy groups and organizations that worked on human rights issues in South Asia, especially those that focused on India and Pakistan. She came across an organization called Justice Upheld, and on its website found the contact details of someone called Jas Uppal.

Fauzia had reached a point where finances meant nothing to her. She would spend money on anything or anyone she thought could help. Calling Uppal was going to cost her since she was based out of London.

The phone rang and a lady on the other side said, 'Hello.'

'Hello, can I please speak to Jas Uppal? I am Fauzia Ansari from Mumbai and I need help regarding my son,' said the determined mother.

Uppal confirmed that it was her, and asked how she could help. Fauzia began narrating her story. She should've been tired by now from repeating the same thing over and over again, but fatigue was the last thing on her mind. She was only thinking about how every moment that she didn't try meant her son continued to suffer in Pakistan.

Uppal heard the anguished Fauzia out and then said, 'I am in London so I can't be there physically for you, but I feel your pain. You have already explored the cops' route, but I think you should also consider the legal route. I have a friend who practises at the Supreme Court. Let me speak to Arvind Sharma first and then I will connect you to him.'

Uppal also started an online petition on Change.org for Hamid's release. She guided Fauzia to approach the United Nations, and when she got a reply to attend their meeting in Geneva, Uppal offered to attend on her behalf. Thus, she was given power of attorney by Fauzia.

A few days later, Uppal connected Fauzia with the Supreme Court advocate Arvind Sharma. He kept the conversation short and asked her to come to Delhi.

Fauzia discussed the matter with her husband and her elder son. They all decided to take the matter to court since there had been no response from anyone. They took a train to Delhi and went directly from the station to meet Sharma.

He had called Fauzia and Nehal to his office on the first floor in the chambers of the Supreme Court at 2 p.m. He was a kind soul, and an impressive and respectful personality. He welcomed them and told them to explain each detail related to Hamid's case. Fauzia introduced herself and presented him a book authored by her, called *Azadi Ki Ladai Mein Musalmanon Ka Yogdan*. It was on the Muslim freedom fighters of undivided India and was published in 2005. She thought it would be a good gesture to give it as a gift.

He listened to Fauzia and Nehal carefully and told them he would help. Fauzia asked him what he would charge. He kindly waived off any fee—the court fee as well as the stationary charges. He said, 'I will file the case in the Supreme Court in Fauzia's name. Before that, we have to serve a notice to the MEA to submit their reply regarding this case; three weeks later, a petition will be filed. Meanwhile, I will draft a petition. You need to sign an undertaking, a *vakalatnama*. Leave the documents with me.'

He added, 'You can attend the hearing. I will inform you in advance and you can come to Delhi accordingly.'

So Advocate Sharma would represent them in court. They signed an undertaking which empowered him to file a petition in the Supreme Court asking the Indian government to pursue the case with Pakistan.

Fauzia and Nehal decided to send Sharma a cheque of 50,000 Indian rupees for all the effort he was making on their account. They felt guilty for making him do so much for them free of cost.

Justice Chandramauli Kumar Prasad and Justice Kurian Joseph heard the matter, and Indira Jaising represented the UPA government. Fauzia and Nehal attended all the hearings. When they reached Delhi for the first one, Sharma took the cheque they had given him out of his pocket and handed it back to Fauzia, saying, 'I told you I will not charge any fee. When Hamid returns, you can throw me a party.'

After a couple of hearings, the court decided that this issue was outside their ambit, and it was for the government to see if they should pursue the matter with Pakistan.

'Another dead end. The courts were our hope of getting the government to persuade Pakistan. Now what do we do?' Fauzia asked her husband.

Everyone in the Ansari household had started wearing a tired and sullen look. All laughter and conversation had died. The one thing that lived on was Fauzia's will, her determination, her prayers.

Slowly, the extended family and family friends started getting to know about Hamid. One day, Fauzia called up Hamid's cousin Shabana as she recollected Hamid mentioning she was a reporter in the newspaper *DNA*. She wanted to check if Hamid had spoken to her.

'Salaam, Fauzia Aunty, how are you?' asked Shabana.

'Things aren't looking up at all.' Fauzia updated Shabana and asked if she had any ideas. 'We have been hitting dead ends. I don't know what to do,' Fauzia replied.

Shabana tried to console her and said, 'Oh my God! I am speechless. I cannot believe that he went through with such a plan. Aunty, I have something to tell you. But believe me, at the time I had no idea what Hamid was up to.'

Fauzia was all ears. Yet another clue. The mystery kept unravelling. 'What is it, Shabana?' she asked.

'Around the middle of last year, Hamid had called me to seek some advice. He said he wanted to travel to Pakistan for some Rotary event but was facing a lot of trouble getting a visa. I told him that I could put him in touch with a friend who had been working tirelessly on India–Pakistan issues. In fact, I told him that he might be able to help and Hamid should seek his guidance,' she said.

'Who is this man? Did Hamid get in touch with him?' Fauzia asked with a sense of urgency.

'His name is Jatin Desai. I don't know if Hamid reached out to him but I did share his number. I will try to find out. Meanwhile, you be strong,' she said as she inquired about how far the case had gone and where it stood.

Fauzia narrated the sequence of events, ending with the fact that the Indian courts' doors had closed for them.

'Aunty, can I tell you something? The story needs to get out. It needs to be covered by the media. The pressure will build on the government then,' said Shabana.

Fauzia did not agree. 'No, beta, if it gets out, I will have to leave my job at the college. Your uncle might also have to quit. Imagine the stigma. Nobody will believe that Hamid went to Pakistan for a girl.'

Shabana told her that they had to get the truth out there before someone else concocted their own facts. 'Imagine if we never get Hamid back because we didn't tell his story.'

That was the last thing Fauzia wanted. She agreed to do as Shabana suggested.

After a few days, on 27 April 2013, Fauzia received a call. The lady on the other side introduced herself as Radhika Ramaswamy from *DNA*. She gave Shabana's reference and told her she wanted to do a story on Hamid.

'Fauzia ji, can I come and meet you?' she asked.

They fixed an appointment for the next evening. She and Nehal returned home from work before it was time for the journalist to come over, and Khalid made sure he was there too. The doorbell rang. Radhika entered the narrow drawing room with its peach-coloured walls. There was a sofa on one side and couches on the other.

Fauzia explained the story to her and insisted that Radhika keep in mind that her son was innocent—and that it was important she understand he had been trapped. 'Please highlight the story so that the government takes action, but please do a positive story. One that will help us trace our son and not get him into further trouble.'

They discussed the details. Khalid showed her the records of Hamid's social media conversations, and Radhika took notes.

Fauzia made a strange request. She said, 'Radhika, will you please hold the story for a few days? Just a few days.'

'But why?' asked Radhika.

'Let my college close for vacations and then you can print it. I don't want to face my principal and colleagues. I am not prepared for it. So please hold it till 1 May. It is just a matter of a few days,' she requested.

Radhika left the house after agreeing.

The next morning, on 28 April 2013, Fauzia saw a headline splashed across the front page of *DNA*, titled 'Goes to Afghanistan for job, Pakistan for girl, then goes missing', with a big photo of Hamid.

Stunned, she stared at it. Nehal and Khalid saw it too and knew all hell had broken loose. Fauzia looked at Khalid with tears in her eyes. 'Couldn't she have waited a few days? I cannot go to college. I won't be able to face my colleagues.'

Khalid tried to convince her that Fauzia had done nothing wrong and had nothing to hide, but Nehal made him understand how her colleagues would look at his mother and her family.

Fauzia called in sick. After putting up a brave front for months, one news report had broken her back. The three of them had dinner in silence that night.

Fauzia went to work the next day with the newspaper in her bag. She met the principal and apprised him of the situation she was facing, and the hard times that had befallen her family.

She pulled out the newspaper and placed it on his table. The principal picked it up and read the story. He told her to be strong for herself and her family.

'Fauzia, I understand your predicament, but many of your colleagues might not, so don't discuss this with anybody. Let me know whenever you need time off,' he said to an already overwhelmed Fauzia.

15

Angel of Hope: Zeenat Shehzadi

Fauzia's college finally closed for the summer and she was spared further humiliation. Nehal resolved to take matters into his own hands so that his wife would not plunge into a depressive state.

The couple had put aside some money to go for Umrah, the holy pilgrimage, to Makkah and Medina in Saudi Arabia. This journey holds immense importance and value for followers of Islam and devout families like the Ansaris. Nehal thought there could be no better time for them to seek help and pray to the Creator.

When they finished breakfast one day, he broached the subject. 'I think we should all go for Umrah,' Nehal said.

Fauzia, who was lost in her thoughts, turned to him with her eyes lit up. She said, 'Yes. I want to go ask Allah for help. Nothing else seems to be working. Maybe the Creator will see the pain of this mother and have some mercy.'

Nehal turned to Khalid and asked, 'Son, what do you think? We should start preparing if we have to go.'

Khalid checked with his parents regarding their finances and learnt that they had saved up to go to Makkah. He knew that they would be keen on going for Hajj, the annual pilgrimage that took place at a particular time of the year. Umrah could be undertaken at any time. But the Hajj period was a long way off, so they decided to go for Umrah.

Khalid found an agent and did all the paperwork to ensure that their trip to Makkah would be smooth. Nehal took leave from work and informed the rest of the family about the trip.

Fauzia, Nehal and Khalid went on this spiritual journey to find help, find their souls, and find their way back to peace—even if it was peace in the form of the knowledge that Hamid might be no more. The family had to reconcile with reality.

27 May 2013

They landed in Jeddah, where the heat was unlike anything they had ever experienced. They were taken to Makkah in a bus and from there to the accommodation booked by the travel agent. They checked in, left their luggage in the room and immediately headed to offer prayers at the Kaaba in the holy mosque.

The Kaaba, a cube-shaped structure made of grey stone and marble, is the holiest shrine for Muslims, located at the centre of the Great Mosque in Makkah. Only followers of the faith are allowed to enter Makkah and Medina, and not non-Muslims. In the eastern corner of the Kaaba is the black stone, which is supposed to be touched and kissed during the seven rounds that pilgrims take of the Kaaba.

28 May 2013

The next day, they again visited the Great Mosque. A sea of people was trying to touch the stone, and the Ansari trio joined in, going around the Kaaba. Fauzia stopped at its threshold, which was called the Multazim, pressing her head to it and wailing out loud. Her sobs and cries were drowned out by the people wailing around her. Nobody cared; nobody looked at her strangely. At the moment when you touched the Kaaba, you were one with the Creator. Nobody else mattered. You ask, you plead, you cry, you let go.

Fauzia held on to the Multazim for hours together and kept saying, 'Allah, save my son. Please bring Hamid back, Allah. Everyone knows I have come to You seeking help and I am sure You will not let me return empty-handed. And it will be an example of Your extreme mercy on Your slaves, increasing everyone's faith in You. I take this *mannat* that when I get my Hamid back, I will come back with him and the entire family for Umrah.'

Time flew but she did not budge until a huge group of pilgrims pushed her out of the inner circle. She moved aside and slowly waded through the sea of people and went out. She saw her husband waving at her so she didn't get lost.

'Thank God you are out. What took you so long?' He rushed to Fauzia with the mobile phone in his hand. 'We are getting constant calls from a Pakistani number,' he had just finished saying when the phone rang again.

Fauzia took the phone from her husband and answered. 'Hello, who is this?'

'Salaam, I am Zeenat Shehzadi, a journalist from Pakistan, and I wanted to cover the story about your son. You must be going through hell. I would like to help trace your boy. But I would need all the details,' she said.

The prayers of the desperate mother had been heard and accepted by Allah. Thanking the Almighty profusely, Fauzia replied, 'Oh, thank you, I have been trying to get someone in Pakistan to help me but to no avail. But how did you get my number?'

'I have been in touch with Jas Uppal for human interest stories. She told me about you and asked if I could help trace your son. Will you tell me what happened?'

Fauzia gave a brief account of the case and said that Hamid had gone there to help a girl. But like every other person to whom she had narrated the story, Zeenat was no different and found this hard to believe. 'How are you so sure that it was for a girl that he entered Pakistan illegally?' she asked.

Fauzia told her she had proof. Zeenat asked for all the documents so she could go through them, and assured her of help if she found it to be a genuine case.

Fauzia said, 'Thank you so much, but I am not in India right now. I am in Saudi Arabia for Umrah. I will save your number and share all my details once we are back in Mumbai.'

The conversation ended there. Fauzia felt like Allah had sent Zeenat to her aid. She turned to the Kaaba and, lifting both hands, said a dua and then hugged Khalid. 'Our prayers are being answered, son,' she said.

~

The three of them returned to Mumbai after fifteen days. Fauzia wasted no time. She went to her room and pulled out all her files, wondering how to send them to Zeenat in Pakistan. She did not know how to scan and email. So she decided to start sending her photos of all the papers, conversations, IDs, etc. through WhatsApp. She spent the entire night doing this.

Fauzia had started snapping at Nehal and Khalid, and telling them she would do whatever it took to bring Hamid home. Khalid had to sit her down and explain that they loved Hamid as much as she did but that did not mean the peace and sanity of the family should be destroyed.

Fauzia heard this and tried to calm down, but found it very difficult. The fear of the unknown was eating away at her more than anything else. She was seeking answers, she was seeking closure.

Meanwhile, reports had started appearing in the Indian media about an Indian national going missing in Pakistan. Some of them were quite detailed. Fauzia picked up a few news articles which explained the entire story and sent them to Zeenat.

A few days went by with no word from Zeenat. And then came the call that Fauzia had been waiting for.

'Salaam, Fauzia ji, this is Zeenat,' she said.

Fauzia heaved a sigh of relief and responded, 'Salaam, Zeenat, how are you? I had been waiting for the past few days hoping to hear from you. Were you able to find anything?'

Zeenat said emphatically, 'Your son has been framed.'

Fauzia's fears were confirmed. 'How do you know? Have you managed to trace him?'

Zeenat told her about what she had found out. This was a very important story for her as she was a budding journalist who, apart from fighting for a just cause, wanted to make a mark.

She said, 'Fauzia ji, I have done my due diligence. I had to, since this is a very complicated story, but what I have found out is shameful.'

'Allah, what are you talking about, Zeenat? Do you know where Hamid is?' Fauzia panicked.

'Well, I don't know where he is exactly but I took the risk of meeting Atta-ur-Rahman. I called on the number you had shared with me. Atta-ur-Rahman picked up the phone and I introduced myself and told him why I was calling. He was shocked to hear someone ask him about Hamid. He said he would not speak on the phone and that if I wanted any information, I should meet him in person. So I went all the way to Karak.'

Fauzia asked how she had managed to convince her parents to be okay with the trip.

'My family has been very supportive, Fauzia ji. We are not very well off. I only have my mother and two brothers. I am the primary financial support for my family. My younger brother, Saddam, is in school, and the older one, Salman, is very bright and in college. I am the eldest.'

She went on, 'So, I took an early morning bus to Karak. My mother accompanied me to the bus stop and waited with me. It was very cold but I knew I had to do this. I wanted to go there and get all the facts. I met Atta at his residence. He is a family man and a reporter in a small media house there. I asked him about Hamid. Fauzia ji, you will be shocked to know that he was looking for money. He said that he was stunned to see that Hamid had left behind a trail. He got very angry. He said he had thought the boy would come with a substantial amount of money and that he would be able to pocket it, but unfortunately, he came with hardly anything. He had no money. Atta had checked all of Hamid's belongings.'

There was no word from the other end, only a sense of intense attention.

'He also told me that he did not want to get into trouble within his own community, so instead of going along with the earlier plan, he

informed the girl's family. He met the father and told him that there was
a boy who was going to come from India for Fiza. It was for the father to
decide how he wanted to handle things,' she said and fell quiet, hearing
sobs on the other end.

Fauzia was choked with emotion and couldn't utter a word. Zeenat
kept calling out her name. 'Hello, Fauzia ji . . . Fauzia ji, please be
strong. Please . . .'

Finally, Fauzia said, 'How greedy can people be? If money was all he
wanted then he should have said that.'

'Money is indeed all he wants,' added Zeenat and very hesitantly
said, 'He has asked for 50,000 rupees up front to divulge any further
information on Hamid.'

'So he knows where Hamid is? Have they kept him hostage or is he
with the Pakistani authorities?' asked Fauzia.

'He refused to give me any information till I make the payment,'
said Zeenat.

Fauzia told her that she would arrange for the money and figure out
how to send it to Pakistan. She was reminded of the fact that Zeenat was
doing all this on her own time and from her own pocket, so she added,
'Zeenat Beta, don't take it the wrong way, but I would also like to pay
you a basic amount for all the trouble you are taking. This is not part
of your job. You are doing more than you should, so please let me help
you on the home front.'

Zeenat was initially not comfortable with this but didn't object to
being paid a small sum that would cover her travel and investigation
costs. Her own means and resources were limited.

She added that Atta had revealed one more name to her—his
accomplice, Abdullah Khattak—but had asked her not to tell anybody
he had given her this information. She told Fauzia that she would go
and meet Abdullah and befriend him. 'Now I need to know what all you
have done so far. Have you sought the legal route? If not, we should.
We should also apply at the Enforced Disappearances Tribunal here,'
said Zeenat.

Hearing somebody speak with purpose brought some relief to Fauzia.
She told her about Adnan Saboor Rohaila and that he was the one who

had initially sent the invitation on behalf of the Rotary to Hamid, but
after he learnt that her son had gone missing, he hadn't done much.

Fauzia shared Barrister Rohaila's details with Zeenat.

Around the second week of June, Zeenat got an appointment with
Barrister Rohaila and went to meet him. She called up later to tell Fauzia
what had transpired. She was unimpressed with the man who seemed
absolutely disinterested in the case. 'Fauzia ji, I went to meet Barrister
Rohaila today and it seems like he hasn't moved on the case at all. He
hasn't even filed a petition yet,' said Zeenat.

The next day, she went to Rohaila's office and told him to file a
habeas corpus petition in the Peshawar High Court.

A few days later, Fauzia called up the barrister to check on the case.
He informed her that he would file the petition but reminded her of his
fee of four thousand dollars.

That was a lot of money but the Ansari family said they would
manage it somehow. Fauzia asked Rohaila how she could make the
payment, and he gave her the contact of a cousin in Dubai and asked
her to send the money to him.

Khalid organized the transfer. He asked his friend in Dubai to
give Rohaila's contact four thousand dollars, and told him his parents
would pay the same amount to his family in India.

Fauzia then called up Zeenat and told her that Rohaila had agreed
to file a habeas corpus petition and that she would have to meet him
with all the relevant documents. Zeenat would be the signing authority,
as Fauzia had given her the power of attorney.

Zeenat handed over all the required documents to Barrister Rohaila.
He prepared a detailed petition and mailed it to Fauzia before filing it in
the Peshawar High Court in Fauzia's name. The court proceedings were
finally initiated, although they progressed at a snail's pace.

By now, Fauzia had opened up all channels: the media, the MEA and
various international organizations as well as the Pakistani authorities.

On 24 June, Fauzia wrote letters to the United Nations Committee
on Enforced Disappearances under the Office of the High Commissioner
for Human Rights (OHCHR). On 13 July, she wrote letters to the then
prime minister, Manmohan Singh, the home minister, the Maharashtra

chief minister, the Mumbai Police commissioner, the chief justice of Pakistan and the Pakistan prime minister. On 18 July, Fauzia and Nehal visited the Red Cross Society in Mumbai.

Around the same time, Fauzia got a call from an unknown number. She picked up, thinking it must be a journalist.

'Hello, I am Jatin Desai, a journalist and someone who knew Hamid. He had come to me seeking guidance on how to go to Pakistan since I closely work on India–Pakistan issues.'

Fauzia was dazed. Who was this man? Hamid had gone to him. How and when? Suddenly, she remembered her conversation with her niece, Shabana, who said she had given Hamid the number of Jatin Desai.

Jatin continued, 'Fauzia ji, I am Jatin Desai, general secretary of the PIPFPD, the Pakistan India People's Forum for Peace and Democracy, and have worked for years on India–Pakistan issues. I am also a journalist. I have been actively working for innocent civilians and fishermen who are in Pakistani and Indian prisons.'

'Jatin ji, so Hamid got in touch with you?'

'I am feeling so guilty and so bad that I am getting in touch with you now. I was not in town and had not seen the reports. As soon as I reached Mumbai and collected my newspapers from the neighbours, I saw the front-page story on Hamid,' said Jatin.

Fauzia asked him about their conversations. What had Hamid wanted to know, and had he told Jatin the purpose of his visit? It turned out that while he had maintained the Rotary pretext with everyone else, he had been dead honest with Jatin, briefly mentioning the fact that his purpose was regarding a girl.

Jatin was clear that this was not a conversation he wanted to have over the phone, and he wanted to do more than just pass on information. He was feeling guilty for not having seen what was coming, and said he was going to help the family in any and every way possible. This chat between him and Fauzia was the beginning of a long struggle and an even longer association.

Meanwhile, the visits from the cops did not stop. They said they were only doing their duty and were very understanding, but the questioning had become tiring.

The next day, Jatin Desai met Fauzia and Nehal at the very same cafe where he had met Hamid Ansari—Fun Republic mall in Andheri.

They sat across the table and Jatin started by apologizing. Fauzia and Nehal insisted that he needn't do that, but they would need to know everything Hamid had told him.

He started, 'I met Hamid three times in this very place; in fact, the first time was at this very table. The first time, Hamid told me the story about the girl and that she was in trouble. He wanted to get a visa but had failed to do so.'

'Did you know he was going to Pakistan? What was your advice to him, Jatin Bhai?' asked Fauzia.

'I told him that India and Pakistan have city-specific visas and getting a visa for a place like Kohat in KPK and the tribal areas was near impossible. At most, people got visas for Islamabad, Lahore, Karachi, and sometimes for Peshawar. But he was determined to go to Pakistan, and I could see that. I was very impressed by his confidence and go-getter attitude. He insisted that I guide him. He logically defended his reason to go to Pakistan. But he was so determined that somewhere he lost his rationality.'

He continued, 'He told me that he had spoken to Rotarians who had promised to accompany him to Peshawar and Kohat. I told him that I was not aware of what they could and could not do, so I would not be able to help.'

'Allah!' Fauzia exclaimed and looked at her husband, who gestured to her to calm down.

'I know, I know I made a mistake. I should've taken your phone numbers to cross-check, but it never struck me. You know, I have worked on the case of Bhavesh Parmar, an Indian who had crossed over into Pakistan. It was a difficult task to bring him back. We lobbied for him with politicians and activists in Pakistan. It was difficult. I should've thought about that. I am so sorry.'

Fauzia placed her hand on her forehead and kept shaking her head in disbelief.

'The third meeting took place after two months, when he came up with the suggestion of entering through Afghanistan. I warned him against doing that. I told him that if he entered illegally from any country and got caught, he would be considered a RAW agent and that they would make his life miserable. But then he mentioned the contacts he had established.' Jatin looked down at his cup of coffee, which had gone cold by now.

'Fauzia ji, I am feeling so bad because I should have informed someone rather than keep it to myself. When I advised him not to go if he did not get a visa, I never thought he would not follow my suggestion,' Jatin said apologetically. He told the Ansaris that he would do whatever was possible to help.

Subsequently, in October, Fauzia received a reply from the United Nations that the case she had filed at the Committee on Enforced Disappearances would be heard; it was registered as Case No. 10003891. She considered this some forward movement at the international platform since there had been no word from the Pakistan government and no response to the numerous note verbales that the Indian government had been sending to Pakistan's MoFA.

At the end of 2013, two things happened: In November, Fauzia filed a petition in the Supreme Court of India. It was a writ petition to direct the MEA through its secretary to take the appropriate steps via diplomatic channels in the Pakistan embassy for tracing the whereabouts of Indian national Hamid Nehal Ansari, missing since 15 November 2012. The other development was Zeenat pursuing Rohaila to file the petition in the Peshawar High Court.

In India, Hamid's story was picking up. The online petition on Change.org got 5000 signatures (3000 offline and 2000 online). Fauzia later submitted the petition to Manmohan Singh and Nawaz Sharif, the respective prime ministers of India and Pakistan.

Zeenat became the reason for Pakistan to finally accept Hamid Ansari's presence in the country. She fought a valiant fight and paid a heavy price.

16

FIA Takes Over

I was a reflection of a man unknown, a soul crushed—unrecognizable, smelly, unbathed, unshaven, lice-infested.

It was the rainy season and the sewer pipes were clogged. One day, water started entering the underground cell from the toilets a floor above. The inmates closer to the staircase started screaming, and before I could react, I felt the stinky, mucky water on my feet. I wanted to throw up; the stench was unbearable. I could see human faeces floating in the water. We all screamed for help, but the commanders and guards had already run upstairs. We waited for them to return.

After an hour, someone came with buckets of water and started cleaning the passageway. He would throw a rag inside every cell he passed, so each prisoner could clean his own cell. Mine was the second cell from the staircase. I stared at the rag and then at the dirty, shit-filled floor, and I couldn't believe what I was going through. I stood there for the longest time. But I eventually had to clean up so I could at least sit. The rag was small and it didn't really help with the mess, but I had nothing else.

This situation cropped up biannually, every April and October. Worse still, we were forced to use the clogged washroom every day, wading through shitty water to relieve ourselves. To top it off, there was no soap.

My solitary confinement continued in this way, 20 feet under. It was now the end of May 2013. One day, an officer made me go with him to the interrogation room. The officers were never in uniform, so I didn't know their names, ranks or departments.

The room had a familiar smell. I was made to sit on a chair. My blindfold was removed, and I saw the officer sitting in front of me with a set of papers.

Without any conversation, he started reading out from them. After some time, it came to me that the first-person account was the statement I had given during a previous interrogation. He finished reading, laid out the papers in front of me and asked me to sign on them. I thought they had finally believed me. I signed the papers with the impatience of a child. The officer then held up my thumb, pressed it on to an ink pad and took my prints on a separate set of papers. I didn't care about documentation any more. I just wanted to get out.

I asked the officer about my release. He replied, '*Humse aise sawal mat kiya karo jiska jawab hum nahi de sakte.*' (Don't ask questions for which I have no answers.)

The ugly old feeling of entrapment was creeping in but I wanted to stay positive. 'They just took my signatures on the right statement. That's a good sign, right,' I thought as I was sent back to my cell for another endless wait.

In the first week of June, I was again summoned to the interrogation room, but this time there was a new face in front of me. A fierce one with a filthy mouth. He hurled abuses at me even before the session began and then asked me to narrate my entire journey here all over again.

I trembled, anticipating torture and abuse. But I went on. As soon as I finished, he stared into my eyes and said, 'And you want me to believe that?'

In his bluster, he inadvertently gave out his name. 'You might have faced many officers but none like me. Nobody stands a chance with lies in front of me. Mallak is known for his brutality. So you either tell me the truth or I will throw you to hungry dogs.'

I was confused. Shaking, I said, 'Sir, my case has been cleared. I have been told that I will be getting an extension on my Afghan visa to be able to cross over . . .'

A roar of laughter interrupted me. The officer laughed hard and abruptly turned to me with bloodshot eyes. He banged his hands on the table and said, 'If that were true then your case wouldn't have come to me.'

Mallak then summoned the previous set of officers handling my case and told them to stop all the facilities that were being provided to me.

This repeated treatment had made me cynical. Yeah right, as if I had been treated royally. What would they take away from me? My dark room, or the worms, mosquitoes, lice, my tattered clothes . . . What?

I soon found out. Even though it was scorching, they took away the pedestal fans from the passageway right outside the cells that kept them ventilated and reduced the stink around us. We were allowed to use the toilet only once a day; at all other times, we had to urinate in plastic bottles kept in a corner of our cells.

With the fans gone, the air in the cell became stale, the stench unbearable, and turned the mosquitoes into fiends. Creepy-crawlies had invaded my body and I had things biting and digging into my skin all the time. I couldn't sleep. The heat was suffocating.

The portions of food I got became smaller and smaller. If I ever made the mistake of asking for more, the guards would say, '*Tu kya yahan humara khana khane aaya hai? Mahmaan aaya hai kya tu yahan?* (Have you come here to eat? Are you a guest?)

The ordeal of going to the toilet once a day and having to do my job in ninety seconds was another form of torture. Ninety seconds for entering the washroom, untying my pyjamas, relieving myself, cleaning myself, putting on the pyjamas again and coming out—all this while listening to the constant banging on the door. Sometimes I was pulled out even before I was done, forcing me to pull up my pyjamas as I was dragged and dumped into the cell.

The first few days of this were a nightmare. Because of the lack of soap to wash my hands, I couldn't get myself to eat initially, but hunger eventually got the best of me. The assault on all my senses had no bounds.

The lonely, excruciating life facing the walls of the cell continued. The prisoners were not allowed to go close to the iron bars and look out. We were not allowed to speak at all. We never saw each other, because we were made to stand or sit facing the wall. Once, a prisoner was caught looking at someone. He was beaten up so badly that his screams haunted me the whole night. Everyone could hear him beg but the guards were merciless.

For months on end, I had no contact with anyone but interrogators. The sound of silence was killing me. I would imagine blue skies, the chirping of birds, the feel of the cool breeze on Marine Drive, the Mumbai rains, my family . . . the good life.

One day, a huge man was put in my cell, the first time I had a cellmate. I was scared. Had he been sent to kill me? It was an unusual occurrence. My vision was blurred without my glasses, and with the darkness in the cell, I was practically blind.

Tall and strapping, with well-trimmed hair and a beard, he did not look like he had been underground for long. Was he one of *them*? Such questions kept popping up in my head.

He came up to me, and, with a heavy voice, asked for a glass of water. I was petrified. We were not allowed to talk to each other. I ran to the iron gate and called the guard to report the matter, lest I get into trouble.

'*Santri* Sahab, he wants water. He needs a glass,' I told the guard.

The guard asked me to share my own glass with him, which I did. He filled it with water and drank half of it, throwing the rest in the corner where my pee bottle was kept. He did all this while inspecting the room. It didn't seem like he was a prisoner.

He then came and sat close to me and started talking. I gestured him to keep quiet, else we would be thrashed. He didn't pay heed.

'I am Mushtaq Shah from Waziristan. What is your name and why are you here?' he whispered.

'I am Hamid Ansari. I am an Indian,' I replied and watched for his reaction.

The moment he heard that, he asked, 'Indian? What was your mission in Pakistan?'

I thought it was a very unusual question. He spoke like a cop, not a criminal. Why would he ask me about my 'mission' and not why I was here? But I told him that I was there to help a friend and was not on any mission.

Barely an hour and a half later, two guards and a commander came and escorted him out of the cell. I found all this very strange.

The next day, after lunch, I heard screams from the interrogation room, but something sounded different. By now, I knew very well the sound made by a belt when it touched flesh. This sounded like the belt was touching the chair.

A while later, a sobbing man was let out of the room. I heard footsteps heading towards my cell, but didn't turn around till the gate opened and the man was pushed in. It was Mushtaq Shah again. The guard asked him to go and sit inside, facing the wall. He obeyed.

After a while, he took my glass and poured himself some water. He said in a coarse voice, '*Ye log itna maarte kyun hain?*' (Why do these people beat us so much?)

He sat close to me and started asking me all kinds of questions. His curiosity was suspicious. I turned around and asked him why he was being held in this godforsaken place. 'Why are you here? What did you do?' I asked.

'I used to train orphaned children to become suicide bombers and supply them to the Taliban,' he said.

I was shocked and angry. I didn't know what to say. He had been using innocent children for crimes. I couldn't bear to be in the cell with such a person. I felt like slapping him but was afraid of the consequences of such an action.

Mushtaq figured out what must be running through my mind and explained, 'My brother was shot by a traffic cop for jumping a signal. He didn't stop. But he was not a terrorist.'

Was he trying to justify his terrorist activities as so-called revenge on the authorities for his brother? Feeling disgusted and angry, I decided I was done listening to him. But he continued with his questions. 'Okay, I am bad. But what are you doing in Pakistan? Are you not an Indian spy? How is that not worse? Anyway, can you help me connect with your people if you get out of here?'

'Like I said earlier, I am not a spy. I came to help someone. And please don't talk to me. I don't want to get into trouble because of you,'

I said and turned the other way. I stared at the wall and wished he would be taken away.

In another hour, he was. That was the last I saw of him. I figured this had been their plan to make me say something that would declare me guilty. But I knew I had to hold on dearly to my truth. Wavering from my statement because of torture would only lead to more torture. If I buckled and said I was an Indian spy then they would ask me my plans, my rank, etc. I would have no answers. I couldn't tell a lieutenant from a major general or a general. Any deviation from the truth would lead to another horrid experience and I was not prepared for that.

But I was also not prepared for the years to come.

The next day, just after my afternoon prayers, I was summoned to the interrogation room by Mallak, who, it turned out, was not as harsh as he seemed. He had, in fact, once opened up and spoken about his own experience with the cops and how he had been picked up on suspicion of being a terrorist. He had been released when they had found nothing against him. The experience had inspired him to join the forces, unlike Mushtaq, who claimed he was seeking revenge.

Mallak spoke with a sense of purpose from across the table. 'Hamid, today is a very important day. I will do something that could show you the doors to freedom.'

I was all ears and nodded.

'I will be conducting a test on you. If you are what you say you are, that is, innocent, you should have no problem going through with it. Have you heard of a lie detector test? Have you undergone any such test before? Do you know how it works?'

'I don't know anything about any such test. Nor have I ever undergone one.' I had nothing to worry about, unless they had rigged the test. I was connected to a machine which was connected to a laptop. My pulse, heartbeat, breathing rate, etc., were monitored through the wires.

The test began with some basic questions.

Is your name Hamid?
Are you a boy?
Are you sitting on a chair?
Are you Indian?

Once they got the parameters right, they started the actual questions, interspersing them with innocuous ones.

The questions had 'yes' or 'no' answers.

Did the Indian government send you to Pakistan?
Were you sent by the army?
Were you sent to build a network for RAW?

When I replied in the negative, they went on to ask:

Were you sent by any organization working against Pakistan?
Are you working against Pakistan on an individual stand?
Were you assisted by someone to enter Pakistan?
Were you funded by someone in Pakistan?
Did you come via the Torkham border?

I didn't know exactly how the machine worked but I knew the readings had to do with my pulse rate. I kept calm and answered honestly. The drill continued for three days, with the same questions being asked in different ways.

Was your mission against Pakistan?
Was Fiza part of your plan?
Do you have a network in Pakistan?
Have you given all the information correctly during your interrogation?
Did you promise to pay Atta-ur-Rahman?
Are you aware of anyone working for India within Pakistan?

They seemed to be struggling to get an answer that would help their cause or lead to a rise in my heart rate. On day three, Mallak looked miffed. He stepped out of the room and then returned and asked if I had taken any medication for fever or headache. He even cross-checked this with the dispenser. Seeing all this, I was reassured that I had passed the lie detector test. I said a little prayer of thanks.

Mallak recognized the relief on my face and was enraged. 'This only proves one thing: You are a very well-trained spy who knows how to dodge the test. It does not prove your innocence, you fool. So don't look so relieved.'

Warning me, he said, 'Hamid, you either accept that you are a spy and turn approver, then we will show some consideration, else I will write such an adverse report on this test that you will never see light again. Ever.'

I kept quiet, my eyes fixed on the ground. The offer of getting out after being labelled a spy was tempting, but I stuck to my stand. The truth wouldn't fail me, or maybe it would. But everything else, including the promise of freedom, was a lie.

I used to observe a fast every Monday and Thursday. On one such day, I was taken to the interrogation room once again, blindfolded and handcuffed. From here on, I would always be blindfolded and handcuffed during interrogation.

The room seemed to be filled with people—four or five of them. Coming from solitary confinement, five was a crowd. I was made to stand in the centre. I could sense the presence of men standing around me. I recognized Mallak's voice. He asked me about my mission again. I repeated my answer: I was in Pakistan to rescue a girl. Suddenly, Mallak pulled my hair vigorously and gave me a resounding slap, which was followed by a barrage of violent attacks.

I didn't know where to cover myself and who to cower from as I was blindfolded. Punches, kicks, rods and sticks rained down on me. When I tried to take cover with my hands and fell on the ground, they asked me to stand. When I was too feeble to even do that, my hands and legs were tied wide apart and the blows kept coming.

The ferocity of this attack made me scream at Mallak, '*Pagal ho gaya hai kya jo itna maar raha hai?*' (Have you gone mad to be beating me like this?)

There was silence in the room. I could feel the disbelief around me. I knew what was to come. Mallak wouldn't tolerate being insulted in front of his juniors.

'Mad?! How dare you call me mad? I will show you what mad is,' he was probably frothing at the mouth. For the next hour, I was beaten to within an inch of my life. One severe blow on my shin almost made me pass out.

The sharp pain led me to think I had broken a bone. I couldn't feel my left leg. Someone said, 'I think his leg is broken.' But that didn't stop him. Mallak made me lie on the ground and poured hot, molten wax on my back.

I screamed all through this time. I lost my voice. My throat hurt. But my ordeal was not over.

After the long torture session, one of the officers asked me, 'So what was your mission here?'

Another asked, 'What has the Indian army taught you?'

'What has RAW asked you to do?' asked one more voice.

Mallak said, 'We have all the proof that you are a spy. It will be better for you to accept it, else you will never go back.'

I insisted that whatever I had told them was the truth. I begged them to believe me.

But then came an unexpected question. 'How much money did you give Atta-ur-Rahman?'

'What? I didn't give him any money,' I said, utterly confused.

I knew they were not convinced. They asked me for my email and other social media IDs and passwords such as for Facebook. I gave them all these details without hesitation.

After a while, I felt a blow across my head. I almost fainted. One of the officers said that the password was incorrect. I was shocked. How could that be possible? I told them that the password was correct to the best of my knowledge and also asked them to allow me to open my email account if they were not able to access it. They did not want to listen. And this was a good excuse for another round of beating the living daylights out of me.

For an investigative team, they were rather dumb. I told them that if the location and device from where one accessed the account was different than usual, Facebook and email servers would not allow access till the user's identity was verified.

There was silence. I also told them that a few months ago one of their officers had told me he sent an email to my parents from my own email ID. So if the password was working then, how could it stop working now? And if it was really not working then the officer was responsible for changing the password.

No one had anything to say on hearing this. The focus shifted to the identity of the officer who had sent the email.

The interrogators called it a day and asked me to be taken back to my cell. I was barely able to stand. As I left, I heard one of them saying, '*Doosre wale ko lao.*' (Get the other guy.)

My ears pricked up. Had I heard them correctly? Limping and dragging my left leg, I walked towards my cell, with the guards pushing me to move fast. I cursed them under my breath.

Once inside, I could finally tend to my wounds. With the taste of blood in my mouth and my throat dry, I asked for some water, but the guard on duty refused, saying he was not authorized to do that.

I simply swallowed a little blood to lubricate my throat. My body was swollen and sore. I heard the azaan and raised my hands to pray and seek forgiveness. It reminded me that God was watching all this cruelty and hearing my prayers.

My entire body was bruised and marked by stripes of black and blue. My feet felt as if they were crushed. Inside the cell, I couldn't stand for namaz, so I sat and offered prayers.

I thought I would die of thirst. The next morning, when they dragged me for my ninety-second bathroom ritual, all I did was drink water from the tap in the loo. As I stepped out, the guard asked me if I had had water inside. I shook my head and looked at the ground. He nodded and dragged me back to my cell.

The entire week, I was in my dark, stinky cell, moaning in pain. A Brufen pill was given to me every evening, without any food. For one whole week, Mallak tortured me—no food, no water. My only access to water was during my daily visit to the toilet.

The following week, the interrogation continued. When I repeated the same things, Mallak surprised me by saying, 'But your friend Atta-ur-Rahman has accepted that you paid him money. So it is clear that you have been lying all along.'

I was speechless. Did they have Atta? Why would he say that? Did he buckle and give a false statement? While I wondered at all this, I heard Mallak say, '*Bandho ise.*' (Tie him up.)

The more I cried, the more he seemed to enjoy it. I tried to control myself and did not shout. I was moved to the dental chair, where the torture continued. I had nothing to add so I kept repeating the same words.

Mallak stopped and said, 'Take him back and get the other one.'

This was the second time I was hearing about the other man. Was it Atta-ur-Rahman? By evening, they started giving me food and water again, but the rude behaviour of the guards and commanders did not change.

Under any and all circumstances, the Pakistani authorities wanted me to accept that I was an Indian spy on a mission to Pakistan. But I thought their strategy was probably to do one last check before releasing me. They wanted to be doubly sure.

I didn't hear from anyone for days. Stuck in that lonely cell, I was losing my mind.

Late one night, the guard raised a sudden alarm. He beat his baton against the iron bars of all the cells, asking people to wake up.

I went to the gate and asked the guard if I had missed the morning azaan. He replied, '*Ye namaz ke liye nahi sehri ke liye uthaya hai. Sehri aane wali hai.*' (This is not for namaz, it is for sehri). Sehri is the early morning meal before the daily fast of the thirty days of Ramzan, the holy month.

I couldn't believe that it was Ramzan and I was still in Pakistan. But the guard thought the concept of sehri was alien to me since none of them thought I was a Muslim.

He politely told me that I could go back to sleep and a separate breakfast would be provided to me at the regular time.

I thought this was another psychological game. But I refused to believe that it was already Ramzan, since in my head the number of days leading up to the holy month were still many. I didn't think so much time had passed. But I also couldn't believe they would fake Ramzan. I decided to play along. I told the guard to give me sehri since I was going to observe the fast like any practising Muslim.

The whole day, I observed if food was served to anyone. There was no lunch.

As per the ritual of Ramzan, we were served iftar in the evening, followed by regular dinner. This routine continued every day, and the fear started settling. After a week or so, I finally accepted that I was wrong and that it was indeed the month of Ramzan.

The realization shattered me. I broke down. My fate looked bleak. I was flooded with memories of home and Ammi laying the table for us all. Of Khalid and I chatting over iftar and even after dinner. The evenings always lit up during Ramzan. How they must all miss me. The fourth empty chair must be killing them.

I started praying day and night, hoping that my prayers would be answered. But the torture continued unabated.

It had been more than eight months since I had brushed my teeth or combed my hair or even shaved. My hair had grown to my shoulders and my beard to my chest. With no proper hygiene and no exposure to sunlight, lice had infested my head, moved from my hair to my beard, from my beard to my chest, and all over my body. I was a feast for blood-sucking parasites.

A person practising Islam knows that pubic and armpit hair should be removed, and it becomes *haram* (unholy) to not do this for more than forty days. I cursed everyone there for being unIslamic and preaching Islam to me.

I was eventually allowed to bathe once a week in peak summer, but without soap. I had to complete defecating and bathing in under two minutes, and wear the same dirty orange uniform again. This made the clothes damp and soon they got sticky and stinky.

August went by, and so did Eid. I got no answer regarding my release or even my case. Strangely, I started praying for an interrogation session because that was the only way I could find out anything.

In mid-September, I was taken back to the interrogation room, blindfolded. Although I had been wishing for it, now I dreaded what it held. From the sound of the footsteps, I figured there were three men.

One of them sat opposite me, while the other two sat to my right. The officer right across from me spoke in a soft voice, 'I have come from a very distant place. And I have been assigned your case. You know what that means?'

I shook my head.

'It means I will be fighting on your behalf, and depending on the verdict, you will either be released or punished,' he said and left without any further interaction, shaking my hand before exiting. In a long,

long time, someone had touched me without any violent motive. It was reassuring to know that this person would fight my case. The devil called hope had resurfaced.

He returned in a week's time and opened a file in which he took notes. I told him the whole story, to which he said, 'If you keep giving this cover story, I will not be able to help you. Tell me the truth.'

He didn't trust me. And I stopped pinning my hopes on him that very moment. These were all psy-ops (psychological operations in spycraft). And I had started recognizing them. The demeanour and body language between us changed.

He started talking about my parents and my brother. This man had come prepared and knew my weaknesses. He blamed me for my family's suffering. The session was a cathartic experience. I was put on an emotional roller coaster and was a wreck for the next few days.

The next time he showed up, I was taken to the interrogation room with other officers. I heard the same officer's voice when he asked about my well-being. I didn't answer. He asked if I was getting food and being allowed to use the bathroom. I reluctantly started answering when he interrupted and, making a disgusted sound, said, '*Uufff! Tumhare muh se itni badbu aati hai, itni kisi ki gaand se nahi aati. Kahin tatti to nahi khate?*' (Goodness, your mouth is stinking. It is worse than someone's arsehole. Do you eat shit?)

The officers in the room started laughing at me. I felt humiliated. He was supposed to be on my side. I felt betrayed and insulted. In a fit of rage, I retorted, '*Aap kya sabki gaand sungte ho jo aapko pata hai kitni badbu aati hai? Aur khane me main wahi khata hu jo aap log pakate ho . . . toh kya aap log tatti pakate ho?*' (Do you smell everyone's arse that you know what an arsehole smells like? And I eat what you guys give me. So do you guys cook shit?)

This was the second time I had lost my cool. The silence in the room reminded me of what was to follow.

'*Achha! Tujhe humara khana tatti lagta hai? Chal ab khada hoja.*' (Oh! So our food is shit to you. We will show you. Get up.)

They made me stand, and the belts, cane sticks, rods, punches and kicks started pouring in from all directions.

During this ordeal, the officer told me that my parents in India were trying to trace me and that they had been told clearly that the Federal Investigating Agency (FIA) was handling the case.

I turned in the direction of the officer's voice and asked how he knew.

My parents knew where I was. Ammi knew. Thank you, Allah.

The officer explained, '*Tumhare ma–baap ne Pakistan High Commission me enquiry ki thi tumhare baare me. Aur yaha se humne jawab bheja hai ki tumhari interrogation FIA wale kar rahe hain aur tum mahfooz ho.*' (Your parents inquired at the Pakistan High Commission. We sent back the message that the FIA is handling the case and you're safe.)

'*Lekin unko kaise pata chala ki main Pakistan mein hoon?*' (How did they find out that I'm in Pakistan?)

'*Tumhara partner Atta-ur-Rahman ne akhbaar mein sab chhapwa diya tha. Daily Express ke 15 August ke ishtihaar me chhapa hai tumhare baare me. Yahan ke akhbaar se wahan ke akhbaar me gaya aur tumhare parents ko pata chal gaya. Zara socho tumhari ma kitni pareshan hai tumhare liye aur tumko unki koi fikr nahi hai. Agar fikr hoti to jaldi jaldi humein sab sach bata dete aur chale jate. Humein koi shouk nahi hai tumhe yahan rakhne ka. Hum tumhari madad kar rahein hain ki tum jald se jald wapas jao lekin tum humein bas cover stories suna rahe ho jo RAW walo ne sikha kar bheja hai. Is tarah chalta raha to zindagi bhar yahin sadte rahoge.*'

(Your partner Atta-ur-Rahman blurted out everything to the media. The *Daily Express* printed the story in the 15 August issue. The Indian newspapers picked up the news and that's how your parents got to know. Imagine how worried your mother must be, and look at you, you are not worried about her. If you were thinking about her, you would've immediately spoken the truth and left this place. We have no interest in keeping you here. We are only trying to help you so you can leave this place at the earliest. But all you do is repeat the cover stories that RAW has trained you to tell. If this carries on, you are going to rot here all your life.)

The session continued with me sticking to my story. As it went on, I got parched and asked for some water. They asked me to open my mouth. As soon as I felt a liquid being poured into it, my throat started burning and I screamed in pain. It was kerosene. They left me half dead, but as they walked out, something gave me the strength to tell them, 'I am still alive. I have not died yet. I will not give up, sir.'

The FIA had taken over my case, which meant serious business. Now I knew that my parents knew, the Indian government knew and the world knew. I prayed to be heard and to get justice.

17

Despair, Reconciliation and Hope

Time had become inconsequential. Darkness engulfed me but a little light flickered inside. My family knew where I was.

One day, I was blindfolded and taken out of my cell. But we weren't walking towards the interrogation room. My heart started racing with fear and excitement. Was it over?

We turned into a room and my blindfold was removed but I was given strict instruction to keep my eyes closed as I was made to sit on a chair. I heard the sound of a shaving machine. I had been told by the guard that those whose heads were shaved were going to be in there for a longer period of time. My shoulder-length hair was a hopeful sign of my impending release and now they were going to take even that away . . .

I resisted, saying I did not want a haircut. I got such a hard slap that my eyes hurt. They held me down and tonsured my head. That was when my hope of being released died.

I was brought back to my cell. One of the guards asked if I had cleaned my pubic hair. My cynical look was self-explanatory. He said that they didn't allow razors to be given to prisoners and the barber would not shave me down there, so he would give me a hair remover cream used by women.

He brought me a bottle labelled 'White Rose'. There were no instructions so I asked him how to use it. He scooped out some on a piece of paper and gave it to me. He instructed, 'Massage the cream on your armpits and down there, leave it for a while and then wipe it away. The hair will come off.'

I went to a corner of my cell and did as instructed. A sweet rosy smell filled the air. I waited for a bit and then wiped the area with my hand. Soon after, my skin started burning and itching. I rubbed and rubbed till it was on fire. The hair didn't come off but I developed a terrible allergic reaction.

The guard came laughing to my cell and said, '*Mazaa aaya?*' (Did you have fun?)

I couldn't believe the viciousness of the man. I was in such pain. One of the other guards took me to the bathroom to rinse the cream off but it didn't help. I couldn't move, sit, stand, walk or even pray.

Gauging the seriousness of the infection, a paramedic was called in after dinner. He came in, laughing, and asked me to remove my clothes. I was fuming and did not listen to him.

I screamed, '*Tum log kaise Musalman ho ki kisi ke kapde utarwate ho?*' (What kind of Muslims are you that you keep making people strip?) He got angry, threw a small pill at me and walked away. My skin took days to heal.

The Peshawar winter beckoned and I was dreading it. The stark difference in weather from Mumbai to Peshawar wasn't easy to get used to. After begging for some warm cover, we were given used sleeping bags. I looked at mine closely and tried to read what was written on it. It had the Chinese flag and Chinese characters imprinted on it. I thought it must have belonged to the Chinese army.

The sleeping bag was so smelly that I wouldn't have touched it in ordinary circumstances, but in this new life, survival was paramount. I got into it and covered my head as well since it was so cold. The first time, I almost threw up. The smell of urine, sweat, dysentery or even semen filled my nostrils. I had to pull my head out to catch my breath, which exposed me to the bone-chilling cold. But I had to make do with what I had. So, with time, I got used to it.

I started exercising in my cell to keep warm, but would pretend to sleep if the guards came close. Twice, a commander warned me not to exercise. How did he know? I found out some days later, when a few men came for inspection. On their way out, a guard told them, 'Sir, the camera in the last cell is not working.' I overheard this. They were not talking about my cell, but that was when I learnt that all the cells were bugged and they had been watching me all along.

Nobody came to my cell for weeks. Every day, every moment weighed heavily on me. One night, I dreamt of Ammi, Abbu, Khalid and all of us together. We had gone for Hajj. I woke up the next morning thinking it was a positive sign. But the days went by and nothing happened. I only thought of my weeping mother and visualized the moment when my father had come to drop me at the airport the first time I flew to Delhi for Kabul. I remembered seeing him through the glass windows as I entered the airport.

My dreams soon turned into nightmares and I began fearing sleep. For nights on end, I would remain awake, which resulted in hallucinations. I started seeing things, imagining things and talking to people who weren't there. I was losing my mind.

At the end of November 2013, I was taken to the interrogation room once again and made to sit on the floor instead of a chair. Then came the voice of an elderly man.

'*Dekh bachhe, meri baat dhyan se sun. Main nahi jaanta ki ab tak yahan tu ne kya bola hai, tera case kya hai. Mere kaam karne ka tareeka baaki afsar se bilkul alag hai. Mujhe ye bataya gaya hai ke tu humare saath cooperate nahi kar raha is liye ab tera case mujhe diya gaya hai. Maine tere jaise bohoton ko theek kiya hai. Tere liye behtar yahi hoga ki tu mujhe sab sach sach bata de, warna tere liye bohot mushkil ho jayegi.*'

(Look, kid, listen to me carefully. I don't know what you've said here till now, or what your case is. I work differently from the other officers. I have been given your case since I have been told you're uncooperative. I've fixed many like you. It'll be good for you if you tell me the truth, else you'll be in a lot of trouble.)

I had no idea what this was all about, so I narrated my entire story to him. No sooner had I finished than I felt the thundering weight of his hand on my cheek, slapping me senseless.

'*Bhenchod, mujhe cover story nahi sunni teri. Samajh aaya tujhe? Sach bata warna yahin marega tu. Bol sach bataega ya aise hi bakwas karta rahega?*' (Fucker, I don't want to listen to your cover story. Do you understand? Tell me the truth or you'll die here. Will you tell me the truth or continue with your bullshit?)

I folded my hands and, with a shiver, told him, *'Sir, mere paas batane ke liye aur kuch nahi hai.'* (Sir, I don't have anything more to tell.)

Another slap and another and another . . . Then the old man left, snarling, *'Ab tujhe mujhse koi nahi bacha sakta.'* (No one can save you from me now.)

They all seemed possessed. While the assaults hurt and always shook me up, over the months, I stopped fearing their threats. I thought to myself, *'Mera Allah mujhe bachaega.'* (My God will save me.)

A few days after this, I was taken back to the interrogation room, where the old officer asked me to repeat my story in detail.

The detailing and cross-questioning was so intense that it took almost a month and involved physical and verbal abuse.

On a cold winter night in December, I was brought into the interrogation room, shivering in my orange cotton uniform, blindfolded. I could hear the voices of three officers in front of me.

One of the officers said, *'Janab, mujhe to badi garmi lag rahi hai aur shayad ise bhi.'* (Sir, I'm feeling quite hot and I think he is too.)

'Koi baat nahi, ye humara mahman hai, iske liye pankha aur AC dono chala do. Aaj iski achhi khatir karni hai jo ye zindagi bhar yaad rakhega.' (Don't worry. He's our guest; turn on the ceiling fan and the air conditioner. Today we will take such good care of him that he'll remember it for life.)

The fan and air conditioner were switched on. As if that wasn't enough, ice-cold water was splashed on me. I felt like I had been stuffed into a chiller. I could feel my brain freeze. My body hurt from the cold, my muscles were giving up, and I was losing sensation in my body.

After a while, I couldn't breathe. I fell to the ground. I was yanked up by the arms and tied to chains hanging from the ceiling. I had no strength left. They poured more water on me because I was passing out.

My lips froze. I couldn't answer their questions. They beat me for not speaking. My chest started hurting as though I was having a heart attack. But the questions about my 'mission' continued.

'Hamid, ab bhi time hai, sab sach sach bata de warna aaj tere jism me itni sui chubo denge ke tu shayad zinda na bache. Agar zinda ghar jana chahta hai toh cover story mat suna aur jaldi se sach bata de. India wale to tujhe aise hi marne chhor denge. Agar India ke kisi major ya general ne tujhse kaha hai ke wo tujhe bacha lenge to tujhse jhooth kaha hai. Tujhe koi nahi bacha sakta.' (Hamid, there's still time, tell me the truth or I'll pierce your body with so many needles, you won't survive. If you want to go home alive, drop your cover story and tell the truth. The Indians have left you to die. If any major or general told you they would save you, they lied. No one can save you.)

'Mujhe jo batana tha, bata chuka hu.' (I've said whatever I had to.)

They were just not ready to believe me. The air conditioner and fan were switched off and I was asked to lie down. The chains were removed and then the ones on the side walls were pulled to cuff my wrists again. I was lying on my back and could sense my body getting warm. They had placed heaters around me and I began to thaw, so it felt good initially. But soon after, the temperature rose and I was literally burning. I started shouting and begged them to stop. My skin felt like a thousand needles were piercing it. I screamed so loud that one of the officers muzzled my mouth with his foot. His boot hit my lip so hard that the skin tore. I could taste blood and feel it swell up.

'What have I done now?' I cried out.

One of the officers replied, 'Well, you have lied to us. Your statements don't match the facts unearthed by us.'

I kept screaming because of the heat and told them that I hadn't lied.

I suddenly felt a hand on my face, rubbing something on it. A man said, *'Ab dekhta hu kaise nahi batayega.'* (Now I'll see how you can hide the truth.)

All hell broke loose. He had put chilli powder on my bruises and wounded lip, making me feel like I was on fire. I couldn't think. I started cursing them till I passed out.

When I gained consciousness, I found myself hanging from the ceiling. The elderly officer pulled my hair to ask me something again, only this time it was a new question. He read out a phone number and asked if I recognized it. I told them that I had only called Atta-ur-Rahman, Zabiullah and Abdullah from my Pakistani number.

I was whacked and told to stop lying. I was confused. Were they trying to set me up with some concocted evidence? I said I didn't know what they were talking about.

Another round of rods and sticks ensued.

And then more questions: 'Why did Atta-ur-Rahman help you, what was his motive?'

I said I didn't know. I only knew that he was helping me on humanitarian grounds. Some of them laughed at my answer.

The officer asked his subordinates to take me away. One of them said, 'Apni nahi to apne ma–baap ki jaan ki soch.' (If not yourself, think about the lives of your parents.)

I was taken back to my cell. I didn't know when I passed out. Around midnight, I woke up. I was burning, as if I was in a furnace. I slid out of the sleeping bag and lay on the cold floor. A while later, a guard came and asked me what I was doing out in the cold. 'Do you have a death wish? Get inside the bag,' he screamed.

I didn't turn, and just said, 'No, I am feeling hot.'

The guard reported the matter to the commander, who came to the cell and asked me to come to the iron bars. He held my wrist and placed the back of his hand on my forehead to check if I was running a fever. I was burning up. The dispenser was called in.

He checked me and said, 'He has a slight fever. Not more than 98 degree Fahrenheit. Give him boiled eggs to eat and a double dose of Ponstan tablets.'

I looked at him and wondered if anybody here had even a grain of humanity in them. How could they be so callous?

The next day, the doctor was called in since I showed no improvement. The dispenser immediately admitted that I was seriously ill. He said, 'Kal raat ise bohot tez bukhar tha. Fir maine do ande diye, to ye theek ho gaya.' (He had a high fever last night. I gave him two eggs and then he felt better.)

I started laughing and repeated what he had said, 'Inhone kal ande diye.' (He laid eggs yesterday.)

Everybody in the room had a hearty laugh. It was the first time I had laughed in a long time.

My health kept deteriorating. I was instructed to sleep on the side and not flat on my back. I gathered they wanted to be sure that I was alive. One day, the dispenser came to collect my blood samples and took me for an X-ray. I was told it was a routine check-up.

I was in bad shape. There were traces of blood in my mucus every time I sneezed. I was given a break from the torture, and that was a relief. But the hiatus was short-lived.

A week later, after dinner, I was taken to the interrogation room again, but it was empty. Late that night, I heard the voice of the same officer who had interrogated me the first time I was brought to the Peshawar underground facility.

He was a humble soul and asked me about my health. I told him that he could see what they had done to me despite me telling them the truth.

To my disbelief, he said, '*Tum bilkul theek ja rahe ho. Tumhara bayan bilkul sahi ja raha hai, koi galati nahi mil rahi hai isme. Bas jo bol rahe ho wahi bolte raho aur kisi aur ki baat par koi tawajjah mat do. Sabka apna apna poochne ka tareeka hota hai.*'

(You're going well. Your statements are going fine, there are no mistakes. Just keep saying whatever you are saying and don't bother about anything else. Everybody has their own way of asking.)

He asked me to rest. I thanked him profusely. I couldn't sleep the entire night out of the satisfaction of knowing something about my case. I was on the right track. I smiled.

The next morning, a fleet of officers entered and the session began. They badgered me with questions for hours. I was kept hungry and thirsty.

They made me lie down on the floor and put drops of water on my face. This continued to a point that I got irritated and asked them to stop. After a while, each drop felt like a sledgehammer.

The questions, abuse and violence continued. I was tossed around like a football. One of the officers used a small metal rod to hit me on my face, head and knuckles. They sounded like bloodthirsty hounds.

I was made to sit on a chair. A weight was bound to my head and my body was strapped to the chair. I thought to myself and prayed, 'Please, not the electric chair.' Even as I had the thought, I heard a button being tapped, and my body convulsed as electricity shot through it.

I thought I would die. I could smell burnt hair; my tongue and mouth felt dry. I couldn't speak.

One of them said, 'Now he will tell the truth.'

'Water . . . water,' I kept saying, and felt a few drops on my lips. That was all.

The whole month of January, till mid-February 2014, went by in this torture. One of the guards told me that when someone was taken to the interrogation room blindfolded, the officers took pictures of the prisoners in their long hair and beards and sent them to headquarters, claiming they had caught a terrorist. It was the usual practice.

I was told that a senior officer was coming and would be taking over my case. My beard and moustache were shaved off but this time my hair was left alone.

Soon after, I was taken to a room which was unusually dark. My blindfold was removed. My eyes couldn't adjust to the darkness even after some time. I suppose not wearing my spectacles for so long had taken a toll on my eyesight.

I could barely see the officer sitting in the room. Without introducing himself, he informed me that he would be responsible for the judgement of this case. I told him about the torture and the abuse I had suffered despite being honest. He said there was a lot more they had to find out. He also added that he would look into my concerns. It was a cold night, and he didn't talk much. He offered me tea and left soon after.

He returned after two days with a bunch of papers. Unlike all the previous officers, his questions didn't start from scratch, but were more specific. He knew the case.

He asked, 'How did you cross the border amid such tight security?'

'Tight security? Where? Sir, I was allowed to enter without a single check on the Dosti bus service. In fact, if you allege that I paid my way through then you should be looking at your guards deployed at the border rather than questioning me. Also, I actually did not pay anybody to enter. I wish I had been checked and not permitted to enter in the first place,' I replied.

'Why were you issued a gratis Afghan visa?' he asked.

Not again, I thought, but I told him, 'I received that type of visa because Afghanistan uses the stamp to convert a visit visa into a business visa. I am not making this up. One of your officers shared this information with me last year during an interrogation.'

He was shocked to know that his own authorities had closed such a big door on them by telling me the truth. Then he paused and stared at me intently. He turned to his papers again and, without looking up, he asked, 'Who other than Atta-ur-Rahman did you call on 11 November 2012 while you were travelling from Peshawar to Rawalpindi?'

I thought of the day and said, 'I only called one number, sir, and that was Atta-ur-Rahman's. First, your officers beat the life out of me, telling me that I had called someone on 13 November, and now you are saying something about 11 November.'

'Did you or did you not?' he asked again, insisting that I ignore past questions.

I thought hard and finally remembered the boy who had borrowed my phone to say he was on his way. Sunny! That was right. That was his name.

'Yes, yes, there was a boy sitting beside me on the bus who made a call to his mother.' I narrated the entire episode.

I saw the disbelief in the officer's eyes. This was followed by many rounds of questions and cross-questioning.

I finally asked him, 'Sir, what is it about the number that makes my case so suspicious? I merely helped a young boy connect with his family. That cannot be such a big crime.'

He then revealed the mystery. 'The number that was dialled from your Pakistani SIM was of someone on Pakistan's most-wanted list. It is a highly suspicious number as all the call records reflect international calls, of which the maximum are from India. We haven't been able to trace the man yet.'

I told him confidently that if he had tracked the number down then there must be a recording of the conversation. 'Sir, please check the voice in the conversation. If it is me, I will accept any punishment you want me to. You can hang me,' I said.

I saw that he somewhat agreed with my argument but did not want to show it. I begged him to believe me, saying that I was just an Indian who had crossed over to help a friend in Pakistan.

His expression changed suddenly. He leaned forward and narrated a personal experience he had had with an Indian that had left him bitter.

He said, *'Hamid, kuch saal pehle main Pakistan air force ke liye kaam karta tha lekin kisi medical reason ki wajah se mujhe ground kar diya gaya. Fir mujhe UN ne chuna tha Africa me peace mission ke liye. Waha alag alag mulkon ki army ek saath mil kar kaam karti thi. Humara jo commanding officer tha wo tumhari army ka ek brigadier tha. Jante ho usne mujhe kya kaha tha? Usne sab ke samne mujhe kaha tha, "Major, I hate you." Aur pata hai maine kya jawab diya use? Maine kaha, "I hate all of you."'* (Hamid, a few years ago I was in the Pakistan air force but was grounded due to medical reasons. Then I was selected for a UN peace mission in Africa. Armies from different countries were working together. Our commanding officer was a brigadier from the Indian army. Do you know what he said to me? In front of everybody, he said, "Major, I hate you." And do you know what I told him? I said, "I hate all of you."'

He continued, 'I hate all Indians. Now your case is with me. You say you are innocent, but the CDR [call detail record] shows that the call to the mysterious number was made from your SIM. So, technically, you had made the call as there is no proof that your phone was borrowed or used by a co-passenger. And that is evidence enough to prove you are guilty of espionage.'

He got up, saying he was not convinced. I told him that my Allah and I knew that I was telling the truth.

A few days later, the torturers led by the elderly officer returned. The violence started. But this time, they used emotional blackmail to coerce me into accepting their version of the story. They started talking about Ammi and Abbu.

They told me that they had been to my house to cross-check and verify things. And that was where they had found my family in a pitiable condition. They even described my father's appearance accurately. I started thinking that they had actually visited my home in Mumbai.

But then they contradicted themselves, saying they had also discovered that my family had contacts within the government and the military. I wondered what they meant. I tried to convince them that we were a simple middle-class family from Mumbai. My parents must have been trying to get the Indian government to help and that was being misinterpreted by the authorities.

They said they had verified my home and seen the family photo of the four of us on the wall. That was where I caught their lie. We did not have any photo frames on our walls. I didn't understand the purpose of these lies.

~

My body was failing me. I started developing a lot of problems; my respiratory tract was dry and I bled from my nose and mouth. I was extremely dehydrated since I had only been having very little water once a day, from the tap in the toilet, ever since December 2012. I couldn't bear to drink from the water bottle in the room since that would mean urinating frequently, and the only way to do that was to pee into the disgusting bottles that contained the urine of previous prisoners.

Then my bottom started hurting. I didn't know why. I pulled out some cotton from my sleeping bag, and hid it under my armpit while being taken to the loo. I used the cotton to wipe my anus to see what was wrong. There was blood. I feared I was dying a slow death.

A few days later, I started throwing up white liquid on an empty stomach. My mouth felt sour and pungent. The dispenser was called in. He checked me and asked me a few questions and then administered some medicine. The guards were told that I was critically dehydrated.

One guard asked me why I was not drinking water. I explained why. He got me a clean bottle of water to drink, and also promised he would allow me to empty the urine bottles into the toilet on a regular basis.

I took a sip and then gulped down the rest of the water in the bottle. This was the first time in fifteen months that I had as much water as I wanted. I could feel it flowing through my veins, trickling down my throat to my stomach and my intestines. My skin felt alive. My entire body had been desperate for water. My nostrils became wet and I could breathe with ease. Slowly and steadily, my body started recovering.

But the guards got tired of taking me to the washroom, and they stopped once they saw I had recovered.

~

Staying in Pakistan, how could one escape the cricket rivalry between the two countries? Around March 2014, one of the guards started excitedly talking about the T20 World Cup. Soon after, one night, I heard an unusual number of gunshots, which was common in Peshawar but not to this extent. When I asked the guard what was happening, he said that Pakistan had won its first match and India had lost its.

The next time I got to know there was a match, I included cricket in my daily prayers. I prayed for India to win. That night there was no gunfire. I figured Pakistan had lost.

The next morning, when the guard came, I asked him for the results. He answered with a sad face, '*Hum haar gaye. India jeet gayi.*' (We lost, India won.) I raised my glass of water to India's win.

A few days later, he told me of a match between India and Pakistan. I was fearful as well as excited. India emerged the winner of that match, and the guards and commanders stopped talking to me. The annoyance reflected in extreme torture during interrogation.

During the beating sessions, one of them said, '*Virat Kohli itne sixer kyun maarta hai? Tum log cricket bhi humare khilaf khelte ho. Tum to pakke dushman ho.*' (Why does Virat Kohli hit so many sixes? You guys even play cricket against us. You are our true enemies.) I was writhing in pain and all I could think of was their juvenility.

Once, when I was being taken to the room, blindfolded, I recognized the elderly officer's ruthless voice from a distance. But on this day, he was rather nice to me. He said that I should repeat what he was saying. Through the gap in the blindfold at the bridge of my nose, I could see he had placed a device on the table. He said, 'Now, when I ask you to speak, say that you have come to Pakistan on a mission. That you deliberately broke the law of the land and that your intentions were not right.'

He said I should start. I heard a click. He was trying to record my statement through wrongful means. So I said, 'Like you asked me to say, sir . . .'

He interrupted and asked me not to say that but just the latter part. I argued and asked how I could do that when it wasn't true. He tried a few times but got frustrated and said that I was trying to be smart by half.

'*Sir, aap hi bolte ho ke sach bolo, main toh wahi bol raha hoon jo sach hai. Yah sari baaten aap hi ne mujhe kahi hai varna main ise kabul nahi karta.*' (Sir, you told me to state the truth, I am only doing that. All this is what you told me to say or I would never have accepted this.)

That session ended in brutal torture, punctuated by slaps and punches. This routine continued till the end of June.

On 26 June 2014, I was taken to the interrogation room, where I heard two new voices. The men posed as being very humble and understanding. They sat with me for a while, bitching about their own officers and colleagues.

After some time, the same senior officer entered the room. Only this time, he greeted me with congratulations. He said that my case had been cleared and my innocence had been proved.

'Really, sir?' I exclaimed, tears rolling down my cheeks. 'When do I go home?'

He replied with a smile, 'Hamid, there are procedures and formalities which need to be fulfilled. So don't rush. You will go home very soon. Your case is nothing for us. You are convicted only for crossing the border illegally without proper travelling documents. I testified that you are clean and innocent. Three or four months or a maximum of six months will be your punishment and then you will be released.'

While my heart fluttered with joy, six more months felt like a lifetime. I asked, 'Sir, I have already spent eighteen months here. Will this not be counted?'

He explained that a remission of the sentence was not in his hands and he left the room, saying, '*Jaise atharah maheene guzre hain, vaise hi baaki time bhi guzar jayega. Bus ab sabr karo.*' (Like these eighteen months, the other six shall also pass. Be patient.)

My happiness knew no bounds. Could this finally be over?

18

Hamid Found, Zeenat Goes Missing

The beginning of 2014 was particularly difficult for the Ansari family in Mumbai. On the work front, both Nehal and Fauzia were facing problems, and the financial constraints and innumerable travels to Delhi were taking a toll.

Their biggest challenge was proving that Hamid was in Pakistan. India's note verbales got no response, and Pakistan continuously denied his presence in the country.

Meanwhile, Zeenat had already written letters to the chief justice of Pakistan and the Supreme Court of Pakistan's human rights cell, the Commission of Inquiry on Enforced Disappearances (CoIoED). She travelled to Islamabad to ensure that the case was heard. Javed Iqbal was then the CoIoED chief (in 2019, he was appointed the National Accountability Bureau Chief). He looked into the case and ordered an inquiry under a JIT (joint investigation team).

In May 2014, the Indian government at the centre changed. The Bharatiya Janata Party (BJP) came into power with a thumping majority. BJP veteran Sushma Swaraj was appointed the external affairs minister. Fauzia went to her husband and said, 'Sushma Swaraj is the new minister. Let's go to Delhi and plead our case with her. She is a woman. She will understand my problem. Please book us on a train to Delhi.'

Nehal agreed that they should take the case and raise it with the new government. Fauzia was in awe of Sushma Swaraj. She thought of her as an inspiration. They sought an appointment with her and waited for a response.

By this time, Fauzia had become familiar with operating Facebook. She made friends on the social media platform to see if anyone could be of help. One day, while she was going through her Facebook page, she learnt that there was a connect between the people of Kashmir and Pakistan-occupied Kashmir, even if limited. She thought of travelling to Srinagar to see if there was any way of getting a contact who could help find her son.

She knew there would be resistance from Nehal. They didn't have the resources to shoot in the dark. But she was determined.

At dinner that night, she broached the topic with him and Khalid. They looked at each other, and then Nehal approached an on-the-edge Fauzia very carefully, 'What will we get by travelling to Srinagar, Fauzia? We don't know anyone there and it will just cost us a lot. Have you established any clear contacts yet?'

Fauzia had tears in her eyes. 'Do you know how long it has been? I don't even know if my son is alive. What do you expect me to do? Just sit and do nothing?'

Khalid saw the situation going out of control and intervened, 'Ammi, you know what Abbu is talking about. You should go anywhere there is a possibility to establish contact or know about Hamid, but just picking up your bags and going to Srinagar makes no sense.'

Fauzia was adamant. She told Nehal that she would spend whatever she had to, go to any place in the world where she could get even a scrap of information about her son. She went to bed without eating.

The men knew that there was no option but to book the tickets. Khalid booked his parents on the Air India flight from Delhi to Srinagar. One of the passengers sitting with them was a Kashmiri. Nehal inquired about affordable lodging and places to eat.

Fauzia, in the window seat, looked out of the window at the valley—snow-peaked mountains, blue skies . . . and Hamid in her thoughts. She struck up a conversation with her co-passenger. 'How does one cross the border to visit Pakistan?' Fauzia asked abruptly.

The middle-aged man was shocked at her question. This was not a question tourists asked. So he hesitantly said, 'Why do you ask?'

By this time, Fauzia had nothing to lose, so she plainly said, 'My son is missing in Pakistan and I am struggling to get him back.'

The man sympathized with her. Fauzia asked him if he could assist them with a contact in Srinagar who could be of any help.

He thought about it, then pulled out his mobile and turned it on. After looking through and typing into his phone for a while, he said, 'Here is a number for a well-known newspaper called *Greater Kashmir*. Just go to their office and meet the editor-in-chief. He might be able to help you. And please don't share your story with anyone you meet. It is a sensitive matter.'

Nehal and Fauzia reached Srinagar around evening. It was raining quite heavily when they stepped out of the airport and it was very chilly. Fauzia and Nehal covered themselves well and looked for a taxi to take them to their lodge, a tiny place in downtown Srinagar.

The next morning, they reached the *Greater Kashmir* office and asked to see the editor-in-chief, Fayaz Ahmad Kaloo. They were made to wait for a while and then taken to his room. Luckily, he was in office at the time. Fauzia started narrating the story to him. As she went on, Kaloo called in one of the journalists, Arif Shafi Wani, to listen to them and write the story. He said there wasn't much they could do to get details about Hamid from across the border but the story would certainly make front-page news the next day.

Fauzia and Nehal returned to Mumbai the next day. They carried a copy of *Greater Kashmir* with a detailed story on the front page headlined 'Another Crossborder Love Story Has a Tragic End'.

~

On 19 May, the first JIT meeting was held in Islamabad, which was presided over by Justice Iqbal himself. Zeenat travelled from Lahore to Islamabad to attend it. Since it was the first meeting, she didn't intervene much but figured out that the authorities were trying to get the JIT case dismissed. She soon figured out what was happening.

At the first meeting itself, the officials were trying to make the case that it was the wrong forum for such a matter. This was a pattern that repeated itself as Zeenat religiously attended every hearing in Islamabad, Kohat, Karak and Peshawar. All her initial efforts were in vain since she would only hear Pakistani authorities denying any knowledge of having Hamid Ansari in their custody.

One of the officials got up during the first meeting and said, 'Sir, we have no information on any such individual in our custody. And even if we did, it cannot be tried under "enforced disappearances" since the said individual, according to claims made, entered Pakistan of his own volition.'

Zeenat pleaded, 'Sir, even if he entered of his own volition and even though he did not have legal travel documents, his family in India and the embassy in Islamabad have to be informed. If not this, what is a case of enforced disappearance?'

Justice Iqbal agreed with the petitioner and said that if there was an Indian national in the Pakistani authorities' custody then they would have to make it public, hence the forming of this JIT stood justified.

Zeenat stepped out of the building and thought that this needed thorough investigation on her part. She called up Atta-ur-Rahman to dig a little more and get some finer points for the next hearing. She also spoke to Fauzia and briefed her. She was as disappointed in the proceedings, as heartbroken as Fauzia was.

The next meeting was scheduled for 4 June. Zeenat went prepared this time. The questioning began again on the issue of Indian national Hamid Ansari ever having entered Pakistan. The officers representing the Pakistani establishment again denied any knowledge of his presence.

Zeenat stood up to speak, being careful with the information she divulged. She asked, 'Wasn't there an arrest made on 14 November from outside KDA Hospital in Kohat? Who was the individual nabbed there? Please share the identity.'

The room fell silent. The officials understood that this journalist knew more than the JIT was supposed to.

One of the officers said they did not have details and would have to check the records at the Kohat police station. So the stumped administration asked for another date for the hearing.

But since the officers sought more time, it was given to them. The third meeting was scheduled for 27 June.

Later, the men representing the establishment asked her how she knew these details. She knew she had to stand her ground and firmly answered that she had her sources and that justice should prevail, even if a man from another country was caught in theirs. 'Everyone has the right to be heard in court and to fight a fair case. If this Indian boy committed a crime then the court will punish him, but to not acknowledge his presence in Pakistan is wrong on so many levels,' she told the officer.

Both parties were never going to be friends—they were standing on two polar ends. The meeting concluded and she left for home. She had a very bad feeling.

~

On 12 June 2014, a Thursday, Fauzia and Nehal decided to go to Delhi and try their luck at meeting Sushma Swaraj without an appointment. When they arrived at New Delhi Railway Station, Fauzia told Nehal they should just go to her residence straightaway. Around 8.30 a.m., the couple reached 8 Safdarjung Road, but to their dismay, they were stopped at the gate.

Fauzia requested the security guards at the gate to let them go in. 'Beta, we are an old couple and have come here to meet Madam all the way from Mumbai. My son is missing and she is our only hope.'

The guard let them in.

Fauzia saw Swaraj meeting people who were there to welcome her as the new foreign minister. Fauzia felt bad that they had come empty-handed. But she ran to the minister with folded hands and tears in her eyes, '*Sab mithai ke saath aaye hain, main aap ke paas aansu ke saath aayi hu.*' (Everybody has come here with sweets, I have come with tears.)

'My son is in trouble. He is stuck in Pakistan,' Fauzia said. Swaraj stopped in her tracks. She turned to Fauzia and put her own hands around her folded ones.

'*Kya hua, mujhe pehle batao? Rona nahi hai. Main hu na,*' she said. (Tell me what the matter is. Don't cry, I am here for you.)

'I have come with a lot of hope to you. My son is in Pakistani custody and they are not even acknowledging his presence there. Please help this mother. I've been running from pillar to post since December 2012. Please, Madam,' pleaded Fauzia.

Swaraj called one of her staff members and asked them to fix an appointment. 'Come to my office today at 4 p.m. I want to sit with you and understand the case first. I assure you, I will do whatever it takes,' Swaraj assured them and moved on to meet other people. Fauzia felt like a weight had been lifted from her shoulders. Finally, a government that was willing to listen. '*Meri Jhansi ki Rani.*' (My warrior queen.) That was what she called Swaraj while Nehal smiled. He was relieved to see Fauzia breathe easy.

Around 9 a.m. Fauzia told her husband that while they waited for the appointment, they should get all the documents together. They took printouts of the important conversations, and also wrote a letter. They submitted these papers at the reception in South Block.

At 3.30 p.m., Fauzia and Nehal went to meet Swaraj, who gave them a patient hearing. She was as surprised as most others to hear that Hamid had crossed over for a girl. But, to Fauzia's surprise, she said, 'I read the entire file you had submitted in the morning. From what I can gather, Hamid was trapped and misled by his friends. As a mother, I can understand what you are going through. I am sure we will bring him back.'

The words 'bring him back' were like music to Fauzia's ears. Nobody in the Indian government had shown such confidence in the fact that Hamid would return. She was in tears.

Swaraj said, 'Don't cry. You have a lot of fight left in you. First fight the good fight and leave the tears for the day you see your son.' She assured them that they would not leave any stone unturned in trying to bring Hamid back.

A fortnight later, Fauzia received the first call from a division in the MEA that she would be associated with till the moment Hamid returned—the PAI (Pakistan–Afghanistan–Iran) desk. The officers handling Pakistan got in touch with her, and Soumya C., deputy secretary, PAI desk, was introduced to her as the point person.

Fauzia was also in constant touch with Fozia Manzoor, counsellor (political) at the Pakistan High Commission. She and Nehal kept writing to her and requesting for a visa to travel to Pakistan.

The pressure was increasing on the Pakistani authorities after news of Hamid started gaining traction and making it to the front pages of all national dailies. Similarly, there was immense pressure from the Indian media and government as well.

~

It was 27 June 2014, and Zeenat was preparing herself for the next JIT hearing. Since the meeting was in Peshawar, she had to travel there from Lahore. Her mother blessed her before she left.

This was a crucial day for the Ansari family. Fauzia called up early in the morning to speak to Zeenat. 'Zeenat Beta, I hope you are fine and all set for the JIT meeting. I just called to wish you the best. May Allah's blessings be upon you,' Fauzia said.

Zeenat entered the office where the meeting was to be held. She was a little nervous because she was going to divulge more information. She thought of the cause and the purpose of her fight and put up a brave front.

The hearing commenced with the presiding officer asking if the details of the individual who was caught in Kohat had been ascertained. The officers representing the forces said that no Indian national was picked up that night.

Zeenat protested that the records of the arrest be provided for the JIT to see. The anger of the officials was quite evident. They insisted that they did not have any Indian and if she had proof then she should come out with it.

Zeenat gave details of how Hamid had entered Pakistan, whom he had met and how he had travelled to Kohat from Karak. She also said that if Hamid's parents were worried thinking he was in Pakistan, and if she was representing them, why hadn't an FIR been lodged yet? That was the least the authorities should be doing.

One of the officials at the JIT warned her, 'Madam Zeenat, I don't think you know what you are doing. This is a very serious case of espionage. Don't meddle in national security matters.'

She was shocked to hear him say that. But she stood her ground because she knew that Hamid was not a spy.

After the fourth hearing on 4 August 2014, an FIR (No. 206) was lodged at the Kohat police station. Zeenat felt like this was a win, because even though there had been no official acceptance of Hamid's presence in Pakistan, there was some forward movement in the case.

Around the same time, Zeenat set up a Facebook page called 'Hamid Nehal Ansari' and started updating all big and small developments regarding the case on it.

In September 2014, Zeenat called and said, 'Fauzia ji, salaam, the JIT is still hitting a dead end. This way, we will never succeed. I think we should consider paying Atta-ur-Rahman and getting some more information before it's too late and he learns of the proceedings that are underway here.'

Fauzia asked Zeenat if that would be risky. 'Zeenat, please be careful. Don't get into trouble yourself. You are our only hope and like a daughter to me,' said Fauzia, who had increasingly become fond of Zeenat and thanked God every day for bringing her into their lives.

They finally decided that Zeenat would go and meet Atta once again and pay him. She called him up and arranged for a meeting, and then informed Fauzia that she was going to Karak. Fauzia was a nervous wreck that entire day since Zeenat's number was unreachable.

~

It was not as cold as one would have expected on 19 September 2014. Zeenat waited with her mother at the bus stop for her trip to Karak. Her mother blessed her and wished her a safe journey. 'Be careful, Zeenat. While Fauzia needs you, your family needs you more. May Allah bring you success.'

Zeenat reached Karak and went to Atta-ur-Rahman's residence. She paid him and he told her exactly what had happened. He mentioned Abdullah Khattak, who was to receive Hamid in Kohat and help him rescue Fiza.

With all honesty, he said that he didn't know why and how Hamid was picked up but that he had informed Fiza's father and that is who must have informed the authorities. 'It could be Abdullah too, you never know,' he added.

Before she left, Atta gave her Abdullah's number, but asked her not to tell anybody that it was him who had revealed the name.

Zeenat did not want to waste time. Since Kohat was an hour away from Karak, she immediately took the bus there and called up Abdullah on the way, introducing herself as a journalist from Lahore, saying she wanted to meet regarding a story. He readily agreed.

They met at the bus stop and went to a dhaba nearby. Zeenat told him why she was there—to track a story about an Indian called Hamid Ansari, who had been written about in the papers. He looked worried and asked her how she knew that he was Hamid's contact. She told him that she was following up with the family back home and they had a few numbers.

'How did they get my number?' He knew very well that he could be in trouble.

Zeenat figured out that he was nervous. 'Abdullah, consider me a friend. You did what was right so you have nothing to worry about. I am just trying to join the dots. How did he manage to enter our country and what was he up to?' she said.

Her words calmed his nerves and he told her, 'Imagine, he thought he could just enter our country and take one of our girls from here. I made sure that didn't happen.'

'Good. But was she not going to be a victim of wani?' she asked while she took out her notepad.

He nodded, embarrassed, but went on, 'Zeenat, whatever may be the case, he shouldn't have thought that he would get away with it. I did what I thought was right.'

'Absolutely, but now I need to know how he planned it and where all he went. I have to recreate the entire story. I will pay you for your help. This is a big story for me and I want to get it right,' she said.

He told her about Hamid's plans, how he had connected with him, and of Palwasha Hotel, where he was taken. He also narrated the entire episode of his arrest. Zeenat listened intently and took notes, occasionally interrupting him for details such as the address of the hotel, time of arrival, last call, etc.

She was also aware of the fact that she needed to travel all the way back to Peshawar. She could not spend the night in Kohat. She thanked Abdullah and gave him some money, and also told him that she would need to call him for her article and would appreciate his cooperation. He was happy to help. He told her that she should just never tell anybody about him.

They parted ways. It was evening. But Zeenat knew what she had to do next. She went straight to Palwasha Hotel and asked the boy at the reception to call the manager. A while later, a young man stepped out.

Zeenat asked them about the Indian who had come there on 14 November 2012. The manager looked shocked but feigned ignorance. Zeenat gave him a knowing look and flashed her press card. 'I am here to do a story and I know everything. So please share whatever information you have. Where is your guest register? Show it to me.'

He hesitated and said, 'We are a small establishment and don't want any trouble. Please don't put this in the paper. We don't want people thinking we allow shady people or terrorists in. We don't know who or where the man was from but we did have him here around that time. He was picked up by the agencies, I think.'

She understood their concern and assured them that she was only trying to find out some details. He pulled out the register and showed it to her.

She went to the entries for 2012 and sifted through them to reach November. When she reached 13 November, she saw that the next page was for 15 November. She looked carefully and ran her fingers through the binding of the register to see the remnants of a torn page.

She looked up at the manager questioningly. He understood what she was asking and said, 'Well, the cops had come to inquire about the man and a few days later some other officers came and tore the page out. They instructed me not to breathe a word to anyone.'

By now, the man was sweating. But Zeenat was unmoved and undeterred. She asked him if he had kept the page with him or the cops had taken it away.

The man was a hotel manager in a small town. He was straight in his ways and didn't mince words. He looked down and then turned around and left, before returning with a sheet of paper in his hand.

'I didn't throw it away since I didn't trust the men. In case someone else came asking for him from the agency then I would have had no proof, that is why I saved this paper. Here it is.' He gave it to Zeenat.

She saw the paper and noticed the name of one guest registered as Hamza. The manager pointed at it and said that that was the guy. Zeenat felt that Hamid obviously must not have revealed his real name. 'Who was here with him?' she asked.

The younger boy who stood beside the manager said, 'I was here that night. There was a local man called Abdullah who had booked the room in advance. This other man looked like an outsider. A city boy from Lahore or Karachi. He checked in and left immediately after. He never returned. Only cops came in late that night to collect his belongings.'

'Where was he taken?'

The manager replied, 'Kohat police station.'

She asked if she could keep the page. The manager refused, since he needed it as evidence. So she took pictures of everything: the register, the area where the tear was visible, the torn page—placing the page on the register to show where it belonged—the manager, the staff, the reception and the hotel. She thought she would require all this as evidence at the JIT hearing.

She went to the Kohat police station and told the officer in charge the purpose of her visit. They took her to the station house officer (SHO), Faiz Ullah Khan.

She sat at his desk and narrated the entire story. This was an official meeting so she told him everything. She told Khan that Hamid's family was really worried and wanted help. She pleaded with the officer that all they wanted was proof he was in Pakistan. Nobody was telling them anything. The family had the right to know.

SHO Faiz Ullah called in his colleagues who had been with him on the night in question. They all sat around the table; the jawans stood. He confirmed to her that there was such an individual, an Indian boy, who had been brought in. 'He looked completely lost but this was a very sensitive case. The IB inspector, Kohat, had brought him in with some other officials. They sat here waiting for other officials from the Inter-services Intelligence [ISI] and Military Intelligence [MI] to come,' he said before Zeenat interrupted.

'Who? Who brought him in?' she asked.

'Naeem Ullah Khan was the IB officer in charge of this district. He has been transferred to some other district. I presume they had a tip-off since they were at the right place at the right time. Anyhow, he was in our custody and we were answerable but they shared nothing with us.'

Zeenat briefed him on the orders of the JIT. She then asked, 'Faiz Ullah Sahab, has an FIR been lodged yet?'

He replied in the negative.

With all the proof and written statements given by the SHO and the other eyewitnesses. Zeenat went to the superintendent of police, investigation wing, in Kohat and ensured that an FIR was lodged.

It read:

FIR number 206 that was lodged on 19 September 2014 under Section 365 of Pakistan Penal Code (PPC) at police station KDA, Kohat.

According to the statement of eyewitnesses SHO Faiz Ullah and Muharrir Fareed Khan, etc. of Police Station KDA, Kohat, the said suspect was taken away from local police by ISI and MI personnel and Inspector IB Kohat Naeem Ullah, for interrogation, but till date the missing Hamid Nehal Ansari has not been returned by these agencies' representatives and IB inspector Naeem Ullah is concealing the facts due to unknown reasons.

It is therefore requested that the concerned authorities of MI and ISI may be directed to return the said person for further legal action into the case.

The entire document was irrefutable proof of Hamid Nehal Ansari's presence in Pakistan. She asked the inspector if she could get a copy. He agreed.

This was a huge breakthrough and Zeenat needed this for the JIT to move forward and order action. To strengthen her case further, she asked Inspector Faiz Ullah if she could get written statements. Surprisingly, he agreed to give it to her in writing that they had indeed caught an Indian on their territory, which was on the record, and handed him over to the intelligence wing of the Pakistan army.

She also got the written statements of Additional Sub-inspector (ASI) Fareed Khan and a few others. They were willing to say the same thing in court. There were two or three more eyewitnesses too. But the FIR was the most important document.

It was late and she couldn't go back, so she stayed the night at a hotel in Kohat. She also thought of making the most of this trip. The next morning, she drew up the courage to find the address of Fiza's father and decided to go to his house.

When she reached, she entered a courtyard, taking note of the high walls and gate. She asked for Sadiq-ur-Rahman. A tall, bald Pathan stepped out of one of the rooms. Zeenat introduced herself, and without giving specifics, asked about the case the family was involved in. He assumed she meant the murder committed by his son.

He looked broken and sad when he said, 'Look at the world we are living in where your own children have no regard for you.'

He spoke a little about the son, but when Zeenat broached the topic of his daughter being given away in wani, he refused to speak.

Zeenat didn't want to push him as the family had already seen enough trouble. She thanked him for his time and left. Next, she went to Fiza's college because it was the same college that Hamid had got an invite from to attend a seminar in Kohat.

She asked the way to the principal's office and went there. Zeenat explained why she had come. The principal began talking about Fiza and her family and saying they had gone through a very difficult time. Zeenat brought up the subject of Hamid, the professor he had invited to the college. The principal said he remembered Fiza as a bright student who wanted to go on to achieve great things professionally, but unfortunately things hadn't gone as planned for her. Zeenat then told him the real purpose of Hamid's visit. He was stunned to know that, and said he felt bad for both Hamid and Fiza and their families for suffering so much. There wasn't much else he could share so she decided to go home.

She had got clinching evidence. With all the written statements and photographs in her possession, she took the last bus from Kohat to Lahore.

The moment she reached home, her mother hugged her and thanked Allah for her safe return. 'I was worried for you. I hope you got what you were looking for.'

Zeenat smiled and grinned from ear to ear. 'That and more, Ammi. This could give us what we want. They will have to accept that Hamid is in Pakistan.'

Zeenat knew that Fauzia would be worried sick and would not sleep till she heard from her, but she was too tired to talk, so she left a message, 'I am home. Please go to sleep. I will talk to you in the morning.'

When they spoke in the morning, Fauzia asked how she was doing. 'I am fine. I got caught up with a lot of things and reached home a day later than I had planned. I hope you are well. I have some good news. In fact, the trip was a very successful one,' she said.

Fauzia repeated the words 'good news' after her with the excitement of a child. They had been hard to come by.

Zeenat told her about all the evidence she had collected and said that it would nail their claim that Hamid was not only in Pakistan but also in the custody of the military. Fauzia started being hopeful again.

Zeenat also told her about her visit to Fiza's home and college. 'The father was very unhappy and sad about his children, and particularly disappointed with his son. But when I mentioned Fiza, he refused to speak. He said that children these days had no regard for their parents.'

She also recounted to Fauzia her interaction with the principal.

Now an emboldened Fauzia thought that pressure had to be built again on the Indian government to take up the matter. She asked her lawyer in Delhi to file a review petition since now there was proof that Hamid was in Pakistan. The attorney said that the Government of India was doing its best and the Supreme Court had opined that they couldn't step in because it seemed like the government was doing all it could.

For Fauzia, the fight was on at many levels. While she was occupied with the search for her son, things at her workplace were bleak. Fauzia was due for promotion as vice principal of her college based on her services and seniority, but she was denied that and forced to refuse the position because she, according to the college, was in deep trouble as her son was held captive in Pakistan. This took a massive toll on her emotionally and impacted her career. She had worked very hard for thirty-six years but in a single sweep her career achievements were taken away from her. Despite the humiliation, she put up a brave front because she had a bigger and more important battle to fight—bringing Hamid back.

Meanwhile, the case in the Pakistan court was not moving forward, and Barrister Rohaila was showing disinterest bordering on disdain. Zeenat was disappointed. She called Fauzia and told her that this way Hamid would never return and that they needed a new lawyer.

Fauzia reached out to Majeed Memon, the only man they knew who could help them on the legal front. He gave them an appointment and they went to his office the next day.

'Majeed Sahab, salaam, we need your help with our legal case in Peshawar. Please help. The lawyer we hired has not given a moment's time to Hamid's case. What do we do?' Fauzia said.

Nehal added, 'He has taken money from us too. We managed to collect it with great difficulty. Now we don't know what to do.'

Majeed Memon thought for a while and then confirmed if the proceedings were going on in Peshawar. On getting an answer in the affirmative, he took out a card from his drawer and handed it over. 'This is Qazi Mohammad Anwar. He is a very well-known and highly respected man in Pakistan. He is a senior counsel who was also a senator and won the Nishan-e-Imtiaz award [an honour given by the Government of Pakistan to military officers of the Pakistan armed forces and civilians who have made outstanding contributions]. Try reaching out to him. He is old but he might put you in touch with someone he knows.'

Memon had hosted Qazi Anwar when he was in Mumbai with delegates of a legal team from Pakistan to India. He had even arranged a meeting for him with Peshawar native and veteran Indian actor Dilip Kumar, who had hosted a party for him.

They spoke for a while and then the couple thanked him and went home. Later that night, Fauzia called up Anwar. She heard the voice of an old man on the other side. She introduced herself and gave the reference of Majeed Memon. He was all ears. Fauzia told him the entire story and sought his legal aid.

Advocate Qazi Anwar heard her out patiently and agreed to help her. When she asked about his fee, he said he would not charge her. He added, 'Behen, don't worry about the money. This is grave injustice done to you and your son. I will surely take up your case. I don't want any fee for this.'

He asked for the case details to be emailed to him. But Fauzia was sceptical. Their current lawyer was a man they had paid and he was still doing precious little—what would a man who wanted to pursue the case without any payment do?

Fauzia discussed this with the family and they came to the conclusion that for now, they should stick with Rohaila. They spoke to Zeenat as well, who was not very happy with the decision, but agreed to give it another shot with the new evidence.

Even if there was little headway in the high court, with the power of attorney given to her, Zeenat was representing the Ansari family at all hearings. She was eager for the next JIT hearing. Fortunately, it was to be held in Islamabad and presided over by Justice Javed Iqbal.

Meanwhile, Zeenat was also trying to connect with officers who could help her get details of that night when Hamid was picked up. She went to the IB office in Kohat and was told that the officer who had been in charge that night, Naeem Ullah, had been transferred.

A few days before the JIT hearing, Fauzia called up the number Zeenat had given her for Justice Iqbal. It was his office number and the staff connected her line to him.

'Salaam, Justice Iqbal here,' he said.

'Salaam sir, this is Fauzia Ansari from Mumbai. I am the helpless mother of Hamid Ansari, whose case you are hearing at the JIT,' Fauzia said and waited for his response.

There was momentary silence before Justice Iqbal replied, 'Yes. I am hearing that case. We are awaiting details from the authorities.'

Fauzia was glad that he hadn't hung up on her. She had faced that many times in her inquiries, but hadn't let that stop her from calling anyone she thought could help. 'Sir, my son is innocent. He was trapped in a wrongful manner by his friends and might have taken some wrong steps to help a girl. But his intentions were not deviant. He had nothing bad in mind. Please help him. We don't know where he is, we don't even know if he is alive,' she said and broke down crying.

'Calm down, Fauzia ji. I will ensure justice is done. If he is in Pakistan, he will be found. Have faith in your strength as a mother and have faith in Allah,' he said.

He said he had to go, but before he could end the call, Fauzia requested him to facilitate a visit to Pakistan for herself and her husband to attend the JIT meeting. He said he would schedule the next meeting in a way that would give Fauzia and her husband enough time to apply for and get visas to travel to Pakistan.

Fauzia was happy to hear this, but unfortunately, the visa didn't come through.

Meanwhile, Zeenat was all set for the big JIT hearing coming up. She had spoken to Fauzia before travelling to Islamabad. At the hearing, Justice Iqbal was first apprised of the case and the actions taken so far.

He asked, 'So, we still do not have any information on this Indian national, Hamid Ansari?'

Even as the official representing the government said 'no', Zeenat intervened and asked for permission to speak. Justice Iqbal turned to her and allowed her to do so.

Zeenat never looked at the officers sitting on the other side. She knew now that the official representing the government was from the intelligence services. But she got up to speak, unafraid.

She held a file in her hand and asked permission to hand it over, which the judge allowed. It had all the details she had gathered, including copies of the photographs she had taken and the written statements of the cops from the Kohat police station.

She could sense a commotion to her left. The officers were discussing the contents of the file. She then sent across another set of papers to the officials. They opened them and looked visibly troubled.

She began, 'Sir, the file that I have just handed over contains written statements of the police officers who had captured, according to their own statement, an Indian national in Kohat on 14 November 2012. It also contains photographs of the register of Palwasha Hotel, where Hamid had checked in. The photos clearly show that the page for that day was torn off the register, but I luckily managed to find the torn page as well. The file also contains a copy of the FIR that was lodged at the Kohat police station on 19 September 2014, which clearly mentions Hamid Ansari's name.'

Justice Iqbal looked at the documents while Zeenat explained the entire trail of events as to how she thought things must have played out, concluding that the written statement clearly mentioned that Hamid Ansari had been taken away by ISI and MI officials.

Looking at the evidence, the judge turned to the officials and said loudly, 'You either didn't do your due diligence or this is a clear case of obfuscation of facts.'

Fuming, he continued, 'Do you have anything to say about the case?'

The officers tried to explain but were not convincing.

Justice Iqbal went red and said, 'These flimsy excuses are not enough. I am under tremendous pressure to act on this case. Hamid Ansari's mother has approached the UN and now the international community is looking into this case. Acknowledge all the events as they happened. Give us a detailed report of your findings. If what Zeenat has shown me is true then we do have an Indian national in our custody, and neither India nor his family has been informed yet.'

The session concluded with one of the officials storming out of the room. Zeenat was worried that this could blow up. She stepped out, praying that she would not be confronted.

Once she was home, she saw a few cops waiting for her. Her mother looked embarrassed since the neighbours had started casting curious glances and asking what the matter was.

When she stepped inside her house, one of the officers asked her to sit. He said, 'Madam, why are you pursuing this Hamid Ansari case?'

She said, 'I am just doing my job.'

Another sleazy-looking cop said, 'Sir, she must be that man's girlfriend.'

Zeenat was shocked to hear such language. Her mother was in tears.

She told them that she knew she was doing the right thing and that they had kept an innocent man in their custody. They should do their job rather than harass honest, decent citizens of the country.

'I know I am fighting for the truth. Hamid's intentions were honourable. I am doing this for my country. I don't want this blot of injustice on my nation,' she said in a firm voice.

After a few heated exchanges, the officers left her house. While they didn't give any specific reason for the visit, the entire household was a little shaken.

Zeenat called up Fauzia to brief her. Fauzia was worried for her but Zeenat said she wanted to focus on the case. She insisted that they needed to change the lawyer in the case that was underway in the Peshawar court.

They decided to appoint Qazi Anwar. The next morning, she called the senior counsel on his mobile. 'Salaam, Qazi Sahab, this is Fauzia Ansari. I had spoken to you regarding my son's case. He is being held in Pakistan, Qazi Sahab, and we need your help.'

He thought about the case for a while and said, 'Yes, yes, I remember. I did agree to fight your case and that too pro bono. I had asked you to send me the details. Why did you delay so much?'

Fauzia apologized profusely and explained that the case was in the middle of a hearing and they had wanted to wait for a while. But now he was their last hope.

He readily agreed. When Fauzia asked him about his fee, he repeated that he would not be charging for it. 'What is important is to find your son first,' he said.

Fauzia told him that Zeenat Shehzadi would meet him to discuss the details. Fauzia then briefed Zeenat on the developments.

The next morning, Zeenat called up Qazi Anwar to fix an appointment. She went to his office with all the documents, petitions, details of the JIT meetings and her own findings.

Qazi Anwar decided to pursue the petition of habeas corpus that Rohaila had already filed rather than going for a fresh application. From then on, he took over the case with his junior advocates. Zeenat was present alongside him at all meetings and hearings at the Peshawar High Court. He was very impressed by the work done by this young journalist.

~

Around November 2014, Fauzia and Nehal were returning to Mumbai after one of their many trips to Delhi. At New Delhi Railway station, Fauzia was lost in her thoughts and tripped on a pothole. An autorickshaw ran over her leg, causing a massive fracture. She fainted.

When she opened her eyes, she was at the trauma centre of a hospital near Old Delhi Railway Station. Her leg was bandaged, and she saw her worried husband at her side.

'What happened?' she asked, a little dazed. Nehal told her that the doctors had recommended surgery. She told him that she wanted to go back to Mumbai for any further medical treatment. Both thought that was the best option since being in Delhi would add to cost and inconvenience. They had nobody in Delhi.

They went back to Mumbai, where she was admitted in hospital. The doctors found a small blood clot in the head, which subsided with medication. The bigger concern was her leg, in which titanium plates and rods had to be inserted since her bones were badly damaged. It hurt Fauzia to take medical leave from her college since she had never done that before. She was shattered. She cried for days, asking God, 'Why me?'

The treatment burnt a hole in their savings. They could also no longer live in their third-floor apartment in a building without an elevator. So they took up a place on rent in another building which had an elevator. To tide over the financial crisis, Nehal sold off a small flat they had bought many years ago as an investment on Mira Road in the faraway suburbs of Mumbai.

In December 2014, the situation caused by Nehal's absence from work due to travel and Fauzia's treatment became untenable. The family decided that it was best if Nehal took up the voluntary retirement scheme (VRS) option. That would bring in some money, and the rest of the expenses would be managed from Fauzia's salary and the rent they were getting from the flat they had moved out of.

~

At the beginning of 2015, Zeenat started being threatened by anonymous callers, warning her against pursuing the case. The threats turned serious when they realized that she would not give up. They told her that she would get into trouble if she did not stop and would have to bear the consequences. She got scared and stopped taking such calls. But the calls continued from multiple numbers.

Zeenat was rattled and expressed concerns about her security to Fauzia.

'Can you take measures to ensure your protection?' Fauzia asked.

'No, no. I will have to be brave and fight the case. The facts are on our side, and we will be fine,' she said to the fretting mother across the border.

The Peshawar High Court was to hear the matter in the first week of June 2015. The famous Qazi Mohammad Anwar was going to represent Fauzia Ansari (the petitioner). Chief Justice Mazhar Alam Miankhel and Justice Muhammad Daud Khan would be hearing the case.

Qazi Anwar, an indomitable presence despite being in his seventies, stood up to argue. A well-known advocate, he was not only respected by his fraternity but also by the judges who had seen him for years.

He pulled out the documents that had already been submitted to the court, the JIT report, Justice Iqbal's ruling which clearly ordered an inquiry, the FIR and the written statements of officials and eyewitnesses at the Kohat police station.

The Kohat police's affidavit was incriminating evidence to prove that Hamid Ansari had visited Kohat and had stayed at a local hotel when the Kohat police, assisted by IB officials, had arrested him.

While the government's counsel repeated the line that investigations were still underway in the matter, Qazi Anwar interjected and said that there was evidence and written statements from the Kohat police station SHO confirming that not only had they nabbed the Indian national without proper legal documents but also that he had been taken away by MI and ISI officials later that night.

He added, 'Whoever enters the country should be treated according to the Passports Act, 1974. My client is worried about her son's prolonged absence.'

Qazi Anwar read out loud an excerpt from FIR No. 206 lodged on 4 August 2014 under Section 365 of the Pakistan Penal Code at the KDA police station in Kohat.

'According to the statement of eyewitnesses SHO Faiz Ullah and Muharrir Fareed Khan, etc. of police station, KDA, Kohat, the said suspect was taken away from local police by ISI and MI personnel and Inspector IB Kohat Naeem Ullah for interrogation, but till date the missing Hamid Nehal Ansari has not been returned by these agencies' representatives and IB inspector Naeem Ullah is concealing facts due to unknown reasons.

'It is therefore requested that the concerned authorities of MI and ISI may be directed to return the said person for further legal action into the case.'

Upon hearing the arguments, the court pulled up the government agencies and directed Additional Advocate General Qaiser Ali Shah to submit the Kohat DPO's report in light of police reports submitted earlier. The court also ordered the federal government to submit the MI report.

Zeenat, present in the courtroom, knew fully well that her work and the JIT FIR were the real reasons they had such a strong case. But she was now terrified every time the phone rang. The court hearing was followed by more threatening calls from unknown numbers.

But she continued following the case very closely, and her Facebook page had become a source of information for any TV or print journalist following the Hamid Ansari case. She kept at it despite the threats.

She kept Fauzia updated about the latest developments. The Pakistani authorities finally had to accept that Hamid was in Pakistan.

Fauzia could see that at long last the case had taken the right direction. She told Zeenat, 'I will always be indebted to you, Zeenat. You are not just a daughter to me, you are a godsend. If you were in front of me, I would have hugged you and kissed your forehead. My blessings will always be with you. It is because of you that the world will soon know that my son is in Pakistan.'

Fauzia called up Justice Javed Iqbal to thank him. Had it not been for him, the entire investigation and narrative would have been steered towards declaring Hamid a spy or a terrorist. He said he was only following the path of justice and truth.

Fauzia also called Majeed Memon to thank him for introducing them to Qazi Anwar.

And finally, she wept her heart out when she called Qazi Anwar. 'You are my saviour. Thank you, Qazi Sahab. I will forever remain in your debt,' she said.

Meanwhile, despite the threatening calls, Zeenat was focused on one thing and one thing alone—to get Hamid and his family justice. In August 2015, she learnt that the Indian high commissioner to Pakistan, T.C.A. Raghavan, was visiting Lahore and would be addressing the Human Rights Commission of Pakistan (HRCP). She decided to go there to ask what the Indian mission was doing.

On 12 August 2015, she attended the meet and asked a question about the case. The Indian high commissioner said they had sent numerous note verbales to the Pakistani government asking about Hamid Ansari's presence in Pakistan, but had got no reply yet.

Later, Zeenat met the high commissioner separately and discussed the case. She apprised the Indian envoy of the developments at JIT and in the Peshawar court. He told her he would ask his office to follow up.

Just as she stepped out of the HRCP building, she was accosted by a bunch of people dressed in white clothes. They blindfolded her and took her to an unknown location.

She was scared and cried endlessly. Her kidnappers told her they were not going to touch her. They just wanted to give her the message that she should withdraw from the Hamid Ansari case completely.

A steady but firm voice said, 'If you continue digging up stuff on the Hamid Ansari case then you and your family will have to pay dearly. This is a serious matter and you had better keep out of it.'

She was questioned about her sources and how she had managed to get all the facts. She answered honestly. She was then released in the same manner and at the same spot where she had been picked up—after six hours of a gruelling and harrowing session. Her blindfold was still on.

Zeenat was a nervous wreck by then but she managed to get home; it was dawn by the time she reached. She went inside crying. Her mother was worried. Her younger brother, Saddam, whom she was very close to, hugged her. She called up Fauzia to tell her what had happened. Everyone was very worried for her safety.

The same morning, Zeenat got ready and left for the enforced disappearances hearing of the JIT being held in Islamabad. She knew this would be an important meeting since the Peshawar High Court had sought details on the basis of the JIT meetings. All the usual officials who attended the hearings were present.

On 19 August 2015, Zeenat was picked up on her way to work in Lahore. Her phone was unreachable when Fauzia tried calling her. Worried, she didn't know whom to call next. She had one other number that Zeenat had used. It belonged to one of her older brothers, Salman, who did not like receiving calls from India since he wished to study abroad someday. So she stopped herself. Zeenat had warned her never to call on that number.

But that evening, she received a call from Salman himself. She didn't pick up the first time but when it rang for the second time, she did.

'Salaam, this is Salman. I am Zeenat's brother. Fauzia Aunty, I have some very bad news about Zeenat. Our neighbours informed us this morning that they saw some men in plain clothes abduct her in a white car. She was going to office in a rickshaw. I am really worried. Have you received any calls?'

Fauzia's heart sank. Her world came crashing down. She said, 'Beta, I have also been trying her number but have not been able to get through. How did this happen? Allah!'

'What do we do now, aunty? I have nobody I can speak to about this,' said Salman.

Fauzia advised him to file a complaint at the nearest police station.

She then called up Jatin Desai and asked him what to do. He told her that they should approach the HRCP and file a missing person report there as well.

A few days later, Fauzia saw news reports with the headline 'Pakistani Reporter Zeenat Shehzadi Missing'.

She started wailing and crying again: 'Allah!' Nehal was in the other room. He came running out and so did Khalid. 'What happened?'

Fauzia was sobbing as she showed her husband the news report. 'First my son and now they have taken my daughter.' She was inconsolable. She wanted to go to Pakistan to be with the mother who had lost her dear daughter for someone she hadn't ever met.

A concerted effort was made to find Zeenat. Desai sourced the contact of renowned lawyer Hina Jilani, Pakistani human rights lawyer Asma Jehangir's sister, and well-known journalist I.A. Rahman, the head of the HRCP. Fauzia requested the HRCP to take up the case of Zeenat Shehzadi.

Hina Jilani heard the entire matter and immediately took up the case after meeting Zeenat's brother. The petitioner in the case was Zeenat's mother.

Rehman and Hina together took up the case with various authorities. Fauzia was in touch with them constantly.

Tragedy had struck twenty-four-year-old Zeenat's family. She was the sole breadwinner of the family. Her younger brother, Saddam, was all of eighteen years old and could not take the news of his sister's abduction. She was his emotional anchor. They were very close.

He started searching for her by asking people. He would ask about Zeenat every time someone came home. He remained mentally disturbed for months, until one day he gave up. In March 2016, he went to his mother and told her, 'Now Zeenat will never return.' Soon after, he committed suicide.

While one family had found their son, another had lost theirs. And both families had lost a precious daughter.

19

Diplomacy and the Media

In June 2014, when Fauzia and Nehal had met Sushma Swaraj in her office, she had read the file that Fauzia had compiled. After her meeting with the family, she had asked her officers where things stood. As someone who followed consular issues very closely, she wanted to know what they had done so far.

Swaraj discussed the matter with the then foreign secretary, Dr S. Jaishankar, the officer in charge of the Pakistan division, and MEA spokesperson Syed Akbaruddin.

'*Iss ladke ko phasaya gaya hai. Case kahan tak pahucha hai?*' (The boy has been lured and trapped. What's the status of the case?)

'Madam, from what we have gathered so far, the boy is being framed but we have no official word from Pakistan on him being in their custody. We have been sending them note verbale after note verbale but we have not heard back yet,' said one of the officials.

'We have to bring him back. That is all I know. He made a mistake but they cannot keep an Indian national for so long without informing us. Tread carefully and let me know what we plan on doing next. *Waapis toh lana hi hoga* [We will have to get him back]', she said in her inimitable way.

She also spoke to the Indian High Commissioner to Pakistan T.C.A. Raghavan in Islamabad to seek a way out.

The Indian mission had not only been writing to Pakistan's MoFA, but also seeking permission to attend the court hearing that was underway in Peshawar, but there was no response to any of India's requests.

One day, India's deputy chief of mission, J.P. Singh, got a call from an unknown number from India. He picked up and a feeble voice on the other side said, 'Hello sir, I am Fauzia Ansari. I am the mother of Hamid Ansari and I am only calling you to help us find our son. I am sorry for calling you on the mobile. But I am desperate to know about my son, sir.'

J.P. Singh had recently joined the mission and was aware of the case but a little flummoxed by the call made to his cell phone. He heard out the anguished mother patiently, like many officials in Delhi had, and then said, 'Fauzia ji, we understand your pain. We are doing all we can. We have sent innumerable letters to Pakistan's foreign office asking about his whereabouts and health. Believe me when I say that we will do everything we can to bring Hamid back. Just be strong.'

'My son is innocent. He just went to help a friend,' she said.

'I understand. But Fauzia ji, can you tell me how you got my number? Did you get it from a journalist or Jatin Desai?' he asked.

Fauzia explained how she had looked for numbers on the MEA website and clicked on the link that led to the Indian High Commission website in Islamabad, where she found an emergency contact number for distressed Indian nationals in Pakistan. She didn't know whom she was speaking to.

'Sir, what is your name? The website only had this number,' she said.

Singh gave her his name and details and told her that he was aware of the case and the mission was working hard on it.

The conversation gave Fauzia some assurance that the mission was trying its best, but their hands were tied too. The India–Pakistan story is that of a complicated relationship with complex layers. Pull one string the wrong way and all efforts unravel. So 'caution' was the mantra.

Meanwhile, the media had started picking up the story, leading to massive pressure on both governments and the Pakistani establishment.

Hamid Ansari had become a common feature in most weekly MEA media briefings. In September 2014, during one such briefing, MEA spokesperson Syed Akbaruddin explained that the parents had found out the whereabouts of their son through his social media account after he was found missing, and discovered that he exchanged a lot of messages with a Pakistani girl.

He said, 'Nehal Hamid Ansari is a sad story because it is the story of a young man who has been missing for two years.'

Akbaruddin also informed the press that Fauzia had moved the Peshawar High Court asking Hamid to be produced in court.

'The matter is in court. His parents have been repeatedly in touch with the MEA on several occasions. I can tell you that we have written to the Pakistan authorities more than fifteen times asking for his whereabouts,' he said.

Journalist Jatin Desai also reached out to his friend and senior journalist Rajdeep Sardesai. He called him up at the end of 2014 to apprise him of Hamid's case and ask for TV coverage.

'Hello, Rajdeep, how are you?' said Jatin.

A surprised Rajdeep responded, 'Hi Jatin. How are you? Long time. How are things on the Indo-Pak front?' He knew that Desai was part of a forum that worked on prisoners and fishermen issues between India and Pakistan.

'Well, not so great. The prisoner issue between India and Pakistan with the current political situation is really not looking good. In fact, I am calling you because there is an Indian boy in Pakistani custody. The parents are very worried. He is an engineer and went there looking for a girl.'

A shocked Rajdeep said, 'What? Are you serious?'

'Yes, yes. He went into Pakistan through Afghanistan and we do not have much clarity from the Pakistan government. Can you do something about it and highlight the issue?' inquired Desai. They agreed to do whatever they could.

Desai emailed Sardesai the articles that had already appeared in various papers. The latter then shared the contact with journalists covering the foreign beat in Delhi, who interviewed the family during their next visit to Delhi. The case of Hamid Ansari made headlines in both India and Pakistan.

During their visit to Delhi in January 2015, Fauzia got in touch with then MEA spokesperson Syed Akbaruddin. A list of prisoners is exchanged between India and Pakistan annually. While the number of prisoners are shared in public, their details and names are not given out. Fauzia reached out to Akbaruddin and sought a meeting to find out if Hamid's name figured on the list. She got an appointment for later that evening. Nehal and Fauzia prepared to go Shastri Bhavan, where the office of the publicity division of the MEA is situated.

Akbaruddin had done his homework on the case. He spoke with JS, PAI, Yash Sinha, and to the officials at the mission to get an update on the issue. The Indian High Commission informed the MEA spokesperson that more than twenty note verbales had been sent to the Pakistan foreign office, the Ministry of Foreign Affairs (MoFA), seeking Hamid's whereabouts, but to no avail.

When Fauzia and Nehal reached Shastri Bhavan, they were escorted to the MEA spokesperson's first-floor office. They entered and sat across him at the table. Fauzia then started telling him of their ordeal. She told him of the list she had learnt about. 'Akbaruddin Sir, is my son on that list? Pakistan has not divulged any information about Hamid so far. This is our only hope.'

He heard Fauzia out patiently but had no good news to offer, 'Fauzia ji, Hamid's name is not on the list. I am sorry. We have been trying very hard to get Pakistan to respond to our note verbales but haven't heard from them yet.'

He assured her that the minister herself was paying personal attention to this case and that the mission was doing everything that was possible diplomatically. They spoke for a while and then a crushed Fauzia left his office along with Nehal.

It was in 2015 when the media, both Indian and Pakistani, started keenly watching the case in the Peshawar court. The media coverage put immense pressure on Pakistan to respond to the habeas corpus petition and accept that Hamid was in their custody. But they held back as long as they could.

The Indian mission asked for permission to attend the Peshawar High Court hearing ahead of the court date but didn't get clearance from the MoFA. The rejection came in the form of silence on the part of Islamabad.

In June 2015, there was a major development where the Peshawar High Court acknowledged Hamid's presence in Pakistan but the Pakistani establishment was yet to admit that they had him.

On 12 August of the same year, Zeenat had met High Commissioner Raghavan just days before she was picked up. This meeting took place at the HRCP, where the Indian envoy also met the likes of Asma Jehangir, Hina Jilani and others. They had discussed Hamid's case in detail. There was consensus on the fact that Hamid had made a mistake by entering Pakistan without documents, but he was not a spy.

The Indian High Commission officials got in touch with legal luminaries in Pakistan to seek advice on the matter. J.P. Singh, along with the visa counsellor, met a well-known human rights activist in Pakistan.

'You know the case of Hamid Ansari. What are our legal options? How should we go about the case?' asked Singh.

She said, as had many others, 'Look, this is a sensitive case. The boy is innocent and we are all following the case. But remember, the moment you guys jump in, they will suspect that he is an asset. You will spoil the case for the poor boy. My advice would be to let the mission look at it as one of the many consular issue cases and leave the legal route to the family.'

The advice of the Pakistani legal luminaries was discussed with the Indian high commissioner and with headquarters in New Delhi. The matter was discussed with Jaishankar as well. There was clarity that too much indulgence from the Indian mission could have an adverse impact on the case. So they maintained a safe distance.

But the note verbales had become more and more specific. From the initial note verbale seeking information about Indian national Hamid Ansari, the missives now cited news reports and asked for details of his whereabouts and his well-being.

The Indian mission could never write to Islamabad directly about Hamid being in their custody because there was no official communication to that effect. So the weekly reminders went on the basis of news reports.

The Indian side also called in Pakistani diplomats and met their envoy in India, Abdul Basit, to seek answers, but all these efforts drew a blank since the military had not given any information on Hamid.

But the mission had to find a way to know what was happening. Serving in India and Pakistan can be the most stifling experience for diplomats on either side. Always walking a thorny path, looking over one's shoulders—that is how they function.

In December 2015, Indian Deputy Chief of Mission J.P. Singh got in touch with Hamid's counsels Rukhshanda Naz and Qazi Anwar. Since they both lived in Peshawar, it was not possible for Indian diplomats to travel to that city without permission from the MoFA so he requested them for a meeting if they were ever in Islamabad.

On one wintry December evening, Singh learnt that Qazi Anwar was in Islamabad and invited him on behalf of the high commissioner to India House. The advocate informed the Indian diplomat that he was in Islamabad for a family function and his wife was travelling with him. The couple was invited for tea.

Since Qazi Anwar did not know the address, he asked for directions.

He was told, 'It is opposite the United Bakery supermarket in Islamabad. The moment you reach the spot, there will be a vehicle waiting to escort your car since it is a high-security zone.'

Qazi Anwar and his wife reached the area and saw a man emerge from a car. He introduced himself as an official of the Indian mission and asked their driver to follow his car.

The moment they entered the street where India House was located, they saw two or three barricades but their car was cleared to enter without being stopped by security.

The bearded dignified man with a walking stick entered the drawing room of the Indian envoy with his wife by his side. He was received by the high commissioner, who apologized for the fact that his own wife was not in town and promised to host them again when she returned.

High Commissioner Raghavan, his deputy, Singh, and the visa counsellor, Prabhat Jain, were present from the Indian side. All of them were very impressed with the senior counsel, who knew exactly what the case was and how to fight it.

They kept it simple and did not discuss the finer details. They just wanted to get acquainted with the man who was fighting an Indian national's case. The high tea ended with Raghavan thanking Qazi Anwar for his efforts.

Raghavan said, for the second time, before seeing the lawyer off, 'We are thankful to you and we shall remain thankful. If I am ever in Peshawar or get permission to travel to Peshawar, I will surely meet you.' He handed the lawyer a box of kaju barfi while seeing him off. He had learnt that the octogenarian loved Indian sweets. The tradition of sending sweets to him has continued ever since.

The moment Qazi Anwar left India House, he saw there were some people waiting for him from Pakistan's intelligence agency. One man stopped his vehicle and asked the driver to roll down the window. He stared into Qazi Anwar's eyes.

'Salaam, *bas yeh janna tha ki aap andar kyun gaye the.*' (Salaam, just wanted to know why you'd gone in.)

Qazi Anwar, without batting an eyelid, said mockingly, '*Hum Indian agent hai. Apni report dene gaye the.*' (I am an Indian agent. I came to give my report.)

The official was stunned by the response and pleaded with Qazi Anwar to tell him. 'Sir, we have to know. Please tell us.'

Qazi Anwar smiled and said, 'I just came to have tea. We didn't discuss any politics. He inquired about my family and thanked me for my efforts in fighting the Hamid Ansari case. He also gave me these lovely Indian sweets.' He showed him the box. The man let his car pass.

The Indian officials also kept in touch with Rukhshanda Naz, who had a lot of experience in India–Pakistan matters. But this was a unique case and she admitted that to the diplomats. When they asked her for advice, she said just a few things.

'Don't worry. It is a fair case and Qazi Anwar is the best you could have got. I know you are also in touch with the family; just assure the mother that the case could not be fought better and we will get him released because he is innocent,' she said.

When asked if the mission could be of any help and if they needed any financial assistance, she said, 'One, the mission should not be proactive. It is a legal case that is being fought well. Secondly, you know Qazi Anwar. He is very different. We have decided to fight it pro bono so no aid is required.'

The Indian side knew that this was a matter of life and death. Any wrong move could land Hamid in a lot of trouble. 'He made a mistake but he should come back, and he should come back alive,' said the Indian official.

It was only around the end of 2015 that the Pakistan MoFA sent a note verbale to the Indian mission. The political officer who received it rushed to the deputy chief of mission's office.

Singh read the note and took it to the high commissioner, whose tenure in Islamabad was nearing its end. 'Sir, MoFA has finally accepted that Hamid Ansari is in their custody. Here is the note verbale which says Indian national Hamid Ansari is in Pakistan's custody and is in good health.' Singh handed over the official document to Raghavan.

The envoy studied the one-line document and looked up to express relief, '*Chalo*, now it is official. At least now we know he is alive and if anything were to happen to him now the state will be responsible. This is huge, J.P. Call up Delhi and inform them,' said the Indian envoy.

Singh called up the officer in charge of the PAI division, Rudendra Tandon, and informed him of the development. He asked Soumya, director, India desk, to inform the mother. The same was conveyed to the foreign secretary and to Sushma Swaraj.

Soumya, who had been in touch with the Ansaris, informed Fauzia of the development but also told her not to mention this to the media. 'Too much media coverage does not always work in our favour. Please keep this information to yourself. The court proceedings are at a crucial stage.'

There was jubilation in the Ansari household. They finally had some information about Hamid but they still weren't aware what the Pakistani officials were doing with him.

On 31 December 2015, Raghavan's tenure ended and he crossed over to India through the Wagah–Attari border. The next high commissioner of India to Pakistan, Gautam Bambawale, was to join in a month's time.

~

The next big breakthrough came on 1 January 2016, with the annual ritual of the prisoners' list exchange. This involves the simultaneous exchange by the foreign ministry of their prisoners' list with the respective mission of the neighbouring country. Each list is handed over to the political officer in the high commissions of India and Pakistan.

That morning, it was handed over to India's first secretary, Raghuram, at Pakistan's MoFA. As he drove back to the Indian High Commission, he saw that the list contained Hamid Ansari's name. Now, it was as official as it could get.

Singh discussed matters with Prabhat Jain, the visa counsellor. This was a major shift. Hamid Ansari was finally 'mainstreamed'.

'The responsibility of his safety now lies with the state of Pakistan,' Singh told the officer.

Soumya apprised Fauzia of the good news and again told her to stay quiet till the court hearing, which was in two weeks, on 13 January 2016.

Sushma Swaraj was apprised of all the developments. During the discussions, one of the officers explained, 'Ma'am, there was no way Hamid Ansari would have been listed had the Pakistani establishment not been satisfied that he is not a spy.'

Another officer added, 'Yes, ma'am, it seems they are satisfied. It is only a matter of time. It is now a judicial case. So let's see what comes up in the next hearing.'

'Will our officers attend the hearing?' she asked.

'Well, they have sought permission from the MoFA in Pakistan to travel to Peshawar and attend the hearing, but like always no word from them yet,' said the joint secretary, PAI.

But there was relief in the MEA that the quiet perseverance of diplomats and the determination of Fauzia Ansari, as well as the stellar team of Qazi Anwar and Rukhshanda Naz, along with the valiant efforts of Zeenat Shehzadi, had paid off.

20

Forced Signatures

26 June 2014

I was counting days. A maximum of 180 days and I would be sent home. Home—just the thought brought back memories of the warmth of my mother, the love of my father, the laughter of my brother.

The guards and commander in the barracks were surprised to see me come out of the interrogation room smiling. Six months—I had to bide my time.

I was told that everybody knew about my impending release, which made me all the more happy. Ramzan was to begin in two days and I looked forward to it.

On the second day of Ramzan, two guards came and told me I was being summoned. I didn't know what to expect as I was blindfolded and taken to the interrogation room. I thought the same senior officer who had visited in February and told me that the case was under him wanted to meet me, but when I entered, I heard the voices of the ruthless elderly interrogating officer and his subordinates.

I gulped in fear. Before I knew it, I was thrown to one end of the room with blows and punches. The elderly officer hurled abuses that I had never heard in my life. They didn't ask me one question, just began with the physical abuse—which was unbearable on an empty stomach.

A massive blow landed on my left eye. It felt like my eyeball had burst. I could see bright flashes, and I lost consciousness. Moments later, I was jolted by a shooting pain. I screamed so loudly that for a moment everybody moved back. In a flash, the pain spread across my head and my face. It was intolerable. I kept shouting.

They all got nervous. If anything happened to me in their custody, they would be held responsible. After a while, the elderly officer asked me, 'Do you want water?'

Through my sniffles and cries, I shouted, 'I am fasting.'

He looked surprised and said, *'Achha haan, to tum Musalman ho. Lekin humein isse koi fark nahi padta kyunki humare liye tum sirf ek Hindustani ho.'* (Oh yes, you are a Muslim. But that doesn't matter to us because for us you are only an Indian.) Saying this, all the officers left me in the room.

The commander-in-charge entered the room and found me lying on the floor, crying in pain. He asked me what the matter was, but since my throat was completely dry I could not speak. He untied my hands and tied them again in the front so I could be a little more comfortable.

After some time, I was taken back to my cell. When my blindfold was removed, the commander noticed that my left eye was completely swollen. He got upset and said, *'Allah ki lanat ho in zalimo par jo Ramzan ka ahtaram bhi nahi karte.'* (Curses be upon these ruthless beings who don't even take into consideration the fact that it is the holy month of Ramzan.)

For a few weeks, I was not able to open my left eye as the pain was terrible. But I remained unaffected by the torture. I prayed and waited for the six months to get over. Among the guards and commanders, some who sympathized with me were warm while others were spiteful.

Sometimes, I would think that this was just a repeat of the vicious circle that I had been put through in the past—being told that I would be going home, only to be tortured more and then some more.

But I brushed aside all the negativity and kept the thought of freedom alive. The entire period of Ramzan (July) and the month of August were peaceful—no interrogation and no torture. The bruises on my left eye healed slowly but I could tell there was something wrong with the eye. I could sense it. I used to pray to God to keep my eyesight intact—it was becoming weaker with each passing day.

At the end of August, each prisoner was taken to the interrogation room one at a time. When it was my turn and I went, my blindfold was removed and I was shown a bunch of photographs on the table.

'Do you recognize any of them?' asked an officer sitting at the table.

I wondered and looked around, confused. What was this now? Wasn't my case cleared? But I was asked to start looking at the photographs carefully.

'What am I looking at and what do I have to find?' I asked.

He didn't answer my question but insisted that I look at the photographs carefully and identify the place and the people.

I failed to answer his questions and was taken back to my cell. I hadn't recognized anyone or anything.

Upon reaching, I asked the guards what this was all about. One of them said that intelligence had been received that an educational institute was going to be targeted by the Taliban.

'What do you mean by that? How would I know what to look for?' I asked with fear of what was to come seeping in. Not me, not again. I had been hoping to be in India by the new year.

One guard said that they were only doing what they were asked to do.

At the end of September, the guards in the facility changed.

31 December 2014

I was asleep and woke up with a start. My dream ended. My mother's lap disappeared, her warmth faded . . . I was left with remorse, with memories of my loving family and thoughts of Fiza.

I was jolted awake by two guards who came to my cell and asked me to get up.

I was back in the interrogation room and thinking, "What a way to start the new year. My blindfold and handcuffs were removed. Across the table was an officer sitting on a chair, surrounded by three or four others who were standing.

There was a blank paper on the table, and the officer pointed at it and said, 'Start making a sketch of all that you saw, the route that you took from Jalalabad to Kohat, whatever you noticed. Draw everything on this piece of paper.'

I looked up, surprised. I recognized that voice. Yes, it was the voice of the elderly officer, the ruthless demon. I looked at him closely to see his appearance. He caught me staring and gave me a stern look. I immediately picked up the pen and started drawing a line.

'Also mark the things you saw on the way,' he added.

I started doing that. I made a rough sketch of the things I remembered seeing—the Torkham border, Haji camp bus depot, shops, trees, farmlands, bridges, etc.

When I handed over the sketch, he looked at it very carefully and after a while asked, *'Jab tu Afghanistan mein tha toh wahan tumne apne phone se bahut si tasveerein li thi lekin Pakistan mein tu ne koi tasveer nahi li. Kyun? Tujhe Pakistan mein koi cheez achhi nahi lagi?'* (When you were in Afghanistan, you took a lot of pictures, but none when you travelled in Pakistan. Why? Didn't you like anything here?)

I replied, *'Main jis raaste par tha us par mujhe aisi koi cheez nahi dikhi. Main apne upar dhyan nahi lana chahta tha. Sath hi main dar gaya tha agar main apna BlackBerry mobile public mein nikalta hoon to shayad koi loot le isliye personal safety ke liye main apna mobile bag se bahar nahi nikala.'* (I didn't find anything interesting in the route that I had taken to really take pictures. Also, I did not want to draw attention to myself. I was afraid of getting mugged in case I took my BlackBerry out. That's the reason I sat quietly through the journey while my phone remained in my bag.)

There were no further questions. The ruthless old officer sat there looking at me for a while and then walked out. I couldn't breathe in his presence. I thought this was one of the last things that they wanted cleared. The 180 days were up and my happiness knew no bounds.

A week had passed, but there was no word on my release, no movement, no paperwork. One week became two. There was no officer to seek an update from.

29 January 2015

At the end of January, there was a sudden commotion in the facility one day. I wanted to look out but desisted. Then came my turn. I was taken to a room (not the interrogation room) and strapped to a chair, both by my wrists and my ankles. My heart sank. Then I heard what I now considered the sound of incarceration—the shaving machine running through my hair. I knew that freedom had eluded me yet again. Tears rolled down my cheeks, but I had no fight left in me. I sat there quietly.

During the haircut, my blindfold was removed but one of the men kept his hand on my eyes.

That evening, I was taken to the interrogation room, where I found three men sitting across the table. My blindfold was removed as I was made to sit. One of them introduced himself as Shahzad and said his subordinates were Bilal and Rashid. He said, 'I am here from the special branch. I hold the power to finalize your case and sign your release, or really screw up your life. Now your fate lies in your own hands. You have to decide what you want to do.'

I was utterly confused. I thought all this had been done and dusted. Shahzad asked me to repeat my entire story from the beginning. I did as I was told. By the end of it, I was drained. Bilal and Rashid took notes.

Then came the cross-questioning. I answered truthfully, as I had done the innumerable times I had been interrogated, questioned and tortured.

Once the Q&A session was over, Bilal and Rashid handed over the notes to Shahzad and left the room. Shahzad said that a senior officer was going to come and talk me through the points. They were unsatisfied with the answers.

I was allowed a short loo break. When the guard escorted me to the washroom, I asked, 'Ye naye log kaun hain?' (Who are these new people?) In a very soft tone he replied, 'Islamabad se bade judge aye hain khaas tere liye. Bas Allah kare aaj tera masla hal ho jaye aur tu apne watan, apne ghar chala jaye.' (These are special judges from Islamabad who have come especially for your case. Allah willing, may your case get solved today and may you return to your country, your home.)

I returned to an empty room.

After some time, another team of three officers entered the room. One of them, an aged-looking officer, sat across the table while his subordinates sat next to me.

He introduced himself as Shams and his juniors as Kamran and Junaid. The pressure tactics to change my statement began. They hurled abuses at me and rejected everything I said. I pleaded with them to believe me.

Shams had a feeble voice and was chewing gum, which made his words incomprehensible. I was on very thin ice so I tried to figure out what he was saying and answered the best that I could.

A while later, Kamran and Junaid tied my hands to a chain bound to the ceiling and started the torture after gagging me with a big piece of cloth, almost choking me. I wanted to scream and cry and just run away. Not again. They threw water at me before hitting me with a belt and a rod. It was one of the worst beatings I had had. My clothes tore at several places.

The same set of questions was repeated. What is your mission? What is your network? For what amount did Atta-ur-Rahman agree to help you? What amount did you pay the soldier at the Torkham border?

The same questions, the same answers, but new wounds, fresh bruises.

The ordeal ended after several hours. They left the room and Shahzad came back. He sat down, shaking his head. 'Hamid, nobody is convinced with this sham of a story. Give up your cover and tell us the truth. We are the Special Branch. We work differently. This is your last opportunity, after which no one will revisit your case for the next five years at least. So your fate is in your own hands,' he said and left the room.

The guard came and unshackled me. I fell to the floor and was carried back to my cell. While closing the door, another guard told me that my partner was in bad shape. My partner? Was he referring to Atta-ur-Rahman? They must have picked him up since they thought he had helped me. I lost all hope of meeting my parents. I was close to giving up on life itself.

The next morning, when I was taken to the washroom, I wrote a message on the bathroom wall with my fingernails, 'I have not accepted.'

I knew Atta-ur-Rahman was educated enough to read English. I hoped that if he ever used this washroom, he would get the message.

Later that afternoon, the same guard told me that 'my partner' had been taken back to the interrogation room by the same set of officers who had come last night. I hoped that he had read the message.

By the end of February, a few prisoners, including me, were shifted to a different facility in the dark of the cold night, blindfolded and handcuffed.

We were taken out of the old building into the open. I could hear vehicles passing by. The smell of diesel and pollution was so pleasant. We seemed to have just crossed the road to reach another building where we were again taken underground.

This was clearly a new facility as construction work was still going on. I could smell fresh paint and a lot of construction dust. We were kept blindfolded even in the cells here for one month. I wondered if Atta-ur-Rahman was also there.

~

On one midsummer day in 2015, a few more prisoners were brought in, and a young boy called Mansoor was put into my cell. Later that night, the subedar came to us and asked if I was Ansari. I nodded. He looked at me carefully and left.

Mansoor started jumping around and said, smiling, 'Something is coming your way. Tomorrow you will go home. The subedar personally came to meet you. This means you will go home.'

Mansoor's words were soothing, but by then I had become so cynical that I saw only negativity in everything. In fact, the visit made me tense and kept me awake all night.

12 May 2015

There was a delay in breakfast being served. We were hungry as it had been over twelve hours since our last meal. After prayers, when the guard was doing his rounds, I inquired about the delay. I was told that some senior officers were expected and that had pushed back the routine. I was pretty sure they had come for me. I lost my appetite despite severe stomach cramps.

The guard came running to open my cell as the commander came and stood in front of the gate. He held my clothes in his hands, the clothes I had been wearing the night I was arrested. I couldn't believe it. I teared up. The end was here.

The gate opened. No blindfold, no handcuff. I was taken to the bathroom and asked to bathe. The guard gave me a bar of soap and asked me to take my time and wash up well. Cold water on the sultry summer morning felt heavenly and the fragrance of soap filled my nostrils, tickling all my senses. I had a nice long bath. When I stepped out, the guard asked me to go back and bathe again. I thought that I still looked dirty, that was why I had been asked to go back in. I did as I was told.

I was so happy. All my pain and frustration was being washed away by the water. After my second bath, I was escorted back to my cell, where the commander was waiting for me with a set of clothes that weren't mine. They seemed to be made of thick material. Maybe they belonged to a prisoner who had been caught during winter. I asked the commander about my clothes. He said that those had been handed over to the authorities, who had asked me to get ready. I was also given a pair of slippers.

I was waiting in my cell when three or four men came with a pair of handcuffs that seemed different, not the kind that were used in this facility. Handcuffed and blindfolded, with my head covered by a black cloth, I was escorted out of the building. I could hear birds, smell fresh air, feel the warmth of sunlight. I could almost taste everything from every pore of my body.

I heard a diesel-belching vehicle drive up to where we were standing. The smell of the burning fuel was like a fragrance to me. As I took a deep breath, a long piece of cloth was put over me, covering my entire body.

One of the officers giggled and said, '*Ansari, aaj toh tune burqa bhi pahan liya.*' (Ansari, you have ended up wearing a burqa too.) I thought it was a burqa since the material was very soft and felt like satin.

I was led to the vehicle and asked to get in. It was a little high off the ground, so I presumed it was an SUV or a pickup truck. There was one officer on either side of me, and one in the front seat.

After some time, the car came to a halt and the driver left the car. I was continuously chanting verses from the Quran. The driver did not return for a couple of minutes and the three other officers in the vehicle were rather quiet. Then they also stepped out. I wondered what was happening. Was there a bomb in the car? Were they going to blow me up? I fretted until they returned and heaved a sigh of relief when they did.

The man sitting to my left told me that a person should always speak the truth before death. I caught on. They were indeed going to kill me. My throat went dry and I could not say anything. But then I thought that if I would be dead either way, I might as well stand up to them.

I told them, 'It is your cruelty and lack of ability to see the truth. You claim to be true Muslims but the Quran says that the Almighty has cursed wrongdoers and their hearts turn black, therefore, they cannot see, hear or speak the truth.'

One tight slap came my way from the left, followed by punches, but the man inflicting the violence was stopped by the officer on my right.

Soon, I was taken out of the car and escorted into a building. We climbed the stairs and entered a room where their voices echoed, so it must have been a huge area. The burqa and blindfold were removed. I saw a large table and a man sitting at the head of it. He was dictating something to another man, who was typing into a computer. I was asked to sit across from them. Two men stood behind me.

The officer who was doing the dictating looked away from the computer and said, 'I am the judge and you are in a court.' I was asked some basic questions: name, profession, nationality, age, qualification.

He sounded professional and respectful as he asked me the purpose of my visit to Pakistan, where I had been kept since 2012, and for how long. While answering his questions, I felt that maybe this judge would do justice.

From the corner of my eye, I saw an army man in uniform get up and walk out of the room. The man I presumed was the judge asked his subordinate to take a printout and hand it to me. I was asked to read it and tell him if it was right or wrong.

I told him that I could not read without my glasses.

'*Chashme lagate ho?* (Do you use spectacles?)' asked the magistrate.

'*Ji, sir.*' (Yes sir.)

'*Door ka hai ya paas ka? Kitna number hai?*' (Is it for distant vision or near?)

'*Sir, door ka hai. Pehle minus 5.5 tha lekin ab shayad aur zyada badh gaya hoga.*' (Sir, it's for distant vision. Earlier it was minus 5.5 but I think it must have increased now.)

'*Tum toh bilkul andhe ho.*' (You are completely blind.)

The magistrate asked his subordinate to increase the font size on the computer and asked me to read from the screen. But the words were still blurred. He then asked for a printout and handed the papers to me. I brought them very close to my face. Slowly, I started reading. To my horror, the statement read that I was an Indian spy sent by the Indian intelligence agency R&AW to build a network in Pakistan and carry out anti-Pakistan activities.

It also said that I already had a network running in Pakistan, funded by India. There were three pages with around eight to ten such points.

I told them that I had not said any of the things written on the paper. The magistrate said that they were checking all possibilities and I had nothing to worry about. But I knew better.

The judge asked me to be taken to another room and got up to leave. As I was being blindfolded, I heard the judge say, '*Mera phone le ao. Colonel Sahab ka phone aata hoga.*' (Get me my phone, Colonel Sir will be calling.)

Why would an army colonel be calling a judge? Was this man a puppet of the Pakistan army? By now I knew that it was all a set-up. I couldn't trust anyone.

In the other room, when my blindfold was removed, I again saw two officers standing behind me. The third officer sat on the table in front, wearing a smug look. It was the same elderly brute.

He asked, 'Do you want to go home or not?'

I wanted to throw up, disgusted with this drill, but I kept a straight face and said, 'Yes, I want to go home at the earliest.'

He put the papers in front of me and said, 'Then sign these documents.'

'What are these papers? I want to read them first,' I said.

One of the officers standing behind me hit me on my head, saying, 'So now you have become so mighty that you want to read the papers?'

The elderly officer said, 'I don't think he wants to go home. His old mother will die waiting for him. And he is so selfish that he wants to read the papers.'

I started crying. They knew how to play me emotionally. I was blindfolded and my face was covered again. They took me back to the vehicle and drove me somewhere. When we reached, they dragged me out and took me to a room. I was made to sit on a chair again, and the cloth covering my face was removed, but not the blindfold. Through the gap between the bridge of my nose and my blindfold, I could see a table in front of me.

The same old officer came in again, kept a few papers on the table and covered them with the file. Now my blindfold was removed. The officer told me that if I wanted to go home, I would have to sign the papers.

I insisted on reading the papers and said that without reading them I would not sign.

'Don't waste our time. Just sign it. They are your releasing documents. Once you sign them, we can start with further paperwork. The judge will leave in some time and your case will get delayed. Don't you know how courts work?'

I bent over the papers holding a pen, trying to buy time and see if they were the same documents that declared me an Indian spy. They were. I put the pen down and said, 'These are the same documents with the false statements. I will not sign them.'

I felt a huge blow to my head. It was something metallic. Maybe the handcuffs that the officer was holding. I was losing consciousness.

They knew there wasn't much they could do so they forcefully took my thumb impressions.

'The work is done,' said one of the officers.

'If only we had one document with his original signatures, we wouldn't have had to go through all this trouble,' said the other, sounding exasperated.

That was the last thing I heard. When I came to my senses, I could hear the azaan from a nearby mosque. I was lying on the floor, blindfolded, my face covered. There was a shooting pain in my head, and then I remembered what had happened.

As I moved, someone asked, '*Theek ho?*' (Are you okay?)

A new voice. I asked for water. Then I heard another voice at a distance ask, 'What is he saying?'

The first man replied, 'He is asking for water.'

The second man replied, '*Rehne de. Kuch bhi dene ki ijazat nahi hai. Ab pani bol raha hai. Fir bathroom ke liye bolega to kaun le jayega ise. Aise hi pada rehne de.*' (Leave him be. We are not supposed to give him anything. If you give him water, the next thing he will want is to go to the loo.)

Because I could hear the azaan, I asked for the sacred direction or qibla, towards which Muslims turn to offer prayers.

He asked '*Qibla jaan kar tujhe kya karna hai?*' (What do you want to do knowing the qibla?)

I said, '*Namaz padhne ke liye.*' (To offer my prayers.)

The man said mockingly, '*Tu kyun namaz padhega?*' (Why will you offer prayers?)

I was irritable and didn't care any longer so I said, '*Koi namaz kyun padhta hai?*' (Why does one offer prayers?)

The man responded, '*Hum to namaz padhte hain, Allah ki ibadat karne ke liye kyuki ham Musalman hain. Tujhe kyun namaz padhni hai?*' (We offer our prayers to worship Allah since we are Muslims. Why do you want to offer prayers?)

I snapped, '*Kisne kaha tumse ke main Musalman nahi hu? Mera rab jaanta hai ke mera imaan kya hai aur mujhe koi zaroorat nahi hai ke main tumhe is baat ka saboot du.*' (Who told you that I am not a Muslim? My

Creator knows my faith in Him and I don't need to provide you with any proof.)

'*Acha! Agar tu Musalman hai to kya teri khatna hui hai?*' (Oh! So if you are a Muslim then have you been circumcised?)

'*Islam kehta hai ke pehla kalma Musalman ki pehchan hai, peshani par sajde ka nishan Musalman ki pehchan hai, insaniyat aur ache akhlaq Musalman ki pehchan hai. Lekin tumhare mulk me to mard ki khatna Musalman ki pehchan hai. Maine pani manga, to tumne ek pyase ko pani dene se mana kiya kyunki baad mein bathroom kaun le jayega. Namaz ke liye qibla ka rukh poocha to wo nahi batate, wazu nahi karne dete. Aur fir tum mere imaan par sawal uthate ho.*' (Islam says that the first declaration of faith, the mark of prostration on the forehead, humanity and truthfulness are the identifications of a Muslim. But circumcision has been made the mark of identification in your country. I asked for water, but you denied water to a thirsty man, worrying about who would take me to the restroom. You did not guide me to the direction of the qibla for prayers, you don't allow me to do my ablutions and then you have the audacity to question my faith.)

But for them an Indian could never be a true Muslim. He said, '*Chup ho ja. Humein mat sikha zyada. Tu to sirf Musalman hone ka natak karta hai. Tu sirf Hindustani hai. Aur har Hindustani humara dushman hai.*' (Shut up and don't try to preach to us. You are just pretending to be a Muslim. For us, you are only an Indian and every Indian is our enemy.)

Saying this, he kicked my face and went away. I did not know which direction I was facing and where I was. But I felt lighter and relaxed after venting my feelings after so many years.

Lying on the ground in that condition, I offered my prayers blindfolded and with my hands tied behind my back. As I finished namaz, I heard someone walk into the room. It was the same interrogating officer, but now his tone had softened. He asked me to get up and congratulated me. He said that I would soon be going home.

I was escorted to a car. It had started drizzling and the weather was quite pleasant. It reminded me of the verses from the Holy Quran that rain was a sign of blessings from Allah Almighty. My heart was satisfied and I was at peace.

I was then taken back to the same prison facility. Lunch was already done so I had to stay hungry that day. But the happiness of going home was enough for me.

My cell mate, Mansoor, asked me what had happened. I simply showed him my thumb, which was painted blue with ink because of the thumb impression. He congratulated me and quickly went to the door and signalled to someone in a cell on the other side. I asked him what he was doing. He said that that was Atta-ur-Rahman, my partner from Karak. I couldn't see him because of my poor eyesight but he recognized me, said Mansoor. I figured he must have read the message on the washroom wall.

Different guards came in and congratulated me for the completion of my case. But none of us knew what exactly had happened. That night, the only question that came to mind was that if they wanted to release me as an innocent person, why did they take my thumb impression on a false statement?

May, June and July passed. There was no movement. In the new facility, Mansoor would talk to Atta-ur-Rahman using sign language, conveying my messages to him and vice versa.

One day, Mansoor conveyed that Atta's message was that my parents had spoken to him and they were very angry with me. I was upset the entire day. I lost my appetite and my sleep.

On 27 July 2015, I was again taken out of the premises. Along with two other officers, the elderly officer accompanied me as we went to CMH Hospital in his car. On reaching, he whispered in my ear that I was being brought here for a medical check-up, as per the release procedure. 'If the doctor asks, say you are absolutely fine, else they will hold you back for longer till the treatment is done.'

I did exactly that. The drill ended and I was taken back. Mansoor communicated the message to Atta, who was glad since he would also be off the hook if I were released.

After a couple of days, another officer came to my cell with my belongings to confirm if they were all mine. He also asked me if anything was missing. I was touching my possessions after two and a half years. It was an emotional moment. I told them everything was intact. I could smell the fragrance of my clothes on my hands.

On 3 August, I was removed from the underground jail. I would never return. It was a bumpy ride in the back of a pickup truck, reminding me of the journey from the Torkham border to Peshawar, which was equally bumpy. Not that I was complaining. This was my road to freedom.

The truck came to a halt after a short drive. I thought it must be at a checkpost, but I was asked to step down, blindfolded and handcuffed. The two men holding me on either side escorted me again into a building and made me sit.

When my blindfold and handcuffs were removed, I found myself in another cell, which was much larger than the underground dungeon I had been in. It also had an attached Indian-style toilet and a concrete elevated area at one corner serving as a bed. When I looked around and walked up to the iron grills, I saw a passageway and a wall made up of concrete trellis on the other side. The best thing I could make out was the absence of cameras.

So I was in another jail facility, but I consoled myself with the thought that it was a temporary arrangement before my release. Besides, I was excited to see blue sky after years. The trellis over the grill opened up to the skies. I couldn't stop looking at the beauty and wonder of this open space.

I thought the borders must have closed since it was late evening and that was why I was being held temporarily in this facility. But the days passed with no word from anyone. I then found out that this place also had an interrogation room, which I was introduced to soon enough.

The interrogating officer here was a lanky young man, a straight shooter. In my head, I named him Afzal.

He introduced himself and said, '*Ye mujhe pata hai ki ab tak tum cover story sunate sunate bachte a rahe ho lekin ab yahan tumhari kahani nahi chalegi. Agar ghar jaana chahte ho to cover story ke bahar aao aur hakikat bata do. Jaise hi tum sach bata doge tumhare saare papers taiyar ho jayenge aur fir Islamabad mein India ke safarat khane se tabadala ki baat shuru ho jayegi. Tum koi pehle jasoos nahi ho jo pakde gaye ho. Tumhare jaise bahut se jasoos humne pakde hain aur India ne humare jasooson ko pakda hai. Lekin jaise hi woh sab sach bata dete hain maheene bhar ke andar andar unka aapas mein tabadala kara diya jata hai. Hum tumhen yahan se chhod denge aur badle mein wahan se apna koi aadmi chhuda lenge. Varna tumhe goli maar ke kisi jungle mein fenk dena humare liye koi badi baat nahi hai. Aur agar meri baat karo to mujhe tumhare vajud se hi taklif ho rahi hai ki mere samne ek Hindustani baitha hai. Agar jaana chahte ho to sach bata do varna hamesha ke liye yahi pade rahoge.'*

(I know that till now you have been telling the cover story. But it will not work here. If you want to go home, tell us the truth. As soon as you tell us the truth, all your papers will be readied. And then the conversation about prisoner exchange will start with the Indian embassy in Islamabad. You are not the first spy to be caught. We have caught many spies like you and India has caught our spies. But as soon as they tell the truth, they are exchanged within a month. We will let you go from here and we will get some of our men released in exchange. Otherwise, it is not a big deal for us to shoot you and throw you into a forest. As for me, your mere presence as an Indian sitting in front of me bothers me. If you want to go, tell the truth, otherwise you will stay here forever.)

The session with Afzal ended and I was taken back to my cell. After a fortnight, I was shifted to another place, which looked like a warehouse for prisoners.

It was a 200-metre-long haunted-looking building divided into eight cells. The prisoners had to follow the same routine of visiting the washroom only once in twenty-four hours, with the time allowed inside a maximum of five minutes. I was kept in the innermost room of this facility. There was no light or fan. It was dingy and stuffy. At one end of the room a bottle was kept for urinating. It was like déjà vu, the only difference being that we were given soap. One bar for everything: bathing, washing clothes, washing utensils.

The only source of fresh air and light was a small ventilator with a really high mesh, close to the ceiling. The place was so dirty that it was as good as sleeping on the muddy ground. Different kinds of insects and rodents also inhabited the place.

We were all given a pair of pyjamas, a short kurta and a plastic plate and cup. The next day, I was taken to get my head shaved. That was it. I was going to be a guest here for much longer than I had thought. Everything I had been told was a farce. I cannot describe the anger I felt. Life no longer made sense.

The system in this facility was different. I was no longer in solitary confinement like at the previous place. I was not always blindfolded. But even though I was alone in my cell, by the end of September, I began talking to my neighbours. I first got the chance to interact with and observe them in the washroom, where we were all taken together for five minutes.

Some of the prisoners were there on charges of breach of national security, such as making fake ID cards and uniforms of the Pakistan army, while some had other serious charges against them. Four prisoners had served in the Pakistan army and were in jail because they had pictures and videos of Taliban leader Mangal Bagh on their phones. I found that unsettling. For a moment, the thought of the Taliban-looking army officer from the Kohat cantonment flashed through my mind. But then again, everything about the Pakistan army was strange. These prisoners were provided with extra facilities like cigarettes, extra food, milk and, best of all, even mobile phones to make short calls.

By the end of September, all prisoners except me had been either shifted or released. The month of October was a lonely one. Solitary confinement again, to the extent that the people on duty almost forgot that I existed. Sometimes they would forget to take me to the washroom; sometimes I had to go hungry.

Alone in the darkness one night, I thought that if I was being left unmonitored for so long, I should at least try to make an escape. One afternoon, after the regular power outage, I tried to climb the grilled gate to the trellis. I was almost there when suddenly, I heard footsteps so I quickly came down and sat in one corner.

The guard came, saw me and went back. I suddenly wondered how he knew what I was up to. Were there CCTV cameras here as well? Then I heard footsteps and chains, the sounds I was dreading. I didn't want to be beaten again.

It was the commander, with the guard right behind him, holding a complicated set of chains. He stepped in and cuffed my feet, and then brought the chains up from my back to my wrists and cuffed me. I was put in shackles, which didn't come off for anything—going to the washroom, bathing, praying, sleeping.

The ceiling had two small openings. From one, I could see blue skies, and occasionally, clouds; and a small leaf from the other. The only thing I looked forward to was the morning anthem or *tarana* that I could hear from a school which I suppose was very close to this facility. '*Lab pe aati hai dua ban ke tamanna meri . . .*' (My longings come to my lips as a supplication of mine . . .) It was the exact interpretation of my condition.

Thoughts of what my fate and the state of my parents would be were killing me. I always prayed for forgiveness from Allah and from Ammi.

One day in mid-November 2015, I heard quick footsteps coming towards me. The guard and commander had come to fetch me and said there was a car waiting for me outside the building. My fear grew as I was blindfolded and handcuffed. All through the ride, everything I had already been through started flashing in front of my eyes.

I figured that I was at the same place where I had met Afzal. I was told that there was another army officer present along with the district magistrate, Bashir Ahmed. The army officer asked me a few questions regarding the statement that I had signed six months ago.

'Sir, I didn't sign any document. They forced my thumb impressions on the papers. I never accepted being an Indian spy. I was beaten and forced, sir,' I pleaded.

He took down the statement that I gave and left. The following week, he returned and removed my blindfold and said, 'Sign here.'

I dreaded asking but did so nonetheless, 'What is this, sir?'

'You can read it and then sign,' he said in a calm tone.

I took my time to read the document. It had the exact version I had narrated. I agreed to sign. Now there was no reason not to.

He took the paper and wished me all the best. The statement was right but everything about me signing any document felt wrong. I didn't know what was coming my way next.

21

Court Martial

December 2015

I told them the truth, but I got no justice. They forced my thumb impressions on papers, yet granted me no relief. Their promises were only lies and deception. I was so angry. It had been more than three years and I had had no legal assistance, no connect with my family. My existence had been wiped off the face of the Earth. And I couldn't do anything about it.

On the evening of 3 December, some guards came to my cell and hurriedly asked me to come with them. As I stepped out of my cell, one of them said, 'Move fast. There is a car waiting outside for you.'

I was blindfolded and handcuffed. I had stopped anticipating positive outcomes so I just wondered, 'Now what?'

I was driven to the same building where I had met the army officer, and made to sit on a chair in a room. I heard the voice of a man in the distance so I figured I must be in a large room. 'Are you Hamid Ansari, son of Nehal Ansari?' the man asked.

He started reading out something I couldn't understand. I moved my head around and tried to concentrate on what he was saying. It was all too technical for me. The man stopped and asked, 'Are you clear on why you are here and the proceedings that are about to begin?'

I was completely at sea. I shook my head and told them that I couldn't fathom a word. Then another voice sitting across from me on a chair said, 'Don't worry. He will read out the statement for you again in simpler language.' Someone else sat next to me and translated every statement into simpler language. I recognized that voice. It belonged to Shahzad, the same army officer who had interrogated me on 29 January 2015.

The voice began reading out the statement again, 'Commencing this court martial session at army headquarters, Peshawar, dated the 16th of November 2015, for civilian Hamid Ansari, son of Nehal Ansari, an Indian national, under charges of espionage . . .'

Shahzad said, '*Koi aisi cheez hai jo tumhein nahi samajh ai?*' (Is there anything that you did not understand?)

I answered, '*Sir, pehle toh aaj 16 November nahi hai. Aaj 3 December hai. Aur dusri baat ki jab aap log mujhe civilian bol rahe hain to phir mera court martial kyun ho raha hai?*' (Sir, first of all, today is 3 December and not 16 November. And secondly, when you guys are addressing me as a civilian then why am I being brought to a court martial?)

There was complete silence in the room for some time and then Shahzad's tone changed to one of extreme displeasure. They had clearly intended to fudge the dates. '*Tumhe kaise pata aaj kaunsi tareekh hai?*' (How do you know what date it is today?)

I said, '*Aapke lower staff ki meherbani hai. Maine unko baat karte suna tha do din pehle. Vah log apni salary ki baat kar rahe the jismein 1 December tareekh ka zikr hua tha.*' (It is the courtesy of your lower staff. Two days ago I overheard them discussing something about their salaries. One of them mentioned the date as 1 December.)

The voice in the distance urged us to continue with the court-martial session. He introduced the officer who would be overseeing the session and declared he would be taking an oath for the same. 'Lieutenant General Jahanzeb Aslam of the Pakistan army, Muslim, will take the oath for justice.'

'*Main, Pakistan army ka Lieutenant General Jahanzeb Aslam, Allah ko hazir aur nazir jankar yeh kasam khata hoon ki main is muqadme mein pura pura insaaf karunga, aur apne auhdey ka najayaz fayda uthakar*' *mulzim ke sath kisi qism ki na-insafi nahi karunga.'* (I, Lieutenant General Jahanzeb Aslam of the Pakistan army, swear by Allah Almighty who is present everywhere and witnessing everything that I will do full justice in this case and will not do any kind of injustice with the accused by taking advantage of my position illegally.)

Lieutenant General Aslam administered the same oath to the other officers participating in the proceedings: Brigadier Zubin Shah, Colonel Ejaz Farooq, Major Ali, Second Major Huzaifa Noorani and Waiting Captain Sahil Khan. Lieutenant General Aslam and Brigadier Shah were presiding as judges of the military court. The colonel was a prosecution lawyer while Major Ali was my defence counsel. The prosecution was asked to read out the charges against me. I was expecting them to call me a spy and an R&AW agent but I was completely blindsided by the charges they were levelling.

Colonel Farooq started with some evidence that he spoke of having found on my phone. According to him, I had taken photographs of the Nowshera Cantonment's main gate.

Aghast and scared, I listened to him carefully but did not utter a word. What and where the hell was this Nowshera Cantonment? When I did not know even that it existed then how could I have taken pictures of the place?

Shahzad explained that I was in possession of a photograph of a cantonment gate. When I argued that I had not taken any such photograph, I was told that I would be given an equal opportunity to defend myself.

The colonel continued, 'I shall try to prove my case with the help of three witnesses: Major Taimur of the FIA, the interrogating officer; District Magistrate Bashir Ahmad; 3. Atta-ur-Rahman.'

He went on to relate a story based on false evidence and lies.

In some time, the azaan was heard from a nearby mosque. I thought they would stop to pray but the proceedings continued unhindered. I said a little prayer and asked God to help me overcome this travesty of justice.

The brigadier asked if I had any questions. I nodded and he allowed me to speak.

I said, 'The prosecution is being handled by a colonel-ranking officer while my side is being pleaded by a major. Isn't this injustice at the beginning itself? How can a major fight an officer he reports to?'

The brigadier answered, 'This is the procedure. Don't worry, justice will be done as we have taken an oath.'

I said, 'I want to have a word with my defence lawyer, Major Ali.'

The brigadier agreed and said that I would get time after he adjourned the proceedings. 'The court martial shall continue tomorrow at 8 a.m. sharp. The suspect civilian Hamid Ansari, son of Nehal Ansari, should be taken to the CMH Hospital for a complete body check-up and then brought to the court martial. All members of the court martial are to be present on time. The court is adjourned till tomorrow.'

I was taken to another room where Major Ali came to meet me. We exchanged pleasantries and then he asked, *'Kya baat karni hai tumhe mujhse?'* (What is it that you want to discuss with me?)

'Is this not a conflict of interest? You are a soldier of the Pakistan army. Why would you go against your own superiors to defend an Indian national who is under suspicion charges of espionage? How can I trust you?' I asked.

He thought about it and then tried to convince me that he would stand by his oath. However, I remained unconvinced. This was all a set-up. And then he said something that confirmed my fears.

Major Ali asked, *'Maan lo agar tum yeh case haar gaye tab tumhara statement kya hoga? Kya tab bhi yehi bologe ke tumhein RAW walon ne nahi bheja hai?'* (Just assume that if you lose this case, what will be your final statement? Will you still say that RAW has not sent you on a mission?)

He was in it to lose, not to win. I asked if spying was the only charge against me or if there were other charges as well.

'What other charges are you talking about?' he inquired.

'Charges of illegally entering Pakistan, possession of the fake CNIC,' I said.

He told me that all other charges had been waived barring this one charge of spying. I wondered how I had been forgiven for the crime

I had actually committed but being charged for one that I had not. Everything was staged.

Major Ali left the room and I was taken back to prison. I was hugely disappointed and also petrified about my fate since it was clear that this was no longer a case of illegal entry—it was of espionage. And by now I knew perfectly well what that meant.

I had lost my appetite and my will to do anything. The curious guards and commander came to my cell to ask me what had happened. The commander figured out there was a problem, so he asked the guards to leave and then put his hand on my shoulder through the iron bars and said, 'Don't worry, Hamid. The chances of you being released are very high. There is word doing the rounds. Just do and say what you have been all this while.'

He left me wondering if that was the truth or if the parallel universe that had been created for me—a mock court and a mockery of a trial—was the real deal.

Captain Sahil Khan arrived early the next morning and escorted me for my medical check-up without letting me have a drop of water or anything to eat. I was blindfolded during all the examinations: blood test, chest X-ray, body weight, pulse, blood pressure and ECG. The technician informed the captain that all reports were normal. I was then taken to the same place where the court martial hearing was to reconvene.

Exactly at 8 a.m. I was made to sit in a freezing cold room. My handcuffs behind my back were tethered to a chain that was held by a soldier. As usual, nothing started on time. We waited while the soldiers behind me chatted away.

I didn't feel very well since I hadn't eaten all morning. My blood pressure fell drastically, to the extent that I could not hold myself up on the chair. The soldiers holding the shackles noticed and informed the superiors. A doctor was called in and I was served water, tea and a few biscuits.

After a while, I heard the azaan for Friday afternoon prayers. I asked the soldier behind me if I could pray. A rough nudge came my way and I was caught off guard, '*Chup chap baithe raho.*' (Stay quiet and keep sitting.) So much for being the Islamic Republic of Pakistan, I thought.

Another hour passed before I heard footsteps and Shahzad's voice saying, '*Ab tak Ansari ka case shuru nahi hua kya?*' (Ansari's case hasn't started yet?)

I couldn't hear the answer that followed, but the guards asked me to get up and took me to another room.

Brigadier Shah said, 'The court martial of civilian Hamid Ansari, son of Nehal Ansari, an Indian national, continues at army headquarters, Peshawar, by 21 Signal Battalion.'

The colonel was asked to initiate the proceedings after the brigadier repeated the charges against me.

Colonel Farooq said, 'Civilian Hamid Ansari, son of Nehal Ansari, was caught in possession of sensitive photographs of the Nowshera Cantonment gate. To prove my point that Hamid Ansari was sent on a mission by Indian intelligence agencies, I would like to call upon my first witness, the investigating officer of FIA, Major Taimur.'

I heard a man take an oath in a familiar voice. I could see flashes of the interrogation in June 2014 when this very officer had sounded convinced with my version and said that he would return with some documents. But he never did.

Major Taimur said, 'I was the interrogating officer for the case of Hamid Ansari and I found out that he was an asset of the Indian intelligence agency. From his BlackBerry, we found three photographs of the Nowshera Cantonment main gate. Sir, this man is highly trained. He suppressed information and dodged us despite all the techniques that we employed. We did detailed investigations from whatever little information he gave us and came to find that Hamid Ansari has more than forty email addresses which he has been using to fool or mislead innocent Pakistani people and get them to join his network.

'A very important point that I present is that anybody who is travelling into another country, especially illegally, would carry enough money to pay people off. But this man had no money on his person or in his belongings during his arrest. How could he have moved or done anything without local support? He has an active network within Pakistan.

'Secondly, sir, Hamid Ansari also claims that he came to rescue a girl called Fiza, a resident of Kohat. But during our investigations, when we went to the girl's residence, she not only denied having any communication with him but also refused to recognize his photo.'

The brigadier turned towards Major Ali and asked him if he would want to cross-question the first witness. He asked the presiding officer, 'Sir, I would like to request that Hamid Ansari defend himself.'

I was stumped. I had not prepared myself and clearly nor had he. What a coward! He must have been one of those soldiers who turned his back and ran away in a battlefield. I had nothing but revulsion for him.

I felt like I was in a feeding arena where the trapdoors had been opened for predators to devour me. I was shifty and didn't know what to do.

My disadvantages were many. Most prominently among them was my blindfold. I requested for it to be removed, and I also asked for pen and paper since I had to argue my own case. But they refused. I wasn't surprised. This entire sham exercise was not to prove me innocent but to create enough impediments to declare me guilty. So I had to rely on my memory and remember every tiny detail I could.

I said, 'Can you please provide me the details of the forty email addresses that you claim are mine?'

Major Taimur read out forty email addresses, all of which had the name 'Ansari' somewhere among them.

I said, 'Clearly, you went through the one email account I shared with you all and found these other email addresses there. They are not mine but of my relatives. You can go back and check. Most are active in Mumbai and other parts of Maharashtra or abroad. Sending or receiving emails automatically adds an email address to the address book. They clearly aren't mine because if they were then you would have had access to all forty of them. Do you have access to the other thirty-nine?'

There was no response. I thought there wouldn't be any so I continued and requested for my wallet and my phone to be presented to the court. 'Sir, please check my wallet. I wasn't penniless when I entered the country. There was 5700 rupees in my wallet. I agree that I didn't have a lot of money but that was because I did not intend to stay in Pakistan beyond one day.

'On the issue of Fiza not knowing me, I would like you to check the messages that we had both exchanged, sir. You will find enough evidence to see that I had only entered Pakistan to rescue her from being a victim of wani. I am sure she must be afraid and must have changed her statement but that does not change my truth, my reality.

'The witness produced by the prosecution was lying on oath, sir. I would request him to be struck off the witness list.'

The brigadier said, 'Even if we reject the three claims of the witness, what about the photograph retrieved from your cell phone? We have forensic reports to prove that it was taken from your phone.'

'I did not click any photograph. I don't even know where Nowshera is located. And if any photograph has been found on my cell phone then it has been clicked after my arrest.'

'But the forensic report clearly says that the photograph was clicked before your arrest.'

'The mobile phone is only an electronic device which can be tampered with easily and its dates can be changed. I request you to provide me with my cell phone containing the photograph and a laptop with an Internet connection; I shall prove that the photograph was clicked after my arrest.'

The brigadier and the colonel both jumped with eagerness. The brigadier said, 'What technology will you use to prove it? Tell us the method and technology and I promise I will help you.'

I figured they were up to something but I knew I was clean so I said, 'I am sorry, sir, I cannot share the technique with you before proving my point. If you really want to help me and do justice then first provide me with the cell phone and a laptop.'

The two senior officers discussed the matter but denied me access to my phone. In all probability, it did not have the photograph they were mentioning and they would have stood exposed.

The brigadier said, 'We don't need you to prove anything that is already proven. We have the forensic report to prove the point.'

I hoped to see my phone once to see what photograph they were talking about. I had to explain the fallacy in their theory. 'Just assume for once that two men are crossing a bridge. One pushes the other off the bridge, into the river. Your forensic report can only show the cause of death. Can it prove whether he slipped accidentally and fell or was pushed by someone or jumped to commit suicide? Similarly, what does your forensic report say about someone tampering with my phone? Was my device tampered with? I am very clear that I did not take the picture that you are using as evidence against me.'

The prosecution was adamant and twisted the entire thing. Colonel Farooq said, 'Do you see, sir, how clever his argument is?'

Brigadier Shah agreed.

Neither was the witness rejected, nor was my argument accepted. It was a trap. They took my argument as proof I had been sent by India's intelligence agency.

Colonel Farooq said, 'I would now like to call upon District Magistrate Bashir Ahmad as my second witness.'

Ahmad was administered the oath and the questions began. He said, 'This Hamid Ansari was brought to my court six months ago, when he accepted all his crimes and recorded a statement in front of me. The statement that he gave me has already been produced in this court.

The brigadier asked, 'Hamid, do you want to say anything about the statement?'

I recognized Ahmad. He was the same officer who had forced my thumb impressions on documents six months ago. I remembered how he had waited to get orders from some brigadier on that day.

Being blindfolded was frustrating. I wanted to take it off so I could see their expressions. I said, 'I have not given any such statement to anyone. Neither have I done it nor did I ever intend to. The statement is completely false and the magistrate himself was typing it when I was produced in his court.'

The brigadier said, 'Would you like to cross-question the witness?'

I nodded and was granted permission.

I asked, 'Sir, that day you were sitting on a chair to do justice. Did I really give such a statement to you?'

I heard giggles instead of an answer.

I persisted, 'Did I sign the statements in your presence? I mean, did you see me signing the statement?'

Ahmad said, 'Sir, he signed the statement in front of me.'

I raised my voice, startling even myself, 'Sir, this witness is also lying. I never signed any documents. They had taken my thumb impressions. But this magistrate says he saw me signing documents.'

The baffled magistrate immediately interrupted, 'No, no, what I meant was thumb impressions. Signatures and thumb impressions are the same thing. I meant I witnessed the episode.'

I argued, 'Oh really! Signatures and thumb impressions are one and the same thing?'

Colonel Farooq interrupted, 'As long as you accept a statement it is one and same thing.'

The brigadier said, 'This is an insignificant point and does not prove anything.'

I said, 'Sir, they were forcing me to sign the documents without letting me read them and when I objected they hit me on the head and took my thumb impressions forcefully while I was semi-conscious. I repeat, this was against my will.'

The brigadier said, 'Hamid Ansari, even if we reject the statement, we still have the photograph.'

I was frustrated and cried, '*Yaar, maine koi photo nahi liya hai. Yeh sab log jhootha drama kar rahe hain.*' (I never took any picture. This is all drama.)

The brigadier screamed, 'What do you mean "jhootha" drama? And I am not your yaar.'

I realized I had got carried away and immediately apologized.

The brigadier then announced a fifteen-minute break. Captain Sahil Khan escorted me to the adjacent room. I told him I wanted to go to the washroom. The captain ordered the guards to take me there. On entering the washroom, one handcuff was removed and the blindfold was simply lifted. When I opened my eyes, I saw one of the soldiers standing in front of me.

I asked him to leave. He wouldn't, so I stepped out without using the loo. The captain came in to ask if I was done. The guard behind me told him that I was acting funny. The captain said, '*Badmashi karte ho?*' (Are you being mischievous with us?) I replied, '*Tum logon mein insaniyat hi nahi hai aur na hi sach bolne ki himmat.*' (You guys lack humanity and the courage to speak the truth.)

The captain figured that something was wrong and asked me what had happened. When I told him, he instructed one of the guards to take me to the washroom and allow me to relieve myself in peace.

The court martial resumed after the break.

Colonel Farooq said, 'I would now like to call upon my third witness, Atta-ur-Rahman.'

Atta-ur-Rahman was administered the oath and the brigadier asked him to give his statement. I was certain which way the narrative was being built, and after all the torture that he had gone through, it was unlikely that he would tell the truth.

Atta-ur-Rahman said, '*Sir ji, ye ladka Hamid Ansari mujhe India se contact kiya karta tha Facebook par aur usne kaha ki iski koi dost Kohat ki rehne wali hai. Woh kisi museebat mein hai aur yeh uski madad karna chahta hai.*

Ladki ke bhai ne apne padosi ka qatal kiya tha to jirge main wani ke mutabik uss ladki ko maqtool ke ghar walon ko diya jana tha. Yeh ladka ussi ki madad karne aaya tha.' (Sir, this boy Hamid Ansari used to contact me from India and tell me that he has a friend in Kohat who is in some trouble and he wants to help her. The girl's brother had killed a neighbour's boy and as per the decision of the village council, the girl was to be given away to the victim's family as per the custom of wani. So this boy had come to help the girl.)

I couldn't believe my ears. Atta was standing by the true story. I was so grateful. I thanked God. I wanted to smile but stopped myself.

Atta-ur-Rahman continued, '*Is ne mujhse kabhi koi aisi baat nahi ki jo Pakistan ke khilaf ho. Yeh mere ghar aaya tha. Jab yeh raat ko so jata tha tab main uska saman check karta tha. Mujhe iske saman mein bhi koi galat cheez nahi mili. Pehli raat jab yeh aaya tha toh iske mobile ki maine talashi li thi. Uske mobile mein bhi mujhe koi galat cheez nahi mili. Main jhooth nahi bolunga. Main is umeed mein tha ke shayad yeh zyada paise leke aata lekin iske paas sirf 6500 rupees the. Mujhe isse koi fayda nahi mil raha tha isliye main aur mere dost Abdullah ne yeh faisla kiya ki hum ise agency ke hath pakadwa denge aur badle mein achha khasa inam lenge.'*

(He never said anything against Pakistan. He came to my house. When he slept at night, I used to check his belongings but did not find anything unacceptable. The first night when he came to my place I even checked his cell phone but didn't see anything suspicious. I will not lie today. I was expecting that he would be carrying a lot of money but he had only 6500 rupees on him. I was not getting any benefit out of him so my friend Abdullah and I decided to get him arrested by the agencies and in return earn a juicy reward.)

I had tears in my eyes. The people I had trusted had betrayed me. Till now, I had been thinking Abdullah had acted alone but now I knew that Atta-ur-Rahman was involved as well. Just for money. I was furious.

Atta-ur-Rahman continued, *'Maine jaan bujh kar ise jaali ID card aur ek SIM card dekar apne ghar se Kohat ke liye ravana kiya. Wahan Abdullah pehle hi agency ko khabar kar chuka tha kyunki jis ladki ki madad karne ye ana chahta tha woh Abdullah ki dur ki rishtedar hai aur iske aane se pehle hi uski shaadi kahin aur kara di gai thi. Main ise sirf paison ke lalach mein yahan bula kar pakadwa na chahta tha par ab main khud bhi fas gaya hoon. Maine kisi terrorist ka saath nahi diya.'*

(I deliberately made a fake ID card and got a SIM card and gave it to him before sending him to Kohat. There, Abdullah had already informed the agencies because the girl Hamid wanted to help was a distant relative of Abdullah and had already been married off even before his arrival. Only out of greed, I wanted to get him here and have him arrested. Now I am stuck in the same pit. But I am sure I did not support a terrorist.)

Atta-ur-Rahman broke down. But I was shocked and couldn't help fixating on the part where he said that Fiza had been married off

long before I came to Pakistan. How could someone be so merciless?
I wanted to strangle him. I felt deceived and like someone had put a
dagger through me and twisted it around to pull all my innards out.
I couldn't breathe. But then he was the only man who had spoken the
truth, my truth.

The brigadier asked me if I wanted to cross-question the witness.
I didn't.

'Hamid, is this animosity that I am sensing?'

I said, '*Chahe is ne mere sath jo bhi kiya ho par maine ise maaf kiya
kyunki maaf karne wala saza dene wale se zyada bada hota hai. Yeh bhi kya
yaad rakhega ki iska pala kisi Indian se padha tha.*' (No matter what he
has done to me but I still forgive him because a forgiver is greater than
a punisher. What would he remember that he had once encountered
an Indian.)

I had not wanted to say this but I did to pinch their egos—that if
an Indian could forgive a Pakistani then the Pakistanis could forgive me
in return. I wanted to convey that it was time to forgive all the wrong
that had been done and move on. If I could be so large-hearted, so could
they. But there were no takers for this sentiment.

Atta-ur-Rahman was sent back and now it was my turn to give a
statement.

The lieutenant general administered the oath to me, 'I, Hamid
Ansari, son of Nehal Ansari, swear by Allah Almighty who is aware of
everything and witnessing everything that I shall speak nothing but
the truth.'

I started, '*Sir, main yahan kisi galat irade se nahi aaya tha. Mujhe
yahi bataya gaya ki meri dost ek aisi musibat mein hai jis se bachne ka uske
paas suicide ke alava koi dusra rasta nahi. Atta-ur-Rahman ne mujhe kaha
ke mujhe khud aana hoga tabhi koi solution nikal sakta hai aur us ladki ki
jaan bach sakti hai. Maine pehle Pakistan ka visa lene ki bohot koshish ki,
lekin nahi mil raha tha.*

'*Atta-ur-Rahman ne mujhe vaada kiya ki woh meri madad karega
aur ussi ne mujhe Afghanistan ke raaste se aane ki salah di. Sirf char din
mein main pakda gaya. Aur ab tak jitne bhi logon ne mera case handle
kiya hai, sab ne mujhe bataya ki main innocent hoon aur mera RAW se*

kuchh lena dena nahi. Mujhe yeh bhi nahi pata hai ke Pakistan mein Nowshera naam ki koi jagah hai to Nowshera Cantonment ke gate ki photo main kaise le sakta hoon. Aur main gate ek aisi cheez hai jo main road per sabke samne hoti hai. Din bhar mein hazaron log dekhte honge. To usmein secrecy jaisi kya cheez hai? Aur main ab bhi kahta hoon ki agar mujhe mera phone aur ek laptop diya jaaye to main yah prove kar sakta hoon ki photo maine nahi liya.

'Main apni galti manta hoon ki main bina visa ke Pakistan mein dakhil hua. Aur iske liye main pichhle teen saal se Pakistan ki qaid mein hoon. Jaise main yahan mere ghar walon ke liye pareshan ho raha hoon vaise hi mere ghar wale bhi mere liye pareshan ho rahe honge. Mere baap ka dard aap hi samajh sakte ho. Aap bhi ek baap ho. Yeh baat har taraf se saabit hai ki maine yahan kisi ka koi nuksan nahi kiya aur jo kanoon toda hai, uski bahut badi saza bhi mil chuki hai aur main apne kiye ki mafi bhi mangta hoon. Lekin ab mujhe pichhle teen saal se insaaf nahi mila. Aapse request karta hun ki ab at least insaaf kare.'

(Sir, I did not come here with any wrong intention. I was told that my friend is in such trouble that she can see no other way out but suicide. Atta-ur-Rahman told me that I should come to Pakistan and only then can we find a solution to the problem and save her life. I tried very hard to get a visa for Pakistan but could not get one. Atta-ur-Rahman promised he would help me and advised me to come to Pakistan through Afghanistan. I was caught in just four days. And so far all the people who have handled my case have told me that I am innocent and have nothing to do with RAW. I do not even know if there is a place named Nowshera in Pakistan, so how can I take a photo of the Nowshera Cantonment gate? And the main gate is something that is in front of everyone on the main road. Thousands of people must be seeing it every day. So what is the secret in that? And I still say that if I am given my phone and a laptop, I can prove that I did not take the photo.

'I admit I made a mistake by entering Pakistan without a visa and for this I have been in a Pakistani prison for the last three years. Just as I am worried for my family members, my family members will also be worrying about me. You can understand my father's pain as you are a father too. It has been proved from all sides that I have not done any harm to anyone here, and I have been punished severely for the law that has been broken. I apologize for my actions. But I have not got justice for the last three years. I request you to at least now give me justice.)

The brigadier asked the prosecution to make their concluding statements. The colonel representing the prosecution said, 'The witness and evidence were produced to the honourable court and I leave the decision to the court.'

The brigadier now turned to the so-called defence and asked for his final points. The major said, 'Whatever the court feels is right as per law.'

The court was adjourned for the day.

Thus ended a cold day with me fighting to prove my innocence on enemy land, hanging on to the last vestiges of truth amid people who adopted a dogmatic approach to the case.

Hungry and tired, I was taken back to the facility.

On 7 December, I was taken back for the hearing. The brigadier had summoned me. 'Do you have anything else to say for us to show mercy on you? Do you plead for mercy?'

I was confused. Blindfolded, I turned left and right to figure what was happening.

The brigadier continued, 'We released a girl named Geeta last month. So, if you come clean then your release is possible.'

I said, 'If you are contemplating my release then you must know that I am innocent. I have apologized for the mistake I committed and have been punished for it for the past three years, sir. I seek justice in your court and plead mercy to Almighty Allah.'

'I know you have not done anything. Because you are not capable of doing anything. But for me you are an Indian and that is crime enough. But if you seek mercy, maybe we can let you go.'

He sounded miffed and ordered that I be taken back. They wanted me to plead for mercy in this case, but that would amount to acceptance of guilt since the charges were of espionage.

I was taken back to the same old haunted warehouse for prisoners. I thought I had fought a good fight. I had proven two witnesses wrong, and thankfully Atta-ur-Rahman had not lied. I believed that the truth would prevail and I would win the case.

~

In mid-December, I was taken to another location. My blindfold was removed and I was handed two sets of documents. 'Sign them,' said the officer. I read the papers. They contained the questions I had been asked during all the interrogations of the past three years. No answers, just questions. So I signed.

Now waiting had in itself become torture. I wanted to know the outcome of the court martial. December and January were unbearable months. The bone-chilling cold took a toll on my health. The echoes of the wind in the corridor made me feel like I was in the wild, with a pack of hyenas waiting to scavenge upon my lifeless body. That was how I looked at the Pakistan army.

I couldn't take the suspense any more. Every time I asked them about my case, it fell on deaf ears. So I decided to protest.

~

It was February 2016 and I was languishing in the cold, dingy cell. I had stopped eating. One of the guards came and asked, 'Why haven't you eaten your food?'

I replied, 'I am on a hunger strike.'

'What?' He thought I was joking.

'I will not eat till I get some answers about my case,' I said as I kept even the bottle of water outside my cell through the iron bars.

He stared at me, amused, and walked away. They all thought it was a gimmick, but three days of me going without food and water got them worried. My health deteriorated drastically. I was anyway skin and bones.

On the third day, an officer whose voice I did not recognize met me and said they were ascertaining details about my case. Meanwhile, I should start eating again.

I said to him, 'Sir, I have proven my innocence. I am not a spy. I have apologized for the mistake of illegal entry into Pakistan. I have paid a heavy price in the form of punishment over the past three years. I might be an Indian but I still have a right to know what is happening about my case.'

He promised to get back to me provided I started eating again. I complied.

On 10 February 2016, I was summoned back to the place I presume was the headquarters. I heard the same captain asking after my health. I told him I was fine and wanted to know the outcome of the court martial.

There was silence as he escorted me to a car. I had experienced the worst on such rides. The same eerie feeling returned. Were they going to kill me? Were they going to release me? Questions galore.

I didn't want to be beaten up again, but I mustered up the courage and asked, 'Sir, am I being released?'

The voice from the front said, 'Oh, I forgot to tell you. You have been sentenced to three years of rigorous imprisonment.'

'What? On what charges? I have spent the last three years in your prison!' I exclaimed.

'The charges that you were tried for—spying,' he said in a calm, no-nonsense tone.

He didn't want any further conversation. But my world had turned topsy-turvy. I was declared a spy despite fighting the charge for three years in the most adverse circumstances, and sentenced to three more years.

Espionage . . . Imprisonment . . . The officer's words kept ringing in my head as we drove on.

22

Qazi Anwar, Rukhshanda Naz and
the Legal Battle

Zeenat was missing—and there was no way to find her. Fauzia now had not one but two children who had gone missing in Pakistan.

It was the last week of August 2015. Fauzia's phone had been buzzing with calls from reporters who wanted to speak to her from India and Pakistan. She spoke to some of them. One asked who she would want rescued first. Without batting an eyelid, she said, 'My priority is Zeenat. She should be rescued. We will fight her case. I hope she comes home soon.'

Meanwhile, she approached the National Commission for Minorities and the NHRC. Every time she was in Delhi, she would try meeting Sushma Swaraj. On most occasions, the minister would meet her, otherwise she would be briefed by the MEA officers handling the case. The number of note verbales sent to the MoFA in Pakistan was only piling up. They shared some of the missives with Fauzia.

All this while, she was also in touch with the Pakistan High Commission in New Delhi, but her requests to meet the high commissioner, Abdul Basit, were in vain. He did not give her an appointment. She was confined to interacting with the visa counsellor.

(Basit eventually met Fauzia twice, about a month before his retirement. He assured her that as he belonged to the same region, he would follow up on the case once he was in Pakistan.)

Meanwhile, Qazi Anwar was fighting the case in Peshawar. The government was not very forthcoming, but the veteran lawyer kept at it.

In Mumbai, Jatin Desai called up Fauzia and told her that he had spoken to the senior advocate and activist Colin Gonsalves, who had offered to help.

Fauzia told Desai, 'Once when Ansari Sahab and I had gone to Delhi to attend the Supreme Court hearing, Colin was present in the courtroom.'

Jatin replied, 'Oh, that is why he said he knew about the case. I thought he had come across the news reports. Anyway, you both should meet him and see how he can help.'

October 2015

The couple went to meet Colin Gonsalves in Delhi, at his office at the Human Rights Law Network, where he welcomed them warmly. A social worker, Zoya, was also present. Fauzia reminded Colin of the day they met in the court room at the time of the hearing; he told her that he distinctly remembered the proceedings and the case. They spoke in detail and Colin told them that he would see what he could do and what needed to be done legally in Pakistan.

Just as they were getting up to leave, Zoya said, 'Fauzia ji, I know someone who has worked a lot on the India–Pakistan front. I would like to introduce you to her. Rita Manchanda, wife of Tapan Bose, is associated with SAFHR [South Asia Forum for Human Rights]. She might be able to help you.'

Fauzia thanked her profusely and got in touch with Rita, who heard her out. Fortunately, Rita was at a workshop in Nepal, where there were participants from Pakistan as well. One person came to mind when she heard of Fauzia's case—Rukhshanda Naz, who had been instrumental in the release of another Indian national, Ashok Kumar, in 1999. He had been arrested in the tribal areas.

Since she was also in Nepal, Rita met Rukhshanda and asked her how she was and what she was doing. Rukhshanda told her that she had been in the UK since 2012 but was now back in Pakistan completing a research paper. Hearing this, Rita said, 'Oh, thank God you are back! We have another case for you.'

Rita introduced Rukhshanda and Fauzia over an email and sent across all the documents that Fauzia had sent her. Rukhshanda went through the documents and connected with Fauzia. They exchanged numbers. Once Rukhshanda was back in Peshawar, Fauzia called her, 'Salaam, Rukhshanda Naz ji, I am so happy that you are looking into our case. Qazi Sahab has agreed to fight the case. I just wanted to know what your fee is going to be. We have to arrange for the money.'

Rukhshanda was quiet for a while and then spoke in her warm, heavy, affable voice, 'Fauzia ji, wa-alaikum-salaam, I am glad to help you in this case. I cannot take money from you. This is a humanitarian matter. Might I also tell you something very important? I am honoured to be part of this case, you know why?'

'Why?' asked a befuddled Fauzia.

'Because Qazi Sahab has taken it up. I have been his student, and nothing is more important for me than standing beside him and fighting this case. And believe me, if he has taken it up, the chances of losing are close to nil,' said Rukhshanda.

Fauzia's grin was almost palpable through the phone. She didn't know how to thank God for such saviours.

Rukhshanda wanted all the case files. Fauzia told her about Shaikh Lateef, whom Zeenat used to be in touch with in the Lahore High Court. He could help her with all the documents there. Rukhshanda called him up and asked him to courier the file, but never received them because he sent them by regular post.

She took printouts of all the documents sent to her via email by Fauzia. She needed to connect with Adnan Saboor Rohaila since the initial petition was his, but she didn't know him. She did know his father, Abdul Rauf Rohaila, and dropped him a message on Facebook. But there was no response.

The next day, Rukhshanda decided to meet Qazi Anwar with all the files. He told her that Abdul Rauf Rohaila had gone for Umrah.

He looked at the file in front of him and asked Rukhshanda, 'Are you convinced?'

Rukhshanda said, 'Yes. I have seen such cases in the past as well. The boy has made a huge mistake for sure, Qazi Sahab. But the family is distraught. The mother is putting up a brave fight. We need to help her.'

'What if there is more to the case?' he asked.

'Qazi Sahab, I don't think it is more than an innocent boy meeting a Pakistani girl online. They got close and she got into trouble with her family and village forcing *sawara* or wani on her. Hamid wanted to save the girl from this humiliation. I have seen many such cases in Khyber Pakhtunkhwa. Consider this a humanitarian case. I have spoken to his mother, Fauzia. She didn't hide anything from me. We have all the documents here and Zeenat has also done a commendable job with her investigations. She ensured an FIR was lodged. We do have a strong case,' she said.

They had a long meeting. The case of Zeenat also came up. Both expressed their worry about what had happened to her.

Rukhshanda and Qazi Anwar were convinced that Hamid Ansari had been trapped. Qazi Anwar asked Rukhshanda to prepare a detailed file of the entire case.

'Rukhshanda, you have handled many cases, even those involving Indians. You know what to do. We have to maintain a very low profile.'

She agreed and went home to prepare a complete record of everything that had happened so far. There was one file in Islamabad at the Missing Persons Commission which Zeenat had registered. She got that, as well as the petition filled out by Rohaila. Additionally, she got all of Hamid's email communications as also all the petitions and letters written by Fauzia.

She spoke to her journalist friend Raza Rumi regarding the case and he suggested that she go through all the news shows that were aired on the Hamid Ansari case. It took her ten to fifteen days to research everything and prepare the documents.

Having Qazi Anwar as the Ansari counsel in itself strengthened the case. There was absolute clarity on how he and Rukhshanda would handle it. Qazi Anwar would be arguing it while Rukhshanda would handle the attorney general's office and the media.

In early December 2015, during the hearings, the judges asked where Hamid was but got no reply from the counsel for the other side. They were procrastinating. This was around the same time that the establishment was holding a court martial in secrecy and forcing Hamid to accept he was guilty of espionage. They were trying to buy time.

After every hearing, Rukhshanda spoke to Fauzia and assured her that they would find Hamid. The FIR had indeed made their case strong. The next hearing was on 13 January 2016.

A restless Rukhshanda wanted to know Hamid's actual status. She went to Qazi Anwar and asked, 'What is happening? Do they have him or not? Is he alive or not?'

He calmly told her that the attorney general's office had informed him of Hamid's presence and that he was alive. 'The next hearing will be very important,' he said.

She also checked with Chief Justice Mazhar Alam Miankhel's office to see where they were on the case. It seemed like they were on the right track.

December 2015

One evening, Rukhshanda was checking her email when she saw an email regarding Hamid Ansari. It was from someone in Mumbai who almost demanded that she help Fauzia. She didn't like the tone of the email and didn't know who the person was so she sent it to Fauzia and Rita, and told them not to share her email ID with anyone.

'We are trying to keep a low profile here. This involves an Indian national. It is a very sensitive matter and I don't want to get involved in any mess,' she told Fauzia and Rita separately.

Both promised that it wouldn't happen again.

She also told them to trust her. '*Mera aitbaar karein. Main Hamid ko zaroor dhund nikalungi.*' (Trust me, I will definitely find Hamid.)

The day of the hearing, 13 January 2016, was a big day.

Qazi Anwar and Rukhshanda were both in court when the two-member bench disposed of the habeas corpus petition filed by Fauzia Ansari against the illegal detention of her son.

They were officially told that the military court had held a trial and sentenced Hamid to three years in prison on charges of espionage. The military establishment also informed the court that he would be shifted to Peshawar Central Prison.

Rukhshanda stepped out and immediately called Fauzia to inform her. Fauzia was in tears. She couldn't believe that their ordeal would soon be over.

'Rukhshanda ji, it has been three years. I cannot believe that it is all over,' Fauzia said with tears in her eyes.

'It is over. Now it is time to celebrate. It is only a matter of time,' she said.

The news started breaking on all channels: 'Pakistan admits to Hamid Ansari's presence in Pakistan', 'Pak reports say he was tried in military court', 'Hamid Ansari sent to Peshawar prison', 'Indian national sentenced in Pakistan'.

Fauzia and Nehal's phones buzzed non-stop with all news channels and newspapers seeking their comments. The Ansaris kept saying only that their long, arduous fight was over and they couldn't wait to see their son, hold their son again.

Fauzia spoke to her family members from whom she was getting constant calls. Desai spoke to the couple as well.

When Rukhshanda and Fauzia spoke next, Fauzia asked, 'But we still don't know how he is, whether it is my Hamid or not.' Doubts had crept in because of the secrecy with which Pakistan had dealt with the case.

Rukhshanda told her that the cops were looking into the files and would give permission for a visit soon.

Then Fauzia calculated three years from the day he had been arrested and told Rukhshanda, 'The three years are over. Does that mean he will be coming back soon?'

Rukhshanda said, 'I will have to get all those details. We don't have them yet since the military is involved.'

When she reached home that afternoon, Rukhshanda's phone rang. The man on the other side introduced himself as a diplomat of the Indian High Commission in Islamabad.

'Rukhshanda Madam, we have been following the case of Indian national Hamid Ansari very closely. You have taken up the case and have fought bravely. I just want to know if you needed any assistance from the mission,' asked the officer.

Rukhshanda thanked him and said that no assistance was required for now but that she would get in touch in case it ever was.

A few days later, when Fauzia was preparing tea, she received messages that Hamid had been shifted to Peshawar Central Prison. But among them were some confusing news reports that he had been sentenced to thirty years in prison. Her heart sank.

She held her head and started weeping. 'My son's life will be ruined.' She called out to her husband and Khalid. The entire family was tense and in shock.

Khalid said that there must have been a mistake and Fauzia should check with the lawyers. She then tried Rukhshanda's number, which was unreachable. Qazi Anwar was not in the country.

The very same day, Rukhshanda had gone to Karachi for the Women's Action Forum convention with her colleague. When she was returning, she realized she had forgotten her suitcase at her friend's residence and was told that her friend would drop it off at Rukhshanda's sister's house. So she told the driver to take her there.

Around 9 p.m., when she entered the house, she saw the television turned to Geo News, which was flashing the headlines: 'Indian national Hamid Ansari sent to Peshawar jail', 'Indian national was sentenced to three years in prison by a military court'.

She immediately called up Fauzia and congratulated her, 'Mubarak ho, Fauzia ji, your son has been shifted to Peshawar jail. You should be happy that he is alive. This is such great news.'

Fauzia broke down and started sobbing. Rukhshanda figured there was something wrong. Even before she could ask, Fauzia said, 'Rukhshanda ji, thirty years! My son has been sentenced to thirty years in prison. His life will be ruined.'

Rukhshanda was confused and corrected Fauzia, 'It is not thirty, it is three years, Fauzia ji. The court said three. Where did you hear thirty?'

Fauzia stopped sniffling and said, 'There are news reports that say thirty. Is it really three?'

Rukhshanda said, 'It is three. I just saw it on Geo News also. I am not in Peshawar but in Karachi. I will rush there tomorrow and let you know if anything has changed. But don't worry. Somebody has got it wrong.'

Rukhshanda immediately called up Sajid, Qazi Anwar's assistance. He informed her that Qazi Sahab had gone for Umrah and would return in ten days.

Rukhshanda was restless. She wanted to return to Peshawar fast to check this news about the sentence. The next day, she took a flight to Islamabad and from there drove to Peshawar. On the way, she saw a candlelight march for the victims of the Army Public School terrorist attack of 2014. The attackers had come through Afghanistan.

When she reached Peshawar, it was late and the jail was closed. She decided to go there first thing the next morning. That evening, she found out that the news about thirty years was wrong and called up Fauzia. 'See, I told you. It is three years and not thirty. Be strong now. This is the final journey of your struggle,' said Rukhshanda.

The next day, Rukhshanda drove to Peshawar Central Prison. She remembered Qazi Anwar's advice not to make it prominent that they were fighting an Indian national's case.

As she stepped out of her black Honda car, she wrapped herself in a white chaddar. After entering the premises, she went to meet her old acquaintance and friend Farooq Sahab, the jail superintendent.

'Salaam, Farooq Sahab, *kaise hain*?' (How are you?)

He looked up and sniffed trouble. 'What mission are you on, Rukhshanda?' he asked with a smile.

With a mischievous look, she said, 'I learnt that you brought in a new guest yesterday.'

He wondered who Rukhshanda was talking about, and then she said, 'The Indian national . . . Hamid Ansari. I hear he has been brought here.'

Farooq looked serious and said, 'Rukhshanda, stay out of this one. *Isme haath mat daal.*' (Don't meddle in these matters.)

He continued, 'I know you have worked many cases, including those of Indians like Ashok Kumar in the 1990s, but this is different and times have changed. There is a difference between then and now.'

Rukhshanda was not one to give up so easily. She said, 'I just need to know whether you have him. Is he alive? And what is the exact sentence by the military court?'

He gave her the look of an elder brother telling his little sister to behave. She thought this would require more work. She took her phone out and showed him Fauzia's messages. 'Look at this poor mother. *Na jeeti hai na marti hai.* (She can neither live nor die.) I promised her that I would confirm that he is alive,' she pleaded.

The cop thought for a bit and said he would try to get permission. Honouring the Pathan culture of respecting women, SP Farooq allowed her to be seated in his office while he stepped out to get an update. 'There is no permission to allow you in. I cannot confirm anything you just said or asked,' he said when he came back.

She returned, disappointed, and called up Fauzia to inform her of the developments. She told her that she could not establish contact but was certain that the sentence was for three years. She was yet to ascertain all the facts.

Rukhshanda called the jail the next day but was informed there was no permission yet. The day after that, she again drove there with two vakalatnamas (power of attorney documents) for Hamid to sign. They would make Qazi Anwar and Rukhshanda his counsels and he could then become a petitioner in his own case. Until now, it had been Fauzia Ansari.

But there was no information on Hamid's status. SP Farooq was a nice man who considered Rukhshanda family. He took the power of attorney papers from her and said, '*Abhi vakalatnama sign mat karo.*' (Don't sign the document.)

He added that during a background check on whether she was associated with Qazi Anwar, they had drawn a blank.

She tried to convince him, saying, 'Farooq Sahab, you know I have just returned from the UK and am doing my own research. I am not a regular employee of Qazi Sahab. I am only assisting him in this case since I was approached for help.'

He told her that there were a few officers who wanted to ask her a few questions. She agreed, since she knew that these checks by agencies were mandatory if anybody took up an Indian's case. He called them in and said, 'You can question her but it will be in my room. Also, remember, she is like my sister.'

He stepped out and the questioning began.

Officer: Why this case?

Rukhshanda: Because they sought my help and I have done similar cases in the past as well.

Officer: Who asked you to help?

Rukhshanda: My friend from India contacted me. She was asked by someone to help. I had helped that friend, Rita Manchanda in the past as well, in the Ashok Kumar case.

Officer: How do you know it is a genuine case?

Rukhshanda: I have inquired about the Ansari family. It is a Muslim family. The boy's grandfather had been a renowned scholar, has written religious books. I never fight a case where I feel there is something fishy.

Officer: Who is paying?

Rukhshanda: I don't take money in such cases.

She then showed the officers Fauzia's WhatsApp messages and said, 'Please see the pain of this poor mother. All she wants to know is whether her son is alive.'

They read the messages carefully and then asked Rukhshanda to hand over all the documents Fauzia had shared. They wanted to see what they were and why Rukhshanda was so convinced of Hamid's innocence.

She called up Fauzia and told her everything. Meanwhile, the date for the next court hearing was approaching. Rukhshanda prepared an entire file for the cops, consuming an entire rim of sheets.

The next morning, an officer called and asked Rukhshanda to drop the file with the guard at the prison gate. She did that and waited for a response.

February 2016

Qazi Anwar and Rukhshanda sat down to strategize. Since they were yet to get clarity on the sentencing and whether the time Hamid had already served would be taken into account, they did not want to waste time.

Pre-empting the move of the other side, Qazi Anwar decided to approach the court to file a petition under Hamid's name under Section 382(B) appealing that the period spent as an undertrial be counted in his sentence.

Meanwhile, he told Rukhshanda that the two of them should get the power of attorney papers signed by Hamid since he would be the petitioner himself this time and not his mother.

Fauzia was getting worried. If he had been sent to civilian prison then why were they not getting access to him? Qazi Anwar spoke to a worried Fauzia. 'Don't worry. We are working to get the time that he has spent included in his sentence. We will be filing a petition of remission of sentence soon. You have been a brave mother. Don't give up now.'

Fauzia replied, 'Nothing would have been possible, Qazi Sahab, had it not been for you, Rukhshanda ji and Zeenat. I hope she comes back soon.'

In the evening, she called up Rukhshanda and started crying. Rukhshanda consoled her, saying, 'Now is not the time to cry. I will make sure I see him, Fauzia ji. He is as much a son to me now. Tell me if and when I meet him what message do you want me to give him?'

Fauzia was quiet for a while, and then, excitedly, with tears rolling down her cheeks, she said, 'Just bless him from my side and tell him that I am waiting and he will be out soon.'

~

It was now March 2016 and there was no word from the jail. Rukhshanda landed up there again one day. It was walking distance from the high court, where she was fighting a case.

She was at the door of her friend SP Farooq's office. He looked up and said, 'Wait, let me check.'

She went in and sat in front of him. 'Farooq Sahab, I promise you that I will only take five minutes. If not as a lawyer, allow me to go in as a human rights activist.'

He was quiet and did not seem comfortable. She convinced him further. 'Farooq Sahab, I have a mother on the other side of the border who only wants to know if he is alive or not. That the man we say has been sent to Peshawar prison is indeed her son. She has a right to know, Farooq Sahab.'

He looked at her intently and she knew he was going to give in. She again pleaded, 'Just five minutes.'

He shook his head at the stubborn lady he had had to deal with for years, and smiled. 'Only five minutes.'

She smiled back. Both parties knew that each other's intentions were in the right place.

He instructed the guards to allow her in. '*Entry karva de.*' (Let her enter.)

One of the constables took her through a door into a room where she had to sign in. When she started writing her details, the man sitting with the register said, '*Yeh toh Indian hai, Nehal Ansari. Aap ka isse kya rishta?*' (This is an Indian national, Nehal Ansari. How are you connected to him?)

She was filling in the column with the heading 'relationship'. As she wrote, she told the guard that her relationship was one of *insaniyat*, or humanity.

They looked at each other. Rukhshanda, who most of the jail employees had seen before, smiled. The constable took her to a small visitor's room. She sat on a chair and waited.

After a while, a thin, young man entered the room wearing plastic slippers and an oversized light-blue salwar kameez. He looked nothing like his photograph. But the beaten-down look with sunken cheeks should have been expected for someone in his situation.

He looked at her suspiciously. She knew he wouldn't trust her, but she was also aware of the limited time she had with him. She offered him a seat beside her and then placed her hand on his head and said, '*Mujhe tumhari ammi ne bheja hai.*' (Your mother has sent me.)

Hamid broke down. She put her hand on his shoulder and consoled him. 'I don't have much time. I just wanted to confirm if it was you. Fauzia ji sent her blessings and a message that she is waiting for you. Everything will be okay. Don't worry, Hamid.'

She asked him if he needed anything. He asked for his glasses, a pair of trousers and a shirt. He wasn't used to wearing salwar kameez.

The constable came in and said it was time to go. Those five minutes were the beginning of a new phase in Hamid's life.

Rukhshanda stepped out of the room, thanked SP Farooq profusely and left. She got into her car and the first thing she did was call Fauzia. 'Salaam, Fauzia ji, how are you? I couldn't wait to get home, so I called as soon as I sat in the car. I just met Hamid.'

Fauzia almost screamed, 'You met Hamid! How did he look? Was he okay? Was he hurt?' She asked so many questions that Rukhshanda had to interrupt. She didn't have the heart to tell her that Hamid looked frail and skeletal, so she said, 'He is very thin but is okay. I touched his head and blessed him on your behalf. I told him "*tumhari ma ney mujhe bheja hai*".'

Fauzia started crying. 'Did he say anything?'

'He just broke down. He cried. I didn't have much time with him,' said Rukhshanda.

'How is his eyesight? Was he wearing his spectacles?' Fauzia asked.

'No, he wasn't,' said Rukhshanda.

'But my Hamid wears spectacles. He cannot see without them. He is practically blind. He has very high power,' she said as doubt crept in. Was it actually her son or someone else?

Rukhshanda figured out what she was thinking and said, 'Fauzia ji, it was Hamid. They must have taken away his glasses. Send me his prescription and I will get glasses made here. Don't worry. Just be thankful that he is alive and safe now.'

Fauzia agreed and thanked Rukhshanda. Nehal was also right there and heard the entire conversation. They both prayed and thanked God, and then informed Khalid that Hamid was fine. The son hugged his mother and kissed her on the forehead. 'Everything will be fine, Ammi,' he said.

Rukhshanda reached home. By then, Fauzia had mailed her the prescription from Hamid's ophthalmologist. She took a printout, went to a store and ordered a pair of glasses for him.

The next day, she met Qazi Sahab and narrated the entire story. He was very glad that she had established contact. When he learnt that Hamid needed glasses, he immediately ordered for another pair to be made at a shop in the market right outside his chambers. Rukhshanda said she had already placed the order, but he insisted that he would visit Hamid too. He took the spectacles, a copy of the Quran and some dates that he had got from Saudi Arabia when he went for Umrah.

Although it was walking distance, Qazi Anwar took his car to prison since it would be allowed inside. Like Rukhshanda, SP Farooq had been his student and had the highest regard for him. His office called up the superintendent's office and informed that Qazi Sahab was on his way.

SP Farooq greeted the senior counsel and asked him the reason for his visit. Qazi Anwar showed him the two sets of papers and said, 'Farooq, Rukhshanda and I are fighting Hamid's case. You are well aware of it. We need him to sign these documents for us and I want to meet the lad.'

Farooq obliged. Hamid was brought into the SP's office, where the formidable Qazi Anwar was waiting.

'Salaam, Hamid, I am Qazi Mohammad Anwar. I am your counsel and I need you to sign these power of attorney papers so we can take your case forward. Also, I've got you a few things that will help you keep your faith intact.'

He handed over a packet with everything he had got, and a box of spectacles, along with a copy of the Quran and 5000 rupees in cash. Hamid opened the box and couldn't have been more thankful.

'Qazi Sahab, thank you so much for everything. Rukhshanda ji also met me. I am finally feeling a bit hopeful.'

'How are you otherwise?'

'Much better knowing that I have people on my side.'

Qazi Anwar gave a knowing nod and said, 'You know, son, I had never set foot inside a prison in the fifty years of my law career.'

Hamid had tears in his eyes. He folded his hands and thanked the elderly gentleman for all his effort. The meeting was brief. Qazi Sahab chatted with Farooq for a while after Hamid was taken back to his cell.

Rukhshanda called her nephew in Islamabad and asked him to shop for warm trousers, shirts, sweatshirts and hoodies. He would send them to her via one of the hourly coaches that ran between Islamabad and Peshawar. While she waited for the glasses to be ready, she picked up biscuits, juice, chips, cake, etc. She also bought a bucket and a mug and pulled out an old saucepan with a lid from her storeroom, the one she had used during her college hostel days.

She went to pick up the glasses and found herself 400 rupees short. When the shopkeeper learnt that they were for an Indian boy she was helping, he said, 'The discount is a gift from me.'

The next day, Rukhshanda put all the stuff in her car and left for court. Later, she went to the jail and Farooq Sahab allowed her to meet Hamid. But he still did not return the vakalatnama to her, saying, 'Wait a little while before you jump in.'

Hamid came into the room and was pleased to see her, but also looked unsure. After three years of torture and deception every step of the way, trusting a stranger was proving to be difficult. But they were both cordial with each other. Rukhshanda tried to break the ice, giving him all the things he had asked for and more. Hamid looked overwhelmed. He said, 'Thank you, aunty.'

Rukhshanda smiled and, with a light pat on his head, said, 'Aunty! Don't call me that. Call me *khaala* [mother's sister].'

They both had a good laugh. Hamid smiled after ages. He felt lighter and Rukhshanda could see that.

It was time to part ways. Rukhshanda asked if he needed anything else. Hesitatingly, Hamid asked, 'Khaala, could you get me an electric kettle? And Millac milk?'

She had the kindest eyes Hamid had ever seen, and an infectious smile. 'Of course, Hamid. The next time I come, I will get you those things.'

She decided that she would also get him some hot food.

~

Meanwhile, Fauzia was getting impatient about the status of her son's sentencing period and date of return. So she researched what to do in such a scenario and then wrote to the HRCP, Amnesty International, Red Cross and the UN.

Finally, around August 2016, she got an email from the HRCP. It was from the director (II). The email had a copy of Hamid's sentencing papers, which clearly spelt out the dates.

To her shock, the letter said that he would have to serve another three years from the date of sentencing. The letter read, 'He has been sentenced to three years in prison from 17 December 2015 to 16 December 2018.'

These dates were important for Pakistan. If they had allowed Hamid's sentence to begin from the date of his capture then it would have made a very strong case at the International Court of Justice (ICJ). In violation of the Vienna Convention, Pakistan had not informed India that they had an Indian in their custody for so long and not given consular access. So they had played smart and kept the past three years open-ended and stated in the official records that the sentence would start from 17 December 2015.

Fauzia stared at the computer screen and wept. She called her husband and showed him the email. Khalid tried to speak to his mother to calm her down, but nothing helped.

For Fauzia to imagine Hamid spending another three years of his life in a Pakistani prison, to not hear his voice for so many years, to not know in which condition he was in, was excruciatingly difficult.

She called up Rukhshanda and Qazi Anwar and asked if anything could be done. They said that they could appeal but that she should still be thankful that in three years he would be back home, unlike many others who had met with a very different fate.

That night, Khalid went to his mother's room, where she sat alone in the dark, and said, 'Ammi, look at the bright side. There is certainty about his return. At least we have it on paper from a Pakistani government authority. This was the first official communication by the Pakistan government saying he will be released on 16 December 2018.'

The next day, Fauzia informed the MEA of the letter, sending them a copy through the mail. She also requested the ministry to take it up with the Pakistan government. They said they would look into it.

Hamid was in the news again, and all channels and newspapers covered the latest. 'Hamid Ansari to be released on 16 December 2018.'

Now began the wait.

23

The Civilian Prisoner

10 February 2016

Three years . . . Three more years . . .

Like cattle, I was pulled out of the car and made to walk, blindfolded and handcuffed. My weak legs were giving way and the walk seemed to be never-ending. But it was raining and the smell of fresh air and the scent of wet soil calmed my disturbed soul. After the long walk, I was taken inside a building and my blindfold was removed. I looked up as my eyes adjusted to the light. I was in a high-ceilinged hall, about four storeys high. The structure looked like a colonial building. I looked around to see a group of men in civilian clothes chained on one side, standing in a queue, while on the other side was a man calling out their names. It was an attendance call.

The captain, who was standing beside me with the other two military men, walked up to a man in police uniform and handed over some papers. He brought a fresh set back to me, saying, 'Here, take these. These are for you. In case you want to file an appeal, you have to do it within forty days. The authorities have been instructed to provide you with your spectacles. You might get access to the embassy officials as well.'

I immediately looked at the papers, which stated three years' rigorous imprisonment and the date of sentencing as 17 December 2015.

The court martial had started with a fabrication of dates; when the final session concluded on 7 December then how could the sentencing date start from 17 December?

Another three years in a jail facility sounded unbearable. I was shaking with fear and rage. I looked at the captain and said, 'You were present during the court martial proceedings. You know I was proven innocent, yet your army has punished me. There is no justice in this land. Allah was watching when the persons at the court martial lied on oath. I am at peace knowing that I did not beg for mercy in front of you people. None of you is worth it. Allah knows I am innocent and He has seen the injustice you did. He will help me. Do me a favour, convey this message to your Brigadier Zubin Shah.'

The man looked at me, bewildered at my audacity, but kept calm. He wished me luck and left the building along with the other two men.

An old policeman came and stood behind me. He said, '*Peshawar Central Prison mein khushamdeed.*' (Welcome to Peshawar Central Prison.)

I thought, 'What a place to be welcomed into.'

This was a civilian prison and I was no longer going to be kept in an underground facility. That came as a relief.

The policeman took me to another officer. My eyes were getting used to the light but I could still only vaguely make out the name on his nameplate: Javed Khan. I had only one thing on my mind: filing an appeal. I had the form in my hand and didn't know if the officer was the final word in these matters, so I said, 'Sir, I need to fill this form to file an appeal . . . the army captain gave it to me.'

He looked at the papers and said that he would get someone to deal with that later. The big hall was the buffer space between two huge gates, one that opened to the outside world and the other that took you inside the jail premises.

Before entering, Javed Khan said, '*Ek baar andar chale jao tab kisi ko bhi yeh mat batana ki tum Indian ho.*' (Once you go inside, don't tell anyone you're Indian.)

'*Sir, mere bolne se hi sab samajh jayenge ki main yaha se nahi hu aur waise bhi jhooth bolke aur bura hi hoga.*' (Sir, the moment I speak, they'll know, and lying will only create trouble for me.)

But the officer insisted that I keep my nationality a secret. 'Just say you are from Karachi. Sindhis more or less talk like you.'

I nodded. He ordered the gates to be opened and I followed him in. It had been three years and three months, and this was the first time I was seeing such a huge, open space.

My eyesight was blurred but the open sky was breathtaking. It was raining, and I looked up as the raindrops fell. My skin tingled as each drop touched me. Trees, mud, the fragrance of freshness. I stared at the plants as though I had never seen one before. I just couldn't move. Then I heard the voice of the officer asking me to follow him. I suddenly realized how cold the water was and started shivering.

The colonial building had its own richness and heritage, and I spotted the Tata Steel signage embossed on the grills. I smiled with pride.

I was taking in as much as I could, but when I looked around for my escort, he was missing. I had lost him. I saw two men wearing red berets with metal emblems on them. I walked up to them and asked if they knew where I could find Javed Khan. One of them asked me where I was from.

'India,' came my prompt response. I had slipped.

They looked at me in disbelief and one of them asked. '*Tu sach mein India se hai? India mein kahan se?*' (Are you really from India? Where in India?)

'*Mumbai se hoon.*' (I'm from Mumbai.)

'*Kabhi kisi film star ko dekha hai? Shah Rukh Khan, Salman Khan, Akshay Kumar . . . kabhi kisi ko dekha hai?*' (Have you ever seen a film star?)

I was frankly getting exasperated. I needed to find the officer. Although starved of a regular conversation, I resisted the temptation to tell them about this one time that I had worked on a Salman Khan project. I said that I had never seen any of the stars.

One of the guards kept his hand on my shoulder and said he would show me the way. They took me to a room with men sitting behind desks in civilian clothes. One of them asked me my name, age, address and other details and I obediently answered.

The moment I said I was from Mumbai, India, all of them stared at me at the same time. And then came a flurry of questions . . . who, what, when, where, how.

In the course of the conversation, I told them that officer Javed Khan had told me not to reveal my nationality for security reasons. They agreed that it was in my best interests.

I asked if it was time for afternoon prayers. They told me that there was a mosque inside the jail premises and I could go there. I asked the computer operator to hold my papers while I offered my prayers and returned; he kindly obliged. I reached the mosque and performed my ablutions before praying.

I was drenched and the mosque was open from all sides. All the others had a quilt or a blanket. I asked the man sitting next to me, 'Where can I get a blanket?'

He looked at me and softly said, 'Son, you have to get it from home.'

'What about those who have nobody outside?' I asked, since that was my truth.

The old man didn't know what to say. I got up and moved to a corner because the chilly breeze was becoming unbearable. The Pakistan army had left me with nothing but a thin, tattered cotton salwar kameez and a pair of broken plastic sandals. I tucked my head between my hands and kept praying to Allah to show some mercy.

There was a tap on my shoulder. I looked up to see the same old man put a coat around me. Gesturing around him, he said, 'This is the place where charity begins. Helping others is the only thing that we can do. *Yeh coat aap rakho. Agar aapne lauta diya toh theek aur agar nahi lauta paaye tab bhi koi baat nahi.*' (Keep this coat. If you're able to return it, that's fine, and even if you can't, that's not a problem.)

The first act of kindness. I was caught off guard. I had forgotten what it felt like just to see kind eyes and hear soft-spoken words. The respectful sentences made me feel like a human being again. I didn't realize I had tears in my eyes till a warm drop fell on my cold, shivering arm.

I thanked him and asked him his name and where I could find him if I wanted to return the jacket.

'Shahid Gul, Barrack No. 2,' he said and left, leaving me warm with his smile and his jacket.

I got up and went to the office area, where I had left my papers. In one cabin, I saw Javed Khan sitting in civilian clothes. He had changed. I thought he must have gone home for lunch and returned.

'Sir, mujhe ab tak koi barrack nahi mili hai. Please mujhe bata dijiye meri barrack kaun si hai. Main bahut thaka hoon aur sona chahta hoon.' (Sir, I have not been assigned a barrack yet. Could you please tell me which barrack to go to? I am really tired and want to rest.)

The three years in solitary confinement had drained my body and my soul. I just wanted to lie down. Officer Khan rang the bell. One of the guards came in. My vision was blurred and he stood at a distance, but I could see something about his skin was different. It seemed to be a colour between dark pink and purple. I had never seen such a thing and wondered if he had had an allergic reaction to something.

'Bahaar, take this man to his barrack,' Officer Khan said to the 'pink' man in their local language (most likely Pashto). He explained which section I was to be taken to.

I left my documents with Javed Khan. While walking into the section where I was to be kept, Bahaar warned me to keep my mouth shut and be extremely careful. 'Stay away from everyone here. They are dangerous people out here.'

But for me, this was a new kind of freedom: no blindfold, no shackles, open spaces, light, trees, open sky. I was happy in my own little way.

We entered a section with three cells and I was free to choose any of them. They could accommodate six to eight prisoners and each of them had a built-in toilet with a three-foot-high wall for privacy. But many other prisoners were already inside and all the cells were crowded. Therefore, there was much resistance in accommodating me.

The guard on duty there helped me enter the first cell. It was filthy, probably constructed at the time of British rule, with dim lights and plastic bags hanging from the ceiling. There were four or five prisoners inside, who stared at me.

They all appeared like criminals, but I could spot the leader—a brawny-looking man who was getting a massage from some others.

Then the questions started. I didn't want trouble, so I told them that I was from Karachi and my case was a visa and passport issue.

They looked confused. One of them asked, 'But why have you been brought to this section?'

I didn't know what he meant and looked at the man quizzically. He continued, 'Why did Bahaar bring you to this section? This is *kasuri chakki* [punishment cell]. Only those who commit a mistake in the jail premises are brought here as a form of punishment.'

He explained that this was a temporary accommodation as it did not have facilities like the rest of the prison: no PCO (calling facility), in-house shop, barber, handicrafts, canteen (other than the mess), television or radio.

Any prisoner caught with something that was not permissible in the rest of the jail was brought here. They could be kept for ten days for possession of a mobile phone, fifteen days for possession of hashish and a month for heroin.

People were also brought here if they got into a fight. But they were released as soon as they produced their willingness to settle, or a *raazi nama*. It was a whole new world. But nothing had been normal for me since December 2012. How could this be different?

I was shocked to see the use of drugs within jail premises. The prisoners told me that the entire network was run by the officer in charge of the '*chakkar*', assistant superintendent Javed Khan. Chakkar was the central office area from where the entire jail was controlled.

By evening, after the azaan, the cell filled up with close to twenty prisoners. There was no space. All the gates were now shut, and many had come in with plastic bags full of grocery items such as vegetables and milk. I asked one of them what they would do with them. He said, 'Have some patience and watch the fun.'

It sounds revolting, but the toilet space was converted into a makeshift kitchen, where arrangements were made for cooking using oil lamps and small utensils. The prisoners were rather creative with space and tools and had not been left wanting for anything. For instance, they used the sharpened rim of a steel glass as a knife to cut vegetables.

The food was shared with everyone, and tea and musical revelry followed the meals. The same utensils were fashioned into musical instruments and everybody sang along. And then, the music faded into the darkness and everyone took their places to sleep. The exact definition of an overcrowded cell dawned on me when I saw everyone sleeping on their sides. There was no space to spread out or even sleep on one's back.

When the room was filled with the sounds of steady breathing and snores, a few prisoners got up and pulled out hidden cigarettes and hashish from their salwars. In some time, the entire cell was filled with a rancid smell. It was suffocating but the smokers couldn't care less.

The person next to me figured out my discomfort and gave me a blanket to beat the cold and smoke. It helped with the former but not with the latter. I tossed and turned all night.

The next morning, we woke up to the sound of a bell ringing. Soon after, the gates of the cells opened and the inmates started stepping out. I sat up and wondered if I could step out too. I hesitantly put one foot out of the door and then the next . . . I was standing outside, under an open sky. I could not believe it. After three years, I took in the fresh morning air and stretched my arms wide. My smile turned into a grin. This was a new world. I wanted to thank the lord for this small piece of freedom.

I took my place in the open space in front of the cells, where everybody was served tea and bread. It was cold but the fresh air was breathtaking. I sat a while longer than the others, contemplating my journey so far and my future.

The next slice of freedom was my washroom visit. For someone trained to finish the job in ninety seconds, I relished the luxury of spending some extra few moments daydreaming in the toilet.

Then came the morning patrol. Javed Khan showed up and asked if I had had any problems. I said I was all right but reminded him of the form that I had to fill for my appeal. I also requested for my spectacles since I couldn't see clearly without them. He nodded and left, following the other guards.

I did a bit of exploring to see what else was there. At the end of the third cell was a locked door. I asked the guard sitting in front of it what was behind it.

He said, 'Why don't you see for yourself?'

I tried to peek through a crack but couldn't make out what it was. But I could figure out a raised platform with a frame on top—a gallows.

I looked at the guard and asked, 'Has it ever been used?'

'The last time it was used was to hang Niaz, the major in the Pakistan air force who was involved in the Musharraf attack case,' he answered.

I stared at the structure, frozen in place. The thought of a human being hanging from that frame made my stomach turn. My imagination ran wild. I lost my appetite. I left to go back to my cell. It was afternoon and lunch was being served, but I was not hungry any more. That entire day, I went without food and water.

In the evening, Javed Khan came for his rounds. I ran to him, more eager than ever now, and reminded him about my appeal. He told me that he would get back to me.

Overhearing our conversation, some inmates inquired about my case. I followed instructions and told them I was from Karachi. Since most of the prisoners were from Peshawar and nearby areas, nobody had any specific questions about Karachi. So I was saved the trouble of lying further. Pathans consider Urdu-speaking people well educated and from the city. The warden was also convinced that I was from Karachi.

Every morning, the cell would open to let out all the prisoners and allow them to stroll on the verandah. I always saw an old man, Ijazat, sitting in a corner of the room under a blanket. He looked sickly, with bloodshot eyes, a long beard and unkempt hair. I went up to him and asked, 'Baba, are you okay?' He snapped at me and said, 'Look at this rabbit asking how the lion is doing.'

Everyone in the room burst into laughter. I didn't understand what he meant. But I was mighty pissed. There was no room for empathy here. The warden later told me that the man needed no sympathy. He had been caught transporting 40 tons of hashish.

'40 tons of drugs?' I exclaimed. 'Yes, he is from Karachi and was caught red-handed with a 40 foot container filled with hashish,' said the warden.

I was on alert the moment I heard him say Karachi. That was a warning to stay away from the old man, or I would be exposed.

I didn't sleep a wink thinking of what else could go wrong and put me in more trouble. I just wanted to go back home. Three years. Or if I was lucky and my appeal was admitted then sooner. I couldn't bear the thought of staying in prison indefinitely. My fate was uncertain. All I could do was pray all night for things to not go wrong this time. The lack of food and sleep left me very weak. The next day, I started hallucinating.

When the guards came in for their rounds, I insisted I had to file an appeal for my case. Javed Khan sent word and I was called to the administrative office. One of the guards took me there. A man was sitting across the table in the room, and Khan introduced me to him.

'This is Goga. I have updated him about your case. Why don't you discuss it in detail and answer all his queries while I finish some work and return.' Goga was a prisoner, but also the most educated man on the premises.

While the two of us were talking, I got dizzy and blacked out. When I opened my eyes, I found myself in a hospital bed on a drip. I couldn't move my hand, which had a cannula inserted in it. I was too weak to move my limbs. I opened my eyes a bit and saw someone coming towards me. Then I dozed off again.

When Javed Khan came to meet me in the hospital the next morning, he smiled at me and asked, 'What happened to you? You are a strong young man, why did you fall unconscious?'

'Lack of food and sleep. I am worried about my case.' I requested him to shift me out of the punishment cell.

He sat in front of me for a moment and then said he would send Goga to file my application.

An hour later, one of the red-beret-wearing guards came to the hospital looking for me. He asked me to come with him to the barracks. 'Why?' I asked.

He said he was just following orders. I was still weak. So he helped me out of bed and we slowly walked to the barracks, where Goga met me again. The guard left us in a room. I asked Goga the difference in the ranks of officers there. Goga was from Rawalpindi and a mere car lifter, but quite knowledgeable.

He pointed at one of the red-bereted men outside the room and said, 'They are not actual guards. The red berets signify prisoners who assist the authorities to earn remission. They are called *numberdar*s and the wardens are called *mulazim*s; they are on the prison payroll.'

I was surprised that inmates could render services within the prison. All these concepts were new to an IT professional from Mumbai who had not seen civilization in the past three years and had then been thrown into this alternate universe. Such learnings were important for my survival.

Goga told me that he was aware of my case through newspaper reports. He offered to help me, pulling out the documents that needed to be filled to appeal to the army headquarters in Rawalpindi challenging the decision of the military court. After that, he escorted me back to Javed Khan's office. I was discharged from hospital and sent back to the punishment cell.

A week passed, and by now everybody had accepted that I was a Pakistani from Karachi. But one morning, a warden came running to me and said, '*Arrey teri photo toh akhbaar mein chhapi hai. Tu toh kehta hai ki tu Karachi ka hai lekin akhbaar mein toh likha hai ki tu India ka jasoos hai.*' (Hey, your photo is in the newspaper. You said you're from Karachi, but this says you are an Indian spy.)

He was loud and undoubtedly within earshot of everyone around me. I stood there exposed. I wanted to cry. I didn't know what was in store for me. I turned to look at a few people who had become my friends.

I expected hateful looks, but most of them looked at me with disappointment—at the fact that I had lied to them. It was not about whether I was from Karachi or India but just the fact that I was dishonest.

I knew that no amount of explaining could salvage my reputation. So I had to reconcile myself with the fact that this disappointment would soon turn to hate and I would have to suffer the consequences.

Many of the prisoners started looking for excuses to be rude or fight with me. But not all of them. There were some who understood my situation. One of them came and sat beside me and said, 'Many hate you for being a spy. But not an Indian spy. Some believe you spied for a Pakistani officer.'

'What?' I asked. I couldn't fathom how they had drawn such a bizarre conclusion.

He explained, 'Last month, a subedar major of the Pakistan army had visited the jail as an undercover prisoner. He visited various cells, and just days later there was a raid by the army and all our mobile phones were confiscated. They also confiscated a large amount of drugs. So most of them believe you were the snitch.'

I couldn't do anything about that. There was no changing anyone's mind now. I was compelled to move to cell two from cell one. Some of the prisoners in cell one warned me that cell two had men who had been in prison for the past ten years and that they were quite 'hungry'.

I didn't know what they meant until one of them tried to act fresh with me. I knew from then on where to sleep, and to be doubly sure, I tied my salwar in double knots. Rape was a real threat. But I was kept safe by my well-wishers.

'Son, the only way you can be safe is if you shift out of the punishment cell. This is not the place for you. Most of the men here are hardened criminals,' said one of the elders.

I was determined to make myself heard. I resorted to a hunger strike. Javed Khan was informed but he remained unfazed. On the fifth day without food, as I lay almost dead on the floor of my cell, there was a commotion outside. Khan was setting right a drug dealer he had caught red-handed.

He was informed about my condition, and he ordered a guard to pick me up and transfer me to the hospital. The senior medical officer came to meet me and asked, 'I heard you were on a hunger strike. Why?'

I told him the entire story. The medical officer called for a meeting with Khan. I pleaded my case in front of him.

He finally agreed to move me out of the punishment section but warned, 'If I catch you with a mobile phone ever then I will teach you such a lesson you will not forget it all your life. Do you understand?'

I was relieved. I smiled and thanked him, promising he would never hear any complaint about me.

He called the head warden and asked him to shift me to the 'death row' section.

'Death row?' I questioned.

'Yes. Don't worry, we are not sending you to the gallows. This is where the death-sentence convicts are kept. They might not be bothered about you since they have bigger worries,' said Khan.

I was shifted directly from the hospital to the death-row section. Before my release from hospital, Goga came to meet me and told me that he was being released in two days on humanitarian grounds. He gave me some clothes and his personal blanket, as well as cash and toiletries.

By the first week of March 2016, I was in the death-row section.

24

From Hamid to 'India'

March 2016

I was shifted to the death-row cell, a place where they kept convicts who had been sentenced to death. I thought this would be a safer place, but lo and behold, I had just taken my first step through the doors when I heard someone say, '*Main jaan se maar dunga, kyunki yeh India ka jasoos hai!*' (I'll kill him! He's an Indian spy.)

What rotten luck! There was no escaping. My Indian identity was becoming difficult to handle. The head warden strictly instructed me not to interact with anyone.

'This is not child's play, my son. These people are hardened criminals, waiting for the gallows. They have nothing to lose. So stay out of their hair,' he warned.

'But they already know I am an Indian. One threatened to kill me, sir,' I said.

'Do not react to anyone and report this matter to Javed Khan first thing tomorrow morning,' he said as he let me into a cell with no other inmate. Back to solitary confinement, I thought. Thanks to Goga, I at least had a blanket.

At 8 a.m. the next morning, the gates to our cells were opened and we were allowed to stroll outside. The other prisoners also stepped out. I was alert, waiting for someone to pick a fight. But nothing happened. Instead, everyone was nice and warm. When death was staring you in the eye, you must only look for solace, introspection and peace, I thought.

A while later, Javed Khan entered the section. He came up to me and asked if everything was fine. I pointed at the man who had threatened me the previous day and told him what he had said.

'His name is Shabib. I will talk to him and I assure you he will not harm you in any way.' Khan delivered the message not just to that man but all the prisoners in that section.

But Shabib was not the kind to let go. After the officer left, he walked up to me, stared me in the eye and said, 'I have read about you in the papers. If it is true, then you better watch out for me.'

'What the papers are saying is absolutely untrue,' I protested, but to no avail.

My one big discovery in that Pakistani prison was the deep sectarian divide in the country. Forget about the sub-sects and minority sects within Islam, Pakistani Muslims were divided between Shias and Sunnis.

I learnt that Shabib, a Shia, was on death row on the charge of murdering a Sunni imam. This would not have been of any consequence to me as an Indian, but because Pakistan was a Sunni-majority nation, I had the advantage of having most of the prisoners on my side. Who knew that these things would matter. But they did.

Every evening, a patrolling guard would check on my well-being and give updates about three high-profile prisoners on his wireless set. I once asked him who the other two were, since I knew I was one of them. He replied, 'It's you, your neighbour Shabib Hussain and Doctor Sahab.' I knew Shabib was a Hizbul commander and a wanted man but not who Doctor Sahab was. He replied, 'Doctor Sahab is Dr Shakil Afridi, the man who informed America about Osama bin Laden.' I was taken aback at the thought that I was sharing prison space with a man who had taken down the Al-Qaeda chief. Why was I on this list, I wondered.

Nobody ever called Dr Afridi by his name. He was known only as Doctor Sahab.

An elderly prisoner named Aamir Ali sat beside me the next day
while I was trying to soak up some sun. He said, 'Son, nobody really
cares why you are here and what you did. Just be careful to not interfere
in their matters while you are in the confines of these walls.'

'But I really am not the person they have made me out to be in the
papers.'

'Like I said, what you did out there is your business but what you
do here is everybody's business,' he said.

He pointed to a man and said, 'You see the fat man over there, that
is Ahsan. Stay away from him. He is pure evil. He was imprisoned at a
very young age for the rape and murder of his own niece, who was just
six years old.'

He started pointing out others in the prison and telling me their
crimes. Not all of them were condemned to death. Of the thirteen
prisoners, six, including me, were kept in this section because we were
under protection. We were called *hifazati* (protected).

The days passed peacefully. It was nice to know that nobody
knew about anybody's case in detail so I was not troubled or harassed.
Necessity became the mother of invention, and I started making things
out of plastic bottles. I borrowed a pair of scissors and cut up the bottles
to make a glass and a mug for the toilet.

The cells were separate for prisoners but the conversations at night
were free-flowing. The entire death-row section was filled with talk and
laughter. But they were strict with the rules—complete silence after
9 p.m.

Around the third week of March, Shabib came to me with a
newspaper in his hand, saying, '*Tumhara ek aur saathi pakda gaya. Woh
bhi RAW ka jasoos hai aur usne har cheez qabool bhi kar li hai.*' (Another
friend of yours from RAW has been caught and he has admitted to
everything.)

In my head, I kept thinking of Atta-ur-Rahman and what purpose
it would serve for him to admit to lies since my case was over.

But then Shabib held up the paper and I read the headline, 'Indian
Spy Kulbhushan Jadhav Caught in Pakistan'. That did sound like

an Indian name. Before I could read further, Shabib walked off with the newspaper.

I thought that the poor man must be another victim of Pakistan's lies. If he had admitted to anything, it must have been under duress, as they had done with me when they forced my thumb impressions on a false statement.

But the news had certainly had an effect on the other prisoners. Their behaviour turned hostile and my worries soared.

One night, as I sat to eat dinner, one of my fellow hifazati prisoners, Saleh, called out for me from his cell and asked me to wait as he wanted to give me some rice he had prepared. The prisoners all had some arrangement within their own cells to cook and smuggle in or buy groceries from the prison guards.

I was excited. Rice was an extravagance. Saleh sent across a big plate to my cell through one of the mulazims who was there on the night shift. I polished off the entire plate and washed it down with green tea given to me by Aamir Ali.

Around midnight, I started feeling uneasy. My entire oesophagus was burning and I felt nauseous, followed by dizzy spells and shivers. I called out to the mulazim, who told me that verbal requests didn't work. The complaint had to be in writing. But I was not allowed pen and paper. He told me that I would have to wait till morning.

'I won't survive the night, please help,' I pleaded. He reprimanded me in a harsh tone and asked me to go to bed.

I vomited violently. It was thick, black viscous fluid . . . I could taste blood in my mouth. A commotion followed, with the mulazim berating me. Hearing the noise, Aamir Ali woke up. Upon learning about my condition, he immediately took his pen and paper and scribbled a note for the doctors.

The jail authorities were sensitive about my protection. Doctors came rushing and carried me to the hospital, where I was admitted for a few days. My entire digestive tract was flushed, and various medications given to me along with saline drips. The entire night, I was attended to by someone or the other as my condition stabilized.

In my semi-conscious state, I heard someone talking about the 'Indian national being poisoned'. A day later, Javed Khan visited me and inquired about everything I had done that night. I told him about the rice and green tea.

He heard me out and said, 'Aamir Ali is okay but don't take anything from Saleh.'

He spoke to the doctor on duty and left. My condition was still not stable and I had a lot of problems swallowing anything, even water. I only had milk. Some prisoners who felt sympathetic towards me sent fruits. By now, word had spread about my true nationality.

On the third day in hospital, one of the guards told me, '*Tumhari mulaqat hai.*' (There is someone to meet you.) Me? I wondered. I had heard these words many times before, but they were never for me. Who could it be? Had my parents come? Was it Fiza? Or had the military guys come back for me? All sorts of questions ran through my mind as I walked like a zombie through the corridors and to the main gate.

I was taken to a small room after security clearance, where I saw a woman sitting on a chair. She looked sophisticated and her head was covered with a white dupatta. Was she an officer, I thought as I greeted her, 'Salaam.'

'Wa-alaikum-salaam, come sit here,' she replied and gestured to the chair beside her.

'*Aap Hamid Ansari ho?*' (Are you Hamid Ansari?)

'*Ji, main Hamid Ansari hoon.*' (Yes, I am Hamid Ansari.) I sat beside her.

'*Beta, mera naam Rukhshanda Naz hai aur mujhe tumhari ammi ne bheja hai.*' (Son, my name is Rukhshanda Naz and I've been sent by your mother.)

I was confused. There were too many questions in my head. What if this was a new ploy of the Pakistan agencies? What if it was a trap?

Hesitantly, I asked, '*Aunty, maaf kariye, main aapko nahi pehchanta.*' (Aunty, forgive me but I don't recognize you.)

'*Haan, main jaanti hoon aap mujhe nahi pehchante hain lekin tumhara case 2013 se chal raha hain. Aap ke vakil ka naam Qazi Anwar hai. Aur main unhi ki assistant hoon. Qazi Sahab ki hi koshish ki vajah se aap ko bahar nikala gaya. Aapki ammi ne aapke liye ek paigam bhi bheja hai. Unhone kaha, mere bacchhe ke sar per maa ka haath rakhna.'* (I know that you don't know me but your case has been on since 2013. Your lawyer is Qazi Anwar. And I'm his assistant. It is due to the efforts of Qazi Sahab that you've been brought here. Your mother has sent a message for you. She said, keep a mother's hand in blessing on my child.) She stood up and placed her hand on my head, like my mother would.

At that moment, I held that hand and broke down. It felt like Ammi herself was there to bless me. Tears rolled down my cheeks.

I asked her, *'Aunty, Ammi kaise hain? Mujhe unki bahut yaad aati hai.'* (Aunty, how's my mother? I remember her all the time.) She consoled me and assured me that I would soon go home and be reunited with my family and that I needed to be strong and wait for the right time.

'I will be coming back to meet you. Is there anything you want?' she inquired.

'I need my glasses and permission to use a pen and paper. Also, can I get permission to call my parents?' I asked. I was desperate to speak to them. Finally, I felt some hope—I would be going back.

It was a brief meeting that didn't last more than five minutes. Before leaving, she gave me hers and Qazi Mohammad Anwar's visiting cards. She then went into the superintendent's cabin.

As I walked back to the prison hospital, I was trying to understand what had just happened. I still didn't trust the lady. She looked like a kind soul but the last three years had taught me a lot. I couldn't bring myself to trust anyone.

After a couple of days, I was discharged and taken back to the death-row enclosure. Javed Khan told me that I was now allowed to use the PCO once a week but only to call my lawyers in Pakistan.

'I will ensure you have some paper and pen to do some writing,' he said, smiling at me as he left the enclosure.

I looked up and thanked the Almighty. Finally, things were changing. There was a sense of freedom but I didn't want to speak or think too soon. So I checked my relief and said that it could just be temporary.

I was never allowed to use the phone unaccompanied. It was always on speaker, and my calls were monitored and recorded by the authorities. The first time I rang Rukhshanda Khaala (as she had instructed me to do), it was surreal. I couldn't believe I had access to the outside world, that someone on this soil was looking out for me.

Meanwhile, things were getting better. The inmates were warming up to me again. One day, a guard came up to me to say, '*Tumhari mulaqat hai.*' (There is someone to meet you.) I was expecting Rukhshanda Khaala. But instead, I was taken to the superintendent's office where an elderly man sat. He had a beard and carried a stick.

I entered the cabin and greeted the superintendent. He greeted me back and signalled towards the sofa. I stepped close and greeted the old man, 'Salaam.'

In a soft voice, he greeted me back and introduced himself as Qazi Mohammed Anwar and told me he had been fighting my case. I remembered what Rukhshanda Khaala had said.

Through my tears, I felt I was looking at a Santa-like figure. I was so relieved. Another assurance. I said, 'I have heard a lot about you. Can I call you Mamu [mother's brother]?'

He seemed to consider this for a moment but happily agreed and said, 'Well, I consider your mother my sister so yes you can call me Mamu. Also, I am here now and you have nothing to worry about.'

He said he was in constant touch with my family and updated me about their well-being. He asked me very briefly about my case and what all had happened to me. Very patiently, he heard everything. He closed his eyes for a few minutes and said, '*Beta, fikr mat karo, tum ghar chale jaaoge.*' (Son, don't worry, you'll go home.)

It was not a very long meeting. Before leaving, he pulled out a case and handed it to me. I was glad to see it contained a pair of spectacles. He then handed me some juice, fruits and dates from the holy city of Makkah in Saudi Arabia, where he had gone for pilgrimage, 5000 rupees in cash and a copy of the Holy Quran.

He asked me to recite a few lines from the Quran. I opened it and read out a few verses. He looked pleased.

Before leaving, he told the SP, 'I have given him 5000 rupees for his expenditure. Ensure that care is taken so nobody treats him like an agent. Look at the option of keeping him in the jail hospital, or with a guard.'

I thanked him for his support and he hugged me like a family elder. I felt like Abbu was right there.

Carrying all the things he had given me, I walked back to the death-row cell with the warden. Everyone was shocked to see that I was carrying so much stuff. They asked if my family members had come to meet me from India. They were curious about Indian goods.

I told them that my lawyer had met me. They looked at me in disbelief but the warden corroborated my statement. He also added that I was richer by 5000 rupees. I felt all eyes turn to me, like I was in a school hostel. Suddenly, all these deprived people wanted to be my best friends. I became the centre of everyone's attention.

But one man, Ahsan, wanted to make a run with all my belongings. He started making provocative statements to turn everybody against me. 'Isn't it strange that this man till some time ago was in military confinement and today he is getting royal treatment in our prison—for spying on our country?' he would say aloud.

The continued repetition of such words did lead to many, including my friend Aamir Ali, distancing themselves from me.

Ahsan also mentioned that lawyers were fighting my case for free, and to top it off, also getting me goodies. Aamir started looking at me as though I was being helped by enemies of the state.

But I needed Aamir to protect myself from Ahsan. The growing distance between us worried me. I also did not believe that my lawyers were fighting the case without taking any fees, but if they were, my respect for them only grew. This was a living example of humanity across the border.

Over time, news had spread all over the jail that an Indian was being kept in the death-row cell. Prisoners from other sections started visiting the section only to see me. I was somewhat surprised when some of them offered me fruits and others gave me money.

I asked one of them, 'Why such kindness to a man from another land?'

One of the older inmates said, 'For us, you are only a helpless human, a creation of the Almighty. Your religion or nationality is not a point of differentiation.'

Another added, '*India Bhai, aap ek musafir ho jo bahut door watan se aaya hai. Aap chahe Hindu ho ya Musalman, yeh aapka zaati maamla hai, lekin humare mein sabse achhi baat hai ki musafir ki qadar karo. Aapko darne ki koi zaroorat nahi hai. Hum Pathan log bahut mehman nawaz hotay hai. Aapko kisi bhi cheez ki zaroorat ho toh humko bejhijak batao.*'

(India, my brother, you are a traveller from a faraway land. Whether you're a Hindu or a Muslim, that's your personal matter, but we respect our guests. We Pathans are very hospitable. Just tell me whatever you need.)

All this attention drove Ahsan up the wall. It had become an ego tussle. His evil words were also worrying the administration. One day, Javed Khan summoned me to his office. When I entered the room, he asked the guard accompanying me to wait outside.

He told me in a grave tone, 'Hamid, you need to be careful. There are people who do not wish you well in the death-row section. Condemned prisoners have nothing to lose, but the first thing they start to lose is their mental balance. They know death awaits them so they will not hesitate to kill someone. So, you need to be aware of your surroundings.'

He didn't take any names but I knew he was referring to Ahsan. I assured him that I would be careful, but I left thinking, 'How?'

I wanted to focus my energies on productive activities, like the skill development lessons that were offered. Aamir came around in time and started teaching me the basic techniques of handicraft using beads.

I started with making bangles and then moved on to wristbands, hairclips, keychains, handbags and clutches. I also learnt crochet and made a lot of functional things.

My days would pass making these items. It became my way of coping. The second most important life skill I learnt was how to make a meal for myself. I sharpened the handle of my steel spoon to work as a knife. The stove was a clay pot filled with coal, which was sold at the prison shop for 100 rupees a pack. The clay pot served various purposes.

Then I started working on getting my friends back. The larger the group, the safer your kitchen. Food always creates bonds when the stomach and the soul are both empty.

The wardens and head wardens were quite cooperative and would get us things from outside if they were not available in the prison shops. Some things like utensils, vegetables, fruits and even medicines were among the permissible items. Of course, their help came at a price.

For other banned items such as phones, CD players and drugs, the inmates would always say, '*Qaid-e-Azam laaega*', referring to the Father of the Nation, Muhammad Ali Jinnah, whose portrait features on Pakistani currencies. This basically meant that it would be brought in by bribing officials. The price of a bribe varied depending on what one wanted to smuggle in. Some of the proscribed items could not be brought in by wardens, and that was when senior wardens, officers, and even assistant or deputy superintendents would get involved. There were code names for various categories of officers who brought in the smuggled goods. Those who managed to get smaller goods were called 'two-wheelers' or 'four-wheelers' and carriers of serious or dangerous things like drugs, weapons, etc. were called 'forty-foot containers'. Corruption was rampant.

While weapons were not allowed, there wasn't a single Pathan in there without a small knife. The authorities knew about it but probably felt there was more peace if everyone was armed. Violence was not an unknown feature of Peshawar prisons; there were stories of a warden being abducted and an assistant superintendent being shot and killed.

The prison was overcrowded, with inmates spilling into the passageways; some even slept in the lavatories since the suffocating cells were unbearable. I felt fortunate to be in the death-row section which was comparatively less crowded.

After Goga's release, I was the only other prisoner who could read and write well enough and explain case papers, which were mostly in English. So prisoners started coming to me for help. They would return the favour in cash or kind; those who couldn't do so would just bless me.

People were very confused about my name. While I called myself Hamid, the local newspapers always referred to me as Nehal Ansari, which was my father's name. The nameplate outside my cell read 'Ansari'.

To avoid confusion, everybody started calling me 'India'. My nation was my identity on this enemy land, where being Indian was not held against me, at least not always.

I started winning the hearts of many, including Shabib, who had once sworn to kill me. He started saying 'India zindabad' when referring to me as I helped him on many occasions. My chest would rise with pride every time I heard anybody say that.

He once said, '*India kitna achha hai. Humne to India ko apna dushman samjha lekin voh hamesha hamari madad karta hai.*' (India is so good. I thought of India as my enemy but he always helps us.)

I couldn't stop smiling. Even Javed Khan, every morning during his rounds, would say, '*Kya haal hai, India?*' (How are you, India?) My response was always an acknowledging smile that life was getting better.

27 April 2016

One morning, I woke to the harsh orders of a numberdar standing at my cell gate. 'Get up, we have to leave,' he shouted. A commotion ensued. I was not able to understand what was happening. I thought maybe Rukhshanda Khaala had come to see me, but when I was taken to the main gate, I was handcuffed to another unknown man and we were rushed out of the jail premises. Once we stepped out, I saw a police van waiting for us. I was confused and scared. Was I being taken to solitary confinement again? I shuddered at the thought.

When I turned my gaze to the man I was handcuffed to, I saw he had some papers in his hand and appeared calm. I whispered, 'Salaam, my name is Hamid. Do you know where they are taking us? What is this about?' He introduced himself as Wasim, a soldier of the Pakistan army. The moment I heard he was from the army, I thought I was in trouble again.

He continued, 'We are being taken to Risalpur for our hearing at the military court. You must have put up an appeal at the GHQ [General Headquarters].' I was puzzled about the fact that I had been given no prior information. I asked, 'If it is about the hearing, why was I not informed in advance? At least I would have been able to prepare my case.'

My questions were met with silence. I was so angry at this demonstration of impropriety.

After a long drive in the rickety van, we reached Risalpur Cadet College. I was under the impression that punctuality would be maintained for the proceedings. But what was to start at 10 a.m. only began at 2.30 p.m. I hoped they would see the truth in my strong arguments. The prosecutor, Major Nadia, not just lacked evidence, but also struggled to prove a motive. All she kept saying was, 'He is very evil, very evil.' Once the arguments were over, we were told that orders would be communicated to us. In the evening, Wasim and I were bundled back into the rickety van and taken to Peshawar Central Prison.

May 2016

Khan Munir, a new prisoner, came into our section. When the others shared his papers with me, it was clear that the man was dangerous and mentally unstable. He was in jail for murdering his childhood friend who had not paid him the 5000 rupees he had won in gambling.

I wanted to stay away from him, but Ahsan looked at the situation as an opportunity and tried to befriend Munir with a glass of juice. But things turned against him when Munir suspected him of poisoning the drink. He attacked Ahsan with the very same glass in which he was served the juice. The others broke up the fight but decided that they should all stay away from Munir.

I kept my distance even though Munir wanted to befriend me. My cold demeanour made his affinity turn to animosity and he started looking at me with anger. It scared me, but I kept a low profile, avoiding eye contact with him.

Ramzan had started, the month when everyone was calm and had a more pious disposition. Then, a transgender person called Jafar was admitted into the death-row section. He was brought in as a hifazati since the authorities could not put him anywhere else, neither the men's barracks nor the women's section. Jafar was booked under 9C for possessing 13 kg of hashish.

He was supposed to be given a separate cell but none was available. The only person who could be moved was me, so I was shifted to another cell with three other inmates, which included Munir. I cursed myself for the hard luck.

I knew this meant trouble. Ahsan had been at work, telling Munir how arrogant I was and that I had taken money from his enemies to kill him. That evening, when I took my belongings to the new cell, I asked Munir to give me some space since his stuff was scattered all over. He snapped, 'There is no space for you here. Go back to India with your stuff.'

'If I could go back to India, I would have gone long ago,' I retorted.

The argument got heated and Munir attacked me. It was the month of Ramzan so I kept my calm. But it didn't help. He leapt on me and tried to bite my neck. I pushed him away, but he succeeded in inflicting enough damage with his teeth and nails.

'*Tune mere burkhilaf se paise liye mujhe marne ke liye. Main tujhe zinda nahi chhodunga.*' (You've taken money from my enemies to kill me. I will kill you.) He was a raging bull, a man possessed. He punched me. I covered my face with my hands; he bit my hand so hard that when I tried to pull it from the grip of his tooth, my skin tore and I started bleeding profusely. Other cellmates rushed to my rescue and separated us, helping get the situation under control.

The wound looked bad; I immediately requested for medical aid but nobody wanted to take the trouble of getting help. It was time to go inside the cell. I refused to go in until I was administered some medical aid.

One of the guards came with a first-aid kit and did a shoddy job of rolling a bandage around the wound after applying some ointment—I was not given any antiseptic or tetanus injection.

'Can I please get a tetanus injection? What if it becomes septic?' I asked.

'Well, that is your problem. You will have to arrange for it yourself. I cannot provide anything beyond basic first aid,' he said and left.

One of the numberdars pointed to a head warden and said, 'That is Arif Kaka. He is a nice soul. He might help.'

I walked up to him and narrated the entire story. 'Arif Kaka, could you please arrange a tetanus injection for me? I need to take it in the next twenty-four hours.'

He agreed and took the money but was a no-show the next day. The twenty-four-hour window ended and my wound started looking ugly. I thought Arif Kaka had cheated me. But he came with the injection the next day. He said, 'Son, I am sorry I couldn't come yesterday. They had deployed me at the outer perimeter.' He returned the change from the purchase but I asked him to keep it for his kindness.

'It's too late for a tetanus injection now. Could you take me to the doctor, Arif Kaka?'

The old man obliged and took me to the prison infirmary. He was the head warden so no one stopped him. The doctor saw the wound on my hand and the injection in the other. He took the medicine from me and said, 'This won't work any more. But you do need some serious cleaning and dressing.'

After finishing the job, he gave me painkillers and sent me back. I was scared to sleep in the same cell as Munir. But there was no option. So I started sleeping during the day and staying awake at night. I would recite the Holy Quran the whole night in order to stay awake.

One day, a guard called out my name and said, '*India, tumhari mulaqat hai.*' (India, there's someone here to meet you.)

I knew it had to be Rukhshanda Khaala. But before I could go to the meeting room, Javed Khan warned me not to talk about the attacks, but I had paid a heavy price for lying the last time so I had no intention of hiding anything from my lawyers. Also, how could I hide my bandaged hand?

I entered the room and Rukhshanda saw me in my battered condition. She looked at my hand and asked, 'What happened, Hamid?'

I told her. She was shocked. She asked, 'Why didn't you inform me earlier?'

'I didn't want everyone to worry but because you are here I cannot lie to you.'

She handed over some eatables, clothes and footwear before leaving. She also brought me the tastiest chicken burger I had ever had, from a chain called Chief Burgers. (They became a regular feature of all her visits.) The meeting ended, but I knew she would not hesitate to take this up with the SP.

On Eid, most restrictions were lifted and prisoners were allowed to move freely around the premises. There were a lot of 'meet and greet' moments across the prison, but for one section—the death-row section. My whole world was now confined to seven cells.

Many prisoners came to visit the condemned people in my section. A number of them gave me Eidi (cash or gifts given to youngsters during Eid). I was very happy. This was turning out to be the best Eid in ages. However, Ahsan did not like that I was getting gifts. His jealous eyes bore into me.

Another prisoner had come to our section, and he kept staring at me, making me very uncomfortable. He wished me Eid and introduced himself as Aasman Khan. As he hugged me, he whispered into my ear, *'Aap India wale ho na? Aapko zameen ke neeche rakha tha 2015 mein? Aur aapke sath aapke dost Atta-ur-Rahman bhi wahan tha.'* (If I am not wrong, you are the Indian guy, aren't you? Weren't you kept in the underground facility in 2015 along with your friend Atta-ur-Rahman?)

I figured he must have been in military custody in the underground cell too. Before I could ask, he said he had been in the opposite cell. But my failing eyesight meant I couldn't have recognized anyone from then. He was a warm young man and offered to help me in any way possible.

'Mujhe Internet connection ke saath phone lake de sakte ho? Ek message ghar bhejna hai. Bahut waqt ho gaya.' (Can you get me a cell phone with an Internet connection? I just want to send a message back home. It's been too long.)

He promptly agreed and asked me to wait. He returned in a while with a phone and said that I should record whatever message I wanted to in the bathroom area of the cell. I went there. Aasman followed with a few of his friends. Ahsan sniffed something suspicious and immediately informed the warden, who came to investigate. Aasman and his friends handled the situation and the warden left.

I quickly recorded an audio message and shared my brother Khalid's number with Aasman. While his heart was in the right place, his technological illiteracy was an impediment. He and his friends left the section, but instead of sending a WhatsApp message to Khalid, he simply sent it as an SMS, which was not delivered. It was an opportunity lost, but I was not willing to take the risk again.

Around the same time, the jail got a new warden, Abdul Samad Baig, who turned out to be an educated graduate. He was placed on duty in my section. A short, stubby man, Baig was empathetic towards me. It was nice to have someone who was caring and understanding as the minder.

It was that time of the week when I could call Rukhshanda Khaala (normally scheduled for Fridays, unless the PCO was not available for some reason). I went to Baig to request him to call the PCO guy. But his demeanour had changed. He looked stern and didn't answer the first time I asked. So I repeated myself, 'Baig Sahab, please call the PCO guy. I need to call my lawyer.'

He looked up and shot off insults at me. I couldn't fathom what was happening. I thought he was putting on an act and kept smiling but soon became aware it wasn't a joke. I calmly asked, 'Baig Sahab, did I do something? Why are you so angry?'

'You are responsible for whatever is happening in Kashmir,' he said.

This was not a joke. He was blaming me for something I had no control over. I tried to reason with him. But it did not help since I knew that his family had come to Pakistan from Jammu and Kashmir in India. He was violently angered by the news coming from Kashmir.

'Baig Sahab, how am I responsible for anything happening in Kashmir? I stay in Mumbai, and for the past three and a half years I have been in Pakistan. Are you out of your mind?'

He got angry when I raised my voice, and said loudly, 'You are the reason for all these problems.'

I lost it. I lashed out at him, 'Javed Sahab, who is just a tenth-pass, is better than you.'

He retaliated, '*Tumhare yahan ke graduate se toh achhe humare tenth-pass hotey hain.*' (Our tenth-grade students are better than your graduates.)

'*Haan, shayad isiliye tum graduate hokar yeh naukri kar rahe ho. Aur mujhe batein sunane se pehle apna ghar bachao. Tumhari toh bibi bhi tumhein chhod kar bhag gai.*' (Maybe you are right. No wonder you are working as a mere guard even after becoming a graduate. And before mocking me, I suggest you save your own home. Even your wife couldn't tolerate you.) I had forgotten all boundaries of decency. There was a rumour going around that Baig's wife had left him, and that he had been denied numerous promotions because he was not considered mentally stable.

All this transpired in front of everyone, leaving Baig red-faced. Since I was a hifazati, Baig could not touch me as per the prison rules. Instead, he started saying loudly, '*India ne Pakistan ko gaali di.*' (India has abused Pakistan)

Where on earth did that come from? Even before I could react, Shabib stormed out of his cell and went back to his old form. '*India, tumne Pakistan ko gaali di, matlab tum pakka jasoos ho. Ab main tumhen zinda nahi chhodunga chahe meri jaan chali jaaye.*' (India, you have abused Pakistan, meaning you are definitely an Indian spy. Now I will not refrain from killing you even if I have to die for it.)

Other inmates joined him. Before I could do anything, they were all on me. I took a few blows before pushing them. In a loud voice, I asked, '*Agar Baig ne tumko yeh bola hai ki maine Pakistan ko gaali di hai to usne tumhen kyun bheja ladne ke liye? Kya woh khud Pakistani nahi hai? Ya fir shayad woh Pakistan ki izzat nahi karta. Varna tumhen bhejne ke bajaye woh khud mere saath ladta.*'

(If I abused Pakistan, why didn't Baig take me on? Why did he have to call you to save the honour of Pakistan or does he not respect his own nation?)

I didn't know how I had managed to think on my feet. But it worked. They started questioning Baig. Meanwhile, I told them exactly what had happened. So they were all the more infuriated. Baig realized things were getting out of hand so he quickly left the compound.

Ahsan then instigated another old inmate, Saeed Omar, who started making obscene gestures at me. I checked him by shouting out loud. If there was one thing I had learnt here, it was that silence was a sign of weakness. After a while, I ignored his gesticulations. But Omar grabbed my neck and tried to overpower me. I lost my balance and fell on the floor. He didn't waste time and bit me hard on my waist. Before I could pull myself out of his grip, he sank his teeth in. I knew the wound would take some serious healing.

What was with this place and everyone trying to bite me? Again, others came to my rescue and I was rushed to the infirmary. Javed Khan was informed and he rushed to the doctor's cabin; the bandaging was done and I was administered a tetanus shot. When Khan inquired about the cause of the fight, Ahsan made it look like I had been picking fights with everyone. Khan warned me to behave and left.

I was working from a position of disadvantage. I wanted to reach out to Rukhshanda Khaala and couldn't wait for my turn at the PCO. When the day finally came, I told her about the second attack. 'Khaala, my life in this section is in danger. Please help me. They want me out.'

She heard me out. She sounded worried but assured me that she would speak to Qazi Sahab and see what they could do.

One day, an inmate, Haseeb, tried to commit suicide, tying the drawstring of his pyjama to the top of the cell's iron bars. I, along with a few others, tried to stop him. Javed Khan rushed to the cell. When he asked Haseeb what the matter was, he pointed at me and said, 'India asked me to hang myself. He said it would be fun.'

I was stunned. I didn't know what was happening. Javed Khan slapped me and ordered that I be shifted to the punishment cell. I was in a state of shock. The guards pulled me and dragged me to kasuri chakki, the same hell-hole I had been in earlier, the overstuffed place where people came and went.

When I was here in February, the number of inmates per cell was about nineteen, and everyone had to sleep on their sides. Now there were twenty-five people in one cell, with some forced to stand through the night. Unfortunately, India had no space to sleep in Pakistan. I was on my feet all night. The next morning, when the cells opened and the prisoners moved out, I took a quick nap.

In all the hullabaloo, I met one inmate called Shahnawaz who was a friend of Goga's and was being released that evening. I asked him for a favour since he seemed like a nice man. 'Shahnawaz Bhai, could you just do me one favour and inform my lawyer that I urgently need to meet her? Please.'

He agreed and took her number from me. He left in the evening. The next day, I waited for Rukhshanda Khaala but nobody came. I was disappointed and thought Shahnawaz might have forgotten or got busy with his family.

I was just done with my afternoon prayers when Javed Khan rushed into the punishment cell and called me. I was being shifted back to the death-row cell. The message had been delivered. I smiled to myself.

On the way, he said, '*Aisa kyun karte ho? Hamari naukri ka sawal hai.*' (Why do you do such things that put my job at risk?)

I replied, '*Sir, nainsaafi to aapne kiya hai. Dusre kaidi bol bhi rahe the ki maine kuchh nahi kiya phir bhi aapne Ahsan ki baat maani.*' (Sir, you were unjust with me. Others said I was not involved, yet you sided with Ahsan.)

He ordered me to change my clothes immediately and come back while he waited outside the section gate. I did as he said and was back in a jiffy.

He told me that the superintendent had summoned me. This was a reconfirmation that my message had been conveyed. I thanked Shahnawaz for being an angel. In the superintendent's office, Rukhshanda Khaala was waiting.

She greeted me and asked, 'What is the matter, Hamid? All okay?'

I narrated the entire incident. Thankfully, cameras were installed in the corridors and they provided proof of a conversation between Ahsan and Haseeb just before the latter's suicide attempt.

There was a need to protect me. It was now a matter of life and death. Javed Khan suggested that I be shifted to Aamir Ali's cell as he had been moved to Adiala jail in Rawalpindi. But the thought of solitary confinement was not appealing at all.

From 10 August 2016, I had a new routine. I was let out when everyone else was in the cell, and when they were out, I was supposed to be inside. It was lonely, and getting any work done became difficult because I had to forever seek favours to get anything during the day. The authorities could not be unfair to the entire section by keeping them inside for the whole day and allowing me to be out. Therefore, I only had freedom for two hours every day—11 a.m. to 1 p.m.—while the others were out for the rest of the day.

I felt deprived of many things. This was the price I had to pay to stay alive.

25

Fight for Remission

August 2016

While the wait had begun for the family in Mumbai, the ordeal was far from over. The next three years were not going to be easy. Qazi Anwar had filed for remission of the sentence but that had failed. Now Fauzia's only worry was her son's safety in a civil prison.

She was haunted by what had happened to Sarabjit Singh in 2013, the Indian prisoner who had been attacked and killed in a Pakistani jail. Every prayer of Fauzia was only for her son's safety.

She was in constant touch with MEA officials, particularly Soumya from the PAI desk. The reason Soumya had been appointed the contact person for Fauzia was clear—the MEA and Sushma Swaraj, the then external affairs minister, wanted a woman to handle the case, someone who could be sensitive to a mother's worries.

But the MEA had not been given consular access yet. All they knew about Hamid's well-being was through his counsels and Fauzia herself. Note verbales requesting consular access had become a regular feature. Barring the one-line confirmation at the end of 2015, there was no further communication from the Pakistan MoFA.

The biggest worry for India was whether Pakistan would honour the court's verdict, or spring a surprise at the end of Hamid's jail sentence.

Indian officials in Islamabad engaged various quarters, political and bureaucratic, to seek clarity on the case. While some were assured that there wouldn't be any impediment, others raised worries. They kept at it, but got no access to the Indian national, a clear violation of the Vienna Convention.

Meanwhile, Rukhshanda had gone to the prison for one of her regular visits and had returned a worried woman. This was the first time she had found out about Hamid being attacked in prison, even though it was the second attack he had faced.

She tried to ascertain details and was told that there had been a brawl. She told Hamid, 'Look, if something happens to you, how will I face your mother? Don't you care about her? What if you die here? You have to ensure that you don't do anything that could lead to an incident.'

Hamid told her the entire story and explained the prejudices he was facing from some inmates.

She felt the pressure of ensuring his safety since she was now involved at a personal level as well. She thought of Fauzia weeping if anything happened to Hamid. How would she tell her about his troubles in jail? She had to first discuss it with Qazi Anwar. He was on holiday in the hills of Nathiya Galli when he received a message from Rukhshanda on his mobile phone. 'Hamid has been attacked in prison. It is serious.'

Qazi Anwar was shocked and called her up. She told him that when she had gone to visit Hamid, his hand was bandaged up. Without wasting a moment, the senior counsel called up the superintendent. 'Farooq, what happened? I just heard that Hamid Ansari has been attacked under your watch.'

'There was a quarrel. One of them beat him up. When I learnt about it, I suspended the warden and got Hamid treated,' said SP Farooq in a meek voice.

'It is not enough. What did you do to that prisoner?'

'He has been put in a cell and given punishment,' said the superintendent, sounding very apologetic.

'Hamid's safety is your responsibility. He has to return to India alive, in one piece, Farooq,' said Qazi Anwar.

Meanwhile, Rukhshanda had to inform the family. Then Hamid was attacked for the third time, when he sent a message to her through Shahnawaz. She rushed to see him then as well. Things were not fine.

She called up Fauzia and told her. By then, news reports had started to emerge. Rukhshanda had informed a few friends in the media of what had happened. It was breaking news everywhere.

Fauzia was distraught. She was living out her worst fears. 'How badly has he been hurt?' she asked Rukhshanda, crying.

'Please be strong. I met Hamid. He is not injured gravely. It is not serious but it will have serious consequences. Qazi Sahab has taken it up with the SP. He has assured Hamid's safety. Fauzia ji, please be strong. You have been so strong until now.'

Fauzia knew that while she was losing strength, she could not afford to lose hope.

'Rukhshanda ji, what should we do now to ensure security?'

Rukhshanda explained to her what Qazi Sahab was planning.

Rukhshanda and Fauzia informed the Indian mission of the attacks. The High Commission sent a fresh note verbale seeking details of the news reports that were emerging of 'Indian national Hamid Nehal Ansari having been attacked' while in their custody in Peshawar Central Prison.

Word reached Sushma Swaraj. She called up the officer in charge at the MEA and High Commissioner Gautam Bambawale, who was briefed by his officers. She asked for a detailed report. The officer told Swaraj that whatever they were picking up was from the counsels. 'Madam, Pakistan has officially not responded to any of our note verbales on Hamid.'

Meanwhile, Qazi Anwar asked Rukhshanda to prepare all the papers and file a writ petition in the Peshawar High Court. It was heard urgently by Chief Justice Yahya Afridi, who summoned the SP.

SP Farooq confirmed to the court that the attacks had occurred but assured the court that such incidents would not take place in future.

The court presented a very strong observation on the matter. 'Hamid is a human being first. Forget about the fact that he is an

Indian. Our Constitution says that fundamental rights are available to a person living in Pakistan. He is in Pakistan and he should be treated like any other Pakistani,' the chief justice told the prison authorities.

Rukhshanda informed Fauzia of the ruling but it did not bring her peace. 'Is there a way to prevent such attacks?' she asked.

'We are looking at those options. For now we need to file a review petition regarding the three-year sentence,' Rukhshanda told Fauzia.

Meanwhile, an Indian diplomat called up Rukhshanda to seek details. They got worried on learning that one of the fights had been because of developments in Kashmir.

Relations between India and Pakistan had dipped to a new low, and that didn't help matters related to consular issues on either side. Kulbhushan Jadhav's arrest and the situation in Kashmir were indeed impacting sensitive cases. For Hamid, this could be life-threatening. That was a real concern which was discussed between New Delhi and the Indian mission in Islamabad.

In October 2016, the counsels filed a review petition, but there was no success in remission or adjustment of the three-year sentence with the time Hamid had already served in Pakistan. The military court said their decision could not be changed or challenged.

The Indian mission was also consulting legal experts, one of whom suggested that Hamid's counsels consider filing a petition for his safety in accordance with the prison manual. The matter was discussed with Rukhshanda, who apprised them that she and Qazi Anwar were preparing for the same.

In November 2016, Qazi Anwar and Rukhshanda Naz filed a petition in the Peshawar High Court for the prison authorities to accord security to Hamid Ansari as per the jail manual.

Fauzia and Nehal did not want to stop at that. They no longer wanted to keep quiet.

'My son's life is in danger. We cannot just sit and do nothing. It is time that India took up the matter with Pakistan or raised it internationally or did something,' she told her husband.

In the extreme winter of December, the couple came to Delhi and held a demonstration at Jantar Mantar. The family was losing a lot of money. They were spending as little as possible and managing with lesser and smaller meals while making sure they were doing everything possible for Hamid's release.

With placards that said 'Justice for Hamid', the couple braved Delhi's winter chill. They were supported by many activists who also began social media hashtags and added to the Facebook page created by Zeenat.

Fauzia and Nehal were also working with Hina Jilani on the matter of finding Zeenat. Fauzia had not forgotten about her. She would routinely ask Rukhshanda about the case in Lahore.

Meanwhile, Fauzia found the phone number of Peshawar Central Prison and started calling to see if she could speak to her son. She cried for help to anyone who picked up the phone on the other side.

One day, an official offered to help Fauzia and shared the contact of a friend, someone who could help Hamid escape. Fauzia prayed and hoped that this was not a dead end. She got in touch with the man later that evening, and he demanded a huge sum of money to help Hamid get out. Fauzia discussed it with her husband. The next day, she called up Rukhshanda.

'Rukhshanda ji, I have some news to share. An officer from the Peshawar jail is offering to help Hamid come back through his friend, but he has asked for a lot.'

Rukhshanda, who was at Qazi Sahab's office, informed him of the same. They spoke for a while and then she responded to Fauzia over the phone.

'Fauzia ji, Qazi Sahab is very clear that this will never work out. Hamid's case is a very sensitive one. No amount of money can help him escape. Whoever is saying this is misleading you. I assure you, if you send any money to them and they try to help Hamid then he will be shot the moment he steps out of prison.'

The thought of Hamid being killed in an encounter came as a shock to Fauzia and she immediately dropped the idea.

January 2017

Around mid-January, Rukhshanda went to visit Hamid, who by then had settled into the ways of the prison since he knew he now had protectors in Pakistan.

She had to go to New Delhi for the book release of *Women IDPs Report—India* as she was part of the Pakistan chapter. She wanted to meet Hamid before she left since she would be meeting his parents in India. She brought him a chicken burger and other food items and also introduced him to Shinwari pulao, Afghani pulao from the famous restaurant, Shinwari. She bought about three or four plates so he could share it with the other prisoners.

She met the superintendent first, who jokingly taunted her, 'Rukhshanda, I have known you for years but you have never brought me any food.'

Both of them had a good laugh. She told him that she was watching over Hamid in Pakistan on behalf of his mother. She bade the officer goodbye and went to fill in the register before entering the meeting room.

As soon as Hamid entered, her smile brightened up the room. He smiled when he saw her and they both greeted each other. She handed over all the things she had brought and told him that he should try the pulao.

'Hamid, I am going to India for the release of my report. I will be meeting your mother and brother, who will come to Delhi to meet me,' she said.

Putting her hand on his head, she said, 'Is there any message for them you want to give me?'

Hamid couldn't believe there was going to be contact with family, the closest he could have got to them. He asked her to wait and rushed to his cell. He returned with a few things—a bowl of kheer (rice pudding) in one hand and some handmade handicraft items in the other.

He smiled sheepishly and placed the bowl in her hand. 'Rukhshanda Khaala, I made some kheer for you. Please have it.'

She smiled and had a spoonful. 'It is very nice, Hamid. What is all this that you have got?'

He kept the things on a chair and told her, 'Khaala, this is for you and my parents.'

He gave her a handmade *tasbih* (prayer beads), a purse and bangles.

'Khaala, the purse is for you. Please give the other things to my family when you go to India,' he said.

He pulled out an old safa (a chequered handkerchief/scarf) and gave it to Rukhshanda. 'This is also for Ammi,' he said.

Rukhshanda did not understand the purpose of an old piece of cloth but didn't want to say anything since it could hold some sentimental value. Since her meetings with Hamid were always monitored, any give and take was thoroughly checked. She wanted to take a picture of him with her but unfortunately couldn't.

She finished her kheer and left with all the items. That evening, she called up Fauzia.

'As-salaam alaykum, Fauzia ji, hope you are well. I am calling to inform you that I will be coming to Delhi on 25 January and it will be nice if you can come to Delhi. We can meet in person finally,' said Rukhshanda.

An ecstatic Fauzia couldn't believe it. 'I can't believe it, Rukhshanda ji, that I will get to finally meet you. Where will you be staying? I am so excited to meet you. I will ask Nehal Sahab to book our tickets immediately.'

'I will be staying at the Islamic Centre, which is close to IIC [India International Centre]. That is where the book release is. I am basically coming on an invitation to attend an event on internally displaced people. I met Hamid today. He is coping well and is very excited that I am going to India. He is sending you a few things. Just pray for his timely release,' Rukhshanda replied.

Fauzia wondered what Hamid was sending from prison. She asked with childish fervour, 'Hamid has sent something for me, for us? What is it?'

'Well, let something be a surprise at least. You will see when we meet. See you in Delhi. The event is on 28 January, a couple of days after your Republic Day,' she said.

Fauzia discussed the trip to Delhi with Nehal. They decided that she would go with Khalid and they would also stay at the Islamic Centre.

Fauzia bought and made things for Rukhshanda with a lot of care. She wanted to gift her the world, but her means were limited so she decided on just a few things. She bought a Punjabi suit, special Lonavla chikki and specially prepared home-made laddoos (sweets) made from dates. She carefully packed one box for her and one for Hamid. She also bought a sweater, a leather jacket, a watch, a pair of jeans and a couple of T-shirts, among other things, for Hamid.

On 25 January, Rukhshanda crossed over to the Indian side from the Wagah–Attari border. At immigration, the moment the officers got to know that she was Hamid Ansari's lawyer, they gave her special treatment. One of them even thanked her for her valiant fight and for standing by the truth. She was touched by all the loving and kind gestures.

At Attari, Rukhshanda was received by Ramesh Yadav from Amritsar, who was also a human rights activist and a friend of Jatin Desai. He had been regularly following up on Hamid's case, and when he learnt of her arrival, he wanted to receive her himself.

She thought, 'What a lovely moment. I wish things were this warm between the two nations at all times.'

Yadav drove her to Amritsar. From there, she took a flight to Delhi, where she was received at the airport by representatives of the event organizers. They drove to the Islamic Centre on Lodhi Road and she checked in. She informed Fauzia that she had landed and looked forward to meeting them.

A few days later, Rukhshanda was at the panel discussion at IIC when she saw two people walk in and sit quietly. She acknowledged the presence of Fauzia and Khalid with a nod when Fauzia gestured a greeting from a distance.

Khalid looked at Rukhshanda and whispered in Fauzia's ears, 'She is much younger than I thought. I was expecting an elderly woman. But, Ammi, she is not that old.'

'Might not be. But look at her achievements. I'm so glad to have her on our side,' Fauzia replied. The two quietly sat and listened to the entire talk.

After it ended and Rukhshanda was done meeting people, she went to Fauzia and Khalid. An emotional Fauzia hugged Rukhshanda and started by thanking her for everything.

In the next session, Rukhshanda and Fauzia sat together. Rukhshanda handed over a bag to Fauzia, saying it was from Hamid. Fauzia was impatient and excited, and started opening it in the seminar hall while sitting by Rukhshanda's side.

Rukhshanda was embarrassed and said, 'Fauzia ji, let's go to our room and then we can talk freely.' The three then moved to the building just down the road.

As soon as they entered the room, Fauzia started looking through the bag. Rukhshanda told her, 'Everything in this has been made by Hamid himself, except for one thing,' she said as she pulled out the safa and handed it to Fauzia. 'I don't know why he sent this. You will have to tell me,' she said.

Fauzia looked at the other contents of the bag. She clutched the bag and hugged it. She kissed the tasbih. Khalid took it from her hand and kept staring at it. He couldn't believe that Hamid had made all these things. He was overwhelmed like his mother. There were tears in his eyes too.

Rukhshanda looked at Khalid and said, 'You have to be strong for your parents and for Hamid. I know it is an emotional moment for you, but your brother will come back.'

'Will he? Will he come back on time? I still worry for his safety. Every day that goes by without incident, I count as a blessing from Allah,' Fauzia said, clutching the piece of cloth.

Rukhshanda asked, 'What is the safa for?'

Fauzia smiled as tears rolled down her cheeks. 'I know my son. He wanted to send something that would bring me closer to him. He has used this, touched it. This is a part of him. That is why he wanted me to have it.'

She kissed the cloth and said, 'Isn't it interesting that in our Quran, there is a chapter on prophets [Joseph] Yusuf PBUH and [Jacob] Yaqub

PBUH where the incarcerated son Yusuf sent his father a tear-filled shirt as a sign that he was alive. The father had turned blind crying for his son but the moment he touched the shirt to his eyes, his sight returned.'

She knew that she was reading too much into Hamid's simple gesture. But there was divinity in what she was experiencing, otherwise how else could she be sitting with a piece of Hamid's cloth when there was hardly any hope of his return a year ago. Now the impossible had turned into reality. For her it was a Yusuf–Yaqub-like miracle.

Rukhshanda was touched by her words. 'You are so connected to your child, Fauzia ji. You are one of the main reasons why I never gave up despite all the adversities. You gave me hope and strength,' she said.

Fauzia asked Khalid to get the gifts from their room. She had made laddoos for Hamid and for Rukhshanda and also got them some dates. She handed these things to the lawyer and said, 'It is not much but whatever little I could manage. Please tell Hamid that we miss him and are waiting for him.'

Fauzia also handed her a letter. 'Please see if he can be given this or at least let him read my letter,' she requested Rukhshanda.

They all had tea and chatted for a while, about Hamid, about her visit and about the fact that Rukhshanda had been in India on its Republic Day.

Rukhshanda went back the very next day, on 29 January 2017. She received the same special treatment at the immigration office on the Indian side.

That week, she took Hamid all the gifts. He was all smiles when he met her and very excited. He knew that his mother would have sent some of his favourite goodies. When Rukhshanda saw him, she could see the anticipation in his eyes.

'Wah, Hamid, you look happy today,' she said, smiling back at him.

Hamid's eyes were glued to the bag she was carrying. 'How is Ammi? How are Abbu and Khalid? Was she looking fine?' She interrupted him.

'Those are a lot of questions in one go. Patience, my boy. They are all fine. Your mother and brother had come to Delhi. Fauzia ji was much relieved after meeting me. And here are the things she sent for you.' She pulled out the box of laddoos, dates and other eatables.

He opened the box and smelt his mother's home-made laddoos. There were tears in his eyes. 'I never thought I would have these again. Sometimes life takes such unexpected turns, Khaala. I am so blessed to have you and Qazi Sahab, because of whom I have this in my hands again.' He gestured at the box.

~

In Mumbai, the family continued to keep up the pressure on the government. The media was following the story. Some journalists covering the foreign beat, in an informal gathering at the Pakistan High Commission in Delhi, discussed the case with High Commissioner Abdul Basit. He was of the opinion that it was a humanitarian case and should be given consideration.

He told one of the journalists, 'The family is in touch with officials of the mission. Unfortunately, I have not been able to meet the parents yet.'

'So, will Hamid return once he finishes his term?' asked a journalist.

'Well, I cannot tell you what the headquarters' decision will be but I will see what I can do,' he assured.

'Please meet his parents. They have stood outside the mission in order to meet you. Just a brief meeting will help,' said the journalist.

'I will ask my staff to look into it,' said Basit.

In March 2017, the Ansaris were in Delhi. They met Sushma Swaraj in her office.

'How are you holding up, Fauzia?' asked the minister.

An emotional Fauzia broke down. 'He was attacked, Madam. I am scared for his life. There has been no movement or assurance from the Pakistani government to ensure his safety. I am very worried.'

Swaraj told Fauzia that they had been working various wheels to secure his timely release. 'We are doing our best. Pakistan is playing its tricks since it has an upper hand. Let me tell you one thing, Fauzia. We will do whatever it takes to bring Hamid back, whether it is bilaterally, or via the International Court of Justice. You have my word,' she emphasized.

As an NCP MP in the Rajya Sabha, lawyer-politician Majeed Memon had raised Hamid's case in Parliament on 9 March 2017. In reply, Swaraj's response was: 'The government continues to seek consular access, and has requested the Pakistani authorities to ensure the safety and security of Shri Ansari while in prison.' Any kind of communication from Swaraj always brought solace to Fauzia. But her struggle was to ensure that Hamid was safe. This time, as always, she and Nehal again tried to secure a meeting with High Commissioner Basit. Surprisingly, they were called to the mission this time.

Her joy knew no bounds. Fauzia and Nehal rushed to meet the Pakistani envoy. The broken souls pleaded with the high commissioner for their son's safety and told him that he had already served more than three years in prison.

'Basit Sahab, can they not consider remission of the rest of Hamid's sentence on humanitarian grounds? My son made a mistake but there was no mal-intent. He has lost so many years. Please help me bring my son back,' she pleaded.

Nehal added, 'Sir, we have lost a lot. We cannot lose our son. Please ensure his safety. You must have heard that he was attacked in prison. Please help us bring him back alive.'

The high commissioner could only assure that justice would be done but could not give his word on when and how Hamid would be released. It was a brief meeting but the parents thought they had achieved a lot.

They went back to Mumbai, but the meetings, media interviews and letters to the premier of Pakistan continued.

It was 20 October 2017, Fauzia's birthday, but she had nothing to celebrate. It was a quiet day and she prayed for Hamid's safety and return. Just then, the phone rang. It was Jatin Desai.

'Fauzia ji, did you hear the great news?' he asked, sounding excited.

'No, Jatin Bhai. What is it?' she asked.

'Zeenat is back. It's all over social media. My friends from Pakistan just informed me. Beena Sarwar has also tweeted about it. She has said that Zeenat should be rushed to the press club to address the media before it is too late,' he said.

Fauzia's heart was racing. She sat on the couch in disbelief.

'Jatin Bhai, this is the best news ever. You have given me the best birthday gift in the world,' she said.

'Is it your birthday? Then there is double the reason for you to celebrate. Your daughter is back,' he said.

They spoke for a while, after which she checked social media for all the details she could gather. Next, she called Rukhshanda and informed her.

'Does Qazi Sahab know, Rukhshanda ji? Please inform him. He treated her like a daughter. I am so relieved. But my heart is still troubled. She was away for two years. I cannot imagine what she must have gone through. Will you go and see how she is doing?' said Fauzia.

Rukhshanda told her that she would go and check on Zeenat and let her know. But when she went to Lahore, she could only meet her mother. Zeenat did not come out. Her mother told Rukhshanda that she was in a state of shock after hearing of her brother's suicide.

'She has gone through a lot and is not in a state to meet anyone. She is depressed. So please let her be,' Zeenat's mother said, teary-eyed.

Rukhshanda hugged the mother and told her that if they ever needed anything then she and Qazi Anwar would be there for them. She asked her to be strong for her daughter. She returned to Peshawar and called up Fauzia.

Both understood the plight of a woman who had lost a son and whose daughter had just returned home after two years.

Allah had heard Fauzia's prayers. Her beloved Zeenat had returned. That night, she prayed Zeenat could again lead the life of a brave woman.

26

From Peshawar to Mardan

August 2016

I found my own routine in Peshawar Central Prison, getting by in the company of some friends but being cautious of others. Life was lonely but I kept myself busy.

One evening, the patrol warden entered my cell and started inspecting my body. 'What happened?' I asked.

'It is all over the TV channels that you have been attacked and are grievously injured. Are you hurt? What happened?' he asked frantically.

I figured that the news had taken its time to reach the media. I lifted my shirt and showed him the bite marks and told him what had happened. I also told him how tiring it had become to be allowed out only for two hours and be dependent on others for sundry chores such as putting out my clothes to dry or getting something from the grocery store.

One day, an army brigadier came to the jail for inspection. By now I knew where the real power was, and so I took the opportunity to request the senior officer to speak to my family. 'Sir, I wanted to request a phone call home. It is a humble request. It has been years,' I pleaded with the officer. He smirked and said brusquely, 'I will see.'

Later, I asked the warden about the sudden army visit and was told that it was regarding the investigations into the 2014 Army Public School incident. 'What incident?' I asked.

'The cruel incident at the Army Public School in December 2014, where children were killed.'

Memories of my solitary confinement in 2014 flashed in front of my eyes. I had been pulled into the investigation room and shown some photographs. The guards were talking about an imminent threat to an educational institution.

'Oh my God! Was it the same attack? How could they succeed when the authorities already knew about it?' I thought.

Days went by, but my request to the senior army officer went unaddressed.

Rainy season was the most difficult time in the prison cell, when all kinds of living creatures made the cell their temporary abode. It didn't help that the entire cell would fill up with water on bad days. I would either spend the night standing or adjusting myself on a broken cooler that I used as a chair to sit. To distract myself from the situation, I would make paper boats and sail them on the water that filled up my cell.

On one such night, I was woken up by a loud thud. Something had fallen through the cracks of the ceiling. It was dark but I had to know what had happened. I saw some movement amid my belongings in their plastic bags. A closer look and I jumped out of my skin. It was a snake!

I screamed for help. The warden came to my rescue. He calmed me down, calling it a mere accident.

I requested Javed Khan to change my timings to the earlier slot, but he refused, saying that this new schedule had been submitted in court and to the interior ministry to ensure my security. 'For any change, we will have to send the request to headquarters,' he said.

The loneliness was taking a toll on my mental health. I had become temperamental and would snap at wardens and inmates alike. I was taken to the doctor, who recommended psychiatric help. But instead of counselling me, they started administering heavy doses of sleeping pills and antidepressants that numbed my nerves. I became a zombie.

Even my paranoia was increasing. Every Saturday, the ophthalmologist visited the jail premises and I would request him for an eye check-up as I was sure my eyesight had become weaker. But he told me that I would have to be taken out of the jail premises for that and he didn't have permission for that. So all I got were eye drops.

In one of my weekly meetings with Rukhshanda Khaala, I complained about this and she ensured I got a proper check-up after the superintendent sought permission from the interior ministry.

1 December 2016

I was taken to Lady Reading hospital in a fleet of elite police-escorted vehicles, and allowed to leave the vehicle only after an entire area of the hospital was cordoned off. With two armed policemen ahead of me, two by my side, two behind me and a senior officer holding the leash to my handcuffs, I was escorted to the ophthalmology department.

I must have looked like a high-profile terrorist to the locals staring at me. While some children on the other side of the building were curious to see me, their mothers were scared and pulled them close. The whole situation seemed unreal.

On reaching the senior ophthalmologist, the officer in charge reported with a smug line, 'He is an Indian.'

The doctor was a thorough professional and said, 'To me he is a patient. Irrespective of his nationality, he is a human being first. Please sit.'

He asked me my name. Hearing a Muslim name, he asked me to recite a few verses from the Quran. I did so. He then looked at the officer and said, 'Well, he might be an Indian but to me he is not only a human being but also a Muslim. He is only a patient to me, and my job is to treat him. So don't try to provoke me by saying who he is or what his crime is.'

I was touched and relieved to see his professionalism. But it also made me fathom how deep-rooted religion was in that country.

After my check-up, I was told that my power had increased from minus 5.5 to minus 7 and the retina of my left eye was severely perforated and would get detached very soon if not treated immediately.

'You need a medical procedure, Hamid. And I need your consent to perform it,' he said.

I was scared. 'Can it not wait till I get home?'

'No. You could lose your vision. It will be a very quick laser surgery to stitch the damaged retina, and the fee will be 600 rupees,' he replied.

I told the doctor that I was an outsider and did not have the money for treatment. He told me not to worry and said he would waive the charges as it was a case from the central prison. He wrote 'from Peshawar prison' on my OPD case papers. I was relieved. The surgery was performed and I was sent back with some eye drops and medication.

Two days later, the dispenser visited me in my cell and handed me a new pair of glasses and the prescribed medicine. 'Do I have to pay for the spectacles?' I asked.

'The fee has been waived as you are a foreigner. The superiors have been kind to you. But that does not mean you get emboldened and start misbehaving,' he chuckled and left.

By now, news of my presence had spread all over the jail. Though I had many well-wishers despite being an Indian, there were also some black sheep waiting for an opportunity to harm me.

An inmate called Haris was now a part of the death-row cell. He was somewhat educated and we got along well. He was always criticizing the Pakistan army and running them down. One day, he came running to my cell and called me near the grill, saying he had some good news. I didn't see why I should be bothered about his good news, so with dull curiosity I asked what it was. He said, '*Maine apne mamu se baat ki hai tumhare bare me aur woh kehte hain ke woh tumhe nikalwa sakte hain.*' (I have spoken to my uncle about you and he says he can get you out.) Had I heard him correctly or was he fooling around? 'How?' was my immediate question without bothering about anything else.

Haris explained, 'My uncle has some contacts in the ISI and he says he will invest money for your release and in return take some profit from you. It's a fair deal. Also, for security, you can pay the amount after release; it's a matter of the trust that I have in you.' That was so caring and benevolent of him. I thought of communicating the matter to Rukhshanda Khaala as finally a door had opened for my early release. When it was my turn at the PCO, I told her what Haris had told me and asked her to find a way. But to my dismay, she asked me to keep away from such matters. However, she said she would seek Qazi Sahab's advice too and update me.

I was a bit angry and disappointed, wondering why they weren't willing to take this option when it was openly available and at such low risk. Other inmates told me that lawyers tended to not do such things as it would spoil their name in the market, because the solution had been offered by someone else and not them. My trust in Rukhshanda Khaala was shaken. When I called her next, she told me, 'Hamid, I spoke to Qazi Sahab and he said that the option you mentioned is fake. Had there been any such way out, we would have taken it a long time back.'

When the call ended, I was still left with a feeling of disappointment, but this time with a doubt in my mind. In the evening, when Haris came to me, I asked him a straight question, 'Haris, tell me honestly, if your uncle is so influential with the ISI, why are you still in prison? He wants to help me but not you?' The shocked look on his face told me a lot. To cover up, he said, 'Haha! Actually, we have a family dispute with him, that is why he is not helping me.' Saying nothing more, he left.

When Rukhshanda Khaala came to meet me next, we discussed the matter again and she told me that she had found out about Haris through her contacts and the offer he had given me was for his own benefit. How? She said there were two things that could happen: Either Haris's uncle would trade me with the ISI for his release, or create a fake encounter case saying that I was trying to escape during a jail transfer; such things were common in Pakistan. She couldn't have told me these details on a call, hence she hadn't explained earlier. I understood what was going on and how some people wanted to use me as bait. From that day onwards, my trust in my counsellors became rock solid and nothing could shake it.

January 2017

The guard came to tell me that my counsel had come to meet me. I was excited to meet Rukhshanda Khaala and get my hands on the lovely food and the chicken burger I loved. She smiled when she saw me and gave me the good news that she was going to India. It was a brief meeting, under observation, as always.

But my heart swelled with joy at what she told me. I gave her the handicrafts I had made and knew they might bring some peace to Ammi. I pulled out the safa that I always wore and packed it with the other things. It was dirty but I knew Ammi would want to hold on to something that I had used. I was happy and excited when Rukhshanda Khaala left. I shared some of the things she had got me with some of the other inmates. It was a good day.

A couple of days later, I was sitting in my cell while the other prisoners were in the lawns. I saw a shadow lurking at the gate. As soon as I turned, a brick came flying in. I ducked and it missed my face by a hair's breadth, but fell on my leg.

I started shouting for help when the warden rushed to the gate of my cell. 'I have been attacked. Help me.' I showed him the brick.

The warden was stunned. 'Did you see who it was?'

'No. But I will not spare him. What time is it?' I asked.

I immediately wrote a note and got him to put it in the complaint box. It would go directly to the superintendent's office.

I knew that the attacks on me were making a lot of news in the media but that didn't stop them coming my way. I was in solitary confinement all day for my safety, but now I felt more vulnerable and exposed than ever.

I wanted some serious action, and when none seemed to be coming my way, I decided to go on a hunger strike again. I got the warden to take all the eatables from my cell and told him, 'I will keep my hunger strike going till you allow me to meet Indian High Commission officials. I don't feel safe here. I want to go home alive.'

The matter was escalated to Javed Khan, who came to meet me the next morning. The matter was discussed with SP Farooq, who ordered an inquiry into the incident. The camera installed outside my cell was for this very purpose. Once they went through the footage, it was clear that Haseeb had attacked me. Javed Khan found out that Ahsan had provoked him.

Khan requested me to break my fast and said, 'I assure you it will not recur, India. Haseeb is not the main cause of all this trouble and the man who did this, Ahsan, will have to pay a heavy price for it. Don't you worry.' Ahsan was locked up for a week.

I was counting days in prison, praying that I could go home when the prison term ended.

Rukhshanda Khaala returned with a lot of things from India, such as my mother's precious date laddoos. I saved every wrapper of the eatables.

As a gesture of gratitude, I shared the special Lonavla chikki with my fellow death-row inmates, some of the wardens and Javed Khan. They had never had something like that and relished every bite.

On 17 February 2017, at 11 a.m., it was time for me to step out of my cell and for the other prisoners to go in. Those were two precious hours for me. Warden Atif Bashir was on duty and today he was unusually slow in opening the cell gate. I waited impatiently with my clothes and utensils that needed to be washed. But as I stepped out, I was hit very hard on the head with a metal object. My head spun.

I turned to see the warden holding a bunch of keys in his hand and coming at me for another blow. I was infuriated. This man was supposed to protect me, instead, he was heading my way like a raging bull. In self-defence, I started throwing my utensils at him.

'I am a prisoner and not your slave,' I shouted.

Then I realized that barring Shabib and Ahsan, everyone was out on the lawns. The others came running, and I thought they would break up the fight but they held me down so Atif could hit me. I couldn't believe I was going through this pain again. I heard Ahsan asking Atif to blow the emergency whistle.

I was trying to put up whatever fight was left in me when the other wardens rushed in, joining in to hit me. I was exhausted trying to fight so many of them so I just gave up and lay there as they hit and kicked me. Someone tried to strangle me. I couldn't breathe. I thought I would not survive this attack.

Suddenly, with all the commotion, some more officers rushed in and stopped the fighting. I was bleeding profusely and was shifted to the emergency ward of the infirmary.

I knew the gravity of the situation. Despite Javed Khan's assurances, I had been attacked. I could soon be dead. All the assistant superintendents and the deputy superintendent, Fayyaz Khan, came to see me.

When they asked me about the incident, I told them, '*Sir, main hukumat ka qaidi hu, kisi ka zaati ghulam nahi. Main khud ke haq me bolunga aur Atif apne haq me. Lekin agar aapko sach janna hai to aap camera ki recording dekh lo.*' (Sir, I am a prisoner here and not somebody's slave. If I say anything, it would be my word against Atif's. Check the camera footage and judge for yourself.)

Later, it was evident that Atif had attacked me first.

When Rukhshanda Khaala came to visit me next, I told her what had happened and showed her my wounds. She was quiet as she listened to me.

'I will raise this matter with the superintendent. You don't look good at all, Hamid. But I have to advise you to not escalate the matter. We are at a critical juncture.'

I was not happy with what she said. Why shouldn't we take it up? Was she on my side or theirs? I asked, 'Why shouldn't we, Khaala?'

She explained, 'Actually, your case of remission is under review. It requires a clean record. These fights and squabbles might hurt the case which has been forwarded to the federal government. If everything goes according to Qazi Sahab and my plans then you could go home by the end of this year and not have to wait till December 2018.'

That made sense. I did want to remain low-key. It helped that I remained in the infirmary for a while. When I was shifted back to the cell, the air between Shabib and Ahsan was hostile. They had apparently had a fallout.

One day, Shabib came to the gate of my cell to chat. 'How are you, India? I just wanted to tell you that the attack on you was planned by Ahsan. You know, the bigger plan was that as soon as you stepped out,

Atif would push you towards our cell and we would hit you on the head with a flat iron pan. Ahsan would not have stopped before killing you but it didn't work out according to him.'

I felt a cold shiver down my spine. How ruthless they were. But I didn't want to engage him so I told him that he was probably saying all this only because he and Ahsan were no longer friends, else he would have been an accomplice in my murder.

I didn't want to be there. I felt unsafe and was losing sleep. It was cruel not to be able to sleep. While I put up a brave front, they had won by draining me emotionally and mentally. But I had to remain calm, as was asked by my counsel.

On 18 August 2017, Javed Khan informed me that I would be shifted out of this prison. I was apprehensive. Being shifted from one prison to another always brought back terrible memories, of uncertainty and a life filled with torture.

Javed Khan saw how I felt. 'You are being shifted to Mardan civil prison. Your rights of having access to legal counsel will be honoured. They have been informed.'

I was relieved. Ahsan, Khan Munir, two more condemned prisoners and I were moved there. I had mixed feelings. I wished that only I had been shifted.

We were all taken there in a police bus with our belongings on a Friday. The journey began at 10 a.m. The metal bus turned into an oven on the freeway in the extreme heat. There was barren land on either side of the road and it seemed never-ending. In fact, on the deserted stretch, it appeared as if the vehicle wasn't moving at all. None of us had carried water with us. We were parched. We were also chained together so we had to coordinate our movements. Either we all had to sit or we all had to stand. But with our belongings also there, there was hardly any space left. The journey was tiring but we were also enjoying being outside the jail premises.

Reading the signboards, we knew when we reached Mardan city. The smell of soil, the sound of horns, the sight of signboards and directions to various cities were novel views. A long road away from the main city road led to the jail. It was newly constructed and had gigantic doors. The bus halted at the main gate and we were asked to exit. It was 2 p.m.

While our belongings were being checked by the authorities, we were taken to the superintendent's cabin. He was a dark man with white hair but he was not old. In a deep, hoarse voice, he asked us to introduce ourselves and our cases. I figured what was coming my way. The moment I introduced myself, there was a silent stare from the senior officer and giggles from the Peshawar inmates.

The prison code of conduct was read out and we were allowed to enter the facility. Concrete, concrete and more concrete was all I could see in that scorching heat.

When all the procedures were over, I saw that I was not being kept with the hardened criminals on death row. My older routine was back and I was no longer condemned to solitary confinement.

But every place has its positives and negatives. Here, one major drawback was that the prison was built on a swamp. It was a concrete jungle, with no greenery and just a few guava saplings and apple trees.

There were three borewells, but the water quality was so bad that you could smell the stench of the swamp in the water. Most of the prisoners suffered from health issues but this was ignored. For the first few days, I threw up constantly. The water was disgusting. I started having severe stomach problems and lost my appetite. One of the prisoners said, 'The water is so contaminated that the health department had inspected it and declared it unfit for human consumption.'

'What did the jail authorities do?' I asked.

'Well, we don't drink the same water as them. So, obviously they did nothing. We are criminals and they think we are dispensable,' he replied.

I was no special case. In forty days after my arrival at Mardan, I lost more than 10 kg. But worse was the fact that there were no medicines available here. The prescriptions flew freely, but when it came to getting medicines, there was nothing.

The dispensers had one common refrain, 'We have ordered medicines worth 1 crore rupees and as soon as they come, we will distribute them.'

Nobody ever saw those medicines. The others at least had family who got them some, but I had nobody, except Rukhshanda Khaala and the hope of her visits, and was left at the mercy of the authorities.

One day, the special secretary to the superintendent came visiting and informed that the inspector general, prisons, was going to visit the inmates and they could directly discuss their problems with him. He walked around, inspecting and listening to the woes of various prisoners. I told him my problems.

He said, 'Don't worry, you will get your medicines.'

That evening, the senior medical officer came to me, accompanied by his subordinates. The doctor asked me if I had prescriptions. I handed them over. He left with them and after ten minutes a subordinate came to me with a bag full of medicines. I wondered about the level of corruption here. If the medicines were there, why weren't the inmates being given these life-saving drugs?

It was nice to see the appreciation for India in some ways. Many spoke highly of Indian medicines. The personal care products were also mainly of Indian origin: Dabur, Parachute and various pharma products. I always wondered how they had reached Pakistan.

November 2017

I was strolling outside my cell in the lawn when a warden came calling for me. 'Superintendent Sahab is calling you to his office,' he said.

When I stepped into the huge room, there were other men present too. I was asked to step closer to the table. Then one officer pulled out a cell phone and dialled a number.

When someone answered on the other end, he said, 'We are here with Hamid Ansari.' I didn't know what was happening. My heart started beating faster. Things could take a steep turn into darkness, madness, hell. I didn't know where this was headed. Was it regarding the remission of my sentence?

The officer then turned on the speaker and said, 'Talk.'

I was shaking. I had to clasp my hands tight to stay in control. 'Hello,' I said.

A meek voice on the other side said, 'Hello . . . Hamid?'

Tears rolled down my cheeks. 'Ammi, I am so sorry. Ammi, please forgive me. I put you and everyone at home through so much trouble.'

I could hear sniffles and sobs. I was embarrassed about speaking in front of so many people but another lesson I had learnt was never to waste an opportunity. So I said whatever came to mind. I was so ashamed of my actions, which had led me and my entire family into trouble.

I could hear everyone on the other side also crying and consoling me. 'Beta, we should thank the Almighty that you are safe. Be strong and patient. I am waiting for you. We have knocked on all doors. With the efforts of both governments, high courts and human rights activists, we will be together very soon,' said Ammi.

It was a brief call but one that gave me the will to carry on with courage. I folded my hands and thanked the officers. It was just the most wonderful thing they had done for me. My mother's voice kept ringing in my head.

The days went by. I witnessed more corruption in the Mardan jail than Peshawar, which was the headquarters and hence under more scrutiny. Since all the senior officers were in Peshawar, the rampant corruption in Mardan went unchecked. Even the surprise checks were a sham; the wardens would inform the prisoners well in advance about the 'surprise' so they would hide contraband in secure places.

There was a thriving drug industry in the jail premises. It was a den of dacoits and drug lords. The head wardens would sell 1 gram of cocaine for 800 rupees; it was actually worth 500 rupees in the market. The buyer of this 1 gram would not use it just for himself. It would be divided into ten equal parts and each part would be resold for 400 rupees. Selling drugs was a very profitable business inside the jail. To avoid trouble and confiscation during checks by honest officers, the prisoners hid drugs inside shoe soles, vegetables, gravy or even shoved it up their bottoms.

This jail was almost empty and prisoners were not allowed to leave their sectors so I thought of putting myself to some good use and requested the authorities to allow me to do some gardening. At first they were hesitant to allow me to have gardening tools, but later reluctantly allowed them upon my insistence.

But like others, I too had to be careful about the elite police and the army dropping in for checks, which were conducted every three months. So I hid my little items inside a wall clock in my cell. Nobody opened the clock to check.

The rather empty prison had started filling up. By the end of December 2017, a bunch of prisoners were brought in from Peshawar and kept in a restricted area. Later, they were released and allowed to mingle with the rest of us.

One of them, Israr, came to me and asked if I was the Indian who had been picked up from Kohat and kept underground. He was a young, inquisitive man, but he knew a lot. Seeing me try to place him, he said, 'I was in the same cell with Atta-ur-Rahman in the underground jail at Peshawar. He told me about you. But he thought you had been released. So how come you are still here?'

I told him what had happened after the military trial. We got talking. There was another prisoner, Yahya Habib Afridi, whom Israr and I befriended. The three of us started spending time together. There was not much to do since handicraft activities were not allowed in the Mardan prison.

Different prisoners were brought in now and then and we would share our stories. Many had been caught during the Zarb-e-Azb operation of the Pakistan army. This anti-terrorist operation, launched on 15 June 2014, was carried out in the tribal areas of north Waziristan along the Afghanistan–Pakistan border to eliminate militants who were attacking Pakistani and NATO forces.

May 2018

During Ramzan, a prisoner called Arbistan from Mohmand district was brought in. One day, we were talking in a group when a light-hearted conversation about Arbistan sounding like a girl because of his voice got out of hand and turned violent. He pounced on me and bit me on the right shoulder. The guards had to break up the fight. From then on, I just stayed away from him.

Just after Ramzan, there was a drastic change in Yahya. He became weak and didn't get up to do anything. He didn't bathe for days and stopped eating. Israr and I got worried and informed the warden but to no avail. Soon, the other prisoners were also concerned. We had a sick man and nobody was bothered.

In October, one of the inmates wrote to the chief justice and the HRCP, complaining about the treatment and lack of medical attention for Yahya. After this, help arrived. He was taken to the hospital. A few days later, they brought Yahya back, handcuffed, on a stretcher, with his nostrils and mouth stuffed with cotton. He was no more. Nobody told us what had happened. I had lost a dear friend.

It was a sad day. Israr and I mourned Yahya's death for days, but we had to move on. I was now counting the days till my release, which was only months away, and I couldn't contain myself. I would speak to Rukhshanda Khaala to get an update on things and tell her that things were fine at my end.

One day I gave one of the wardens 300 rupees and requested him to get me a new towel as my old one was torn. The next day, he returned with a towel and told me it had cost 250 rupees. I told him to keep the rest. But he smiled and put the entire 300 rupees in my hand and said, 'When the shopkeeper found out that the towel was for the Indian in our jail, he asked me to tell you it's a gift from him. He didn't charge me. So, here is the towel and the money. Consider it a gift.'

I was touched. These little things made my days less hurtful.

Winter was approaching and the temperature had started dipping. The cold in Mardan was far more severe than in Peshawar. The snow-capped mountains of Malakand brought in chilling winds that made the entire prison feel like a mortuary. The thick fog cover wouldn't clear till noon every day, and even after that, it would never be a clear day.

At night, we covered the entrance gate of our cell with plastic sheets so we wouldn't freeze to death. I missed the warm Mumbai

weather. I would dream of being home, in the warmth of my house
and with my family.

November 2018

I was always on alert. With prisoners coming in from all parts of
Pakistan, my security was in question. Nobody could anticipate how
they would react to an Indian among them. To avoid any untoward
incident so close to my release, the prison authorities shifted me to an
empty barrack. But an empty barrack with no plastic sheets was like a
death warrant. It was very cold.

I had one plastic sheet to put at the gate of my cell, but the entire
barracks had four such gates and forty-eight windows—it was impossible
to insulate the entire area. I did my best to seal my cell but the barracks
were a wind turbine with so much ventilation.

It didn't help that the head warden assigned to my barracks hated
me. I had been moved to avoid any altercation with the other prisoners,
but here the warden himself was hostile and would ill-treat me.

One day, he came up to me and said, '*Ansari, mujhe tumko dekhne
se hi nafrat ho rahi hai. Agar meri duty nahi hoti to main khud tumhe mar
deta kyuki tum ek Indian ho.*' (Ansari, whenever I look at you, I am filled
with hatred. If it wasn't my duty, I would've killed you because you're
an Indian.)

I asked him, 'What did I do?'

He replied, '*Mere walid sahab 1971 ki ladai me pakde gaye the. Kisi
dalle Pakistani general ne un sab ka sauda kiya tha. Lekin tumhare mulk
walo ne unke saath janwaro wala sulook kiya tha . . . mere walid ko khana
nahi diya is liye main tumhe khana nahi dunga . . .*' (My father was a PoW
in the 1971 war. Some corrupt Pakistani general gave them all up. Your
people treated them like animals. They didn't give my father food, so
I'm not going to give you any food.)

I waited for my turn to use the PCO. That week, I used my call
facility to speak to Qazi Sahab and told him what was happening. I
also asked him about the delay in my release. I was worried about the
newspaper reports of the one-month extension given to the authorities

to complete paperwork. I also informed the deputy superintendent
about the head warden, following which someone new was assigned.

December 2018

Qazi Sahab came to Mardan, accompanied by the district nizam,
Himayatullah Mayar, and his assistant, Tufail. They had a conversation
with the prison authorities.

A senior warden came to me a day later and asked me to go with
him. I was shifted to the prison hospital for the last week of my stay
in Mardan.

27

Homecoming

In 2017, there were a number of changes in terms of foreign ministry officials and missions in India and Pakistan. Deepak Mittal took over as the new joint secretary of the MEA's PAI desk in February. In August, Raveesh Kumar became the new MEA spokesperson, taking over from Gopal Baglay, who was the deputy chief of mission in Islamabad when news of Hamid's arrest had first emerged. In September, Ajay Bisaria replaced Gautam Bambawale as the new Indian envoy to Pakistan.

Around October, Mohamad Faisal assumed charge as the new spokesperson of the Pakistan MoFA. He was already director general of the South Asia and SAARC division of the ministry. In November, Sohail Mahmood replaced Abdul Basit as the Pakistan high commissioner to India. He later went on to become the foreign secretary.

Fozia Manzoor in the Pakistan High Commission, Soumya in the PAI division of the MEA and J.P. Singh in the Indian mission in Islamabad were the constants in Fauzia Ansari's life. They all played a role in Hamid's homecoming.

The news of Hamid's transfer to the Mardan prison got the MEA worried. They had no clue why it had been done. Fauzia called up Soumya and broke down, 'Hamid has been moved to the Mardan prison.

What is happening, Soumya Madam? I am scared. Will they do to him what they did to Sarabjit? What should we do?'

Soumya tried to console her and told her that they were trying to find out what had happened. She asked her not to worry. J.P. Singh and Prabhat Jain at the Indian High Commission in Islamabad started making calls to ascertain details. They also called Rukhshanda Naz.

Soumya informed Deepak Mittal, who had a conversation with officials in Islamabad. He checked if Foreign Secretary Dr S. Jaishankar was in office and went to brief him. Dr Jaishankar asked Mittal to find out what was happening. They had to know before word got out in the media.

Rukhshanda Naz spoke to Qazi Anwar, who called up SP Farooq, and was informed that Hamid had been shifted to the district jail at Mardan, 40 km from Peshawar, along with all the inmates at Peshawar Central Prison. Everyone was being transferred to different prisons across the country. The same was conveyed by Rukhshanda to Fauzia and the Indian mission.

Around the same time, Qazi Anwar received a call from Hamid. This was rare, as he normally spoke to Rukhshanda. Qazi Anwar understood that it must be a grave matter, and he was right. Hamid informed his counsel that he was being kept in a high-security cell with militants. Hamid was worried that clubbing him with terrorists could affect his case, so he had repeatedly requested the prison authorities to move him out. He raised the matter with Qazi Anwar and Rukhshanda. This was around the same time he was facing threats from the head warden.

Qazi Anwar immediately filed another writ petition regarding Hamid's safety. Word got out and it was covered by all news agencies in Pakistan, and picked up by the Indian media as well. The high court summoned the Mardan jail superintendent and directed him to move Hamid to a safe cell. The superintendent told the court that there was no space, and that was why Hamid had to be kept there. He also informed the court that Hamid was respected by the other inmates, adding that Hamid had started leading prayers in the evening. 'They consider him an imam,' said the superintendent.

Qazi Anwar told the court, 'I am not concerned about whether he is giving sermons. I am only bothered about his safety.'

The court repeated its order.

Meanwhile, Qazi Anwar and Rukhshanda Naz put up another petition seeking that the term 'anti-State activity' be removed from the ruling since Hamid was not a spy and had not indulged in any anti-Pakistan activity. He did enter Pakistan illegally, so they called it 'illegal' activity under the Passports Act. The MEA sent note verbales to the Pakistan MoFA, seeking an official response and reasons for his transfer, but they got no reply.

For the Ansari family in Mumbai, the main concern was Hamid's safety. Every day, Fauzia would wake up to a new struggle, a new fight. Holding her 'Justice for Hamid' placard, she would travel across the country. She had all the things she needed in a bag she carried everywhere: documents, photographs of Hamid, placards and 'Save Hamid' pamphlets.

In their meetings with Pakistani officials in Delhi, the Ansaris would always request for visas or a call with Hamid to be facilitated. News of him being attacked increased Fauzia's anxiety. She would go to the media seeking coverage of the case so that pressure continued to build on the Pakistan government. In one of her studio conversations with Rajdeep Sardesai, she reiterated, 'All I request is for them to let me talk to my son once. This is a request from a mother.'

She said the same thing to reporters while waiting outside the Pakistan High Commission with 'Justice for Hamid' placards. 'I am begging Pakistan to allow me to hear my son's voice. He was attacked again. News reports say he is seriously injured. I just want to see for myself if he is okay. There is no news from any quarter. If I can't see him then at least they should facilitate a call.'

The pressure on Pakistan was mounting. The officials there knew that it was only a matter of time that the boy would be back in India, but the continuous negative coverage wasn't helping its case at a time when they were firefighting on other fronts. Relations with India were at a real low after the terrorist attacks in India and India's boycott of the SAARC summit.

Once, when they were outside the Pakistan High Commission in Delhi, Fauzia and Nehal were called in for their first meeting with High Commissioner Sohail Mahmood. Fauzia had read up on him and learnt that, like her, he was a student of history. She mentioned that to him and said that she would one day like to visit Pakistan to study the Sindhu civilization. The envoy was pleased with the conversation and assured Fauzia of all help. 'We are trying to do our best. It doesn't help if you take matters to the media. We are bound by rules,' he explained.

Mahmood was constantly in touch with headquarters on the matter. He had been more accommodating than the previous envoys, none of whom had the advantage of the court case having concluded. Mahmood looked at the case from a humanitarian angle. Around the same time, news came of Pakistan allowing Kulbhushan Jadhav's mother and wife to visit Islamabad. Fauzia immediately called up Soumya in the MEA and messaged Fozia Manzoor, expressing disappointment over this other family getting precedence over them.

Many news networks reached out to Fauzia Ansari for comments and she told them, 'I am happy for Kulbhushan's mother for getting the opportunity to meet her son. I wish that Pakistan had paid heed to my requests as well. I am disappointed that they have not allowed me to visit or talk to my son. Our case has been going on since 2012 and this case is relatively new. But I'm happy for her.'

A few days later, Manzoor called her up and asked when they would be in Delhi next. Fauzia said they would be there any time they were required. Manzoor asked them to inform her once there was a confirmation on the dates. The couple immediately booked the first available train to Delhi and messaged the officer that they would arrive on 6 November. Fauzia messaged Soumya and apprised her of the latest development and requested a meeting with her.

Manzoor asked the Ansaris to be at the Pakistan High Commission at 11 a.m. on 6 November 2017. This was the first time that mission had called them for a meeting. They were hopeful of getting visas and so went well prepared. Fauzia told Nehal, 'Please keep our passports, bank passbooks, printouts of bank statements, money to buy something for Hamid and our lawyers there. Also, let's take the contact details of Qazi Sahab and Rukhshanda ji in case we need them in the visa form.'

Fauzia was very happy. She was hopeful of reaching out to the new high commissioner for a visa to visit Hamid, whom she was desperate to see. Nehal was also excited. But on the day of their travel, the train to Delhi got slightly delayed due to unfavourable weather conditions. They managed to make it to the high commission slightly after 11 a.m., by which time Manzoor had called them a couple of times to inquire about their whereabouts. They were very anxious.

Mahmood had been working the wheels. He told the Pakistan administration that there was one more year to go for Hamid's release, and the negative coverage was not helping. He wanted clearance for a phone conversation between Fauzia and Hamid.

The MoFA, particularly Pakistan's adviser to Prime Minister Nawaz Sharif, Sartaj Aziz, decided to take up the matter for political clearance, most importantly from security agencies. Senior Indian journalists who were known to Nawaz Sharif were writing about and doing news shows on Hamid. An atmosphere was building up to douse the burning 'Save Hamid' flames in the Indian media and certain quarters of the Pakistani media.

Soumya was in constant touch with Manzoor in the Pakistani mission. She impressed upon the latter that the pressure was immense and that they had to do something about it. 'The least Pakistan can do is let the family talk to Hamid. We have not got consular access yet and we have no hopes of getting it. But the counsels are in touch with Hamid. We know he is alive and okay, but what do you tell a mother who has not heard her son's voice for five years now? Please see if something can be done,' said the Indian official.

'We are trying to get clearances for the same. There are procedures and protocol in place. You do understand. I can tell you this much, Sohail Sahab has taken a personal interest in the case and really wants this one request to work out. Let's see what instructions we get from Islamabad. We are hopeful,' said Manzoor.

Soumya informed Mittal about the development. It was possible that the Pakistani envoy was trying to clear the way for a conversation.

That was a positive signal. But the uncertainty of Hamid's fate lurked large. The Indian side still didn't have access to the Indian national. It engaged many quarters only to find out if Pakistan would honour the court's ruling.

Meanwhile, as soon as Fauzia and Nehal reached the Pakistan High Commission, a staff member received the couple at the reception and took them to Manzoor's office. Manzoor was busy on the phone. Fauzia waited for her to wrap up the calls and attend to them. On one of the calls, she spoke briefly and then got up to give the mobile to Fauzia, saying, '*Lijiye, Fauzia Sahiba, Hamid se baat karen.*' (Here, Fauzia Madam, speak to Hamid.)

The confused mother looked at the officer and asked, '*Kaun Hamid?*' (Hamid who?)

She thought it was some officer on the other side till Manzoor said, '*Aapka beta Hamid.*' (Your son Hamid.)

Fauzia started trembling. The phone was shaking in her hand and she started to weep. In a faint voice, she said, 'Hello, Hamid?'

When she heard her son's voice for the first time in so long, she couldn't believe it. She was not prepared for this.

Nehal also wanted to hear his son's voice so they stuck the phone between their ears and spoke to him. While Hamid kept apologizing, the Ansaris were ecstatic. They couldn't believe that they were finally speaking to Hamid, even for a brief conversation.

Fauzia folded her hands and thanked the officer and also asked her to convey their sincerest gratitude to the high commissioner.

Manzoor said, '*Fauzia Sahiba, aap khud kyun nahi bol deti high commissioner sahab ko?* [Why don't you tell the high commissioner yourself?] It is because of him that you could speak to your son.'

They couldn't believe how the day was panning out. An emotional Fauzia nodded to that proposition.

Manzoor asked permission for the meeting. After getting the nod, she took the couple to Sohail Mahmood's office. He was sitting behind his desk and got up to receive them, gesturing them to sit on a couch.

Fauzia started by thanking him. 'Thank you, Sohail Sahab, for helping us. I can't tell you how indebted we are for your kindness. You felt the pain of a mother. I only wish you the best.'

Nehal added, 'We cannot repay your kindness, sir. We had been struggling for years to connect with Hamid and you made it happen.'

Fauzia said, 'I troubled you a lot for a visa but after today I don't see the need. You all have done everything I couldn't have done even if I myself had gone to Pakistan. So I would only like to thank you for being there.'

Mahmood said, 'It is not me. All credit goes to Fozia Manzoor, who has been at it. She followed the case and ensured that it got the humanitarian focus it required. So you should be thanking her.'

They spoke for a little while and then the couple left. The Ansaris once again thanked Manzoor for her perseverance. She strictly asked the Ansaris not to inform the media. The Pakistan High Commission was tired of all the media attention on this one story. 'It is important that this remain a quiet affair. So please do not tell anyone. It is important.'

Fauzia agreed but told Manzoor, 'Not the media, but I have to inform my government.' Manzoor allowed that.

As soon as they stepped out of the high commission building, the Ansaris called Soumya and informed her. Fauzia asked her if she wanted to meet. She said, 'Consider us your family. This is your home. You can come anytime you wish to.'

Since it was already lunchtime, they first went to a small hotel in Paharganj and checked in. They had lunch, and then reached the MEA around 3 p.m. They narrated the entire conversation to Soumya. She told the Ansaris to inform the ministry in advance rather than after any visit to the Pakistan High Commission. She told Mittal who further informed Sushma Swaraj of the development. The minister was relieved and said, 'It is good to know that they have spoken, and that despite the attacks, he is fine. I agree with the other side on one count. The family should stop speaking to the media too frequently. It might not be good for the case.'

December 2017

A journalist called up Fauzia and told her that the adviser to Pakistan's prime minister, Sartaj Aziz, was going to be in Amritsar for the Heart of Asia conference and they could go there to meet him. For Fauzia, meeting anyone to secure Hamid's safety in prison, where he had to stay for another year, was a priority.

Fauzia and Nehal reached Amritsar on the day of the conference even as news channels broadcast footage on the Hamid Ansari case. Both of them, through the media, requested a meeting with Aziz.

The day after the conference, before going back to Pakistan, Aziz was supposed to visit Harmandir Sahib (Golden Temple), as per reports in the media. Fauzia and Nehal went there and sat in the gurdwara compound.

When it was time for namaz, the Ansaris spread their prayer mat in front of the gurdwara and offered their prayers as the media looked on. The sight of this Muslim couple offering namaz at a gurdwara was quite a sight, and a symbol of what India is all about.

After their prayers, they waited, holding the same placards with the same plea: seeking assurances of Hamid's safety and the remission of his sentence. They wanted to fight till the very end, until their son was back on Indian soil.

February 2018

All through the year, Fauzia and Nehal travelled and met anybody they thought could reach out to the powers that be in Pakistan. They attended a seminar in New Delhi on India–Pakistan prisoners' issues and met legal delegates from Pakistan, such as Justice Aslam Zahid, deputy high commissioner of Pakistan. They then decided to focus on the timely repatriation of Hamid and became regular visitors to the MEA and the Pakistan High Commission in Delhi.

Meanwhile, Imran Khan's party Pakistan Tehreek-e-Insaf won the general elections in July and he became the new prime minister. This, in a way, was good news for the Ansaris as some Indian journalists personally knew him, Rajdeep Sardesai among them. When Fauzia and Nehal were in Delhi next, they met Sardesai and requested him to reach out to the new prime minister. Sardesai promised that he would raise the issue at the first opportunity he got.

That opportunity came with some good news when Pakistan announced the opening up of the Kartarpur corridor to facilitate the visit of Sikh pilgrims to Kartarpur Sahib Gurdwara on the Pakistani side of the Punjab. Sardesai, along with many other Indian journalists, got the opportunity to go to Pakistan on 28 November 2018 for the inaugural ceremony.

The Indian media's press interaction with Khan was the window of opportunity that Sardesai had been waiting for. When it was his turn, he asked, 'There is a young Indian who has been kept in a Pakistani jail because he strayed into your country after he fell in love with a girl. 16 December is when he is officially supposed to be released. India says it has written sixty-six letters asking for consular access. His name is Hamid Ansari. I know his mother, she broke down twice in front of me last month when we spoke. I request you, sir, please look at his case in as humane a manner as possible.'

Khan assured him he would do so. 'Rajdeep, this is the first time I have heard of him. We will do our best,' he said.

This was the first political assurance on Hamid Ansari which was on the record. When the Ansaris heard of it, they immediately looked up the press interaction and were relieved.

~

In Mardan, Hamid was waiting eagerly for his release. Some prisoners would keep telling him that he was lucky to be going home as most of those who were released were immediately picked up from outside the prison itself. That scared him but he didn't want negative thoughts to crowd his mind when he was so close to home.

Qazi Anwar went to meet Hamid in Mardan. He told him to be prepared for a new life, a new journey, and then went to ask the superintendent if everything was in place. He was told they were ready at their end and would proceed with Hamid's release as soon as they got orders from headquarters. His release papers had not reached them yet.

A week before the release date, the Indian mission started reaching out to the Pakistan MoFA for the modalities of repatriation.

The efforts were met with silence. Indian high commission officials were in regular touch with the DGSA and its spokesperson, Dr Faisal, and the director of the India desk, Dr Fareeha Bugti. But there was no response. Closer to the date, in a press conference, the Pakistan MoFA spokesperson said, 'Yes, his sentence has been completed and we are processing his papers.'

India was convinced that he would be released and that a decision had been taken at the political level for the officer to make that statement. That was a certainty. It was only a matter of time. But when? That question remained unanswered. Ajay Bisaria discussed the matter at the highest level in the Pakistan MoFA. They needed to know when. New Delhi was asking for information.

16 December 2018

The Indian mission was worried. J.P. Singh spoke to Rukhshanda Naz, and there was a media blitzkrieg. Fauzia was on all TV channels saying that her son should have returned by now.

Qazi Anwar picked up the phone to find out since the confusion was killing everyone. Superintendent Farooq said, 'Qazi Sahab, 18 December is when he was received at the Peshawar Central Prison and so we will count the three-year sentence from that date and not from 15 December, when he was actually sentenced.'

The same was conveyed to the Indian officials by Rukhshanda. 'The officials will go to Mardan on 18 December. He will be released the day after. You should make preparations. Mubarak.'

But the Indian side had to do its due diligence, so a note verbale was sent seeking an explanation. On the phone, one of the diplomats was told that as per the India–Pakistan bilateral agreement, it took one month for the paperwork and procedures to be completed.

The Indian side felt that Pakistan was going to hold Hamid back or delay repatriation further. So they activated the media, which went to town about Pakistan's violations.

Hamid had not been transferred to the Peshawar prison in December. He had only been taken to the civilian facility in March 2016.

So the argument of the Pakistani authorities was false. But nobody knew the exact date of his transfer. They had to rely on the dates given by Pakistan.

When the Ansaris were informed by Rukhshanda of the release date, their joy knew no bounds. They immediately informed Jatin Desai, who decided to travel with them to receive Hamid. Khalid asked the parents to go ahead and said he would fly directly to Amritsar or Chandigarh once the news was confirmed. They all offered prayers and thanked God.

Rukhshanda did not want Hamid to return to his country in tattered clothes. She knew that the world would be watching, so she picked up a suit for Hamid along with a Peshawari cap.

She drove to Mardan and handed these items over to the authorities so they could give them to him.

17 December 2018

Fauzia, Nehal and Jatin Desai left for Delhi. After reaching, they visited the Pakistan High Commission where they met Pakistani diplomats, including High Commissioner Sohail Mahmood, who assured them of Hamid's release and repatriation on the given date, which was 18 December.

He looked at the elderly couple and said, 'Consider Hamid's case a unique one, as Hamid was innocent and got sympathy and help from both countries. Let Hamid be a symbol of peace and love in the region.'

Fauzia left for Amritsar with this message of peace. Nehal called up Khalid and told him to reach by the morning of 18 December. Fauzia then called Rukhshanda and told her that they were going to the border.

'Will I see you there?' she asked Rukhshanda.

'I would have wanted nothing more than to see Hamid off. But I have been advised not to go to the border. I have been told to not come into the limelight since that would put me in danger. But I am so excited to hear this good news. I went shopping for Hamid and gave him new clothes to wear,' she replied.

Fauzia was in tears and said, 'He may have lost some years but he found another mother in you, Rukhshanda ji. Thank you for everything.'

The Indian High Commission received a note verbale from the Pakistan MoFA on Hamid Ansari. This was the second official note on him, after they had acknowledged his presence in Pakistan and in their custody in the first. The note read that Hamid Nehal Ansari would be 'repatriated'.

One of the Indian officials met the MoFA director to discuss modalities and told her that they would need time to prepare.

'Give us enough time for our man to reach Wagah. We have to issue emergency certificates and documents to cross the border. We can only make them after seeing and identifying the person,' conveyed the official.

Late that night, J.P. Singh received a call from Dr Faisal, informing him that Hamid would be repatriated the next day and that an operational director in the MoFA was coordinating with the political officer.

Singh said, 'We would need permission for the concerned officers to travel to Wagah.'

Dr Faisal replied, 'Yes, those modalities are being discussed. Send the officers' details.'

Singh thanked Dr Faisal. It was around 11 p.m. when the Indian diplomat called up High Commissioner Ajay Bisaria to discuss who should be sent. They didn't want to send a senior officer and make it a high-profile case. Till Hamid was in Pakistan, the case could turn any which way. Therefore, they wanted it to be a low-profile crossover. Three names were sent for the repatriation process to Pakistan's MoFA: Shubham Singh (second secretary at the Indian High Commission), a staff officer and a driver.

28

The Final Journey

December, 2018

This was the final leg of my journey, which began in the Mardan jail hospital. The hospital had a barrack for senior citizens adjacent to it. Many came to meet me when they learnt that an Indian was there. They had so many stories about India and their families across the border. One of these persons was in the merchant navy and had visited the Mumbai port in the early eighties and he shared his pleasant experience with me. He was full of praises for India and Indians. He said to me, '*Beta, jab bhi tum wapas jao, Hindustan ko humara salaam bolna.*' (Son, whenever you return, give India my salutations.)

I was pleasantly surprised to hear such words from a Pakistani. I asked, '*Baba, aap aisi baat bol rahe ho?*' (Baba, how is it that you're saying this?)

'*Beta, hum to gareeb awam hain. Hum to Hindustan se aaj bhi utni hi mohabbat karte hain jitni pehle karte the. Akhir 1947 se pehle to ye sab ek hi tha. Siyasatdano ne apne laalach ke liye masoom awam ko apas me bat diya hai. Sach poocho toh humari awam Hindustan se pyar karti hai, dushmani to siyasi aur fauj ke aala level par hai.*'

(Son, we are poor citizens. I love India today as much as I used to earlier. After all, before 1947 this was all one. Politicians divided our innocent population into two for their own benefit. If you ask me, the people of Pakistan still love India. Enmity is at the political and military level.)

After getting to know I was from Mumbai, the people from the senior citizen ward wanted me to carry greetings to cricketer Virat Kohli. They wanted me to do the same for Indian TV actor Mona Singh for her serial *Kya Hua Tera Wada*, which aired on ATV in Pakistan.

There was a world of difference between how the older generation viewed India–Pakistan and how the present generation treated the same relations. The older lot still had a lot of love left in them while those closer to my generation seemed to have fallen for the hate narrative. I only wished that things got better between the two countries.

Imagine for an Indian to be in Pakistan during such hostile times. I had had such varied experiences—one set of people considered me one of their own while the other didn't even consider me Muslim because I was Indian.

But for me, this journey was coming to an end. I was going home. To my people, my land, my life.

16 December

I saw my case file in Peshawar and in Mardan, and on both occasions I had seen it clearly mentioned that my date of release would be 16 December 2018. I thought I would go home on that day. I was told that I would first be shifted to Peshawar and then to either Adiala jail in Rawalpindi or the Indian High Commission in Islamabad or straight to Wagah. But nobody came for me.

I started fretting. I didn't know what was happening and took to praying. Seeing me worried, the elderly ward in-charge came to me and said, 'I have worked at various prisons for more than twelve years and have seen many releases. Your release is getting delayed as it is a Sunday today and no releases happen on holidays. But if someone's release date falls on a holiday, he is released on the prior working day, provided all the documents are in order. Even a spelling mistake in your name can become the cause for a delay in release. It is not the mistake of the jail authorities. Don't worry, son, you will be released on the day that's written in your destiny.' I accepted these words and tried to control my emotions.

17 December

Every passing hour would break my heart and leave me feeling even more humiliated since I had told everyone of my release date. The delay raised a concern in their hearts. By afternoon, some of them told me that I could still be under suspicion, which may be why the ISI had not released me; this was a normal practice in Pakistan for cases involving the army. These words broke me.

The hours passed with no outcome. I was sitting in a corner of the verandah of the ward when the ward helper and a patient inmate, Shariq, came to console me. He started telling my about how he had been shot by three bullets which punctured his lungs, yet his enemies could not kill him as Allah was his saviour. His words motivated me and brought back some hope.

Soon, it was time for evening prayers, after which everyone would be locked up. But at 5 p.m., a numberdar came to the ward calling out for me and asking me to hurry up. I was happy that the moment had finally come. I asked him if it was my release and if I could collect my belongings. But he disappointed me by saying that it was not what I was thinking. Instead, I had been summoned by the deputy superintendent.

Any event at this time was significant. While escorting me to the deputy's office, even the numberdar expressed his concerns over my release. We reached the office area and I was asked to wait outside. Through the side window I could see that the deputy was on a call. But the conversation grabbed my attention. 'Major Usman, Hamid Ansari is still in our custody. We have not released him since his releasing documents have not arrived yet. We shall keep you informed.' The district magistrate had spoken to some colonel and now the deputy was talking to a major. It felt like something big had shattered and broken inside me. My throat went dry and eyes welled up. I had to control myself.

The deputy concluded his call and waved at me, signalling me to wait. He then came out with some carry bags and gave them to me. With his hand on my shoulder, he directed me to a private area. He wanted to tell me something in person. 'Hamid, these are a few clothes that your lawyer Rukhshanda Madam has dropped off and she wants you to wear them at the time of your release. She has also conveyed a very important message for you. There could be a sea of media on either side. Whatever you say to them can have major repercussions. You are smart enough to understand the message. The delay in your release was a strategic move for your safety. We are expecting something big. Don't share this news with anyone. You don't know who could be jealous of your release and try to harm you during the night. All the best.'

He patted me on my back and left. On my way to the ward, the numberdar asked me about the bags and the conversation with the deputy. I simply told him that I had been given some winter clothes that I had asked for. I repeated the same thing to my fellow inmates.

At about 8.30 p.m., while we were chit-chatting and eating in the cell, we heard a commotion outside. The warden told us that the superintendent had entered the premises and ordered us to stop the noise and sleep. 'What could have brought the superintendent here at such an odd hour?' I wondered. I could only think that all these events were somehow connected to my release.

18 December

At 6.30 a.m., there was a knock on the door of the ward. I was awake for my morning prayers. I saw the deputy superintendent and the warden outside. He said, 'Hamid, you have thirty minutes to get ready, not a minute more. The team has arrived to take you to Wagah border.'

I jumped up in excitement. I got ready in the blink of an eye, wearing my new suit and Peshawari cap with pride. The deputy was surprised at my speed.

Everybody else was still asleep. I woke up the ward in-charge and bade him goodbye. It was still dark outside. When I reached the deputy's office, I remembered that I had forgotten my wallet. I went back to get it and remembered the day in 2012 when I had missed my flight to Kabul because I had forgotten my wallet at home. I had a sinking feeling with that memory. I prayed it was not an omen. I had seen and suffered enough.

At the office, the second deputy was doing some paperwork, along with his assistant superintendent, who was holding the register for prisoner data. There were two other officers who were engrossed in paperwork as well. They made me sign a few documents that only had my personal details and some important dates like when I was sentenced and when I would be released.

I requested a call to Rukhshanda Khaala but was told that for security reasons, the repatriation was being done at such an odd hour that any call would be monitored, so it was best not to make a call. I asked for my belongings that had been confiscated at the time of my arrest. But the deputy said he had no order to release anything. I was hurt and angry. I only wanted the things I had come there with. 'What a shame, I am leaving this country after six years and they don't have the decency to return what is mine. So petty,' I thought, but didn't let that dampen my spirits.

The deputy asked the other officers to be very careful and take all precautions during the transfer. One of the officers ordered that the cell phones of all those who were present in the team escorting me be collected and kept safely in custody.

I finally hugged and bade goodbye to all the jail authorities present at that hour. When I stepped out of the main gates, it was pitch dark and extremely cold. With floodlights on the jail gates, I could see it was foggy and there were approximately twenty-five to thirty heavily armed men and a fleet of eight or ten armoured vehicles. The officers and I sat in one of the high-security vehicles and were driven out of Mardan Central Prison. The moment we left the building, I smiled. These were my final hours in Pakistan.

The deputy told me that I would be handed over to the Punjab Police at Attock for the rest of the journey. After an hour's drive, the convoy came to a halt. In front of it stood a bus with 'Punjab Police' written on it. We had entered the Punjab province from Khyber

Pakhtunkhwa, and this was the handover. I was asked to step out and sit inside the bus with a constable. There were two elite police cars in front and two behind the bus. The deputy inspector general of the area was also part of the convoy.

The drive from Attock to Wagah took approximately seven hours. It was a non-stop journey with no tea halts, no refreshments, no toilet breaks.

At one point, the bus came to a halt. I looked outside the grilled windows and saw that it was secluded outside. Since it was an odd hour and the weather was foggy, there were hardly any vehicles. A team of the elite police force surrounded the bus and were fidgeting with their rifles. In a worried tone, I asked the constable if it was a refreshment halt. He asked his colleagues but even they were clueless. Stories of fake encounters and words of the investigating officers of the military intelligence and the FIA started flashing through my mind, 'You will never go home alive.' I said a small prayer and shared my fears with the constable. He laughed and said that if they wanted to stage an encounter, they would not have made such security arrangements. I also told him the deputy's words regarding my delayed release. He explained that if anyone would have been planning to harm me in any way, they would have laid a trap. So this delay was to foil any possible accident.

After some time, one of the guards outside told us that there was a flat tyre and the extra tyre had to be fetched from the nearest police line since they did not have any spares. What luck! Why was my freedom getting delayed again and again? After a couple of hours, the journey resumed.

Halfway through, I dozed off. I was not interested in the view. The only view I was interested in was of the border where I would be able to see the Indian flag fluttering on the other side and my family waiting to receive me.

I was woken up on hearing the constable shouting at passing cars. He said, 'People have been turning around to see who is in the bus in such a heavily guarded convoy. So I am just shouting back at them that if they are so interested, why don't they come inside the bus.'

I smiled and added, 'They must think it is Nawaz Sharif's convoy to transfer him from one jail to another.'

I noticed that whenever we entered a new district, its DIG would join the caravan while the previous district's DIG would leave. I saw villages, farmland, ponds, cattle and lands that did not appear so different yet were so alien. There were a lot of similarities with India in clothing, speech and food. We crossed three major rivers, Jhelum, Chenab and Ravi. I had studied about them in school and when I looked at them, I was forced to imagine the undivided India of the British era. The winds of love that reached Peshawar and Mardan must have touched their hearts as well. No wonder the old captain told me that the country's poor civilians loved India, but it was the politics and army that separated us. These could also be the civilians that my inmates spoke about.

By 5.30 p.m., we reached the Wagah border. I was immediately taken inside a building. I could not see the Indian side yet. I was taken into a room where there were a handful of mediapersons and army men holding cameras, recording my every move.

An officer wearing a black suit and spectacles walked up to me and introduced himself. 'Hi, Hamid. I am Shubham Singh from the Indian High Commission. How are you? I want to confirm your identity with the documents I have.'

I finally breathed easy. I was meeting an Indian after six years. We shook hands and he handed me a bag of gifts from the mission. We sat down at a table. He proceeded to confirm my identity to hand over the emergency certificate for me to cross over.

By this time, the mediapersons started asking me questions. They asked me to hold up my travel document for photographs and inquired about my experience in Pakistan. After the brief media interaction, Shubham Singh and I started walking towards immigration, but we were suddenly asked to turn back.

Shubham resisted this break in procedure and asked, 'Why are you asking us to turn back? The procedure is done and we should be allowed to go to the other building for Hamid to go through immigration.'

But the officer asked him to leave the building. 'Please leave. Your work here is done. You can meet him at the border. Please leave.'

The Indian diplomat couldn't do much. Later, I found out he had stepped out and called J.P. Singh. 'Sir, they have kept him in a separate building after I finished the paperwork. He has the travel documents but they are not taking him for immigration yet.'

'What did they tell you?' asked Singh.

'They have asked me to go to the final gate and wait there,' he replied.

Singh told him to do as they said but keep tabs on the situation. Everyone had to be cautious.

After the Indian diplomat left, the mediapersons again began asking me questions. It was an old tactic to pressure someone into accepting guilt before allowing them their freedom.

One of them said, 'You better speak the truth now or it will not take us much to make a call and take you back to solitary confinement.'

I was tired of these antics and replied, 'For the past six years, you guys have been punishing me on false grounds, completely ignoring the truth. That's all you can do, so I don't care if you repeat it again.'

The Pakistanis probably knew that I hadn't budged from my stance in six years, and I wasn't going to do so on the day of my release. They asked the media to step out and an officer in civilian clothes told me that there was a huge swarm of media personnel outside and that we would have to dodge them to reach the final gate.

We ran in the opposite direction of the crowd. A few steps away from the India–Pakistan gate, I was overwhelmed. There were too many people. I had been expecting just my family. At the gate, officers from the Indian side stepped forward to exchange some documents with the Pakistanis.

While the formalities were being carried out, I saw my parents walk out from behind the stands where the retreat ceremony took place every day. My mother had her eyes fixed on the gate. She saw me standing with the officers. At first, I could not recognize Ammi, Abbu and

Khalid; they had become so weak and their physical appearance seemed to have changed, but the emotion on their faces was unmistakeable. I was filled with guilt and happiness at the same time. I couldn't contain my excitement.

I was seeing my family for the first time in six long years. The sight was so mesmerizing that I lost focus of everything else. I wanted to rush to them but I was held back for the procedures to be completed. I pleaded with the officers to let me go to my parents. They asked me to be patient. It was a matter of a few minutes.

On the other side, I could see Ammi getting impatient. So were Abbu and Khalid. Ammi opened her arms, waiting to hug me. I had tears in my eyes. I couldn't believe that all this was real. My heart was racing and my hands shook while I completed the paperwork.

As soon as it was done, I was released and handed over to the Indian authorities. I could see the warm smiles of the officers on the Indian side, an acknowledgement that I was one of them. They welcomed me back. My heart wouldn't stop racing. My head spun as the door opened to the Indian side of the border and I saw Ammi with her arms open, waiting for me. I ran and hugged her. I began crying, begging for forgiveness. 'Ammi, I am so sorry . . . so sorry . . . please forgive me,' I cried into her shoulders.

I felt her hand on my head and then my face, and I knew everything would be fine.

I hugged my brother and father. I could see some other familiar faces, like Jatin Desai, around us, but also some new and unfamiliar ones. There was a flood of tears of joy and emotion.

But for now, I didn't care about anyone but the three most precious people in my life. It was finally over. I was home. I kept hugging my mother. A rebirth, a new life.

It was like I had a 360-degree view of a sea of people and flashes of my own past. I could feel it all play out in front of my eyes in fast and slow motion. I could hear the sound of silence, with nothing but the desire to thank the Almighty. There was a sense of divinity that enveloped the space where I stood with my family. I looked up to the sky and turned to my mother. She guided us all to offer grace.

The four of us bowed down to thank the Almighty and kissed the Indian soil.

The experience was surreal, magical and yet so real.

This was my most treasured moment. I got my mother and my motherland back.

A Note from the Parents

A child is the most valuable asset for the parents. He is the joy, hope and support of their lives. If something untoward happens to the child, the whole family is shaken.

The period of six years and more, when our beloved son Hamid suddenly went missing, was a black shadow, a nightmare, the most horrible phase of our lives. It was as if time had stopped; our daily routine was centred around trying to find him. A deafening silence crept into our lifeless movements.

Happiness, chaos, festivals, social gatherings, joy, smiles had all vanished from our lives. Our every breath was focused only on searching for Hamid. Every passing day and night was making us physically weak but mentally strong. Each new day brought new hope, and a new way; the daily struggle became the mantra of our lives.

We understood the silence, the unspoken words between us. Our world was limited to three people: Nehal, Fauzia and Khalid. Our tears had stopped, words had lost their meaning. The sleepless nights, the stressful days, the gloomy faces, the teary eyes, the choked throats, the hypocrites we met, the wolves in disguise, the sudden distances of friends and the boycott of our very own people couldn't further enhance our pain as we had already reached its limit; nothing could affect us more.

The six years of pain and agony taught us the realities of practical life. One can easily distinguish between friends and foes in such situations. Many had joined their helping hands with ours but many had also withdrawn them. When the sun is burning above your head, your own shadow also leaves you. A different kind of look in the eyes of our acquaintances, an unknown fear and the anxiety of uncertainty compelled us to stay secluded.

We were badly shaken and in physical, mental, emotional, social and financial turmoil. We had lost everything, but not hope. Our silent prayers and tears were our only strength. It's miraculous but true that the day someone taunted us saying that Hamid was no more and would never return, and the Pakistani military would never send him back in one piece, in a mother's restless dreams, Hamid would appear, hale and hearty. This was the divine signal and a ray of hope.

We were searching for a needle in a haystack, but it was not impossible because many good people had joined our efforts. We searched and found them on the Internet and requested them for help. They were not relatives; they were from different parts of the world. But all of them were real human beings. Humanity was above all for them.

They knew that Hamid's intention was noble, based on humanity; to save a life, he had risked his own.

We got help from many corners. The media became our voice. We knocked on every door within our reach—the Internet, Google search, from social media to the international stage, Facebook, WhatsApp, Twitter, online petitions, dharnas, protests, emails, Gmail, videos, appeals, NGOs, visits, rituals and charities.

The news of Hamid's presence in Pakistan was confirmed by the Pakistani government in December 2015. It was a big relief; this gave us the assurance that Hamid would return.

Finally, with the efforts of many people, the #bringhamidback struggle was successful. Hamid was repatriated back to India on 18 December 2018.

We find it difficult to express our experiences of six years in a few pages. It was a long struggle of 2255 days. And even though Hamid is back home, the chapter has not ended there. It is the beginning of a new life for a person who has suffered the trauma of a long detention. He should be welcomed and accepted with a big heart by all. It is the combined responsibility of the family, society and government to rehabilitate and help him be strong physically, mentally, emotionally and financially. Only then can he stand on his own feet and live a normal life.

Mumbai
October 2020

Fauzia Ansari and Nehal Ansari

Acknowledgements

For all those who lent helping hands and did not find a mention in the book

From India

I, on behalf of my family, must thank the citizens of my beloved country who stood by my side when I needed them the most.

Adv. Jayesh C. Mirani, president of the All Maharashtra Human Rights Welfare Association, who filed a petition in the National Human Rights Commission and the Supreme Court of Pakistan's Human Rights Cell, and approached the United Nations as a member.

Colonel (retd) Bhatia, the Indian army officer who wrote to his Pakistani friends to search for me.

Haris Bhai, a hotelier in Delhi who occasionally hosted my parents whenever they visited him.

Journalists Rakesh Tripathi, Rashmi Talwar, Sarvesh Tiwari, Vidya and many more who followed the case from beginning to end.

Shabnam Hashmi of ANHAD and her subordinates who helped arrange a dharna and was with the family the whole day at Jantar Mantar in New Delhi to express her solidarity.

Maharashtra Police, Mumbai Police and officers on duty at Versova police station, CBI, CID officers on duty, ADG Sanjeev Kumar, Spl IGP Sunil Ramanand, SP Vijay Patil, SP Pournima Gaikwad, additional SP K.V. Nigde, deputy SP Vijay G. Pawar and IPS (retd) Habib Ansari and many others working on this case, who were all very humble and helpful.

Peace activists Sudheendra Kulkarni, Vijayan, Jibin Robin, Ravi Nitesh, Devika Mittal, Shivam Vij, Kavita Srivastava, Ovais Sultan Ahmed, Sampa Arya, Abid Syed and Dalbeer Kaur (sister of Sarabjit Singh) tried to help in their own ways.

Principal Ajay Kaul of Clara's College of Commerce helped by introducing Afghani businessperson Amanullah Nizami, hoping he would be of help.

Qari Najmul Hassan, a close family associate in Saudi Arabia who tried to contact people from Khyber Pakhtunkhwa, Pakistan, residing in Saudi Arabia.

From Pakistan

My family and I thank the officials of the Pakistan High Commission in New Delhi who helped my parents and treated the case from an absolutely humane angle.

Special thanks also to many other civilians from Pakistan who contributed in their special ways.

Late Adv. Sultan Mehmood helped and guided Zeenat in Hamid's case.

Beena Sarwar and I.A. Rehman Saheb wrote articles in Pakistan's leading newspapers and also followed Zeenat's case when she went missing.

Hina Jilani stood in solidarity with me and followed Zeenat Shehzadi's missing case through the Human Rights Commission of Pakistan until her recovery.

Gratitude to Pakistani peace activists of civil society, Ansar Burney, Late Asma Jehangir, Deip Saeeda, Karamat Ali, Sarim Burney Trust, Taimur Ajmal, Mohammad Tufail and Waheedullah Khan.

Rehan Allahwala made an online appeal and circulated my mother's appeal videos on social media.

Khalid Mahmood, Malik Jamshed and a few other journalists wrote articles and raised the issue of my arrest in newspapers in Pakistan.

Special thanks also to the family members of Adv. Rukhshanda Naz and Zeenat Shehzadi.

From the Middle East

Special thanks also to those who helped establish communication between our contacts in India and Pakistan, especially when direct communications were not possible from India.

Amanullah Nezami from Riyadh, Saudi Arabia, offered all his help and assisted Zeenat's family after she went missing.

Late Mehmood Bhai from Dubai spoke to Atta-ur-Rehman on the phone.

My cousin Tarique Ansari and Mukhtar Naik from Qatar who helped my mother, extending all kinds of assistance whenever needed.

Extending our gratitude to our family friend Umer Bhai from Jeddah, Saudi Arabia, who helped on various occasions.

Hamid Ansari